Lea**ne Routledg** Literary

D1494334

The Routledge Dictionary of Literary Terms is a twenty-first century upda.. .. .. er Fowler's seminal *Dictionary of Modern Critical Terms*. Bringing together original entries written by such celebrated theorists as Terry Eagleton and Malcolm Bradbury with new definitions of current terms and controversies, this is the essential reference book for students of literature at all levels.

This book includes:

- New definitions of contemporary critical issues such as 'Cybercriticism' and 'Globalization'.
- An exhaustive range of entries, covering numerous aspects to such topics as genre, form, cultural theory and literary technique.
- Complete coverage of traditional and radical approaches to the study and production of literature.
- Thorough accounts of critical terminology and analyses of key academic debates.
- Full cross-referencing throughout and suggestions for further reading.

Peter Childs is Professor of Modern English Literature at the University of Gloucestershire. His recent publications include *Modernism* (Routledge, 2000) and *Contemporary Novelists: British Fiction Since 1970* (Palgrave, 2004).

Roger Fowler (1939–99), the distinguished and long-serving Professor of English and Linguistics at the University of East Anglia, was the editor of the original *Dictionary of Modern Critical Terms* (Routledge, 1973, 1987).

Also available from Routledge

Poetry: The Basics
Jeffrey Wainwright
0–415–28764–2

Shakespeare: The Basics
Sean McEvoy
0–415–21289–8

Literary Theory: The Basics
Hans Bertens
0–415–18664–1

Contemporary British Novelists
Nick Rennison
0–415–21709–1

The Routledge Companion to Postmodernism (Second Edition)
Edited by Stuart Sim
0–415–33359–8

The Routledge Companion to Russian Literature
Edited by Neil Cornwell
0–415–23366–6

Who's Who in Contemporary Women's Writing
Edited by
Jane Eldridge Miller
0–415–15981–4

Who's Who in Lesbian and Gay Writing
Gabriele Griffin
0–415–15984–9

Who's Who in Dickens
Donald Hawes
0–415–26029–9

Who's Who in Shakespeare
Peter Quennell and
Hamish Johnson
0–415–26035–3

Who's Who in Twentieth-Century World Poetry
Edited by Mark Willhardt
and Alan Michael Parker
0–415–16356–0

The Routledge Dictionary of Literary Terms

Peter Childs
and
Roger Fowler

**Based on
*A Dictionary of
Modern Critical Terms*,
edited by Roger Fowler**

Routledge
Taylor & Francis Group
LONDON AND NEW YORK

First published in 1973 as *A Dictionary of Modern Critical Terms*
Revised edition published in 1987
by Routledge & Kegan Paul Ltd

This edition published 2006
by Routledge
2 Park Square, Milton Park, Abingdon, Oxon OX14 4RN

Simultaneously published in the USA and Canada
by Routledge
270 Madison Ave, New York, NY 10016

Routledge is an imprint of the Taylor & Francis Group

© Routledge 1973, 1987, 2006

Typeset in Times New Roman by
Newgen Imaging Systems (P) Ltd, Chennai, India
Printed and bound in Great Britain by
MPG Books Ltd, Bodmin

British Library Cataloguing in Publication Data
A catalogue record for this book is available
from the British Library

Library of Congress Cataloging in Publication Data
The Routledge dictionary of literary terms / [edited by]
Peter Childs and Roger Fowler.
    p. cm.
'Based on A Dictionary of Modern Critical Terms, edited by
Roger Fowler.' Rev. ed. of: A dictionary of modern critical terms.
Rev. and enl. ed. 1987.
    Includes bibliographical references.
    1. Literature – Terminology. 2. English language – Terms and
phrases. 3. Literary form – Terminology. 4. Criticism – Terminology.
I. Childs, Peter. II. Fowler, Roger. III. Dictionary of modern
critical terms.

PN41.D4794 2005
803–dc22   2005006915

ISBN 0–415–36117–6 (hbk)
ISBN 0–415–34017–9 (pbk)

To Claire Philpott, with thanks

Contents

Note on the style of references

Cross-references give the article to which the reader is referred in SMALL CAPITALS.

Further reading is suggested wherever appropriate, sometimes within the text and sometimes at the end of articles, whichever is stylistically more suitable. Dates of first editions are given when they are significant, but usually the most accessible and convenient modern reprintings and translations are cited.

List of terms

A

Absurd The theatre of the absurd was a term, derived from Camus and popularized by Martin Esslin's book *The Theatre of the Absurd* (1961), applied to a group of dramatists whose work emerged during the early 1950s (though Beckett's *Waiting for Godot* and Ionesco's *The Bald Prima Donna* were actually written in the late 1940s). In *The Myth of Sisyphus* (1942) Camus defined the absurd as the tension which emerges from the individual's determination to discover purpose and order in a world which steadfastly refuses to evidence either. To writers like Ionesco and Beckett this paradox leaves human actions, aspirations and emotions merely ironical. The redeeming message no longer comes from God but is delivered by a deaf mute to a collection of empty chairs (*The Chairs*, 1952); human qualities, such as perseverance and courage, no longer function except as derisory comments on the individual's impotence (*Happy Days*, 1961); basic instincts and responses, the motor forces of the individual, become the source of misery (*Act Without Words*, 1957). Camus himself could see a limited transcendence in the ability to recognize and even exalt in the absurd (*The Outsider*, 1942) or in the minimal consolation of stoicism (*Cross Purpose*, 1944). But he came to feel that absurdity implied a world which appeared to sanction Nazi brutality as easily as it did individual acts of violence. From an examination of the nature of absurdity, therefore, he moved towards liberal humanism: 'The end of the movement of absurdity, of rebellion, etc....is compassion...that is to say, in the last analysis, love'. For writers like Beckett and Ionesco such a dialectical shift was simply faith. For to the 'absurd' dramatist it is axiomatic that humans live in an entropic world in which communication is impossible and illusion preferred to reality. The individual has no genuine scope for action (Hamm sits lame and blind in *Endgame*, 1958; Winnie is buried to the neck in sand in *Happy Days*; the protagonist of Ionesco's *The New Tenant* (written 1953, produced 1957) is submerged beneath proliferating furniture); individuals are the victims of their metaphysical situation. Logically, the plays abandon linear plot, plausible character development and rational language. In contrast to Camus's work their style directly reflects their subject.

The term 'absurd drama', applied by Esslin to dramatists as diverse as Beckett, Ionesco, Adamov, Genet, Arrabal and Simpson, is something of a blunt weapon. Esslin had a disturbing if understandable tendency to trace the origins of the absurd in an incredible array of writers some of whom do not properly belong in a theatre which is convinced of the unbridgeable gulf between aspiration and fulfilment, the impossibility of communication or the futility of human relationships. In other words he is not always completely scrupulous in distinguishing between style and content. In his revised edition of his book, however, he has shown a commendable desire to underline the deficiencies of a term which, while proving a useful means of approaching dramatists intent on forging new drama, was never intended as a substitute for stringent analysis of the work of individual writers.

See Martin Esslin, *The Theatre of the Absurd* (2004); J. L. Styan, *Modern Drama in Theory and Practice: Symbolism, Surrealism and the Absurd* (1983).

CWEB

Action   See DRAMA.

Actor   See DRAMA.

Aestheticism   A sensibility, a philosophy of life and of art, and an English literary and artistic movement, culminating in the 1890s, with Oscar Wilde as its most extravagant exponent and Walter Pater its acknowledged philosopher. Other names commonly associated are those of the members of the Pre-Raphaelite Brotherhood, Swinburne, Arthur Symons, Ernest Dowson, Lionel Johnson, Andrew Lang, William Sharp, John Addington Symonds and the early Yeats. Aubrey Beardsley and J. McNeill Whistler are representative of the same trend in the fine arts.

For the Aesthete whose creed is to be derived from Pater's conclusion to *The Renaissance* (1873), reality amounts to sharp, fleeting impressions, images and sensations arrested by the creative individual from an experience in constant flux. The life of art, or the art of life, which the Aesthete wishes to equate, is ideally a form of purified ecstasy that flourishes only when removed from the roughness of the stereotyped world of actuality and the orthodoxy of philosophical systems and fixed points of view. The quest for unadulterated beauty is recommended as the finest occupation individuals can find for themselves during the 'indefinite reprieve' from death which their lives are. Pater's phrase, 'the love of art for its own sake', a version of the French *l'art pour l'art*, has served the Aesthetes as a slogan, implying the repudiation of the 'heresy of instruction'

(Baudelaire's *l'hérésie de l'enseignement*). Art, Whistler wrote in his 'Ten o'clock' lecture (1885), is 'selfishly occupied with her own perfection only' and has 'no desire to teach'. As a fashionable fad, English Aestheticism was brought to a halt with the trial of Oscar Wilde in 1896.

Aestheticism, as a stage in the development of Romanticism, is not limited to England. Profoundly a movement of reaction and protest, it reflects the growing apprehension of the nineteenth-century artist at the vulgarization of values and commercialization of art accompanying the rise of the middle class and the spread of democracy ('a new class, who discovered the cheap, and foresaw fortune in the facture of the sham' = Whistler). The hostility of an alienated minority towards bourgeois 'Religion of Progress' ('Industry and Progress,' Baudelaire wrote, 'those despotic enemies of all poetry') prompted an indulgence in the decadent, the archaic and the morbid. The Death of God, as proclaimed by Nietzsche among others, turned the Aesthete towards the occult and the transcendental in an attempt to make a thoroughly spiritualized art substitute for the old faith. The *fin-de-siècle* witnesses the proclamation of an elitist 'new hedonism' determined, in the words of Oscar Wilde, 'never to accept any theory or system that would involve the sacrifice of any mode of passionate experience'.

Philosophy provides the theoretical mainstay of the prevalent moods. Kant's postulate (*Critique of Judgement*, 1790) of the disinterestedness of the aesthetical judgement, and the irrelevance of concepts to the intuitions of the imagination, is taken up and carried further by Schopenhauer. In the latter's thought, an 'absolute' Art removes the mind from a despicable life and frees it from its bondage to the will. Since music is the most immaterial art, as well as the most removed from quotidian reality, it becomes the ideal. Schopenhauer declares that 'to become like music is the aspiration of all arts', which is echoed by Nietzsche in *The Birth of Tragedy from the Spirit of Music* (1872), by Verlaine in '*de la musique avant toute chose*', and by Pater in his equally famous 'All art constantly aspires towards the condition of music' (*The Renaissance*, 1873). The ensuing cult of pure or 'essential' form is as characteristic of symbolism and literary Impressionism as it is of the entire English 1890s. This, in turn, leads to the devaluation of the subject matter in favour of personal, innovatory techniques and the subtleties of exquisite execution.

See Madeleine L. Cazamian, *Le Roman et les idées en Angleterre, vol. 2: L'Anti-intellectualisme et l'esthéticisme* (1880–1900) (1935); L. Eckhoff, *The Aesthetic Movement in English Literature* (1959); Graham Hough, *The Last Romantics* (1949); H. Jackson, *The Eighteen-Nineties* (1913); R. V. Johnson, *Aestheticism* (1969); Talia Schaffer and Kathy Alexis Psomiades (eds), *Women and British Aestheticism* (2000).

NZ

Aesthetics (The study of the beautiful.) A subject that has developed, especially in Germany, into a formidable one. Lack of space forbids any attempt to deal with its philosophical and psychological problems here; but some discrimination may be made to clarify and amplify its use as a critical term.

First, *aesthetic pleasure* may be distinguished from other pleasures – according to the Kantian definition now widely accepted – as that which is disinterested, the result of perceiving something not as a means but as an end in itself, not as useful but as ornamental, not as instrument but as achievement. To perceive it so is to perceive its 'beauty' (if it turns out to have any). Such beauty, being the counterpart to use or purpose, which largely depend on content, must spring from formal qualities, as must the special pleasures its perception gives rise to. Non-moral, non-utilitarian and non-acquisitive, this is the purest of the pleasures, the one least exposed to bias from areas outside the work of art (and therefore the one most appropriate for defining what 'art' is; see ART). Second, aesthetic pleasure may be distinguished from *aesthetic appreciation*. The former emphasizes one's experience of the work, which may be mistaken, untutored or injudicious; the latter emphasizes the characteristics of the work, and implies a critical assessment of their 'beauty'. Third, both presuppose *aesthetic attention*. Unless a work is regarded in the way indicated above – for what it is, not for what it is up to – its aesthetic qualities, if any, are likely to go unperceived. For this reason works where the subject, or manner, deeply involves the reader are less likely to give aesthetic pleasure or to prompt aesthetic appreciation than those that encourage aesthetic attention by formal devices that lend *aesthetic distance*.

Finally, *aesthetic merit* should be distinguished from aesthetic qualities and reactions, for a work might possess genuine aesthetic qualities, properly provide for their appreciation, yet in fact be a poor specimen of its kind. Merit and pleasure, too, are not necessarily related. An untrained or naturally crude sensibility could clearly be aesthetically pleased by a crude work – and so, in certain circumstances, could a trained and refined sensibility (though it would *appreciate* the work for what it was).

Aesthesis (aesthetic perception) is normally a blend of aesthetic pleasure and appreciation, and may be of three kinds: *aesthesis of composition*, resulting from purely formal harmonies of part and part, or parts and whole, and more characteristic of the fine arts than of literature; *aesthesis of complementarity*, resulting from the matching of form and content; and *aesthesis of condensation*, resulting from the perception of aesthetic qualities in part of a work only (a minimal instance, strictly speaking, of either of the other two modes).

The *Aesthetic Movement*, or *Art for art's sake*, which started in France during the latter part of the nineteenth century and flourished in England in the 1880s and 1890s, was less concerned with such niceties than with a general reaction against the Art for morality's sake so characteristic of the earlier part of the century. When Wilde averred that 'all art is quite useless' he spoke truly – if art is defined in aesthetic terms. But the pleasures of literature are usually multiple and its proper appreciation therefore rarely limited to the aesthetic. Critics, such as Paul de Man and Terry Eagleton, have argued that the aesthetic is primarily an ideological category reflecting and promoting Western bourgeois taste. See also PLEASURE.

See Monroe C. Beardsley, *Aesthetics* (1958); P. Guyer, *Kant and the Claims of Taste* (1979); *British Journal of Aesthetics* (*passim*); Anne Sheppard, *Aesthetics: An Introduction to the Philosophy of Art* (1987); Terry Eagleton, *The Ideology of the Aesthetic* (1990); Paul De Man, *Aesthetic Ideology* (1997); Jesse Matz, *Literary Impressionism and Modernist Aesthetics* (2001).

AER

Affective fallacy   See EFFECT.

Aktualisace   See FOREGROUNDING.

Alienation effect   See CONTRADICTION, EPIC THEATRE.

Allegory   A Major symbolic mode which fell into some critical disrepute in the mid-twentieth century ('dissociated', 'naive', 'mechanical', 'abstract') though it flourished in satire, underground literature and science fiction. It is often defined as an 'extended metaphor' in which characters, actions and scenery are systematically symbolic, referring to spiritual, political, psychological confrontations (Bunyan's *Pilgrim's Progress*, Orwell's *1984*). Historically the rise of allegory accompanies the inward-looking psychologizing tendencies of late antiquity and medieval Christianity (see C. S. Lewis, *The Allegory of Love*, 1938). The 'hero' is typically a cypher (Spenser's Guyon, Christian in Bunyan, Winston Smith in *1984*), a proxy for the reader, because the action is assumed to take place in the mind and imagination of the audience; 'characters' other than the hero are, rather like Jonsonian HUMOURS, demonically possessed by fear, desire or need. (It is often misleadingly suggested that they 'represent' vices and virtues, but when successful they *are* jealousy, greed, modesty, etc. with intervals of neutrality where they get the plot moving or are spectators to the obsessions of other characters.) Allegory's distinctive feature is that it is a structural, rather than a textural symbolism; it is a large-scale exposition in which problems are conceptualized and analysed into their constituent parts in order to be stated, if not solved. The typical plot is one in which the 'innocent' – Gulliver, Alice, the Lady in Milton's 'Comus', K. in Kafka's *The Castle* – is 'put through' a series of experiences (tests, traps, fantasy gratifications) which add up to an imaginative analysis of contemporary 'reality'.

Many of the attitudes which characterized MODERNISM and NEW CRITICISM were explicitly hostile to the intentionalist and individualist assumptions allegory makes – that the emotive power of literature can be channelled and directed, that the work itself is the means to an end (saving souls, 'to fashion a gentleman', etc.). Pound's strictures against the abstract ('dim lands *of peace*'); Richards's insistence that poetry is 'data' not rationalist scaffolding; Yeats's stress on the mysteriousness of the genuine literary symbol – all seem to label allegory as the product of a now untenable idealism. But the clear-cut distinction between 'the music of ideas' (Richards on Eliot) and the 'dark conceit' of allegory is harder to make in practice than in theory: Yeats's *A Vision* systematized and expounded the mystery of his symbols much as Spenser did in *The Faerie Queene*. Cleanth Brooks in *The Well Wrought Urn* (1947) allegorized all the poems he explicated, so that they become 'parables about the nature of poetry', and Northrop Frye in *The Anatomy of Criticism* (1957) summed up this tendency by pointing out that all analysis was covert allegorizing. But though the common distinction between allegory and symbolism falsifies the facts of literary experience when it claims an impossible instantaneity and universality for the symbol (symbolism can be grossly schematic – cf. Hemingway or Steinbeck), and accuses allegory of arid rationalism, there is a genuine distinction to be made.

Two main strands in the modernist aesthetic, the doctrine of the autonomy of the artefact and the association of literature with collective and recurrent 'myth', combined to leave little room and few terms for allegory. Modernist critics were equipped to talk about the textural enactment of content, and about the largest (mythic) patterns into which literature falls, but were not at ease in the area between the two where form and content are often increasingly at odds, and which involves argument, discursiveness, paraphrasable opinion. Allegorists, like satirists (and the two are often the same) employ myths rhetorically, rather than respectfully embodying them (John Barth, *Giles Goat Boy*, 1966). More recently, critics, such as Craig Owens have allied postmodernist writing with allegory because of its tendency towards irony and parody. See also MYTH, SYMBOL.

See Angus Fletcher, *Allegory, the Theory of a Symbolic Mode* (1964); Northrop Frye, 'Levels of meaning in literature', *Kenyon Review* (1950), 246–62; A. D. Nuttall, *Two Concepts of Allegory* (1967); Edmund Spenser, 'A Letter of the Author's…to Sir Walter Raleigh' (1596); Craig Owens, 'The allegorical impulse: toward a theory of postmodernism' in Scott Bryson *et al.* (eds), *Beyond Recognition* (1992); Theresa M. Kelley, *Reinventing Allegory* (1997).

LS

Alliteration   See TEXTURE.

Alterity   The dictionary definition of the term alterity is 'the state of being other or different; diversity, otherness'. Its use as an alternative (which, as it happens, is a term cognate to alterity) to 'otherness' has emerged from changes in twentieth-century philosophy that have shifted the conceptualization of identity from the Cartesian humanist proposition of a self-contained consciousness located in the individual mind, based on the proposition 'I think therefore I am', to subjectivity located in social contexts that are discursively and ideologically constituted. In this latter perspective, the formation of the Other is inseparably involved in the formation of the Self for it is only through the discursive construction of this Other that the Self can be defined as an 'identity'. The 'Other' then is not something outside or beyond the Self as the traditional Cartesian perspective would have it; rather, it is deeply implicated within the Self. Its philosophical status must, accordingly, shift from being an epistemic question to an ethical one. In short, the philosophical 'problem' of the Other is no longer of the sort that involves a coherent Self-asking 'How can I know the Other?' Rather, the questions become 'What is my relationship to the Other?' and 'How should I act towards the Other?' The term alterity here becomes useful because it suggests that the Other involved in these questions is neither merely an abstract proposition, nor is it unrelated and therefore irrelevant to considerations of the Self. The Other's difference is therefore not absolute but relative; it is determined by series of cultural, economic, political and moral differences. It is this emphasis on relationality that gives alterity its value in contemporary theory.

This is particularly marked in post-colonialism, which seeks to deconstruct the 'Othering' process that Gayatri Spivak argues is the manner through which colonial identities formed themselves within an ideology of racial and cultural hierarchy. Colonized Others functioned within this discourse to propagate a sense of selfhood amongst colonizers that imagined itself to be utterly and absolutely different from the colonized. The colonized Other is deployed as an 'inscrutable' figure that is unknown and unknowable – that is, as an epistemological question. This is particularly apparent in such colonial fictions as E. M. Forster's *A Passage to India* and Joseph Conrad's *Heart of Darkness*, both of which rehearse the limits of colonial knowledge. Significantly, this discourse positions the Other outside of discourse and so involves a certain cultural solipsism in which the difference of the Other functions only insofar as

it resolves (or, interestingly, does not resolve) questions within the colonial Self. In other words, the only perspective that matters is the colonial one; it cannot, or rather refuses, to recognize the perspective of the colonized.

To use the term Other in this context is to run the risk of reinscribing this Othering process instead of dismantling the very binaries on which such discourse rests. Alterity offers the opportunity to see colonial discourse and its Others in a relational manner, each constituting the other whilst simultaneously respecting difference, thereby avoiding the trap of collapsing all distinctions into an abstract, ahistorical homogeneity. This respect for the difference of the Other opens up a space for recognition of mutual interaction and dialogue. See also HYBRIDITY, ORIENTALISM, POSTCOLONIALISM, OTHER.

See Gayatri Chakravorty Spivak, *The Spivak Reader* (1996); Michael T. Taussig, *Mimesis and Alterity: A Particular History of the Senses* (1993).

AM

Ambiguity   If opposed to 'clarity', ambiguity would be considered a fault. Modernist criticism turned it into a virtue, equivalent roughly to 'richness' or 'wit'. This reversal of normal connotations was made possible by two factors: I. A. Richards's argument that what is required of scientific language (e.g. lucidity) is not necessarily demanded in poetry (see LANGUAGE); and William Empson's promotion of the concept in *Seven Types of Ambiguity*, first published in 1930. Following Empson, ambiguity came to be regarded as a defining linguistic characteristic of poetry.

Ambiguity is not a specific figurative device which may be chosen at will for decoration; it is not, says Empson, 'a thing to be attempted'. Rather, it is a natural characteristic of language which becomes heightened and significant in verse. The link between content and form is indirect and arbitrary; hence syntactic 'accidents' may occur, syntax realizing two or more meanings in the same signal. Linguists say that one 'surface structure' may conceal two or more 'deep structures' (the reverse situation is PARAPHRASE). Ambiguity is common in ordinary language, but we do not notice it because context usually selects just one of the alternative meanings ('disambiguates'). It is of several kinds: *homophony*, the convergence of unrelated meanings in one form (*bank*, *plane*); *polysemy*, a scatter of more or less connected meanings around one word (*bachelor*, *record*); purely syntactic ambiguity, as in *Visiting relatives can be boring* or *old men and women*.

Verse tends to be more ambiguous than prose or conversation, for several reasons: it is less redundant; context is inaccessible or irrelevant; verse displays extra levels of structure and can be 'parsed' in more ways. Empson sums this up: 'ambiguity is a phenomenon of compression'. Deletion of words for metrical/stylistic reasons leads to ambivalence, as in Empson's example from Browning:

> I want to know a butcher paints,
> A baker rhymes for his pursuit...

So does a line-break at a crucial syntactic point:

> If it were done, when 'tis done, then 'twere well
> It were done quickly.

Since we are disposed to assume multiple meaning in verse, we consent to read in extra meanings. The leaves in Shakespeare's Sonnet 73 ('yellow...or none, or few') are simultaneously the leaves of the autumn metaphor and the poet's writings – leaves of a book.

The problem is justification, selection; Empson's reading of 'trammel up the consequence' is clearly fantastic. What control is there over the desire to spawn meanings?

The doctrine of ambiguity is not a licence for self-indulgence, free association producing a mushy poem, an arbitrary heap of meanings. Multiple meanings must be justified by their interrelationships. We must neither impose meanings without control, nor reject all meanings but one; instead, we must reject all meanings but those which interact wittily. In the same sonnet we find 'those boughs which shake against the cold'. *Shake* is either passive – the boughs being ravaged by the cold wind – or active and defiant, the shaking of a fist, a gesture against approaching death. This is a common syntactic ambiguity: the diametrically opposed meanings capture the conflict between decay and energy which the poem embodies. Here we have not merely *mentioned* the double meaning, but *used* it in relation to the poem's theme. Ambiguity in this usage resembles and informs the New Critics' TENSION, IRONY, PARADOX; it comes nearer than any of them to providing a linguistic explanation for poetic complexity and wit, for it springs from the familiar resources of ordinary language.

RGF

Analysis The purpose of analysis, according to William Empson, 'is to show the modes of action of a poetical effect'. And in the work of Empson (*Seven Types of Ambiguity*, 1930) and Richards (*Practical Criticism*, 1929) it is a conviction of criticism that these effects are accessible to reason, and not mysteries reserved for silent appreciation. 'The reasons that make a line of verse likely to give pleasure...are like the reasons for anything else; one can reason about them' (*Seven Types*). Empson's major achievement was his demonstration that these modes of action were capable of description in terms of effects of language. The conviction that the forms and meanings of literature are linguistically generated gives to the business of analysis its centrality in New Criticism. For the classical idea of language as the dress of thought had for long limited literary analysis to the categorization of stylistic features, the description of decorative externals. So long as the reality of the work lay 'beyond' language it had no objective existence, it could not be analysed. Traditional stylistics concerned itself with classification and comparison of types of prosody, diction, imagery, etc. without attempting to show how these features co-operated in creating the 'meaning' of a work. The tradition of *explication de texte* in French education, in which the 'texte' often seems almost incidental to the categorized information that is hung about it, demonstrated the consequences of this dualistic form–content model of language. What is offered is what Ian Watt called 'explanation...a mere making plain by spreading out'; Watt's critical analysis demands, on the other hand, 'explication...a progressive unfolding of a series of literary implications' ('The first paragraph of *The Ambassadors*', *Essays in Criticism*, 10, 1960). But explication, or as W. K. Wimsatt refined it 'the *explicit*ation of the implicit or the interpretation of the structural and formal, the truth of the poem under its aspect of coherence' (*The Verbal Icon*, 1954), had to wait upon a language theory that would abandon this dualism and redefine 'meaning' as a totality, of linguistic relationships (see LANGUAGE). If language in poetry could be conceived of not as the dress but as the body of meaning, then

analysis had access to the fact of the poem, not simply to its incidentals. It could account for its 'modes of action'.

In fact the essential conceptual metaphors had been available to criticism since Coleridge; Romantic theories of poetry as holistic and organic, with their controlling analogies of plants and trees, had supplanted the classical form–content dichotomies. But so long as these vitally interdependent 'parts and whole' were unlocated except as metaphysical abstractions, their relationships remained unanalysable. However, the revolutions in philosophy of Frege and Wittgenstein, and in linguistics of Saussure, substituted for the 'referential' or 'representational' model of language an idea of meaning as a result of complex interaction. Criticism took the point that if the meaning of a word is everything it does in a particular CONTEXT, then analysis of the words of a poem, of their total interinanimation, would be nothing less than an account of the poem itself. The metaphysical abstractions which Romantic theory identified as the form of poetry could now be located as linguistic realities, and since language has a public existence, independent of the psychologies of poet or reader, they were open to analysis.

The analytic tradition that descended from Richards and Empson, known in England (and particularly at the University of Cambridge) as *Practical Criticism* and in America as the NEW CRITICISM, was primarily concerned with semantic explorations. Its key terms – AMBIGUITY, PARADOX, TENSION, gesture – emerged from a new awareness of multiplicity and complexity of meaning in literature. This tradition (and its modern offshoot which relies explicitly on the techniques and conceptual framework of linguistics: see LANGUAGE) has been attacked for its tendency to stick close to the lower levels of verbal structure; for its apparent neglect of value-judgements; for its alleged inability to account for the larger-scale structures of long works; for a necessary preference for short, complex, highly textured lyric poems. For examples of structural analysis beyond purely verbal structure, see Vladimir Propp, *The Morphology of the Folk-Tale* (1st Russian edn, 1928; English trans. 1958; French trans. of the 2nd Russian edn, 1970); Roland Barthes, *S/Z* (1970).

See Martin Montgomery, *Advanced Reading Skills for Students of English Literature* (2000); Steven Cohan and Linda M. Shires, *Telling Stories: Theoretical Analysis of Narrative Fiction* (1998)

PM

Anticlimax   See DÉNOUEMENT.

Anti-hero   See HERO.

Apocalyptic literature   There exists a body of biblical literature, canonical and apocryphal, conventionally called apocalyptic (from the Greek, meaning unveiling, uncovering). The Old Testament Book of Daniel and the New Testament Book of Revelation are the best known of these. They are characterized by an interest in the revelation of future events, as in prophecy. As a kind of systematized prophetic writing, the literature of apocalypse takes a wide view of human history, which it schematizes and periodizes, and an especial interest in eschatology, in the 'latter days', the end of historical time, the last judgement. These revelations are part of a hitherto secret knowledge. They tend to affect an esoteric, visionary, symbolic and fantastic scenario, a cast of animals, angels, stars and numbers, which are to be understood symbolically. The struggle between good and evil powers in the latter days of a terminal period culminates in a final judgement,

the resurrection of the dead and the installation of a messianic kingdom. All these elements are not necessarily present in any one work, and it can be convenient to use the term even where a deliberate frustration of a conventional apocalyptic expectation may be at issue.

Apocalyptic types characterize historical periods of upheaval and crisis, and interest in apocalyptic literature of the past has also occurred in such periods. Similarly, critics of secular literature in the twentieth century became sensitized to the apocalyptic elements in works not formally of the type, but whose language, particularly imagery, touches on the themes of revelation, renovation and ending. Frank Kermode's *The Sense of an Ending* (1967) is the most notable of these, using the 'ways in which...we have imagined the ends of the world' as a taking-off point for a study of fictional endings and fictional structures generally. For him, the literature of apocalypse is a 'radical instance' of fiction, depending 'on a concord of imaginatively recorded past and imaginatively predicted future'. Awareness of apocalyptic types in fiction, he claims, has concentrated on 'crisis, decadence and empire, and...disconfirmation, the inevitable fate of detailed eschatological predictions'.

In using apocalypse as a type of fiction criticism may merely be using a congenial language to define the literature of its own time – including that of the past felt to be 'relevant' – in terms acceptable to its own sense of crisis. It seems also true that there has been a social history of apocalyptic fictions in Anglo-American literature, for while apocalypse seems almost allied with 'progressive' forces in Elizabethan times, as in Spenser's *The Faerie Queene*, it is entertained later with mixed fascination and horror by writers who project the

Final End as an image of the abortion rather than the consummation of current trends of history. In his essay, 'The end of the world', reprinted in *Errand Into The Wilderness* (1964), Perry Miller provided not only a summary of English and American apocalyptic literature, but also an insight into the gradual transition in expectations and reasons for the desirability of this typology. His focus was particularly on the period between the Elizabethan and the Modern and on the figures of Jonathan Edwards, 'the greatest artist of the apocalypse' in America, and Edgar Allan Poe, whose eschatological stories pinpoint a transition in the handling of apocalyptic materials, foreshadowing more modern attitudes to a world-consuming holocaust.

Apocalyptic writing has come to be understood in terms of writing an end point rather than the end of the world. The twentieth century was notable for a number of moments of apocalyptic writing from the modernists, such as Lawrence, through the News Apocalypse poets at mid-century, to millennial pictures of destruction in a wide range of writers, from Angela Carter and Martin Amis to Zadie Smith. The subject has thus been taken up in some studies of ECO-CRITICISM in recent decades.

See Frank Kermode, 'D. H. Lawrence and the Apocalyptic Types' in *Modern Essays* (1971); Arthur Edward Salmon, *Poets of the Apocalypse* (1983); Morton Paley, *Apocalypse and Millennium in English Romantic Poetry* (1990); David Seed (ed.), *Imagining Apocalypse* (1999); Greg Garrard, *Ecocriticism* (2004).

AMG

Aporia   See DECONSTRUCTION.

Appreciation   See   AESTHETICS, EVALUATION.

Archaism   The use of forms whose obsoleteness or obsolescence is manifest and thus immediately subject to the reader's scrutiny. It can be mere whimsical display: Thackeray sometimes lapses into language quaint in his own time and irrelevant to the cast of mind of his characters, thus evoking a simple, ultimately repetitive response and impeding any probing of the more complex implications of characters and plot. In general, archaism's tendency is to be a simplifying device: one's experience of the language of one's own time and place is of something richly and variously suggestive, closely related to one's experience and knowledge, capable of complexity of organization and delicate flexibility, spontaneously understandable and usable, whereas archaism refers back to a linguistic or cultural system which it cannot totally reconstruct, and archaic forms may thus seem impoverished, rigid and ponderous. The consistent archaism of the Authorized Version (1611) of the Bible interposes a unified tone of solemnity between the varied subject-matter and the audience, making its response more uniform because more uncomplex. More sophisticated, and richly fruitful, uses of archaic language are commonly found in canonical authors, invoking and incorporating the values of older literary traditions: Spenser, Shakespeare, Milton, Wordsworth, T. S. Eliot provide many examples.

Archaism can arouse an often vague delight in the familiar but long forgotten, yet as it refers back to the unknown can also be made frightening: Thomas Mann, in *Doctor Faustus* (1947), exploits this paradox to reveal affinities between cautious, conservative habits of mind and dangerous primitivism. Except in regionalist writers, cultural archaism is not commonly combined with consistent linguistic archaism, but it too can be a simplifying device: many historical novels exploit the reader's unfamiliarity with the culture described to give an uncomplex, idealized and sometimes monumental and intriguingly remote impression of human emotions, such as heroism, nostalgic yearning and guilt.

See Colin Burrow, *Epic Romance: Homer to Milton* (1993); John N. Wall, *Transformations of the Word: Spenser, Herbert, Vaughan* (1988).

MHP

Archetype   See MYTH.

Aristotelian criticism   See CHICAGO CRITICS.

Art   Like 'good', 'Art', it seems must be simply a commendatory word covering a multitude of incompatible meanings. What commends itself to one's taste is to another distasteful, for such commendation is subjective. Nor can there be agreement about objectively commendatory characteristics, for qualities perfectly appropriate to a good comic drama cannot be so to a love lyric or a tragic novel. In any case commendatory definitions are persuasive, and therefore however descriptive they purport to be, they are always prescriptive, and thus provocative, in effect.

The pull of common usage is probably too strong to allow this distracting commendatory element to be eliminated, but perhaps the following stipulative definition will serve useful: *any work characterized by an obvious aesthetic element is to be deemed a work of art*. This definition is minimally commendatory, for it does not imply that the aesthetic element defining a literary work as 'art' need be its most valuable characteristic, or that all works, even of creative literature, *ought* to be works of 'art' as defined. It is not essentialist in so far as *any* form, whether in drama, narrative or lyric, and *any* content in combination with it, may give

rise to aesthetic effects, so allowing dissimilar works all to be classed as works of art yet without the disrespect to their differences that comes from concentrating attention on some alleged metaphysical common property. It is descriptive rather than prescriptive in so far as aesthetic appreciation depends on describable formal qualities (see AESTHETICS). Finally, such a definition is consonant with the commonest use of this word in literary history, 'Art for art's sake'.

The usefulness of this definition is both negative and positive. Negatively, by drastically reducing the value-connotations of 'art', it avoids that metaphysical discussion which distracts attention from more concrete critical issues. Positively, by leaving open the possibility of good, bad or indifferent art (accordingly to the quality of the aesthetic element) and also by not pre-empting the possibility of factors other than 'art' being more pleasurable or important, it encourages full and varied critical appreciation.

See E. H. Gombrich, *Art and Illusion* (1960); R. Wollheim, *Art and its Objects* (1968); *British Journal of Aesthetics*; Mieke Bal, *Reading 'Rembrandt'* (1991); A. S. Byatt, *Portraits in Fiction* (2001); Antonella Braida and Guiliana Pieri (eds), *Image and Word: Reflections of Art and Literature* (2003).

AER

Assonance   See TEXTURE.

Atmosphere   A vague term with diminishing currency, atmosphere is created where the overtones of the words and ideas employed reinforce one another. The paradox of 'atmospheric' literature is that although (like almost all writing) it is linear, one word following another, it gives an appearance of stasis. Such German Romantics as Brentano and Eichendorff often use rhyme-words closely related in emotional colouring, so that the second rhyme-word, in recalling the first, includes it; thus a progressively all-engulfing sense of expansion is achieved. This, combined with effects of ebb and flow as one rhyme is replaced by another, eliminates a risk of 'atmospheric' writing, namely that it will seem aimless and meagrely repetitious, and sustains the paradox (exploited more complexly by some authors, for example, Hardy) of a movement which is no movement.

Atmosphere is often created by the viewing of ordinary events from an unusual angle, giving them an air of mystery: in Alain-Fournier's *Le Grand Meaulnes* (1913) even everyday happenings at school (which themselves evoke nostalgia in the reader) are mysterious because the child's understanding is insufficiently developed to work out to his own satisfaction how they are affecting him.

MHP

Author   According to common sense, authors are people who write books. But this is an activity subject to considerable historical variation, and one development in criticism has been to attend to this variation: to analyse the shifting identity of the author in relation to different institutions – the church, the court, the publishing house, the university. This analysis includes among its concerns the effects of print technology upon authorship, and the emergence in the nineteenth century of authors as a distinct professional group with legally protected rights of property in what they wrote. Another aspect of this history is the changing cultural image of authorship. Again the variation here is considerable, ranging from the scribe, to the artisan skilled in rhetoric, to the figure who imitates either nature or established models of excellence, to the seer who produces forms of writing deemed equivalent to new forms of consciousness, endowed with powers of prophecy or moral wisdom. This history demonstrates the problematic relationship between writing and authorship: are all writers authors or only some? What, in any given period, makes the difference? Nor is it a history characterized by the simple succession of one image of authorship by another: for example, the fascination with literary works as the product of divinely inspired genius which emerged in late eighteenth-century Europe revives themes found in Longinus and Plato.

The history of the practice and concept of authorship is valuable to students of literature because ideas and fantasies about the author have determined how we read and value literary works. If we regard literature as the product of genius, we approach it with reverence and an expectation of revelation. Or the logic of critical argument could be organized around the idea that the author is the sole or privileged arbiter of meaning. To discover the meaning of a work might be regarded as equivalent to understanding what the author did intend or might have intended in writing it. The problem of how to decode the author's INTENTIONS is itself the subject of extensive critical debate. What is the relevance of biographical information? Can we discern the author's intentions by analysing the literary work as a series of speech acts, each with an intended force? Can we know an author's intention without access to the historical context in which he or she wrote? What are the effects of PSYCHO-ANALYTIC criticism which introduces the idea of unconscious motivation into an account of authorship?

These questions continue to preoccupy literary critics, testifying to the power of the author in critical argument and in the wider culture. Our contemporary fascination with authors is long-standing, going back at least to the eighteenth century when Samuel Johnson produced a classic of biographical criticism, *The Lives of the English Poets* (1779–81). ROMANTIC theory introduced the analogy between divine and literary creativity, and this theological aura around authorship was renewed by MODERNIST accounts of the impersonality of the great writer. Authors have become heroic figures in modern culture: whether as rebels or reactionaries; because they write books, authors are expected to have wise things to say about a whole range of political and personal dilemmas.

But modern criticism has not simply underwritten the authority of authors. In a famous essay, 'The Intentional Fallacy' (1954), the American critics Wimsatt and Beardsley issued a dictat forbidding critics to refer to authorial intentions in the analysis of literature: a literary work contained all the information necessary for its understanding in the words on the page, so appeals to authorial intention were at best irrelevant, at worst misleading. The argument is valuable in so far as it warns against replacing the interpretation of texts with an interpretation of the author's life. It founders, however, for various reasons: the words on the page do not simply begin and end there, and understanding them requires reference to historical and social contexts, which are not so constant as Wimsatt and Beardsley believe. Nor can meaning be so readily divorced from intention. According to speech act theory, to understand the meaning of an utterance requires that we understand the intention of someone in uttering it. The problem with literary texts is identifying who that someone is, given the multiple displacements of the author into narrator, persona, characters, statements of traditional wisdom and other forms of quotation. Where do we find Dostoevsky amid the multiple voices which make up *Crime and Punishment*? Where do we find Chaucer in the *Canterbury Tales*?

The impossibility of answering these questions is the starting point for Roland Barthes's polemical essay 'The Death of the Author'. According to Barthes the author is an ideological construct whose purpose is to legitimate a practice of writing and reading which always pursues 'the voice of a single, person, the author "confiding" in us'. Barthes proposes an alternative account: the text is irreducibly plural, a weave of voices or codes which cannot be tied to a single point of expressive origin in the author. Reading is not about the discovery of a single hidden voice or meaning, but a production working with the multiple codes that compose a text. Traditional assumptions about the origin and the unity of a text are reversed:

> The reader is the space on which all the quotations that make up a writing are inscribed without any of them being lost; a text's unity lies not in its origin but in its destination. Yet this destination cannot any longer be personal: the reader is without history, biography, psychology; he is simply that someone who holds together in a single field all the traces by which the text is constituted.

Barthes's stress upon the anonymity of the reader recalls T. S. Eliot's earlier account of the impersonality of the author in 'Tradition and the Individual Talent' (1919). Barthes shifts the terms of a Modernist poetics on to the side of the READER; the meaning of a text is volatile, varying according to the different occasions of reading and without reference to an authority which will fix meaning. Barthes's paradoxical transformation of authors into readers liberates us from the oppressive reverence for authorial creativity and wisdom, but it excludes important questions from the critical agenda: what is it that brings a particular person at a particular time to write? What do we make of the phenomenon of originality or of the fact that literary works have stylistic signatures which enable us to distinguish the work of one author from another? Turning authors into cults is not going to answer these questions, but neither is banishing them altogether from the discourse of literary criticism. See also CREATION, DECONSTRUCTION, DIALOGIC STRUCTURE, DISCOURSE, READER.

See J. Bayley, *The Characters of Love* (1960); R. Barthes, 'The Death of the Author' in *Image-Music-Text* (trans. 1977) and *S/Z* (1970, trans. 1975); M. Foucault, 'What is an author?' (1969) in *Language, Counter-Memory and Practice* (1977); P. Parrinder, *Authors and Authority* (1977); Sean Burke, *Authorship: From Plato to the Postmodern – A Reader* (1995).

JC

Autobiography   See BIOGRAPHY.

B

Ballad   The term has three meanings of different scope. The widest is that of any set of words for a tune. The narrowest refers to the English and Scottish *traditional ballad*, a specific form of narrative poem which became a part of the larger world of folk song. The ballad is not peculiar to England and Scotland, but is found throughout Europe and in post-settlement America. In Britain, the traditional ballad first appears in the later Middle Ages, probably in the fifteenth century, when the minstrels, declining in social status and circulation, began to carry to a wider audience their narrative art in folk songs based on strong symmetrically constructed stories in a simplified four-line stanza. Then ballads were increasingly sung at every level of society by non-professionals. By the end of the seventeenth century, emphasis had shifted to the music as the prime formative constituent and more ballads used refrains, meaningless vocables like 'fal-lal', common-places and formulae, 'filler lines' to give the singer time to arrange the next stanza, and the peculiarly effective structure known as 'incremental repetition':

> He was a braw gallant,
> And he rade at the ring;
> And the bonny Earl of Murray
> Oh he might have been a king!

> He was a braw gallant
> And he played at the ba;
> And the bonny Earl of Murray
> Was the flower among them a'.

The traditional ballads as a whole have certain well-marked characteristics. They deal with episodes of well-known stories, condensed and impersonally presented, often by means of juxtaposed pictures or direct speech of the persons involved:

> The king sits in Dunfermline town
> Drinking the blude-red wine;
> 'O whare will I get a skeely skipper
> To sail this new ship o' mine?' ...

> Our king has written a braid letter,
> And seal'd it with his hand,
> And sent it to Sir Patrick Spens,
> Was walking on the strand...

There is little psychological comment, and the 'meaning' is realized through directly rendered action, and cryptic references to the larger context of related events. There is a 'ballad form' and a 'ballad world', both of supreme imaginative interest. The traditional ballads became admired literary objects in the eighteenth century, and numerous collections were made and published from then on. The most famous is Francis J. Child's five volumes of *The English and Scottish Popular Ballads* (1882–98). Such study tended to treat the ballads as timeless, though later discussion, based on the invaluable work of scores of collectors, such as Bishop Percy (*Reliques of Ancient English Poetry*, 1765), Sir Walter Scott (*Minstrelsy of the Scottish Borders*, 1802–3) and Child himself, has begun to establish the evolution of style in the ballads. The Romantics were interested in the ballads as folk-art and monuments of the heroic past. The *literary ballad*, with no music, had a vogue at the end of the eighteenth century and for another century, the best known of such works being Coleridge's *Ancient Mariner* and Keats's 'La Belle Dame sans Merci'. The older study of ballads had the disadvantage of treating 'collected' ballads both as written texts – though any written form poorly represents the 'performed' ballad in its musical and dramatic strength – and as fossil objects of a dead art.

Before the end of the eighteenth century the third meaning of the word was the most common: any doggerel verses set to one of several well-known tunes, such as 'Packington's Pound'. These were the sheet ballads, broadside ballads sold in roughly printed sheets, or stall-ballads hawked around the countryside at fairs or from door to door. The ballad-singer sang to collect customers for his wares, which dealt with murders, political events, prodigies. Such ballads were 'low-falutin', mostly realistic, irreverent, ironic, sometimes seditious. From this kind of production come the miners' ballads, work songs, protest songs, party political attacks which have had popular revival on the contemporary 'folk scene'.

The European settlement of America has also produced large bodies of distinctive ballads in the New World, particularly in the United States. The ballads in English consist either of transplanted traditional ballads which successive waves of immigrants, to Virginia in the seventeenth and eighteenth centuries, for example, have taken with them, or of indigenous ballads which have been and still are produced among West Virginian miners, the cowboys of the South West or African Americans. Versions of traditional ballads have been collected in the remoter parts and more isolated communities of the United States, such as portions of the Atlantic coast and the Central West, or the mountain people of the Appalachians, and these have been an important source for British as well as American ballad scholars. The changes which took place in the texts by transmission in America, modifications, for example, of the importance of rank in the narrative and modulations of names, provide valuable material for the study of ballad tradition. American sources often preserve archaic forms of European tunes, and musical works are rich and distinguished. The words, it has been said, are often preserved in relatively impoverished forms. An interesting reverse transplanting of traditional material is to be noticed in the way modern American recordings frequently introduce Scottish and English listeners and singers to forgotten or half-forgotten ballads. Indigenous American ballads include broadsides of the Revolutionary Period and the Civil War.

See D. C. Fowler, *A Literary History of the Popular Ballad* (1968); M. J. C. Hodgart, *The Ballads* (1950); V. de Sola Pinto and A. E. Rodway, *The Common Muse* (1950); Nicola Trott and Seamus Perry (eds), *1800: The New Lyrical Ballads* (2001); Joseph Harris, *The Ballad and Oral Literature* (1991); Susan Gilbert, *Ballad* (2005).

AMR

Baroque   A term denoting a distinctive style deeply characteristic of the seventeenth century, long since firmly established for critics of art and music, whose application to literature has been problematic and controversial. However, it has offered possibilities for cultural analysis. Like ROMANTICISM, it submits to an enormous number of seemingly disconnected and even contradictory usages, as phrases like 'Baroque grandeur', 'Baroque eccentricity', 'Baroque mysticism', 'Baroque exuberance' attest; it is even more polymorphously perverse in its frequent appearances outside the seventeenth century in labels like 'The Contemporary Baroque'.

Art historians have generally agreed to regard the Baroque as the third Renaissance style, setting in around 1600, with its centre in Rome and its quintessential representative in Bernini, and with important Catholic and post-tridentine tendencies. Musicologists associate the Baroque with the advent of Monteverdi, the birth of operatic recitative and *concertante* style, and with figured bass. The essential features of the works of art produced can perhaps best be suggested in a short space by means of semantic clusters, obviously shading into each other, with appropriate illustrations: *solidity*, massiveness, size, intimidation (St Peter's, Rome); *ornament*, playfulness, wit, fancifulness (Bavarian and Austrian Baroque); *mysticism*, ecstasy, inwardness, transcendence (Bernini's St Teresa); *drama*, human warmth, fleshiness (the paintings of Caravaggio); *illusion*, *trompe l'oeil* (the Heaven Room in Burghley House). It is important to add, as a further defining feature, that Baroque works of art unify, or attempt to unify, such elements in simple, massive organization: solidity *carries* ornament, for instance, rather than being swamped by it (consider Baroque columns, or the function of the figured bass in Bach).

The most fruitful approach to the relations between literature and other arts is likely to be one that attempts to 'translate' the stylistic elements of one art form into those of another. To give examples: it seems legitimate and useful to regard the frequent literary use of oxymoron and paradox in the seventeenth century as a counterpart to the dramatic use of chiaroscuro in Baroque painting, or to see a correspondence between the 'play within a play' form in seventeenth-century drama and the construction of Bernini's St Teresa chapel. In the case of Baroque, it is helpful to be also aware of the term MANNERISM. The features of Donne's poetry, for instance, that have sometimes been referred to as 'Baroque'

might more fruitfully be considered in relation to the art of Parmigianino or Giulio Romano.

Besides setting a challenge of an interdisciplinary nature, the use of the word *baroque* outside the seventeenth-century context involves other problems that reach out as far as the theory of history. Some critics (e.g. Hauser, *Mannerism*, 1965) have seen 'Baroque' as a recurrent phenomenon, a constant tendency of the human spirit. This requires very cautious handling indeed; if one can posit a 'Baroque spirit' it seems most fruitful to regard it as historically activated, as a last energetic assertion of the Renaissance faith in the fundamental interconnectedness of phenomena – one that is conveyed above all in a fleshly solidity of realization, accessible to a wider audience than were the *arcanae* of Florentine neo-Platonists.

In the 1960s and 1970s, there was a contemporary vogue of Baroque imitation and pastiche among writers preoccupied with illusion and sham, such as John Barth, Iris Murdoch and Gunther Grass. In many ways, however, this was failed Baroque – the inflated or sentimental rhetoric that generated, for instance, the stylistic conventions of religious kitsch – that fascinated and stimulated the ironic use of the self-evidently bad or hollow. The best Baroque art – the work of Bernini, Rembrandt, Milton, Monteverdi, Bach – is of a different order of intensity and grandeur.

See L. L. Martz, *The Wit of Love* (1969); W. Sypher, *Four Stages of Renaissance Style* (1955); Joseph M. Levine, *Between the Ancients and the Moderns: Baroque Culture in Restoration England* (1999); J. Douglas Canfield, *The Baroque in Neoclassical Literature* (2003).

MAH

Belief Since I. A. Richards's *Principles of Literary Criticism* (1924), critics have usually been wary of detailed explorations into reader psychology: 'willing suspension of disbelief' (Coleridge) is now more often alluded to than investigated. It implies a contract between author and reader: the reader is encouraged to imagine that what is portrayed is real or possible rather than remain querulously aware of its fictionality and impossibility, and hopes thereby to attain satisfactions and discoveries for which involvement, not distance, is required. Total delusion is rarely achieved (we do not rush on stage to whisper in the tragic hero's ear) and would probably be psychologically damaging: literature may help us to recognize and explore our fantasies without giving way to them.

The means by which belief is encouraged are diverse. Perhaps the best known is *verisimilitude*, an attempt to satisfy even the rational, sceptical reader that the events and characters portrayed is very possible (e.g. typical of a certain milieu or recurrent human tendencies). Other means are less rational, such as the non-intellectual appeal of intellectual ideas, sometimes reinforced by incidental sensuous and motor attractiveness (e.g. the power, lilt and sound-quality of Hugo's verse is sometimes seen as giving convincingness to his ideas). Another, frequent in tragedy and linked to wish-fulfilment, is an appeal to the desire to believe in human dignity and value.

A reader's willingness to believe provides various possibilities for manipulating responses. Some writers (e.g. Arnim and Hoffmann in their use of 'Romantic irony', and many comic novelists in their alternations of sympathy and mocking distance) use techniques which destroy belief, or which continually play off our wish to believe against our wish to be sceptical, calling both in question and requiring a complex, questioning response. Some (e.g. Céline) display an innocuousness which at first creates uncritical belief but of whose implications the reader becomes increasingly suspicious. Others, by undermining confidence in the world presented, induce us to transfer our belief to the narrator or author as the only reliable authority.

See Michael Bell, *Literature, Modernism and Myth: Belief and Responsibility in the Twentieth Century* (1997); Volney P. Gay, *Joy and the Objects of Psychoanalysis: Literature, Belief and Neurosis* (2001).

MHP

Bildungsroman Often literally translated as a 'novel of growth' the term applies more broadly to fiction detailing personal development or educational maturation. As a literary genre, the form originated in Germany towards the end of the eighteenth century and Johann Wolfgang von Goethe's *Wilhelm Meister's Apprenticeship* (1795–6) is commonly regarded as the prototype. Goethe's attention to the gradual growth to self-awareness of his protagonist depends on a harmonious negotiation of interior and exterior selfhoods, a reconciliation that involves the balancing of social role with individual fulfilment. Crucial to that holistic rapprochement is the educative journey that the hero undergoes: completion through enlightenment has been, from its earliest days, a cornerstone of the *Bildungsroman*. The focus on the integration of the self and society made the genre a particularly apposite embodiment of bourgeois capitalistic values and the apotheosis of the form in the mid-nineteenth century reflects both the wide-ranging social impacts of revolutionary and industrial histories and the difficulties of positioning subjectivity within this rapidly changing geo-political environment. In Britain, the *Bildungsroman* became synonymous with a certain sense of social dislocation as is discernible in some classic accounts of problematic identity and stifled individuation, such as Charles Dickens's *David Copperfield* (1850) and, *Great Expectations* (1861) and Samuel Butler's *The Way of All Flesh* (1903). George Eliot's *Middlemarch* (1871–2) typifies the Victorian embracing of the genre as an ambivalent site of psychosocial interaction. The story of the idealistic Dorothea Brooke's relationships with the pedantic Casaubon, the artistic Will Laidslaw and the ambitious Tertius Lydgate revolve around the political manoeuvrings of the years preceding the Reform Act of 1832. Social, economic, scientific and religious orthodoxies are brought into a jarring conflict that reveals not just the web of societal connections but also a nation in a process of transition. Elsewhere in Europe, the nineteenth century saw the publication of *Bildungsromane* more overtly transgressive in the arenas of sexuality and sexual politics. Gustave Flaubert's *Madame Bovary* (1857) and Leo Tolstoy's *Anna Karenina* (1874–6) present women as the models of psychological growth whose development intrinsically involves the fulfilment of a sexualized subjectivity, a self-realization that flies in the face of social convention.

Twentieth-century interpretations of the genre have seen its subversion, fragmentation and reinvention but have not diminished its compelling narrative importance. Modernism's addiction to the revelation of the interior life tended to focus attention away from the social interaction of the individual and towards the ineffability of the fractured self. One notable exception is D. H. Lawrence's *Sons and Lovers* (1913), which charts the growth to emotional maturity of Paul Morel against the backdrop of financial hardship, industrial pragmatism and social upheaval. The modernist *Bildungsroman* enabled the presentation of an apolitical consciousness focalized on self-knowledge and exploration. It lent itself particularly to the articulation of contemporary women's experiences, but rather than showing psychosocial integration, implied the impossibility of female individuation under the auspices of a patriarchal hegemony. Both Virginia Woolf's *The Voyage Out* (1915) and May Sinclair's *The Life and Death of Harriett Frean* (1922) declare female growth impractical through the channels of conventional marriage and domesticity. The development of the self as a creative and artistic force, so intrinsic to modernism's denunciation of the dogmatism of science, gives the form a sub-generic life in the shape of the *Künstlerroman* ('novel of the artist'), which addresses the struggle to fulfil an artistic potential. James Joyce's *A Portrait of the Artist as a Young Man* (1916) is perhaps the most celebrated incarnation of this offshoot of the *Bildungsroman* but Thomas Mann's *Doktor Faustus* (1947) is also a pertinent example of the form.

Postmodernism's attention to the suppressed narratives of marginalized groups has further expanded the envisioning potential of the *Bildungsroman*. Feminist interpretations have been joined by gay and lesbian rewritings, such as Jeannette Winterson's *Oranges Are Not The Only Fruit* (1985) and Alan Hollinghurst's *The Swimming-Pool Library* (1988) in an open renunciation of the traditionally conservative values of the genre. Non-white *Bildungsromane*, such as Chinua Achebe's *Things Fall Apart* (1958) and J. M. Coetzee's *The Life and Times of Michael K.* (1983) explore the experience of self-realization under the oppressive regimes of political intolerance, whilst Salman Rushdie's *Midnight's Children* (1981) offers a transgressive undermining by problematizing the very notion of identity. Postmodernism's cynicism towards fixed and stable subjectivity constitutes a serious ideological blow to the relevance of the *Bildungsroman*, but rather than dispense with the genre altogether, contemporary writers appear intent on redeveloping it for the twenty-first century.

See Michael Beddow, *The Fiction of Humanity: Studies in the Bildungsroman from Wieland to Thomas Mann* (1982); Franco Moretti, *The Way of the World: The Bildungsroman in European Culture* (1987); Martin Swales, *The German Bildungsroman from Wieland to Hesse* (1978); Marc Redfield, *Phantom Formations: Aesthetic Ideology and the Bildungsroman* (1996).

DL

Biography   In post-classical Europe the literary recording of people's lives begins with the search, for example, in the Lives of the Saints and the stories of the rise and fall of princes. Medieval historians like Geoffrey of Monmouth, Matthew Paris and others, bring a concern with human failings and strengths to their histories which often overrides their objectivity. But it is not until the sixteenth century that the first recognizable biographies appear. Cardinal Morton's *Life of Richard III* (1513?), wrongly attributed to Thomas More; Roper's *Life of More* (1535?); and Cavendish's *Life of Wolsey* (1554–7) are variously claimed as the first true biography, though no one could claim that the genre was established in the eyes of a readership. The seventeenth century saw Bacon's *Life of Henry VIII* (1621), Walton's *Lives* (1640–78) and,

best-known of all perhaps, Aubrey's *Minutes of Lives* which he began collecting in the 1660s and in which he persisted till his death. It is in Aubrey that we first hear the real human voice commenting with a sly smugness, a gossipy humour and a delight in the oddity of human nature on the affairs and misalliances of those he minuted. But it is in the eighteenth century and with Dr Johnson's *Lives of the Poets* (1779–81) that the form is established beyond a doubt with his claim for its recognition as a literary form in its own right and his insistence on its peculiar virtue being that it alone of literary forms seeks to tell the literal, unvarnished truth. It was fitting that the founder of the form should be repaid by becoming the subject of what is perhaps the best known of all biographies, Boswell's *Life of Johnson* (1791).

In the nineteenth century, biography continued to flourish (e.g. Lockhart's *Life of Scott* (1837, 1838), Gilchrist's *Life of Blake* (1863)) but now it was also showing its potential influence on the structures of fiction. Wordsworth's *Prelude*, the novels of Dickens and those of the Brontës all show in various ways the intimacy which grew up between experience and invention during and after the Romantic period. This process continued until the end of the century, culminating perhaps in that most literary of biographies, Gosse's *Father and Son* (1907) and that most biographical of novels, Butler's *The Way of All Flesh* (1903). But if the hybrids flourished so did the thing itself, and Lytton Strachey's *Eminent Victorians* (1918) established the standards both in reasoned objectivity and in witty skill for all those who were to follow him. The modern biography was established.

The main claim of modern biographers has been an objectivity towards the chosen subject, asserting that by choosing the form they deal in *fact*, not fiction. This claim may seem dubious if we compare the methods and presuppositions with the autobiographer, who also claims to tell the whole truth and nothing but the truth. (Vladimir Nabokov has great fun with this claim in his autobiography *Speak Memory*, 1966.) A much more naïve judgement emerges from H. G. Wells's *Experiment in Autobiography* (1934) when he wishes the novel could more closely resemble the biography since the latter is more 'truthful': 'Who would read a novel if we were permitted to write biography all out?' This completely begs the question of the selection and presentation of the material; it presupposes that the only limitations to biographers' truth telling are the range of their knowledge and licence of their society to publish it. It ignores the central issue of what kind of reality language can sustain.

In the mid-twentieth century, a wide interest was shown in the interchangeability of fictional and documentary techniques. Novelists experimented with 'factual subjects' (e.g. Truman Capote's *In Cold Blood*, 1966), while social scientists went to the novel for structures which enabled them to relate patterns of behaviour not amenable to the sequential logic of analytic prose discourse (e.g. Oscar Lewis, *The Children of Sanchez*, 1962). The traditional distinctions between biography, personal history (diary/confession) and novel (especially first-person narrative and/or tape-recorded novels) begin to be questioned. For writers in African countries (Achebe, Ngugi, Soyinka) and in Negro American circles (Baldwin, John Williams, Jean Tooner) autobiographical art is not a device for summing up the accumulated wisdom of a lifetime but a means of defining identity. The distinction between novel and autobiography becomes almost meaningless in this context. A novel like Ralph Ellison's *Invisible Man* (1965) and an autobiography like J. P. Clark's *America, Their America* (1964) are united beyond their different forms in a single gesture of passionate self-exposure.

Work in England began to show this influence too: Alexander Trocchi's *Cain's Book* (1960) and Jeff Nuttall's *Bomb Culture* (1968) continued a tradition whose roots run back through Kerouac to Henry Miller. This trend has continued in the extension of the 'hybrid' book whose format disdains to answer the query, fact or fiction?

Modern biography is now quite likely to acknowledge a degree of artifice in its writing, with some authors showing an imaginative, inventive and speculative approach to literary biography in such works as Peter Ackroyd's *Dickens* (1990) and D. J. Taylor's *Thackeray* (1999). The late twentieth century was also notable for an increase in a 'life-writing' approach to fiction and non-fiction. Such books use the autobiographical mode and are written in a meditative, confessional style, while their authors often seek neither to equate the narrator with themselves nor to pretend that the narrator is simply a fictional character. Books in this mode range from Martin Amis's literary 'autobiography' *Experience* (2000) to semi-autobiographical novels such as V. S. Naipaul's *The Enigma of Arrival* (1987). Feminist critics have also attacked the traditional emphases of biographical and autobiographical writing for their masculinist stresses on action and public recognition over interpersonal relationships and reproductive life.

See also FICTION, NOVEL.

See Leon Edel, *Literary Biography* (1957); Paul Murray Kendall, *The Art of Biography* (1965); H. G. Nicholson, *The Development of English Biography* (1959); Lytton Strachey, *Biographical Essays* (modern collection, 1969); Adriana Cavarero (Paul Kottman, trans.), *Relating Narrative* (2000); Liz Stanley, *The Auto/biographical: Theory and Practice of Feminist Auto/biography* (1992).

GG

Burlesque   See PARODY.

C

Cacophony   See TEXTURE.

Caricature   See PARODY.

Carnival   See DIALOGIC STRUCTURE.

Catastrophe   See DÉNOUEMENT, DRAMA.

Catharsis   The most disputed part of Aristotle's definition of tragedy is his statement that it is an action 'through pity and fear effecting a catharsis of these emotions'. Traditionally *catharsis* is rendered as 'purgation' and refers to the psychological effect of tragedy on the audience. Against Plato's condemnation of art for unhealthily stimulating emotions which should be suppressed, Aristotle argues that audiences are not inflamed or depressed by the spectacle of suffering in tragedy, but in some way released. Our subjective, potentially morbid, emotions are extended outward, through pity for the tragic hero, in an enlargement, a leading out, of the soul (*psychogogia*). So tragedy moves us towards psychic harmony. A related, but less psychological, interpretation puts catharsis into the context of Aristotle's argument that the pleasure peculiar to tragedy arises from the fact that our emotion is authorized and released by an intellectually conditioned structure of action. In fiction, unlike reality, we feel the emotion *and* see its place in a sequence of probability and necessity.

Alternatively catharsis may be seen, as by G. Else (*Aristotle's 'Poetics'*, 1957), not as the end result, but as a process operating through the 'structure of events' which purifies, not the audience, but the events themselves. The tragic hero's pollution (typically from the murder of a blood relation) is shown, through the structure of discovery and recognition, and the hero's subsequent remorse, to be in some measure undeserved. So catharsis is the purification of the hero which enables us to go beyond *fear*, our horror at the events, to *pity* born of understanding; the poet's structure leads our reason to judge our emotion. See also PLOT, TRAGEDY.

See Humphry House, *Aristotle's 'Poetics'* (1956); A. K. Abdulla, *Catharsis in Literature* (1985); Dana F. Sutton, *The Catharsis of Comedy: Greek Studies: Interdisciplinary Approaches* (1994).

PM

Cento(nism)   See PASTICHE.

Character   The fictional representation of a person, which is likely to change, both as a presence in literature and as an object of critical attention, much as it changes in society. Ideas of the place of the human in the social order, of human individuality and self-determination, clearly shift historically; and this is often mimed in literature by the relation of characters to actions or webs of story. The idea of character often attaches, therefore, to the personalizing or humanizing dimension of literature; thus naturalism, which tends to create plots in which characters are not self-determining agents but in ironic relationships to larger sequences of force, seems a remarkably impersonal writing. Yet, individual identity is often partly an attribute of social interaction, of the play of the social drama; this too is mimed in the dramatic character of much literature. In plays the paradox is compounded by the fact that characters are not simply represented verbally but impersonated by actors – a situation often used (as in much Shakespearean drama) to explore the paradoxes of being or identity themselves.

If the idea of character undergoes variation in different phases of literature, so it does in criticism. Neo-classical criticism tends to interpret characters as representatives of general human types and roles; romantic, to isolate and humanize them (see A. C. Bradley, *Shakespearean Tragedy*, 1904) and even separate them from the surrounding fictional determinants or dramatic design as 'living' people; modern, to regard them as humanized outcroppings from some larger verbal design. 'Characters' are by definition in determined contexts (i.e. they are parts of a literary sequence, involved in a plot), and can hence arouse liberal issues about the individualism of selves: as happened in the 1960s (in, for example, John Bayley, *The Characters of Love*, 1960 and W. J. Harvey, *Character and the Novel*, 1965) where an intrinsic association between humanist realism and literature was suggested, and the loss in fiction of what Iris Murdoch called 'the difficulty and complexity of the moral life and the opacity of persons' explored. Indeed 'liberal' character was a central aspect of artistic attention: hence, perhaps, Henry James's attempt (in parallel to that of his character Ralph Touchett) to set Isobel Archer 'free' in *The Portrait of a Lady*. Many fictional actions were in this sense portraits, aspects of the tendency of literature to personalize experience, in which the following out of the growth of a character was a primary cause of the work, the basis of its form.

But (as Henry James indicated) there are characters and characters in fiction; we recognize some as of the centre and others as of the circumference. Some are characters in the Aristotelian sense (i.e. detailed figures with their own motives and capacity for distinctive speech and independent action); some are enabling aspects of story, minor figures, stereotypes; there are some to whose perceptions we give credence (from poetic speakers to characters like Anne Elliot in *Persuasion*) and some we regard as a contextual society; some who partake in and are changed in the action (heroes, protagonists) and confidantes or devices. Literature is dramatic as well as personal; and the dramatic play of characters in a sequence frequently involves various levels of aesthetic impersonality. Hence there are always variables of closeness to and distance from them (a fact which has enabled much Shakespearean criticism). The complex of impersonation, role and mask; the complex of the personality and impersonality of identity or of the dimensions of the unconscious; the complex of that spectrum running from character as separate existence to character as qualities, moral attributes: all of these have been essential areas of exploration for drama, poetry, fiction.

'Character' has perhaps been the most mimetic term in the critical vocabulary, and hence one of the most difficult to contain within the fictional environment; yet, it is an essential condition of fictional existence that a character is so contained. In this sense the representation of persons in literature is a simultaneous process of their humanization and their dehumanization. See also DIALOGIC STRUCTURE, HERO, NARRATIVE.

See Northrop Frye, *Anatomy of Criticism* (1957); Erving Goffman, *The Presentation of Self in Everyday Life* (1959); Leo Lowenthal, *Literature and the Image of Man* (1957); Ortega y Gasset, *The Dehumanisation of Art* (1948).

The concept of 'character' came under attack for methodological and ideological reasons in STRUCTURALIST and POST-STRUCTURALIST theory. In the work of Roland Barthes, for example, we find 'character' dispersed into the constitutive 'indices' or 'semes' of narrative discourse. See Barthes, 'Introduction to the structural analysis of narratives' (1966), trans. in *Image-Music-Text* (1977) and *S/Z* (1970, trans. 1975). Representative of a more radical critique of this humanistic notion is Cixous, 'The character of "character" ', *New Literary History*, 5 (1978).

See John V. Knapp, *Literary Character* (1993); Robert Higbie, *Character and Structure in the English Novel* (1989).

MSB

Chicago critics   A group of critics, literary scholars and philosophers who came together first at the University of Chicago in the mid-1930s; included R. S. Crane, W. R. Keast, Richard McKeon, Norman Maclean, Elder Olson and Bernard Weinberg; are best known through the collective volume *Critics and Criticism* (1952); and have had a continuing influence on criticism. Their contribution to literary study lies in the philosophical clarity with which they attempted two main tasks. One was a close analysis, historical and synchronic, of criticism itself, to find out the kind of thing it was and the kind of thing it was studying; the second was an attempt to derive from that analysis a usable, coherent poetics. Participating in the general tendency of modern American criticism towards theory (as compared with the English tendency towards critical pragmatism), these critics dissented from several NEW CRITICAL emphases – stress on symbolism, paradox and the iconic nature of literature and the pre-eminent concern with lyric rather than narrative

or dramatic forms. What distinguished 'Chicago' theory was that it was holistic (concerned with the complete, dynamic structure of works) and typificatory (concerned to identify general kinds or species of works). It is thus that it was *neo*-Aristotelian: following Aristotle's ideal of a poetics always being derived from existing works, it was empirically plural, regarding criticism as secondary analysis, and so continually opened by the ever-growing variety of literature. Neo-Aristotelian poetics goes beyond the Aristotelian base to the extent that it draws on a vastly larger and more various literary corpus than Aristotle knew.

The neo-Aristotelian attitude in criticism was this: critical discourse, ostensibly a dialogue, actually conceals a multitude of differing presumptions about the genesis, nature and effect of a poem (i.e. any fiction) and sees it according to a wide variety of metaphors and analogies, often derived from extra-literary schemes of knowledge, and often dependent on self-invigorating dialectical pairs (form–content, tenor–vehicle, structure–texture) which are at best local expedients of composition rather than central features of artistic ordering. For critical dialogue, we have to know what kind of thing a poem is, to have a poetics based on the nature of the object. Hence the need for a pluralizable and pragmatic poetics which is still a poetics capable of emerging with general principles, a responsive theory of parts which are capable of creating concrete wholes in the given case, but will not predetermine the basis of coherence according to prescriptive assumption. The neo-Aristotelian poetics turns primarily on the notion of plot as a complex of matter *and* means: the basis of unifying coherence which has reference both to composition, to significant authorial choice, *and* the range of matters imitated.

The result is a remarkably sophisticated notion of the relation of parts to wholes – one of the most promising modern bases for deriving a *literary* (as opposed to a linguistically or scientifically based) ontology. The risk is that the approach can become a ponderous applied method rather than a critical sympathy; it led to some rather heavy works (Sheldon Sacks, *Fiction and the Shape of Belief*, 1964) as well as more famous critical endeavours (Wayne C. Booth, *The Rhetoric of Fiction*, 1961). Crane, especially in *The Languages of Criticism and the Structure of Poetry* (1953) and some essays in *The Idea of the Humanities* (1966), was the best exemplar; also see Elder Olson, *The Poetry of Dylan Thomas* (1962) and *Tragedy and the Theory of Drama* (1961) and Bernard Weinberg, *History of Literary Criticism in the Italian Renaissance* (1961). For an unsympathetic view see W. K. Wimsatt, Jr, *The Verbal Icon* (1954), 41–65.

MSB

Chorus A band of dancers and singers at the festivals of the gods; also, their song. According to Aristotle, Greek tragedy evolved from the choric song of the Dithyramb. Incorporated in fifth-century drama, the chorus, male or female, represents the voice of a collective personality commenting on events and interpreting the moral and religious wisdom of the play. In Aeschylus, it still has some direct influence on the action. With Euripides, who curtailed its function, it loses some of its mythic solemnity but takes on a new lyrical beauty. In post-Euripidean tragedy, it apparently became mere ornamental interlude.

In later drama, the chorus was never to regain its original significance. In Elizabethan tragedy, it is sometimes reduced to a single actor, but larger choruses also exist (e.g. Norton and Sackville's *Gorboduc*). Milton (*Samson Agonistes*), Racine (*Esther, Athalie*) and in the nineteenth century, Swinburne (*Atalanta in Calydon, Erectheus*) use it in an attempt to revive or imitate the spirit and procedures of the Greek theatre. Rare in twentieth-century drama, it appears in Eliot's *Murder in the Cathedral*, and in *The Family Reunion*, where the cast itself assumes the role of chorus. But it survives in opera.

Interpretations of the nature and function of the chorus vary. A. W. Schiegel considered it the 'idealized spectator'. Nietzsche, who attacked the democratic conception of the chorus as representing the populace over and against the noble realm of the play, maintained that it posits a reality set apart from quotidian reality, affirming the timeless, indestructible force of Nature. English critics, such as Lowes Dickinson and Gilbert Murray, pointed out that through the chorus the poets could speak in their own person and impose upon the whole tragedy any tone they desired.

See Reginald William Boteler Burton, *The Chorus in Sophocles' Tragedies* (1980); Cynthia P. Gardiner, *The Sophoclean Chorus: A Study of Character and Function* (1994).

NZ

Classic Matthew Arnold, in *The Study of Poetry*, says that 'the true and right meaning of the word *classic, classical*, is that the work in question belongs to the class of the very best'; and as T. S. Eliot observed (*What is a Classic?*) classic status can be known 'only by hindsight and in historical perspective'. A critic for whom the term *classic* is important is likely to be a conserver of the canons of art: and the scholars of Alexandria who invented the classic status of earlier Greek literature held it fast in an elaborate mesh of formal rules which they then tried to use as the basis of their own work, thus ensuring its own classic status. The Romans, inheriting this classificatory system of rhetorical terms, based their own upon them and reinforced the 'classic' status of Greek literature, which they imitated with a recurrent sense of inferiority. For us 'the classics' means first the literature of both Greece and Rome: but 'a classic' is nowadays likely to signify a work about the status of which there is general agreement, often unenthusiastic (Arnold perhaps used the term thus when he called Dryden and Pope 'classics of our prose'). A turning-point in the conception of classic status may have occurred in the neo-classical eighteenth century when deference to the rules of rhetoric, enshrined in the much-imitated *Ars Poetica* of Horace and in Aristotle's *Poetics* and sustaining an aristocratic culture, gave way to that sense of cultural diffusion that enabled Dr Johnson to invoke the general admiration for Gray's 'Elegy' as real evidence of its excellence. Since Arnold's time the term *classic* has lost effectiveness in proportion as moral criticism has waned. Where there is no critical consensus or (in Johnson's phrase) 'common pursuit of true judgement' the term is of doubtful use. Eliot, in *What is a Classic?* cites 'a very interesting book called *A Guide to the Classics* which tells you how to pick the Derby winner': and his own argument for the classic status of Virgil is clearly shaped by extra-literary concerns. In general the term is too readily used as a substitute for criticism, and to endorse received judgements.

Nevertheless an impulse towards *classicism* as fostering the virtues of formal discipline, impersonality, objectivity, and the eschewal of the eccentric and self-indulgent has since the time of Goethe (who defined the classical as the healthy, the romantic as the sick) served to check the individualistic aesthetics of romantic conceptions of 'genius'. Pushkin's work displays a classicism of this kind, often manifesting itself through SATIRE, as in the case of much eighteenth-century neo-classical writing. The revolt of many twentieth-century writers against their late romantic predecessors either enlisted the literature of classical antiquity as an aid to objectivity or universality (Joyce's use of Homer in *Ulysses*, or Pound's of Sextus Propertius) or contained lyric sensibility within the disciplined forms of a deliberate doctrine of classical impersonality. Eliot's theory of the OBJECTIVE CORRELATIVE is neo-classical in this sense, as is his insistence on the separation in great literature of the man who suffers from the mind which creates. A neo-classicism of this kind also underlies IMAGIST theory and practice. It was Eliot's elaboration of this new classicism into a Virgilian absolutism and orthodoxy extending beyond the frontiers of literature that prompted D. H. Lawrence's expostulation that 'This classiosity is bunkum, and still more *cowardice*' (*Collected Letters*, p. 753); and it is true that such neo-classical phenomena as neo-Aristotelianism in criticism run deliberately counter to the eclecticism of the culture they spring from, rather than constituting an authoritative definition of literary norms (as did the neo-classicism of Dryden, Pope and Boileau). Such phenomena amount in essence to a renewed emphasis on the importance of style and technique.

See Matthew Arnold, *Essays in Criticism, Second Series* (1888); T. S. Eliot, *Selected Essays* (3rd edn, 1951); T. S. Eliot, *What is a Classic?* (1945); H. M. Peyre, *Qu'est-ce que le classicisme?* (1933); S. Vines, *The Course*

of English Classicism (1930); Italo
Calvino, *Why Read the Classics?* (2000).

GMH

Closure   See DECONSTRUCTION.

Code   See CREATION, SEMIOTICS.

Cohesion   See DISCOURSE.

Comedy   Arouses and vicariously
satisfies the human instinct for mischief.
The playing of tricks on unsuspecting
victims, whether by other characters (e.g.
Palaestrio in Plautus's *Miles Gloriosus*) or
quirks of chance (e.g. Goldoni's *I due
Gemelli veneziani*) or both, recurs continually in comedy. The tendency to derive
delight from watching characters who
come to find situations difficult and
problematical (although to the audience
they are clear and simple) can go beyond
mischief and draw on more dubious
emotions, such as delight in sadistic and
voyeuristic observation of another's dis-
comfiture. A situation which to a comic
character seems dangerous (likely to
erode or destroy self-esteem, comfort,
amatory adventures or worldly success),
but which implies no great threat to the
audience or humanity in general, is a
typical comic situation. Indeed, one characteristic of comedy (especially of comic
drama, since it is frequently enacted at
speed) is its ability to blur the distinction
between harmless mischievous enjoyment
and sado-voyeuristic satisfaction. When
(as frequently in Molière) a master beats
his servant, or when a fop is humiliated in
a Restoration comedy, our amusement is
spontaneous and unreflecting. This casts
doubt on the supposedly intellectual and
unemotional appeal of comedy which,
according to some, derives from the
absence of any deep sympathy and the
distance which comedy sets up between
characters and audience. The tempo
leaves us no time to puzzle over our
reactions and motives.

Rapidity can also be exploited more
positively. If we are made to associate
things which at first seemed dissimilar,
the enjoyment of comedy can become
more than an exercise in self-indulgence.
A comic dramatist may choose simply to
indulge our preconceptions of the comic:
those who watch a third Whitehall farce
know from the previous two exactly what
forms of enjoyment to expect. But the
comic dramatist may also aim to extend
our awareness of comedy, so that we see
analogies between what we regard as
ridiculous and what previously we
regarded as having value. The effect of
this may sometimes be to blur distinctions
(e.g. Aristophanes, in *The Clouds*, falsely
equates Socrates's style of philosophy
with that of the sophists); at other times
self-seeking and self-adulation can be
revealed behind an impressive exterior
(Molière's treatment of a hypocrite in
Tartuffe, and Kleist's of a village magis-
trate in *Der zerbrochene Krug*, illustrate
ways in which respected social roles can
be manipulated and misused). Comedy in
itself is thus neither morally useful nor
immoral: it can perpetuate and extend
misconceptions as well as ridicule them.
Sometimes, however, dramatists use the
irresponsible instinctual speed of comedy
to lead the audience to a more complex
intellectual awareness. Besides manipulating audience responses, many comic
writers have developed various devices
for making us conscious that manipula-
tions of various sorts are taking place and
roles being adopted: the use of disguise
and masks is an obvious example (*Love's
Labour's Lost*).

Such awareness of complexities, when
it occurs, is normally available only to the
audience; rarely does it leave an imprint
of uneasiness on the language of the
plays. The language of comedy is fluent
and articulate: characters do not feel a
need to develop exploratory, stretching

uses of language to account for themselves and the world around them, but are satisfied that the relationships between them and the world are simple and comprehensible. Unlike tragic heroes, comic characters do not face up to the task of reconciling inconsistencies in their own nature (Harpagon, in Molière's *L'Avare*, feels no discrepancy between his selfish avarice and his desire to marry an emotionally lively young woman). Comic characters are, however, usually more than willing to face up to the task of defending themselves, particularly in the cut-and-thrust of dramatic dialogue. Even comic butts share this articulateness: they may be fools, but they are normally capable of speaking the same language as their more perspicacious opponents (e.g. the language of abuse in Molière or the language of pun and conceit in Shakespeare). Comic dialogue is frequently a battle which needs evenly balanced opponents to sustain its momentum. With dialogue and characterization, as with other aspects of comedy, it is perhaps by examining an author's capacity to generate pace, and the repetitiveness or increasing subtlety of the ways in which writers exploit it, that one can best arrive at an assessment of them as comic dramatists. See also FARCE.

See Henri Bergson, *Le Rire* (1899); Maurice Charney, *Comedy High and Low* (1978); Robert W. Corrigan (ed.), *Comedy: Meaning and Form* (1965); Paul Lauter (ed.), *Theories of Comedy* (1964); Elder Olson, *The Theory of Comedy* (1968); Harry Levin, *Playboys and Killjoys: An Essay on the Theory and Practice of Comedy* (1994); Ronald P. Draper, *Shakespeare: The Comedies* (2000).

MHP

Comedy of manners See MANNERS.

Comparative literature Techniques of comparison have formed a common part of the literary critic's analytic and evaluative process: in discussing one work, critics frequently have in mind, and almost as frequently appeal to, works in the same or another language. Comparative literature systematically extends this latter tendency, aiming to enhance awareness of the qualities of one work by using the products of another linguistic culture as an illuminating context; or studying some broad topic or theme as it is realized ('transformed') in the literatures of different languages. It is worth insisting on comparative literature's kinship with criticism in general, for there is evidently a danger that its exponents may seek to argue an unnatural distinctiveness in their activities (this urge to establish a distinct identity is the source of many unfruitfully abstract justifications of comparative literature); and on the other hand a danger that its opponents may regard the discipline as nothing more than demonstration of 'affinities' and 'influences' among different literatures – an activity which is not critical at all, belonging rather to the categorizing spirit of literary history.

Comparative literature is often discussed as if it were analogous with comparative philology or comparative religion: but it lacks, fortunately or unfortunately, the academic establishment of these disciplines. The idea that a work of literature yields a richer significance when placed alongside another, each serving as a way of talking about the other, has more to do with the approaches of NEW CRITICISM, and with Eliot's assertion that 'comparison and analysis are the chief tools of the critic', than with traditional literary scholarship, since intrinsic criteria of value help to shape such comparisons. This is not to deny, of course, that an imposing family tree is available to show how a shared European culture in medieval times (and later) took for granted what must now be painfully recreated: a culture in which to consider Chaucer, for instance, only in an English context would have seemed as senseless as to explain him away by reference to his French or Italian sources. On the world-historical showing the nationalist nineteenth century and the critical aftermath, stressing the need for a high degree of linguistic and cultural inwardness on the part of the reader – who cannot, the argument goes, be expected to attain this in a foreign culture except in unusual circumstances – can be seen as a Romantic aberration, wrongly at odds with the internationalist aspirations of European culture which received a supreme formulation in the Enlightenment. But although an ideology of internationalism underlies comparative literary studies, and many of its more impressive exponents have been European Marxists, such studies clearly need to assimilate, not reject, the admirable critical work done, for example, in England by critics whose high degree of sensitivity to literature in their own language has not been accompanied by a developed critical interest in another literature.

The presumptuousness of comparing literary works across languages can be avoided if emphasis is shifted from the smaller units of the literary work ('texture') to the larger ('structure'). Style can be described in terms of chapters as well as sentences: and the failure of many critics who approach novels as 'dramatic poems' can be explained as a consequence of over-insistent application to the minutiae of metaphoric language. The analogy with linguistics is fruitful: one needs as exact as possible an apparatus for describing the structure of a literary work, its 'grammar'. The term 'morphology' was appropriated by the Russian anthropologist Vladimir Propp (*The*

Morphology of the Folk-Tale, first published 1928, trans. 1958) to describe the large metamorphoses undergone by certain themes or topoi in folk narratives, when it became clear to him that it was unproductive to compare (or indeed to describe) 'images' or 'characters' – local and partial phenomena. He discovered that one tale about a rabbit, for instance, might be radically different from another such: but that one could compare tales in terms of *patterns* of activities, what one might call 'fields', generated by the topos as it underwent changes of role and relationship: its morphology, in fact. It is evident that where narrative fiction is concerned a close study of the style of any given episode of a large structure will be of questionable validity unless the analysis can refer to the relationship of this episode to the whole work conceived as a coherent utterance: and that this pattern, often unperceived, is likely to yield more significance than local texture minutely analysed. In other words, a satisfactory account of a novel could consist, more than is usually the case, in an account of its 'plot' (the morphology of its fable, the pattern of formal changes), and there is no reason why this should not be perceived and described in a translated text as well as in a text in the original. Characteristic devices can be perceived in works which are products of similar phases of civilization (the devices used by Tolstoy and George Eliot to assert the religious significance of life against the small agnostic ego are comparable). To such a degree may this comparability exist that comparative analysis can invoke a concept of an underlying MYTH which has structured the works in a given way, as suggested by the work of Lévi-Strauss. In the case of poetry, too, verbal texture can be considered as one manifestation of the total structure of the poem: but since many forms and stanza-patterns are common to the whole European tradition, where they engender comparable formal problems, comparative analysis will be rewarding to the critic who reads the language in question. In many cases the study of translations becomes a comparative critical exercise of great value, even for readers who lack the original: intelligent students of literature can benefit from a systematic comparison of three significant translations of Homer (e.g. Dryden, Pope and Cowper) even if they do not know Greek. The Chomskyan concept of deep structure can also offer an impetus to comparative criticism, since it facilitates the comparison of works whose surface structures may be dissimilar (an example that springs to mind is Melville's *Bartleby* and Gogol's *The Overcoat*: dissimilar in detail, these two masterpieces have a profound kinship which seems inadequately described in terms of 'theme' but may be more convincingly described in terms of generative grammar).

See Henry Gifford, *Comparative Literature* (1969); Marius Guyard, *La Littérature comparie* (1961); Leo Spitzer, *Linguistics and Literary History* (1948); N. P. Stallknecht and H. Frenz, *Comparative Literature: Method and Perspective* (1961); René Wellek and Austin Warren, *Theory of Literature* (1963). Steven Totosy De Zepetnek, *Comparative Literature and Comparative Cultural Studies* (2002); E. S. Shaffer (ed.), *Comparative Criticism: Fantastic Currencies in Comparative Literature – Gothic to Postmodern* (2002). Relevant journals include *Comparative Criticism*, *Comparative Literature*, *Comparative Literature Studies*, *Comparison*.

GMH

Competence, literary See POETICS, STRUCTURALISM.

Complaint See ELEGY.

Conceit A characteristic feature of much Renaissance lyric poetry, the conceit is a way of apprehending and expressing the subject which pleases and illuminates by its ingenious aptness. It belongs therefore to a kind of poetry which is avowedly artificial, which is not 'the spontaneous overflow of powerful feeling' of Wordsworth but instead invites the reader's appreciation of virtuosity and inventiveness. Like WIT and 'fancy', terms to which it is closely related, the word 'conceit' itself refers to the mental act of conception or understanding, and it implies an artful varying of the ordinary, not only in verbal expression, but in the way the subject has been conceived.

Although conceits may take the form of paradox ('The truest poetry is the most feigning') or hyperbole ('An hundred years should go to praise/Thine Eyes, and on thy Forehead Gaze'), they commonly involve metaphorical or analogical correspondences, which may be paradoxical or hyperbolical in character, for example:

> Full gently now she takes him by the hand,
> A lily prison'd in a gaol of snow,
> Or ivory in an alabaster band;
> So white a friend engirts so white a foe.
>
> (Shakespeare)

> For I am every dead thing,
> In whom love wrought new Alchimie.
> For his art did expresse
> A quintessence even from nothingnesse,
> From dull privations, and leane emptinesse:
> He ruin'd mee, and I am re-begot
> Of absence, darknesse, death; things which are not.
>
> (Donne)

As these examples illustrate, the conceit belongs as much to the courtly style of the Elizabethans as it does to the wit of the Metaphysical poets; yet, the former presents a series of emblematic pictures, while the latter realizes its object in the conceptual terms of a philosophical definition.

A single conceit may provide the basis of a whole poem (as in Sidney's sonnet, 'With how sad steps, O moon, thou climb'st the skies', or in Donne's 'The Flea'), or a poem may consist of a string of different conceits on a single subject (Crashaw's 'The Weeper', Herbert's 'Prayer'). The conceit may be sustained and elaborated at length, especially if it derives from a familiar or conventional motif (such as the innumerable variations on the 'blazon' or descriptive praise of the lady in Elizabethan love sonnets), or it may be confined to a single striking figure (such as Marvell's image of the fishermen carrying their coracles over their heads: 'Have shod their heads in their canoes/Like the Antipodes in shoes'). It may even be altogether implicit, like the unspoken pun on 'host' which underlies Herbert's 'Love'.

The conceit went out of fashion when it was generally felt that ingenuity or surprise were effects less suited to poetry than a sense of the natural. Like the pun, which suffered disfavour at the same time, it came to be regarded as a form of bad taste. But in the twentieth century, with its taste for singularity and shock in art, the conceit returned to poetry, nowhere more so than in the work of T. S. Eliot, himself a great admirer of seventeenth-century wit. The famous image from the beginning of 'The Love Song of J. Alfred Prufrock' describing the evening 'spread out against the sky/Like a patient etherised upon a table', is a good example of the conceit's appeal to the reader's mental acuity as much as feeling. For as the Renaissance itself insisted, however far-fetched or elaborate the conceit, its success depends upon how appropriate its extravagance and ingenuity are. True artifice in this kind of poetry demands of the poet a precise balance of fancy and judgement. See also WIT.

See M. Praz, *Studies in Seventeenth-Century Imagery* (1964); K. K. Ruthven, *The Conceit* (1969); R. Tuve, *Elizabethan and Metaphysical Imagery* (1961); George Williamson, *Six Metaphysical Poets: A Reader's Guide* (2001).

DJP

Concrete poetry   Conceives of the poem as ideogram; as an instantly assimilable, visually ordered text in which the word stands both as physical spatial object, and as a plurality of simultaneously existing meanings. Preoccupations with both typographical form and semantic content create confusions in which the text is seen as being somehow 'between poetry and painting', readers being unsure whether they are confronted with a picture for reading, or a poem for looking at. At its mimetic extreme, the structure of the concrete poem either echoes its semantic content, in the manner of Apollinaire's '*Il pleut*', or else becomes its semantic content; in the words of the painter Stella: 'a picture of its own structure'.

The concrete poem's aesthetic is not that of accumulative, discursive, linear writing, but that of the 'constellation'; Max Bense explains: 'It is not the awareness of words following one after the other that is its primary constructive principle, but the perception of its togetherness. The word is not used as an intentional carrier of meaning.' Bense's 'abstract' texts seem very close to the 'silence of form' that Roland Barthes believes attainable 'only by the complete abandonment of communication'.

Despite such formal preoccupations not all concrete poetry rejects communication; indeed the semantic extremes of concrete poetry, via its spatial 'grammar', come closer than any other mode of writing to the elusive meaningful semantic simultaneity that Barthes lauds as 'colourless writing'; writing in which each word is 'an unexpected object, a Pandora's box from which fly all the potentialities of language'. The elusiveness of 'writing degree zero' may be explained by the fact that traditional syntax, and the logical form of linear writing, simply does not permit a statement of the several simultaneously existing semantic realities making up the 'potentialities' of the word.

The eye may perceive two objects, the mind may conceive two concepts, but such pluralistic observations transcend the possibilities and patterns of linear language which must choose to record first one observation and then the other; a distortion which turns simultaneity into the sequential. Attempting to simultaneously evoke all the potentialities of language, rejecting the internal ordering of sequential linear language, yet, still working within its confines, the Surrealists abandoned logical order for the 'super-real' semantic impressionism of 'automatic writing', while Joyce, Helms, Eliot and Burroughs remixed fragments of words and phrases in order to exchange old semantic potentialities for those of their new hybrid creations. Mallarmé achieved a relatively non-sequential and non-linear simultaneity of pluralistic semantic potentialities in his poem '*Un Coup de Dés*' whose pages, though precisely sequentially ordered, proffered scattered spatially punctuated words permitting permutation in a number of non-sequential readings.

Concrete Poetry finally attained a truly poly-semantic 'Pandora's box' of potentialities of meaning, synthesizing the typographical discoveries of the DADA and Futurist poetries, and adopting the single page as 'working area', transcending the sequential, and creating simultaneity, by rejecting linear order and spatially punctuating the liberated word, henceforth an object to be read freely in all directions, and as such a semantic object capable of presenting both vertical and horizontal linguistic potentialities. Whilst the scale of Concrete Poetry (one page) marks this genre with the limitations of minimal rather than of epic literature, it is significantly symptomatic of a mode of writing permitting the presentation of unprecedented semantic simultaneity. Concrete Poetry has offered important pointers to a visual writing transcending the limitations of sequential language.

See Stephen Bann (ed.), *Concrete Poetry: An International Anthology* (1967); Mary Ellen Solt, *Concrete Poetry: A World View* (1968); Emmett Williams (ed.), *An Anthology of Concrete Poetry* (1967); K. D. Jackson, Eric Vos and J. Drucker (eds), *Experimental – Visual-Concrete: Avant-Garde Poetry Since the 1960s* (1996).

NCPZ

Consonance See TEXTURE.

Context A central notion of modern philosophical linguistics, and by extension, of modern literary criticism too. Contextual theories of meaning assert that concepts precede percepts; that association can only take place between universals, not discrete impressions; and that all discourse is over-determined, having a multiplicity of meaning. In literary criticism the effect of these doctrines has been to extend the use of the word 'meaning' to cover all aspects of interpretation and to promote the false dictum 'The meaning of a word is its use in the language'.

What should be substituted for this is the sentence 'The interpretation of an utterance is dependent upon a knowledge of the contexts within which it occurs.' The problem may be seen at its most acute in the use of puns, and is discussed by Paul Ziff in his *Semantic Analysis* (1960). As Ziff points out, knowing the meaning of the words will not help one to understand the remark 'England had at least one laudable bishop'. It is also necessary to catch the pun. The range of contexts within which utterances occur extends from the narrowly linguistic (phonetic or morphological) to the broadly philosophical, and the task of literary criticism can be seen, in part, as the need to relate words, phrases, sentences and other parts of literary works to their linguistic contexts. The other, more open-ended part of criticism involves relating the works themselves to relevant psychological, social and historical contexts. The obvious difficulty of interpretation arises from the need to assess the claims of conflicting contexts, though throughout the twentieth century an increasing emphasis by Formalists, New Critics and Structuralists, on the 'foregrounded' or 'aesthetic' elements of literature at the expense of 'utilitarian' or 'referential' ones, resulted in a general lack of interest in the broader, human contexts within which literature is produced and consumed.

In an attempt to correct this imbalance, David Lodge suggests in his book *The Modes of Modern Writing: Metaphor, Metonymy, and the Typology of Modern Literature* (1977), that when literary texts work properly 'it is because the systematic foregrounding also supplies the place of the absent context of facts and logical entailments which validates nonliterary discourse; one might say that it folds the context back into the message, limits and orders the context in a system of dynamic interrelationships between the text's component parts and thus contrives to state the universal in the particular' (p. 8). See also DISCOURSE.

BCL

Contradiction   From Aristotle to Coleridge, Hegel to T. S. Eliot, literary criticism tended to conceive of the literary work as an achieved unity, often of an ORGANIC or 'spontaneous' kind. Developments in MARXIST, SEMIOTIC and DECONSTRUCTIVE criticism have queried this view, regarding it as a misleading, and potentially mystifying, account of the nature of literary texts. Emphasis shifted instead to the multiple, conflicting and uneven character of such texts, which may well *attempt* to resolve into harmony materials which nevertheless remain stubbornly various and irreducible.

Deconstructive criticism has characteristically fastened upon those aspects of a literary work which appear to an orthodox eye fragmentary, marginal or contingent, and shown how the implications of such fragments may begin to deconstruct or unravel the 'official', unifying logic on which the text is founded. Expelled by that logic to the text's boundaries, such unconsidered trifles return to plague and subvert the literary work's ruling categories. For Marxist criticism, this process has ideological relevance. Literary texts, like all ideological practices, seek an imaginary reconciliation of real contradictions; the classical REALIST work, in particular, strives for a symmetrical 'closure' or 'totality' within which such contradictions can be contained. But in its striving for such unity, a literary work may paradoxically begin to highlight its limits, throwing into relief those irresolvable problems or incompatible interests which nothing short of an *historical* transformation could adequately tackle.

In granting ideology a determinate form, the work unwittingly reveals that ideology's absences and silences, those things of which it must at all cost not speak, and so begins to come apart at the seams. All ideologies are constituted by certain definite exclusions, certain 'not-saids' which they could not articulate without risk to the power-systems they support. In daily life, this is not often obvious; but once an ideology is objectified in literature, its limits – and consequently that which it excludes – also become more visible. A literary text, then, may find itself twisting into incoherence or self-contradiction, struggling unsuccessfully to unify its conflicting elements.

For much Marxist and deconstructive criticism, this is true of any literary writing whatsoever. But there are also literary works which are, as it were, conscious of this fact, which renounce the illusory ideal of unity in order to expose contradictions and leave them unresolved. In much MODERNIST writing, the fundamental contradiction of all realist literature – that it is at once FICTION and pretends not to be – is candidly put on show, so that the text becomes as much about its own process of production as about a stable reality beyond it. In the hands of Marxist writers, such devices have been turned to political use. For Bertolt Brecht, the point of theatre is not to provide the audience with a neatly unified product to be unproblematically consumed, but to reflect in its own conflicting, irregular forms something of the contradictory character of social reality itself. 'Montage' – the abrupt linking of discrete images – and the 'alienation effect', in which the actor at once exposes a reality and reveals that this exposure is fictional, are examples of such techniques. By articulating contradictions, the Brechtian drama hopes to throw the audience into conflict and division, undermining their consoling expectations of harmony and forcing them to ponder the many-sided, dialectical nature of history itself. See also EPIC THEATRE.

See Leon Trotsky, *Literature and Revolution* (1971); Lucien Goldmann, *The Hidden God* (1967); Christopher Caudwell, *Illusion and Reality* (1937).

TE

Convention A generalizing term which isolates frequently occurring similarities in a large number of works. If critics are concerned to categorize a work, they will describe it as belonging within a convention which in this sense is a subcategory of TRADITION. If, on the other hand, they are more concerned to describe the individual work, they will point out that this or that element is conventional without implying that the whole work is thus defined as belonging within that convention. *As You Like It* 'belongs within the pastoral convention': or *As You Like It* 'has this or that element of pastoral', but is more usefully categorized in some other way. Clearly it is largely a matter of how all-pervasive the conventional element is.

It is tempting to distinguish between conventions of form and conventional content. A convention in the first sense is any accepted manner, hallowed by long practice, of conveying meaning. The second sense coincides with ordinary usage and means a generally accepted, standard, view or attitude. But it is as difficult to keep these two meanings separate, as it is generally to separate medium and meaning. Take an example of what seems a purely technical convention: the invisible fourth wall separating the real world of the theatre audience from the imaginary world of the play. Even in this case it might be argued, as Brecht argues, that the technical convention tends to express, and foster as immutable truth, views which are mere conventions in the second sense.

The pastoral convention shows clearly how manner and meaning are inextricably entwined, and demonstrates too the positive and negative values of both aspects. The conventionality of meaning allows for stylistic brilliance. We are so familiar with the broad meaning that we can appreciate aesthetically the subtle expression of fine nuances – the variations on a theme – as we cannot so easily in new un-assimilated areas of discourse. On the other hand, the conventional style or form may function like a shorthand. It allows an author to introduce huge areas of meaning very concisely by virtue of the accretions of connotation and resonance it has acquired. In a negative way, such manipulation of a literary convention is a powerful weapon of the ironist.

The drawbacks are obvious. The convention may become exhausted, the language and form too mannered: a stylistic rigor mortis revealing dead attitudes and emotions (see MANNERISM). The accretions of meaning may be too heavy or centrifugal, so that works seem abstruse or vague. The language may be so weighed down by conventional associations that it cannot absorb and express new meaning, even through irony. Conventional attitudes from the past may blind to present truths. *Conventional* commonly has such pejorative undertones and in this sense is opposed to *original* (see ORIGINALITY).

See M. C. Bradbrook, *Themes and Conventions of Elizabethan Tragedy* (1952); Bertolt Brecht, trans. and ed. J. Willett, *Brecht on Theatre* (1964); W. Empson, *Some Versions of Pastoral* (1935); Richard Taylor, *Understanding the Elements of Literature: Its Forms,* *Techniques and Cultural Conventions* (1982); Peter J. Rabinowitz, *Before Reading: Narrative Conventions and the Politics of Interpretation* (1997).

EJB

Couplet In English verse, a unit consisting of a pair of lines of the same length, linked by rhyme. The couplet may be *closed* if the sense and syntax are complete within the metrical unit, or *open* if the couplet is itself a part of a longer unit. There are two chief kinds of couplets; other experiments have proved unsuccessful. The older in English is the *octosyllabic* or *four-stress* couplet, perhaps based on a common Latin hymn metre, which became a staple form of English medieval narrative verse in works like *The Lay of Havelock the Dane*, remaining a popular form into the eighteenth century. The two great practitioners of the four-stress couplet both show the strengths of the couplet as a form: pithy memorability of wit in closed units, and sinuous flexibility in the open structure. The craggy couplets of Samuel Butler's influential work, *Hudibras* (1663–78) came to be known as 'Hudibrastics':

> And Pulpit, Drum Ecclesiastick,
> Was beat with Fist, instead of a stick.

Swift forms a link with the older masters of the shorter couplet in his satirical narratives like *Baucis and Philemon*, or in straight SATIRE ('Verses on the death of Dr Swift'):

> My female Friends, whose tender Hearts
> Have better learn'd to act their Parts,
> Receive the News in doleful Dumps:
> 'The Dean is dead, (and what is Trumps?)
> The Lord have Mercy on his Soul!'
> (Ladies I'll venture for the Vole.*)
>   * grand slam

The *decasyllabic* or *five-stress* couplet is most commonly thought of as the English couplet form. It seems to have been introduced into English by Chaucer in the 'Prologue to the Legend of Good Women' (*c.*1375), as an imitation of a French metre. In the Restoration theatre, it became the staple equivalent of the French dramatic Alexandrines of Racine and others: hence the term, from its association with those heroic tragedies, 'heroic couplet'. Early in the seventeenth century, Wailer adjusted and regularized the syllabic structure to match English stress structure, and in the hands of Dryden and Pope the 'heroic couplet' became one of the most disciplined and effective verse forms. As with all formalist art, it allows great sophistication and power to develop from almost imperceptible signals, such as small variations in placing the *caesura* or pause, or from pressing the strict form into unusual uses (Pope, 'Epistle to Bathurst'):

> 'God cannot love (says Blunt, with tearless eyes)
> The wretch he starves' – and piously denies:
> But the good Bishop, with a meeker air,
> Admits, and leaves them, Providence's care.

AMR

Creation   The metaphor of creation has traditionally dominated discussions of literary authorship, with strong implications of the mysterious, possibly transcendental nature of such activity. MARXIST CRITICISM has identified the roots of the notion as essentially theological: the hidden model of literary creativity is the Divine Author, conjuring his handiwork – the world – *ex nihilo*. Viewing such an idea as a fundamental mystification of the process of writing, Marxist criticism (in particular the work of Pierre Macherey) preferred to substitute the concept of literary production, which suggests the essentially ordinary, accessible nature of fiction making. Production is understood as the general activity of purposive transformation of raw materials, whether this be economic, political, cultural or theoretical; and it is seen as possessing a triple structure. All production entails:

1   certain specific raw materials to be transformed;
2   certain determinate techniques of transformation; and
3   a definitive product.

Because of the intervention of stage 2, this product can in no way be reduced to the 'expression', 'reflection' or mere *re*production of the initial raw materials.

Literary raw materials, for Marxist criticism, are essentially of two kinds. On the one hand there is the specific historical experience available to a given writer, which will always be *ideologically* informed, directly or indirectly relevant to the processes of political, cultural and sexual power. On the other hand there are previous writings, equally ideologically formed, which the writer may also transform through *intertextuality*. These raw materials are never 'innocent' or easily pliable: they come to the literary productive process with specific degrees of resistance, particular valences and tendencies of their own. The 'techniques of literary production', always part of a certain LITERARY MODE OF PRODUCTION, can then be grasped as the codes, conventions and devices historically available to a particular literary producer. These techniques, equally, are never ideologically neutral: they encode and secrete particular ways of seeing which have complex relations to social power-systems and power-struggles. Since a particular literary device or convention may belong to an ideology other than that to which its raw material belongs, one can expect that the ideology of the end product is especially complex.

Such a view of literary production renders writing amenable to analysis by 'decentring' the individual AUTHOR, who can then be seen not as the unique, privileged 'creator' of the text, but as a particular analysable element in its constitution, a 'code' or ideological sub-formation in itself. How important this 'authorial ideology' is in the production of the text will be generically and historically variable: more important, obviously, in ROMANTIC lyricism than in medieval religious verse. Such a decentring of the author finds parallels in STRUCTURALIST, POST-STRUCTURALIST and DECONSTRUCTIVE criticism, where the 'author' is no more than one text among others; the 'author's life' will not provide us with a firm foundation for the meaning of the work, since this itself is only textually available to us. Post-structuralist criticism, in its concern with the potentially infinite productivity of language, and PSYCHOANALYSIS, which sees the dream as itself the product of a 'dream-work' or determinate process of labour, both tend to converge with Marxist criticism in its dethronement – to many still scandalous – of the 'creative author'.

See L. Althusser, *Lenin and Philosophy* (1971); R. Coward and J. Ellis, *Language and Materialism* (1977); T. Eagleton, *Criticism and Ideology* (1976); F. Jameson, *The Political Unconscious* (1981); P. Macherey, *A Theory of Literary Production* (1978); P. Macherey and E. Balibar, 'Literature as ideological form' in R. Young (ed.), *Untying the Text* (1981).

TE

Criticism 'To criticize', etymologically, meant 'to analyse' and later,

'to judge'. If usage were to be restricted to both these meanings some coherence could be given to a now dangerously over-extended term. Literary *scholarship* and literary *history*, then, should be so named and should be regarded as complementary to literary *criticism*, not as part of it. *Critical theory* too should be distinguished from criticism, since it concerns itself with the analysis of concepts rather than works. It is a philosophical activity which should underlie criticism but, again, should not be regarded as part of it. Similarly, *metacriticism* is probably the better name for what has been called *extrinsic criticism*: the practice of using literary works for some extra-literary end, such as gaining insight into authors or their readers or society, amplifying studies of ethics, religion, psychology and so on. *Structuralist criticism*, so called, since it regards literature only as a manifestation of its environment and is therefore intent on using it merely as evidence – a piece in the jigsaw 'structure' of society – is a type of metacriticism. Arguably, *(intrinsic) criticism* must precede metacriticism, as no literary work can constitute valid evidence in any more general field until its own workings have been assessed. It is usually desirable that critical appreciation of meaning should be complemented by metacritical study of relevant significance; that a grasp of literary identity should lead to discussion of extra-literary relationships. But the two activities, despite some overlapping, should not be confounded under one term; nor should the extra-literary end in view be allowed to bias the critical activity (by pre-selecting the aspects considered to be central) or to blind the metacritic to the possibility of other significances, other standards (for literary works are multifaceted and multivalent).

'Extrinsic criticism' has been used for that criticism which relies heavily on information drawn from outside the literary work, and is contrasted with an 'intrinsic criticism' which does not. Sometimes the same terms are also used to distinguish criticism that deals mainly with content (attitudes, ideas, subject-matter) from that dealing mainly with form. These usages evidently do not correspond to the difference between metacriticism and criticism, since a work grasped without the aid of external scholarship could then be put to some meta-critical end and, contrariwise, a good deal of scholarly information might be necessary to appreciate a work in and for itself. The distinction therefore is between two critical approaches to a work, not between a critical and an extra-critical use of it. *External criticism* and *internal criticism* thus seem to be preferable terms. And the second distinction mentioned is made more clearly by the terms *contentual criticism* and *formal criticism*. The term 'extrinsic criticism' is better used, if at all, only as a synonym for metacriticism, and '(intrinsic) criticism', with or without the brackets, only as the contrary of metacriticism.

The distinction of *ends*, which marks off various kinds of criticism from various kinds of metacriticism, may be matched by a broad distinction of *means*: *objective* or *subjective*. Metacriticism can obviously attain objectivity more easily than criticism (but has to be based on the latter). External criticism seems to encourage objectivity, internal criticism subjectivity. But within the field of internal criticism, though, it is clearly easier to be objective about form (as formal criticism is technical) than about content. Equally clearly, none of these approaches actually compels the critic to adopt one attitude or the other. However, *impressionistic criticism* and *affective criticism* – since they limit themselves by definition to judgement from immediate personal reaction – are necessarily subjective. *Practical criticism* and *judicial criticism* – since they seek consensus-judgements based on analytical or other evidence – are necessarily objective in their aims.

As with metacriticism and criticism, there is inevitably some overlapping of objective and subjective methods. Objectivity, in the arts, can be defined only as the attempt to be unbiased, uneccentric, about personal reactions, the attempt to get them right, so that they may constitute valid evidence not mere opinion. It cannot imply their exclusion; criticism that excluded them would not be criticism at all, for they *are* much of the literary work. Similarly the most impressionistic of critics must refer, at least implicitly, to some recognizable (and therefore objective) characteristics of the work if their impressions of it are to carry any weight as criticism and not be discounted as mere autobiography. Nevertheless, the perceived existence of objective criticism led to claims that criticism could be, or should be, a science. Alternatively, the existence of subjective criticism has led to claims that criticism is, or should be, an art, parallel to literature rather than a commentary parasitic upon it. But both the etymology of the word and all the various traditional practices that have come under it, indicate 'criticism' to be an activity dealing with fictions but not itself fictional; it has rarely been considered strictly creative, rather than re-creative. Analysis or judgement are already varied enough to strain the viability of 'criticism' as a useful term. Yet, the number of critical approaches, from practical criticism to ECO-CRITICISM, continues to grow. See also ANALYSIS, CRITIQUE, DECONSTRUCTION, EVALUATION, HERMENEUTICS.

See Gary Day, *Re-reading Leavis: 'Culture' and Literary Criticism* (1996);

E. D. Hirsch, Jr, *Validity in Interpretation* (1967); Allan Rodway, *The Truths of Fiction* (1970); R. Wellek, *A History of Modern Criticism* (1961); René Wellek and Austin Warren, *Theory of Literature* (3rd edn, 1963); W. K. Wimsatt, Jr and C. Brooks, *Literary Criticism: A Short History* (1962); D. Lodge (ed.), *Twentieth Century Literary Criticism* (1972); A. Jefferson and D. Robey (eds), *Modern Literary Theory* (1982). Jerome J. McGann, *A Critique of Modern Textual Criticism* (1992). See C. Belsey, *Critical Practice* (1980) or R. Fowler, *Linguistic Criticism* (1986) for alternative conceptions of 'criticism'.

AER

Critique A word that comes into the English language from French early in the eighteenth century. The *Oxford English Dictionary* cites, among other examples, the following quotation from Addison: 'I should as soon expect to see a Critique on the Posie of a Ring, as on the inscription of a medal'. Here 'critique' refers to a piece of writing, in the manner of an essay or review, concerned with the description and judgement of a work of art or literature. The connection with writing about literature is maintained in the transfer of the word from noun to verb, as in the further example from the *OED*, 'Hogg's tales are critiqued by himself in Blackwoods' (1831). This usage, although it has died out in England, continues in the United States where it is still possible to 'critique' a poem and to write a 'critique' of a novel.

The precise reasons for borrowing 'critique' from French are difficult to discern. The word appears in English during a period when a new form of literary culture is appearing, marked by the emergence of reviews, such as the *Spectator* and the *Tatler*, and by new audiences for literary works, who are felt to need guidance in matters of taste and judgement. Literature becomes a two-fold process: the production of novels, plays, poetry and works of philosophy and history, and the production of a commentary on them in the form of essays and reviews. Critique, then, may have been a useful word to describe this relatively new kind of writing, a literature about literature, concerned with matters of taste, judgement, and advertisement, a new form for the promotion and circulation of opinion.

A new meaning for critique emerged in England during the nineteenth century, and again, the reasons for this have to do with intellectual developments outside England. In the late eighteenth century the German philosopher Kant published a series of what, in translation, became known as critiques. A word recently borrowed from French was used to translate the German word *Kritik*. The provenance of critique moved away from literature and towards philosophy, where it designated a mode of inquiry designed to reveal the conditions of existence for certain ideas and perceptions. Kantian critique was concerned to discover the nature and limits of human understanding, and found these in what were claimed as the fundamental structures of the human mind. Marx changed the direction of critique by locating such fundamental structures not in the human mind but in the economic organization of society. This became, however mediately, the explanatory ground for why we think, feel and act the way we do, and in Marx's writing critique became closely concerned with *ideology*: the purpose of critique was to reveal ideology at work in thought by referring it to its base in economically determined antagonisms of class. Marx's writing forms one episode in the transformation of Kantian critique into what has subsequently become known as the sociology of knowledge. Weber and Durkheim are also central figures in the transformation. Although the three writers do not necessarily agree about what the relevant social context is for explaining why we think as we do, they do share a sense that it is in some concept of social structure that an explanation is to be found.

Literary criticism has developed various affiliations with the different modes of critique. An early equivalent for the Kantian critique can be found in ROMANTIC theories of IMAGINATION which attempt to locate the origins of literature in a faculty which is ambiguously placed between a human and a divine mind. Since then, the different modalities of critique – Marxism, feminism, linguistics, structuralism, psychoanalysis – have all, in combination or separately, produced critical theory which is concerned not only with the detailed analysis and evaluation of literary works but also with their conditions of existence, whether these are discovered in the structures of culture or language, in the laws of narrative, or the ideologies produced by class-divided societies. It is possible, therefore, to distinguish between those forms of literary criticism which bear some affiliation to critique and those which do not concern themselves with reflexive thought, preferring instead to carry out routine maintenance of a literary canon whose own creation is not subject to inquiry. But there are other and equally important kinds of distinction to be made, notably between those kinds of critique and criticism which put in question forms of political power, and those which locate the fundamental questions outside the realm of politics, in certain (claimed) invariant properties of culture, language or the human unconscious. Critique

reproduces today a division – and a point of transgression – which characterized its eighteenth-century origins. As Paul Connerton has noted (Introduction to *Critical Sociology*, 1976), in the eighteenth century 'The process of critique claimed to subject to its judgement all spheres of life which were accessible to reason; but it renounced any attempt to touch on the political sphere.' But this self-denying ordinance was not maintained for long. Critique increasingly concerned itself with politics and laid the intellectual foundations for the French Revolution. Then, as now, when critique, and the forms of literary criticism associated with it, question the prevailing distribution of political power, the alarm bells start to ring. By contrast, the apolitical forms of critique are a tolerated part of the intellectual scene. But this distinction between the political and the apolitical is not itself invariable and we cannot necessarily know in advance what form of critique will strike a political nerve. See also DECONSTRUCTION, DISCOURSE, FEMINIST CRITICISM, MARXIST CRITICISM, PSYCHOLOGY AND PSYCHOANALYSIS and references.

Some examples of work which, in various ways, presupposes critique as a goal, would include C. Belsey, *Critical Practice* (1980); T. Eagleton, *Criticism and Ideology* (1976); A. Easthope, *Poetry as Discourse* (1983); R. Fowler, *Literature as Social Discourse* (1981), *Linguistic Criticism* (1986); P. Widdowson (ed.), *Re-Reading English* (1982); Deborah Cameron (ed.), *The Feminist Critique of Language: A Reader* (1998).

JC

Cultural criticism This term is an extremely broad and generally unhelpful appellation given to an amorphous body of critical practices that explore the functioning of culture not purely in its

Arnoldian sense of the best of a civilization, but as a holistic study of the whole range of a society's products. As a field, Cultural Studies, emerged during the late-1950s across the English-speaking world and, though it frequently developed out of academic departments of English Literature, it very often stood in opposition to the conservative dominance of those programmes of study by the literary canon. Where 'English Literature' explicitly suggested an accepted, ideologically driven hierarchy of cultural production and signification, 'Cultural Studies' tended to gravitate towards those forms of expression that were conventionally deemed (often pejoratively) to be popular. Thus critics focused attention on the arenas of mass culture and took as their texts newspapers, magazines and popular literary genres, such as the romance, the detective story or the western, as well as non-literary forms, such as radio, television, film, music, advertising and fashion. In fact the remit of Cultural Studies extended to all forms of articulation that reflected a society's idiosyncratic character and therefore included the analysis of art and architecture as well as subcultural expressions of resistance, such as the Goth and Punk phenomena.

The academic credentials of the discipline were established along the lines of Raymond Williams's argument that 'culture' was the outcome of a whole way of life rather than being simply the selected highlights of a society's most intellectually, philosophically or artistically enlightened citizens. Culture as a conglomeration of disparate and antagonistic forces reflected the vitality and vibrancy of a society at a given moment and, by de-emphasizing the prior claim to supremacy of high culture, revealed both the ideological bent of that society and the voices that sought to resist the dominant superstructure. This line of thinking, which is often referred to as 'culturalist' derives partly from the disciplines of sociology, anthropology and history, which, during the period 1960–80 focused serious attention on what became known as 'history from underneath' – social, particularly working class history that situated the average person rather than the elevated or monarchical orders as the barometer of social change. This branch of Cultural Studies which took a broadly socio-historical stance was methodologically distinct from the 'structuralist' branch which owed much to the development of linguistics, of literary theory and of semiotics. This group of critics, employing the work of Louis Althusser, Roland Barthes and Michel Foucault, examined the position of the subject as an effect of the ideological structures and institutions that formed it. The subject is a product of a matrix of persuasive political, ethical, educational, historical, ethnographic and demographic forces that frame a view of reality as 'normal' and situate the individual as both subject of and subject to a particular social and cultural order. The products of that order are interpreted as discourses that underlie but also reinforce the dominant cultural codes. Adherents of the 'structuralist' branch of the discipline tend to examine forms of discursive practice for the collective conventions that they implicitly or explicitly supported.

In Britain the most celebrated institution for research in the field since the mid-1960s was the Centre for Contemporary Cultural Studies at the University of Birmingham. Set up under the directorship of Richard Hoggart, its period of greatest prominence came during the 1970s under the stewardship of Stuart Hall. It established itself as a pioneering centre for cultural research with the publication of collectively edited works such as *Resistance through Rituals: Youth Sub-Cultures in Post-War Britain* (1976), *On Ideology* (1978) and *Working Class Culture* (1979), and paved the way for the acceptance of Cultural Studies as a serious academic programme across higher education. It has sadly been disbanded in recent years. In the United States the field came to prominence during the 1980s and 1990s and provided a forum for a new interdisciplinary momentum. The intellectual fragmentation that attended postmodernism's disquisition of the metanarrative encouraged a productive dialogue between feminist scholars, literary critics, philosophers, Marxists, postcolonialists, New Historicists and sociologists that explored the interventions between, and interdependences of academic territories. In recent years the subject has expanded in its intellectual remit (analysing for instance the impacts of the internet and hypertextuality on the consumption and signification of culture) and in its popularity amongst new generations of scholars and students. See also CULTURE and CRITICISM.

See Louis Althusser, *Ideology and Ideological State Apparatuses* (1970); Catherine Belsey, *Critical Practice* (1980); Antony Easthope, *Literary into Cultural Studies* (1991); Antony Easthope and Kate McGowan (eds), *A Cultural Studies Reader: Texts and Textuality* (1992); John Fiske, *Understanding Popular Culture* (1989); Stuart Hall, *Cultural Studies: The Two Paradigms* (1980); Laura Mulvey, *Visual Pleasure and Narrative Cinema* (1975); Raymond Williams, *Culture and Society, 1780–1950* (1958).

DL

Cultural materialism That which looks for the dissident elements in a text – is often compared and contrasted with new historicism. Both are reactions to the view that literature can be studied in isolation from its social and political contexts. However, both cultural materialists and new historicists did not merely want to situate literature in its context but to question the whole idea of the work and its 'background'. They argued that this was a false distinction and that the relationship between the text and its context was mutually constitutive, the text helped shape the context as the context helped shape the text. Cultural materialists and new historicists are also interested in the relationship between literature and power. They agree that literature can be used to legitimize power but where new historicists believe that the challenge literature poses for power is ultimately contained, cultural materialists believe that literature has the potential to subvert it. So where a new historicist would argue that Shakespeare's *Henry V* ultimately asserts the value of monarchy even though it questions it, a cultural materialist would claim that the critique of kingship has consequences beyond the play. In particular, they would highlight the subversive elements in the play in order to make us think about the role of royalty today.

The term cultural materialism was coined by the critic Raymond Williams (1921–88) in *Marxism and Literature* (1977) and he used it to describe the material effect that culture has in social life. This is most easily seen in the case of IDEOLOGY which constitutes us in such a way that we happily assent to the authority that governs us. The education system, which is of part what the French Marxist Louis Althusser (1918–90) called 'the ideological state apparatus', uses culture to instil in us the belief that we are free individuals living in a democratic society and that great art, with its timeless truths of human nature, transcends mere politics. Consequently, and here is the material bit, we behave in ways – voting, earning a living, getting married, setting up a home, shopping – that help to perpetuate that society. While acknowledging that ideology indeed has this effect, the cultural materialist would also argue that it can be challenged. Instead of ideology, they prefer the term HEGEMONY, which derives from the Italian philosopher Antonio Gramsci (1891–1937), because it emphasized how the dominant and subordinate groups in society were in constant conflict with each other whereas ideology, particularly in the work of Althusser, seemed to allow no room for opposition to the *status quo*.

What particularly interests culture materialists is the role art and literature plays in the struggle between dominant and subordinate groups. Cultural materialists start with the idea that literature is used to support the system. For example, the role of Shakespeare in schools and universities is to promote Englishness and to justify the principle of hierarchy in all areas of social life from class to sexuality. Having shown how an author or a work is used to transmit the values of the establishment, the cultural materialist then wants to disrupt this transmission by pointing out those meanings in a work that a more conventional reading would either overlook or ignore. An example would be the murderers whom Macbeth employs to kill Banquo. The desperation that makes them accept this commission is born partly of their impoverished status brought about by the enclosure movements which deprived many people of their livelihood. By drawing attention to such details in a work, the cultural materialist not only recovers the repressed voices of history, here the 'masterless men', but also relates them to

similar issues in the present, for example, homelessness.

Although cultural materialists initially focussed on Shakespeare their work has now expanded to take in everything from *The Canterbury Tales* to crime fiction. There is no doubt that cultural materialism has energized literary studies – not least in its interrogation of the concept of 'literature' and how that has privileged certain forms of writing at the expense of others. However, cultural materialists do operate with a rather simplistic model of reading – are all works really no more than a struggle between dominant and subordinate readings? – and, moreover, they have very little to say about the language of the works they study. Finally, they may exaggerate the claims they make on behalf of cultural materialism as a means of social change. Some things have got better in Britain in the last thirty years and some have got worse. But how much of either is due to cultural materialism remains to be seen. See HISTORICISM.

See Jonathan Dollimore and Alan Sinfield (eds), *Political Shakespeare: Essays in Cultural Materialism* (2nd edn, 1994); Kiernan Ryan (ed.), *New Historicism and Cultural Materialism: A Reader* (1996).

GD

Culture Metaphorically, a cultivation (*agri-cultura*); the cultivation of values; by extension, a body of values cultivated, See Raymond Williams, *Culture and Society, 1780–1950* (1959) and *The Long Revolution* (1961). More recently, sociologists and anthropologists have employed the term to denote the totality of customs and institutions of a human group (cf. SOCIETY).

Literary criticism has traditionally concerned itself with culture as a body of values, especially those values transmitted from the past to the future through imaginative works. Culture in this sense implies the accumulation of discriminations. It implies a selective social structure, since it distinguishes passive recipients of social perspectives from those who cultivate an awareness of such perspectives. This, in turn, implies a teaching and learning process, and generates theories of a distinctive class with a duty to protect and disseminate traditions. Such an embodiment of the standards reinforces the traditional personal dimension of culture, as implicit in the underlying metaphoric skein (a 'cultivated' or 'cultured' person). It becomes simultaneously a code of values and a mode of perception. So, concepts like SENSIBILITY and taste evolve. Matthew Arnold (*Culture and Anarchy*, 1869 and *Essays in Criticism*, 1889) represents the classic statement of this view of culture.

At first this version of culture seems isolated from the alternative, 'scientific' version, namely, culture as the totality of human habits, customs and artefacts. See, for example, M. F. Ashley Montague, *Culture and the Evolution of Man* (1962) and *Culture: Man's Adaptive Dimension* (1968). But the critical and scientific definitions overlap, despite the apparent central difference that one claims to be evaluatory and the other descriptive. It is arguable that the distinctions depend on the isolation of certain phenomena as expressions of human value, and the false rejection of others (institutions, social habits, political movements, etc.). A communal act, for example, the founding of the trades unions, clearly part of the sociological dimension of 'culture', is an embodiment of cultural *values* as much as a novel or a painting. It involves a radical change of sensibility and may be said to be an expression of cultural advancement in the widest sense.

Debate has increased with the growth of mass communication. Films, television, the Internet – the whole range of devices for the distribution of images and information – call into question traditional standards and accepted forms. In the face of this threat to its standards, literary criticism failed to create the necessary models to investigate the new phenomena. Critics discovered that it was necessary to turn to other disciplines, such as sociology, to find tools to aid their work. A pioneer in this field was Richard Hoggart, whose *The Uses of Literacy* (1957) led to a widespread interest in what had previously been dismissed by all but the most acute (e.g. George Orwell) as pulp-art. Cross-fertilization between mass- and minority-art, and between its audiences, necessitated rejection of the old pyramidical structure of high-, middle- and low-brow, as conceived by the first critical response (e.g. Q. D. Leavis's *Fiction and the Reading Public*, 1932). As all art-forms began to overlap it became increasingly apparent that pigeon-holing was not enough. As Williams said, the mass-minority split is not the cure of our plight but its symptom (Raymond Williams, *Communications*, rev. edn, 1966). Modern cultural discussions stress the rejection of the past and the increasing disengagement of modernist and postmodernist thought (Bernard Bergonzi (ed.), *Innovations*, 1968), such that the central cultural metaphor of unfolding growth starts to disappear entirely in an age wedded increasingly to violent change.

In recent decades, 'culture' has bifurcated into its older associations with an over-arching, largely national or ethnic, collective of practices and signs, and a now-more-common reference to smaller, local socio-anthropological phenomena that might range from bikers' culture to a drinking culture. The rise of cultural studies has also contributed to a partial shift in usage from a nature/culture division to one of art/culture within the general perception of a widespread Western consumer culture. Critics from Gramsci to Bourdieu have analysed the value-laden aspects of the usage of the word, while migration, diaspora and GLOBALIZATION have highlighted the proliferation of hybrid and pluralized cultural identities.

See also SOCIETY and CULTURAL CRITICISM.

For the etymology and semantic development of the term, see R. Williams, 'Culture' in his *Keywords* (1976); his *Culture* (1981) is a book-length treatment with full bibliography. See also Dick Hebdidge, *Subculture: The Meaning of Style* (1979); Simon During (ed.), *The Cultural Studies Reader* (1999); Michèle Barrett, *Imagination in Theory* (1999).

GG

Cybercriticism   A term that is invoked in modern critical discourse in two distinct but related ways. The first (which is less usual) refers to the use of mechanical aids in the analysis of literary texts and the influence of such technology upon both the subject matter and the methods of literary criticism.

Literary historians point to the example of the radical changes wrought upon established medieval practices by the invention of the printing press in the fifteenth century. A similar paradigm shift was widely felt to be in the offing in the latter part of the twentieth century with the invention of the microcomputer and the advent of the World Wide Web. Supporters suggested that the meaning of texts (and of reading) might no longer be confined to the limits of the human imagination; rather, new and different kinds of analyses would change the way in which

literary texts were approached, and this would have implications for the meanings produced by such texts as well as the underlying attitudes and practices upon which such meanings depend. The development of online literary criticism has certainly altered many aspects of traditional critical discourse, especially in an academic context; a researcher can discover relatively quickly, for example, how frequently Shakespeare employs a certain word or phrase or metaphor. What happens to such information afterwards is another question. Opponents maintain that the greatest use to which digital technology has been put is undergraduate plagiarism, and that such a development is indicative of the essential incompatibility between electronic print media and the critical imagination.

The second (more usual) use of 'cybercriticism' refers to analysis which focuses upon the developing interaction of human life and the great variety of mechanical technology which humans have employed throughout history. Mary Shelley's *Frankenstein* (1818) is regarded as a key moment in this tradition. With the advent of digitalization towards the end of the twentieth century, the question of the interaction between human consciousness and mechanical activity became acute. Co-terminous developments in medicine (such as cloning and the mapping of the human genome), science (advances in Artificial Intelligence and computer technology) and philosophy (the vogue for various 'post-humanist' systems) combined to produce a general 'postmodernist' cultural climate in which both the meaning and the limits of the human were constantly brought into question.

Many of the issues that animate this latter form of cybercriticism emerged in the first instance in the imaginative writing of figures, such as William Gibson, Ursula K. le Guin and Philip K. Dick. The influential 'cyber' strand of science fiction interfaces with 'postmodernism' in their mutual concern with the impact of technology upon the human condition. Dick is responsible for one of the most influential of all 'cyber' texts: *Do Androids Dream of Electric Sheep?* (1967), adapted by British director Ridley Scott into the influential film *Blade Runner* (1982). Dick poses the question of what it might mean to be human in the high technological age, asking what will occur to the species when it evolves to the point at which it is capable of artificially engineering those capacities and attributes we have been encouraged to consider as the most deeply, the most undeniably human.

By focusing upon the absolute interpenetration of the human and the mechanical, cybercriticism claims to represent an assault upon all the categories which have traditionally exercised the critical imagination. For cybercritics, the medium/message dialectic becomes the central focus rather than a marginal consideration; this issue may be traced all the way back to *Genesis* in which it figures as a relationship between God (the original) and Man (the copy). Cybercriticism overlaps with ecocriticism insofar as both look to expose the 'human' as a contingent historical effect rather than a timeless essential quality. This effect (they claim) has been gained throughout history at the expense of the 'non-human' (the mechanical or the animal) – again, *Do Androids Dream of Electric Sheep?* constitutes a key meditation on this point.

Opponents have been inclined to regard the 'post-humanism' touted by cybercritics (and ecocritics) as a thinly disguised form of 'anti-humanism' – another trendy attack upon the Enlightenment tradition of critical reason. This latter discourse, maintains its adherents, is not the great demon represented by pessimistic postmodernists; rather, in a world in which uncontrolled technology is rushing human civilization towards collapse, critical reason remains the best hope for the species. See also ECOCRITICISM, POSTMODERNISM.

See Mike Featherstone and Roger Burrows (eds), *Cyberspace/Cyberbodies/Cyberpunk: Cultures of Technological Embodiment* (1995); Donna Haraway, *Simians, Cyborgs, and Women: The Reinvention of Nature* (1991); Andrew Milner, *Literature, Culture and Society* (1996).

GS

D

Dada Received its enigmatic name in February 1916; was a reaction against the brutality of war, the expediency of art and literature and the dangerous inadequacy of rational thought; in fact it spat out its contempt for the spiritual and moral decadence of a whole intellectual, cultural and social system. Born in neutral Zurich in the middle of the anarchic destruction of the Great War, it expressed its disgust with a morally culpable bourgeoisie and a spiritually nerveless art which had no objective beyond a simplistic social photography, a faith in its own function as anodyne and a reprehensible dedication to self-fulfilment. With unabashed relish Dada declared its negative intent: it wished, apparently, to destroy art along with bourgeois society, but in truth it opposed itself to the abuse of art rather than art itself, to society rather than humanity. Its exponents were poets and artists (Marcel Duchamp, Hugo Ball, Tristan Tzara, Richard Huelsenbeck, Man Ray, Max Ernst) who professed to despise art and literature but who, paradoxically, expressed their contempt in terms which identified them as part of the modernist movement. Its chief weapons – manifesto, phonetic poetry, simultaneous poem, noise music and provocative public spectacle – were all borrowed directly from the Futurists and stood as an image of the dissolution which seemed the central fact of modern existence. Their commitment to experimental modes, and the vitality of their performances, however, seemed to indicate a more fundamental faith in the possibility of opposing historical entropy with energy and concern if not with the self-contained structure of art itself.

When Dada found itself outflanked by the more coherent and purposeful experiments of the Surrealists it was laid to rest in 1922. But, as an attitude of mind rather than a formal movement, its subversive energy could not be contained by the incantations of a mock funeral service. In the 1960s American artists, writers, actors and musicians laid claim to the excitement and commitment of Futurists, Dadaists and Surrealists alike and approximated their experiments in the technique of Pop Art, happenings and the multimedia performance. See also SURREALISM.

See C. W. E. Bigsby, *Dada and Surrealism* (1972); Hans Richter, *Dada: Art and Anti-art* (1965); William S. Rubin, *Dada, Surrealism and their Heritage* (1968); S. Foster and R. Kuenzl (eds), *Dada Spectrum* (1979) (contains extensive bibliography); R. Sheppard (ed.), *Dada: Studies of a Movement* (1979), *New Studies in Dada* (1981); R. Short, *Dada and Surrealism* (1980), *Modernism, Dada, Postmodernism* (2000); D. Tashjian, *Skyscraper Primitives* (1975).

CWEB

Decentring See AUTHOR, CREATION, DECONSTRUCTION, DISCOURSE.

Deconstruction Refers to a philosophical activity initiated by Jacques Derrida in France; the first major publications appeared in the late 1960s. It is a critique of concepts and hierarchies which, according to Derrida, are essential to traditional criteria of certainty, identity and truth; but which, nevertheless, achieve their status only by repressing and forgetting other elements which thus become the un-thought, and sometimes the unthinkable, of Western philosophy. Derrida, following Nietzsche and Heidegger, tries to expose and explain this partiality, which he calls 'logocentrism'. Both aspects of this name – the fact of being centred, and of the logos as centre – are significant. Logos is a Greek term that can specifically mean 'word', but also carries implications of rationality and wisdom in general, and is sometimes reified as a cosmic intellectual principle. Early Christianity, in its drive to contain and supplant classical philosophy, adapted logos for the Word of God, thus annexing the principle of wisdom to the creative divine utterance, as in the Fourth Gospel. God is the only self-sufficient being; his word, as both source and standard of meaning, is the only self-sufficient discourse.

The logos casts a long shadow: a whole series of preferences is seen to derive, nostalgically, from its value judgements. Speech, as unmediated expression, is privileged in relation to writing, which appears as a suspect supplement to the authenticity of utterance – a distinction already evident in Greek thought. A desire for self-sufficiency, for the unqualified and unmediated, shows itself in attitudes to meaning, in the search for absolute knowledge, original truth, or determinate signification; and in attitudes to existence, in the search for unified being or a self-knowing reflexive consciousness. It is as if the urge of every entity – signified or existent – is to be *present to itself* in a way that makes it self-confirming and self-sufficient. 'Presence' is thus a prime value for logocentrism, which itself forms 'the matrix of every idealism'. And the various systems which function as 'centrisms' of whatever kind are attempts to delimit realms of security in which the proliferating play of

meaning is closed by the presence of a centre as guarantor of signification.

Derrida's approach to these desires is sceptical; but simply to equate deconstruction and scepticism is to miss the point. The critique of logocentrism or of a metaphysics of presence cannot take place from a privileged position outside the traditions it questions, for there is no such outside; the traces are too deep in language and thought. But just because ideal logocentrism is never actually achieved, the language will also carry traces of its repressed other, of the un-thought. And hence Derrida's philosophical practice involves a close textual criticism in order to trace the contradiction that shadows the text's coherence and 'expresses the force of a desire'. This undermining from within is the first stage of deconstruction, and usually subverts a privileged term: thus 'nature' is shown as always already contaminated by 'culture', 'speech' by 'writing', and so on. Writing (*écriture*), necessarily caught up in the play of signification, takes the place of pure speech as a norm for language. But Derrida is not concerned with simple binary reversals of value, which would merely offer another centred structure. He therefore releases his 'undecideables', radically unstable terms which act to disrupt systematization. The most important of these is 'differance', a coinage which plays on two meanings of the French *différer*: difference – between signs as the basis of signification (see SEMIOTICS), and deferment – deferment of presence by the sign which always refers to another sign, not to the thing itself. Derrida's 'mis-spelling' cannot be heard in French pronunciation; it exists only as written, emphasizing writing and textuality at the expense of speech. And so that 'differance' cannot be recuperated as a centre, he insists that it is neither word, concept nor origin: at most, a condition of the possibility of meaning, which resists hypostatization. The artifice and even frivolity of its neologism act to prevent it being taken as a master key to any structure. Indeed, the use of neologisms, puns and etymologies, as well as individually opaque styles, is common among deconstructive writers.

As we have seen, the power of logocentrism is not total. Certain texts appear 'to mark and to organize a structure of resistance to the philosophical conceptuality that allegedly dominated or comprehended them'. There is a distinction between this latter group and those texts that simply contain an inherent contradiction or *aporia*. The *aporia* is a built-in deconstruction, as it were; but the 'resistant' texts go further and begin their own critique. They include (only in part) the writings of Nietzsche and Heidegger, Freud and Saussure. They also include some 'literary' texts – Derrida distrusts the category, but finds in Artaud, Mallarmé and others 'the demonstration and practical deconstruction of the *representation* of what was done with literature'.

The relevance to literary studies, then, is not through a critical method (which is not on offer as such) nor in the finality of given interpretations (there are no final interpretations) but in the theoretical and conceptual insights of deconstruction. There are specific points at which Derrida's argument overlaps with more narrow literary concerns: the treatment of nature in Rousseau, for example (*Of Grammatology*, 1967, trans. 1976); or the treatment of mimesis in Mallarmé (*Dissemination*, 1972, trans. 1981). A great deal of modern writing has turned around problems of representation and consciousness, and these are extensively discussed by Derrida through his critical involvement with phenomenology, semiotics and psychoanalysis. Many critical issues are open to a deconstructive approach; thus the concern with authors evinces a desire for origin, to serve as interpretive closure; and realist representation is precisely an illusion of presence. In general, Derrida's way of thinking radically revises what a reader expects to do with a text.

The specific use of deconstruction in literary argument grew in the United States, following pioneer work by Paul de Man and J. Hillis Miller at Yale. There is a dubious tendency in de Man to privilege literature in general as a self-deconstructing discourse; but this does not destroy the brilliance of individual readings which, in their aporetic ensemble, make the text 'unreadable' in terms of closure (*Allegories of Reading*, 1979). Similarly, Hillis Miller argues that 'The fault of premature closure is intrinsic to criticism' (*Fiction and Repetition*, 1982). Besides generating new readings, mainly of nineteenth- and twentieth-century material, American deconstruction has enlivened debate about critical principles. The refusal of final meaning caused a certain institutional anxiety about anarchic individualism – understandably so, perhaps, in view of the polemical mannerism of deconstructionist style for those who do not enjoy it. But the absence of absolute criteria for interpretation does not mean total freedom; it is precisely the pressure of pre-existent discourse that deconstruction re-marks in its critique of origin. In a recent interview, Derrida says that 'Meaning...does not depend on the subjective identity but on the field of different forces, which produce interpretations' (*The Literary Review* 14, 1980, p. 21).

Deconstruction, as a set of popular clichés, soon palls. Simply to demonstrate logocentrism becomes a tautologous exercise. But the major examples of deconstructive practice retain their power. Few theoretical approaches have combined such challenging abstraction with such intense textual work. Not the least of its values lies in the learning and wit of its principal practitioners. 'To write on their plan, it was at least necessary to read and think.' See also DISCOURSE, POST-STRUCTURALISM, DIFFERENCE, PSYCHOLOGY AND PSYCHOANALYSIS.

For overviews see M. McQuillan (ed.), *Deconstruction: A Reader* (2000) and N. Royle (ed.), *Deconstructions: A User's Guide* (2000). The most approachable of Derrida's texts is *Positions* (1972, trans. 1981); there are excellent translators' introductions to the English versions of *Dissemination* (Barbara Johnson) and *Of Grammatology* (Gayatri Spivak). Christopher Norris, *Deconstruction: Theory and Practice* (1982) is a general account from a literary standpoint. For examples of effects on criticism see Barbara Johnson, *The Critical Difference: Essays in the Contemporary Rhetoric of Reading* (1980), Gregory L. Ulmer, *Applied Grammatology: Post(e)-Pedagogy from Jacques Derrida to Joseph Beuys* (1985) and Martin McQuillan, *Deconstruction: A Reader* (2001). Relevant journals include *Glyph* and the *Oxford Literary Review*.

EC

Decorum   The appropriateness of manner to ideas or situation, defined by the Elizabethan critic Puttenham as 'this good grace of every thing in his kinde'. It is primarily associated with the tradition of classical rhetoric and courtly values underlying Renaissance literature. Nevertheless, as a principle of propriety and appropriateness its validity is not confined to one period. It has, too, both

aesthetic and moral considerations, as a criterion of right relationships whether between style and subject matter or in the fulfilment of social obligations.

Sensitivity to decorum is likely to be greater when and where the observance of formal conventions is felt to be important; in art and life the concept of what is fitting implies a sense of established or accepted values. Thus by the critical canons of neo-classicism, decorum regulated the distinctions between literary genres, determining what kinds of style and subject were in keeping with each other: an elevated style for epic, for instance, to match the heroic proportions of character and action, but a mean style for comedy, in which ignoble vices and follies were ridiculed. By such canons Shakespeare's drama was held to be essentially indecorous, since it persistently mingled tragedy with comedy, and high style with low; Dr Johnson's objection to the word 'blanket' in *Macbeth* is a celebrated example of what neo-classical taste felt to be a breach of decorum.

The vagaries of Shakespeare's critical reputation illustrate how the principle of decorum can atrophy and become mechanical in its application. Indeed an application of inappropriate critical criteria is in itself a form of indecorum, and in this respect we can understand why writers in any age who depart radically from accepted conventions are likely to be judged indecorous by their contemporaries. Donne, whose love poetry 'perplexes the minds of the fair sex with nice speculations about philosophy', as Dryden put it, deliberately flouted the established decorum of courtly tradition, while the Wordsworth of *Lyrical Ballads* and the Eliot of *The Waste Land* were felt by most of their first readers not only to be abandoning conventional ideas of decorum but also to be defying any principle whatsoever of fitness and formal coherence. Such cases remind us that the sense of decorum lies not in the rigid prescription of absolute law but in a tactful and flexible judgement. 'For otherwise seems the decorum,' wrote Puttenham, 'to a weake and ignorant judgement then it doth to one of better knowledge and experience; which sheweth that it resteth in the discerning part of the minde.'

DJP

Defamiliarization   See FORMALISM.

Dénouement   French metaphor, literally 'unravelling', derived from the Latin for 'knot'; synonym 'catastrophe'. First used in French with reference to drama in 1636, adopted in English in 1752, to denote the neat end of a plot, the final resolution of all conflicts in a play, the tying up of loose ends, usually in the last act or even scene. Like all conclusions, dénouements have a reputation for difficulty, and even great playwrights (such as Shakespeare and Molière) have been criticized for the unconvincing artificiality of theirs. But as with other elements of dramaturgy once thought essential, the traditional type of dénouement is generally avoided by contemporary writers, for example, Samuel Beckett in *Waiting for Godot* (1955) and Harold Pinter in *The Caretaker* (1960) both opt for open, ambiguous endings which resolve nothing – anticlimax in place of striking climax. By extension, the term 'dénouement' is also applied sometimes to the unravelling of plots in narrative fiction. See also NARRATIVE STRUCTURE and CLOSURE.

See William Archer, *Play-Making* (1912), 253.

JWJF

Deviation   See FOREGROUNDING, POETIC LICENCE.

Dialogic structure   The term 'dialogic' is uniquely associated with the work of the Russian scholar Mikhail Bakhtin, and in particular his theorization of the novel in *Problems of Dostoevsky's Poetics*. The dialogic principle is central to Bakhtin's extensive and polemical theory of language and consciousness. Dialogue, he writes,

is not a means for revealing, for bringing to the surface the already ready-made character of a person; no, in dialogue a person not only shows himself outwardly, but he becomes for the first time that which he is, not only for others but for himself as well. To be means to communicate dialogically.

There can be no such ready-made character existing somehow prior to the linguistic, social operations of the dialogue with the other. And likewise, before we can use words for inner self-expression we must have developed language through dialogue with other people. Bakhtin is not merely talking about dialogue in the ordinary sense in which two or more people talk with each other. He is addressing the prior issue as to how such dialogues are in the first place enabled or even possible. They are so because, in his view, language is constitutively intersubjective (therefore social) and logically precedes subjectivity. It is never neutral, unaddressed, exempt from the aspirations of others. In his word, it is dialogic.

The polemical thrust of Bakhtin's theory lies in his pervasive suggestion that our hallowed autonomous individuality is an illusion; that in fact the 'I' that speaks is speaking simultaneously a polyphony of languages derived from diverse social contexts and origins. In reality each of us is a 'we' and not an 'I'. Without ever using religious terminology, Bakhtin nonetheless assigns to this fact of life an exalted value: and he turns to the study of genre in literature, to the novel in particular, to raise the question of the degree to which texts embrace or efface this value. He uses the term *monological* to designate the reduction of potentially multiple 'voices' (or characters) into a single authoritative voice. This voice is sometimes inescapable. The apparent polyphony of drama, for example, remains tied to the fact that the dramatist imposes upon characters what they must say. But the technical resources of narrative in prose (the varieties of indirect discourse in particular) do have an inherent capacity to represent languages other than the author's. Bakhtin celebrates the novel as the genre most capable of technically dismantling the dictatorial authorial voice that regulates and resolves any interplay of other voices in the text.

The dialogical text remains, nonetheless, the exception rather than the norm; it is perhaps better described as an experimental possibility: the writer thinking, as it were, in points of view, consciousnesses, voices, as, for example, Richardson did in the epistolary form of *Clarissa*. In Bakhtin's account, however, this possibility has a long and rich historical foundation in the genres of the Socratic dialogue and the ancient Menippean SATIRE, the latter being directly rooted in the world of *carnival* folklore. In the carnival the social hierarchies of everyday life – their solemnities and pieties and etiquettes as well as all ready-made truths – are profaned and literally outspoken by normally suppressed voices and energies demanding equal dialogic status. In this world-turned-upside-down, ideas and truths are endlessly tested and contested, and thus

de-privileged. In Dostoevsky Bakhtin found a paradigmatic polyphonic structure where the other voices in the text come into their own, as it were; they acquire the status of fully fledged verbal and conceptual centres whose relationship, both amongst themselves and with the author's voice, is dialogic and carnivalized, and thus not susceptible to subordination or reification. Raskolnikov, as with all the other characters, is a subject and not an object: therefore never exhaustively known or defined as he would be were the implied author to have the first and last word about him.

The dialogic or polyphonic text thus puts the much-argued issue of the author's 'disappearance' into a significantly new light. The character ceases to be the object of the choices and plans open to the implied author. Many critics in the Western tradition have argued (Wayne C. Booth, for example, in *The Rhetoric of Fiction*) that only these choices and plans can guarantee the 'unity' of the text and justify the ways of the author to the reader. Bakhtin challenges these long-held assumptions radically: the monological text is a partial report. There is even an attractive value-judgement implicit in Bakhtin's constant invitation to us to distinguish more keenly between those techniques that favour polyphony and those that easily give the final word to the monologue.

See M. Bakhtin, trans. C. Emerson, *Problems of Dostoevsky's Poetics* (1984); M. Bakhtin, *Rabelais and his World* (1965); V. N. Voloshinov, *Marxism and the Philosophy of Language* (1973); M. Holquist (ed.), *The Dialogic Imagination: Four Essays by M. Bakhtin* (1981); K. Clark and M. Holquist, *Mikhail Bakhtin* (1984); T. Todorov, *Mikhail Bakhtin: The Dialogical Principle* (1984).

TM

Diction Aristotle's low ranking of diction (*lexis*) among the six elements of tragedy implies an idea of the poet clothing the essential form, the structure of action, character and thought, in appropriate language: the selection of words is secondary to the imaginative design. This dualistic view of language as the dress of thought lies behind traditional critical attitudes to diction in poetry. It is customary to speak of the archaic diction in *The Faerie Queene* or the Latinate diction of *Paradise Lost* as if these were stylistic incidentals. In the eighteenth century, the idea of 'poetic diction' emerged: poets like Thomas Gray asserted that the language of poetry was necessarily specialized and remote from 'ordinary' language. It was this 'poetic diction', with its elaborate devices of archaism, Latinity and circumlocution, that Wordsworth attacked as artificial and unnatural; he denied any 'essential difference between the language of prose and metrical composition'. But the idea that there is a special language for poetry persisted; I. A. Richards, in *Principles of Literary Criticism* (1924), attempted to separate poetry from other forms of discourse in his theory of the emotive and scientific uses of language. However, as Elder Olson points out, 'there are no necessary differences between poetic diction, as diction, and the diction of any other kind of composition. There are no devices of language which can be pointed to as distinctively poetic' ('William Empson, contemporary criticism, and poetic diction' in R. S. Crane's *Critics and Criticism*, 1957). But Olson's neo-Aristotelian relegation of language to the least important place among the parts of poetry revived the dualism that generated the concept of 'poetic diction'. His argument that 'the chair is not wood but wooden; poetry is not words but verbal' suggests that the 'matter' of poetry, language, is as incidental to its essential form as wood to the chair; chairs can be made out of many materials and remain chairs. But it is difficult to imagine poetry 'made out of' anything other than language. In fact descriptive criticism would prefer the organic analogies of Romantic poetics, and assert that language is no more incidental to poetry than wood is to *trees*.

The new attitudes to language of the later Richards (*Philosophy of Rhetoric*, 1936) and William Empson (*Seven Types of Ambiguity*, 1930) relocated diction at the centre of critical attention. For if 'meaning' is the result of the total activity of all the words in a context, and not something pre-existing expression, then statements about the meaning and form of poems are implicitly statements about organizations of words: diction, the choice of words, is a fundamental element of meaning. Winifred Nowottny (*The Language Poets Use*, 1962) points out that diction determines the personae of poetry, the voices the poet adopts, and argues that poetry differs from other utterances in its ability to create its own context, to speak with any voice. Indeed, far from being restricted to a 'poetic diction', it is uniquely free 'to raid other forms of language at will'; poetry can take its words from any style of language, literary or other. Once in the poem, however, words are characteristically 'used to induce or define attitudes other than those in which everyday language allows us inertly to rest'. See also ANALYSIS, CHICAGO CRITICS, LANGUAGE, NEW CRITICISM.

See Emerson R. Marks, *Taming the Chaos: English Poetic Diction Theory Since the Renaissance* (1997).

PM

Différance See DECONSTRUCTION, FEMINIST CRITICISM.

Difference Not confined to a single theoretical school or perspective, the notion of difference would be difficult to underestimate in terms of its importance within modern thought. In the twentieth century, this concept first came to prominence in the work of the French linguist Ferdinand de Saussure. In his *Course in General Linguistics* (1913), Saussure debunks referential theories of language by arguing that 'in language there are only differences, and no positive terms'. In other words, there are no inherent qualities within a sign that demand that it refer to one specific referent. According to this relational theory of language, meaning is generated only through the difference *between* signs. Yet, according to the deconstructive critic Jacques Derrida, Saussure is unable to acknowledge the most radical implications of his own argument. As Derrida demonstrates, Saussure effectively severs the sign from its extra-textual referent but continues to maintain the unity of signifier and signified as established by their conventional spoken usage. In order to destabilize the sign itself, Derrida puts forward the 'concept' of différance. Suspended between its two senses of differing and deferring, this neologism represents the non-originary origins of a generalized system of language that encompasses both speech and writing; where meaning is never located within the sign as a self-sufficient entity but is, rather, constituted through the differential play between an infinite number of signifiers and signified. As a result, meaning is always deferred. Thus, the 'concept' of *différance* represents a powerful critique of PRESENCE and its associated values.

Building on the work of Saussure, STRUCTURALISM focuses its attention not on the intricacies of any individual text or social phenomenon, but on the relation between various texts and different social phenomena. Espousing a supposedly scientific view of the world, it concentrates on the binary oppositions and systems of similarity and difference that supposedly generate meaning. The move from structuralism to POST-STRUCTURALISM entails a recognition that binary oppositions are also hierarchies where one element is always privileged over the other. This recognition opens the door to a variety of political readings concerning the construction and representation of difference, especially in relation to the dominant norms. As this norm is often represented as white, male and heterosexual, the concept of difference has been particularly useful to feminist, queer and postcolonial critics. Such critics have played a key role in identifying and exploring the excluded or repressed term within the hierarchy.

It is important to note, however, that the concept of difference is employed in a variety of ways. Feminist theories offer a case in point. While certain branches of feminist criticism have made a strategic and political decision to emphasize the difference between men and women in order to consolidate a more positive and self-determined conception of 'woman', others have employed the concept of difference to challenge the ESSENTIALISM of such a position. It is now widely recognized that language does not simply reflect the world but actually constitutes it. This means that language does not represent pre-existing differences (between, for example, men and women). Rather, such differences are themselves the product of the language system that organizes our thoughts and perceptions (see DISCOURSE). Thus, the notion of linguistic difference represents a profound challenge to the essentialist view that men and women are fundamentally different creatures, each possessing certain unalterable and innate characteristics. Instead, such critics concentrate on the ways in which such differences are constructed and represented in language. Finally, certain recent feminist theories use the term difference more broadly to refer not only to the differences between groups but also to differences *within* groups. Emphasizing diversity rather than sameness, this use of the term recognizes that class, racial, local and national differences fracture any generalized notion of what it is to be a woman.

It is also important to recognize that the concept of difference plays a pivotal role in the construction of our subjectivity. According to post-structuralist thought, the SUBJECT is, precisely, a construction and, most obviously, a construction of language (we are born into a language system that pre-dates and shapes us). Moreover, each subject – like the linguistic sign – depends upon its relation to, and differences from, other subjects. Thus, we are all constituted through relations of both similarity and difference and our sense of what we are depends, in part, on what we are not. Group identities are predicated on the same principles. To identify yourself as a member of a group is to claim certain similarities with its other members, but it is also, and equally, to differentiate yourself from other groups and their members. As a result, constructions of the self are always bound up with an other that both constitutes and destabilizes the boundaries by which we are constituted. See also ESSENTIALISM, DECONSTRUCTION, HYBRIDITY, STRUCTURALISM and THE OTHER.

See M. Currie, *Difference* (2004).

JA

Differend   Differend is a term given by the French philosopher Jean-François Lyotard (1924–98) to the point of difference that arises between two disputant agencies who do not possess common terms of reference within which to conduct their dispute. Any attempt to describe or analyse the disagreement will always be unjust, because it will always function to sanction one side of the conflict, while implicitly proscribing and/or marginalizing the other.

Lyotard's work engages with a long European philosophical tradition (including most centrally the thought of Immanuel Kant [1724–1804] in the latter part of the eighteenth century and that of Ludwig Wittgenstein [1889–1951] in the first part of the twentieth) focussed on the intersection of culture, politics and ethics. He began his career as a philosophy teacher with strong left-wing affiliations. As with many of the key names in the development of modern European cultural theory, a pivotal moment for Lyotard was the Paris riots of 1968. Frustrated with the failure of the 'real' revolution, a generation of erstwhile activists turned their energies to expediting a 'revolution in the text' which would in turn precipitate the 'revolution in the head' that they understood to be a necessary preamble for any programme of social change. Lyotard's own work belongs to (and is one of the key components in the formulation of) the moment of 'postmodernism' – a moment he shares (despite widespread antipathy towards the term) with fellow French intellectuals Jacques Derrida and Michel Foucault, as well as the German Jürgen Habermas (1929–) and the American Fredric Jameson.

Like many modern philosophers and social theorists, Lyotard looks for, and invariably finds, support for his philosophical speculations in literature. Great writing (such as that of Marcel Proust [1871–1922] or James Joyce

[1882–1941]) invariably functions to reveal (although not to 'represent' in the accepted literary sense) a differend – a mode of being in the world which is not amenable to the traditional discourses of narrative, language or character. Like the critical theorist or the radical philosopher, the task of the great writer (regardless of intention or affiliation) should be to bear witness to the differend; the task of the responsible reader, meanwhile, should be to transpose literary effects into a discourse of social justice. In between these two categories, however, there exists another figure, one whose institutional identity militates against the survival of the differend: the critic. The traditional role of the critic has been to sit in judgement upon the literary text – that is, to bring a particular array of skills and knowledge to bear upon the text so that its secret may be revealed, its 'meaning' discovered. Traditional critical practice, in other words, is by definition opposed to the differend. Critical language represents the arbitrary power which will always attempt to (re)solve the differend with reference to one or another privileged subject (the author or the reader), or some favoured external political narrative, such as Marxism.

The differend, for Lyotard, is an injustice suffered by those whose signifying system is silenced by established representations of 'reality'; as such, it is part of an ethical programme in which 'the unpresentable' – that which is silenced in every discursive event – is witnessed and activated as an element within the process of judgement. For others, however, postmodernism *à la* Lyotard is a profoundly pessimistic proposition, one based upon a denial of the Enlightenment concept of rational critique and a long tradition of organized political dissent. The key figure here is Habermas, whose theory of social justice is founded upon a notion of democratic consensus formed by subjects who, although perhaps characterized by incommensurate language systems when they first encounter, are willing to work to find common terms of reference within which they may communicate effectively. Although wide-ranging in both implication and application, the differences between Lyotard (broadly representing postmodernism) and Habermas (broadly representing an ongoing modernism grounded in the responsible human subject) stem from radically different ways of understanding how language functions in relation to reality, and more finely still, from mutually exclusive apprehensions of the individual word as it relates to the other words with which it is surrounded and to the 'real' world it ostensibly represents. See also POSTMODERNISM and POST-STRUCTURALISM.

See Jürgen Habermas, *The Philosophical Discourse of Modernity: Twelve Lectures* (1987); Jean-François Lyotard, *The Postmodern Condition: A Report on Knowledge* (1984), *The Differend: Phrases in Dispute* (1988); Bill Readings, *Introducing Lyotard: Art and Politics* (1991).

GS

Dirge See ELEGY.

Disbelief See BELIEF.

Discourse Up until the later part of the twentieth century, 'discourse' had its traditional meaning: the ordered exposition in writing or speech of a particular subject, a practice familiarly associated with writers, such as Descartes and Machiavelli. In recent decades the term has been used with increasing frequency and with new kinds of meaning, reflecting in part the effect on critical vocabulary of work done within and across the boundaries of various disciplines: linguistics, philosophy, literary criticism, history, psychoanalysis and sociology. The term now represents the meeting-ground for diverse inquiries into the nature and use of language; but it has meant different things when spoken in a French or an Anglo-American accent.

A basic motive in the formulation of discourse in Anglo-American research has been to discover the regularities and constraints at work in units of language larger than the sentence. This has meant a redefinition of the goals of linguistic inquiry as formulated by Chomsky. Whereas Chomsky had given priority to a description of our knowledge of the grammaticality of sentences, work on discourse stressed the importance of a description of communicative competence, our ability to combine sentences, to relate them coherently to the topics of discourse, and to say the right thing at the right time. A string of grammatically well-formed sentences does not necessarily constitute a successful act of communication. To reply to the question 'What is your name?' by saying 'The cows are under the bridge' is not, ordinarily, to respond appropriately, even though both question and answer are grammatically correct. Such an exchange might make sense in the context of a surrealist novel or of schizophrenic language, but normally discourse is cohesive, and one of the aims of discourse analysis is to show how a knowledge of conventions for links between sentences and for links with context is a necessary condition of successful communication (see M. A. K. Halliday and R. Hasan, *Cohesion in English*, 1976).

A concern for understanding language in the context of communicative use has been central to the contemporary conception of discourse. What is understood as the context of communication has varied from one field of inquiry to another. In the philosophy of language, the theory of the speech act, notably developed in the work of Austin and Searle, has been incorporated into this expanded definition of discourse. Speech act theory is, in part, a reaction against the impoverished conception of language inherited from logical positivism whereby the meaningful use of language consists in the utterance of statements about the world that can be either confirmed or disconfirmed. Austin and then Searle proposed that language use was not simply a matter of making true or false statements about the world, but also a kind of action, the expression of an intention in relation to a person or state of affairs. To understand the meaning of an utterance requires more than knowing what it refers to; it is also to understand its 'force', whether it be promising, commanding, questioning or any one of a number of what Austin and Searle called 'illocutionary acts'. Although working with invented examples of utterance, speech act theory has made a good case for describing the necessary conditions for a successful or 'felicitous' act of communication, a task neglected not only by linguistic philosophy but also by the Chomskyan grammar of sentences (see J. R. Searle, *Speech Acts*, 1969).

Three other related areas of inquiry need to be noted: the ethnography of speaking, conversational analysis and functional linguistics. The first of these, through the development of such concepts as speech community and speech style, has refined our understanding of language as a force in social life, and notably the way that language contributes to the definition of social identity and difference (see J. J. Gumperz and D. Hymes, *Directions in Sociolinguistics*,

1972). Conversational analysis poses various questions – what are the constitutive events in a conversation, how do we recognize that it is our turn to speak, who controls the topic of conversation – in an effort to identify the regularities and constraints at work in examples of actual conversation (M. Coulthard, *Introduction to Discourse Analysis*, 1977; M. Coulthard and M. Montgomery, *Studies in Discourse Analysis*, 1981). The premiss of functional linguistics has been usefully described by its principal exponent, M. A. K. Halliday: 'The particular form taken by the grammatical system of language is closely related to the social and personal needs that language is required to serve.' Given that our language allows us to make the same proposition in different forms – 'John loved Mary', 'Mary was loved by John' – functional linguistics investigates what it is that determines one realization over another. The question of determination here is complex: preference for one grammatical form can be partly understood in terms of the immediate speech context, but implicated in that and surrounding it are other contexts of power and politics. Functional linguistics can alert us to the operations of ideology in language, whether it be in everyday usage or in literature. For example, the use of nominalization and personification – 'The stock market had a good day today' – can obscure the issue of who immediately profits; compare as an alternative realization 'Today a number of stock brokers and speculators made a lot of money'. Besides enriching our understanding of the social context of communication, functional linguistics, conversational analysis and the ethnography of speaking have opened up a critical potential for discourse analysis because of their capacity to illuminate language use as a process in which inequalities of power and position are negotiated and contested (M. A. K. Halliday, *Language as Social Semiotic*, 1978; R. Fowler, R. Hodge, G. Kress and T. Trew, *Language and Control*, 1979).

The work described above had a considerable effect on literary study. At one level the refinement of the analysis of spoken language contributed a new set of techniques for the close reading of literary language. Work done in the analysis of conversation allowed a more discriminating description of dialogue in drama (D. Burton, *Dialogue and Discourse*, 1980). Speech act theory produced a diversified if unstable set of categories which can be used in the analysis of the intentions and verbal actions encoded in the rhetorical strategies of literature (R. Ohmann, 'Speech, action and style', in S. Chatman (ed.), *Literary Style: A Symposium*, 1971). At another level discourse analysis provided a global model for literature itself, one which describes literary works not as iconic objects set apart from a world of intention and effect, but as a socially determined communicative practice between reader and writer, and, as such, analogous to other forms of communication (R. Fowler, *Literature as Social Discourse*, 1981).

Working from a different perspective, discourse is a key term in the writings of the French philosopher and historian, Michel Foucault. The place of discourse in Foucault's own work can be crudely described through two intertwined concerns. The first is with discourse as an historical phenomenon, an emphasis that has been marginal to the main body of Anglo-American work. For Foucault there is no general theory of discourse or language, only the historically grounded description of various discourses or 'discursive practices'. These latter consist in a certain regularity of statements which then define an object – whether it be sexuality or madness, criminality or economics – and supply a set of concepts which can be used to analyse the object, to delimit what can and cannot be said about it, and to demarcate who can say it. But the regularity which produces a discursive practice should not be confused with a logical or systematic coherence. It is an historical event, not the realization of some pre-existent system. The analysis of discourse is a matter of research into the historical conditions which permitted, but did not guarantee, its appearance. As discourse defines its object, there are no criteria of truth external to it: the truth of a discourse is, according to Foucault, akin to a rhetorical imposition. We believe a discourse about sexuality to be true because we have no alternative. Truth is the unrecognized fiction of a successful discourse.

The second concern, already indicated in Foucault's attitude towards the concept of truth, is a radical scepticism about many basic assumptions in intellectual history, literary criticism and linguistics. In literary criticism Foucault has unpacked and criticized the assumptions at work in such terms as 'tradition' and 'author'. Foucault sees the idea of tradition as bestowing a specious unity upon works whose difference is then obscured for the sake of a myth of a unified development of literature which transcends the abrupt discontinuities between diverse social formations. Similarly, the idea of the 'author' is historicized: 'Even within our civilization the same type of texts have not always required authors; there was a time when these texts which we now call "literary" (stories, folk-tales, epics, and tragedies) were accepted, circulated, and valorized without any question about the identity of their author' (M. Foucault, 'What is an author?', 1969; see AUTHOR). The fact that literature and authors have become so closely identified needs to be explained as the condition of a discursive practice which may itself be historically transient.

Foucault's critique of our common sense about authors is consonant with another important component of his conception of discourse. For Foucault, discourse is at once a denial and a critique of a canonical assumption in our thinking about literature and language, the assumption that these are expressive activities, either in the sense that they express emotions and ideas 'within' the individual, or in the sense that acts of expression, and notably acts of literary expression, are a means of self-realization. The different 'discursive practices' within a society afford various 'subject positions' which permit us to write or speak in certain ways about certain subjects. But this cannot be equated with acts of expression or self-realization. The opposite is true: 'discourse is not the majestically unfolding manifestation of a thinking, knowing subject, but on the contrary, a totality in which the dispersion of the subject, and his discontinuity with himself may be determined' (Foucault, *The Archaeology of Knowledge*, 1969, trans. 1972). This account of discourse expressly challenges the commonly held assumption that literature is the expressive use of language *par excellence*. For Foucault this would simply be another myth about literature in our cultural epoch, one that could be traced in the genealogy of an ideal of expressive selfhood in the forms of lyric poetry. Conceived as discourse, literature no more expresses us, either as writers or readers, than do the leaves on a tree express themselves when they are blown by the wind.

Although Foucaultian discourse opposes traditional conceptions of the literary, his work can be read as the theoretical equivalent of a contemporary practice of literary writing which itself traces the disappearance of the expressive subject (the works of the American writers John Ashberry and Thomas Pynchon would be a case in point). More generally, work done around a conception of discourse has permitted a rethinking of notions of literary form. Instead of seeing the literary work as an ideal aesthetic harmony, or the equally ideal resolution of psychological tensions in the author or reader, discourse theory conceives of the literary work as an instance of the historically variable institution of literature, an institution which mediates relations between writer and reader in different ways at different times, and in so doing, echoes, transforms or challenges the uneven distribution of power within societies. See also C. Belsey, *Critical Practice* (1980); A. Easthope, *Poetry as Discourse* (1983); Sara Mills, *Discourse* (1997), *Michel Foucault* (2003).

JC

Dissemination As a term employed by the deconstructive critic Jacques Derrida, dissemination designates the idea that meaning is never stable, or fixed, but is, rather, dispersed or scattered throughout the language system. Thus, like the notion of UNDECIDABILITY (to which it is related), dissemination calls into question the possibility of definition itself. For this reason, it is best conceived of as an effect of writing. It is, however, essential to recognize that Derrida extends the traditional understanding of writing (the graphic signifier of the spoken word) to include a system of difference, deferral and spacing that encompasses language in general. In other words, whether we are dealing with speech or writing, meaning is never located in any one sign but is, rather, produced by the difference between that sign and all the other signs in the language system. Caught in a concatenation of signification, meaning is always on the move, always deferred.

Inevitably, this radical re-conception of writing and signification has a profound impact on traditional, logocentric understandings of meaning and interpretation. As Derrida suggests in his essay '*Différance*' (1982):

> the first consequence to be drawn from this is that the signified concept is never present in and of itself, in a sufficient presence that would refer only to itself. Essentially and lawfully, every concept is inscribed in a chain or in a system within which it refers to the other, to other concepts, by means of the systematic play of differences.

This 'play of differences' is, moreover, infinite; without origin or end. Nor can it ever be brought under control – anchored or arrested – by any external point of reference that, escaping its play, would allow the signifier to be reduced, or sublimated, into its signified. As a result of this disseminating force of writing, our desire for a stable, self-present meaning is always frustrated. Thus, the notion of dissemination plays a key role in Derrida's critique of the logocentric valorization of PRESENCE and all its associated values. More generally, this concept subverts, resists and disrupts any attempt at mastery or totalization. As Barbara Johnson suggests in the Translator's Introduction to *Dissemination* (1981), it is what 'foils the attempt to process in an orderly way toward meaning or knowledge, what breaks the circuit of intentions or expectations through some ungovernable excess or loss'.

As is the case with all of the key terms within Derrida's vocabulary, it is impossible to extricate the concept of dissemination from the chain of signification in which it is embedded. Thus we must turn to his text of this title and, more specifically, to his deconstruction of the speech/writing opposition within Plato's *Phaedrus*. Concentrating on a family scene – of good and bad fathers, legitimate and illegitimate sons, good and bad writing – Derrida employs the notion of dis*sem*ination in order to demonstrate how, for Plato, both *semen* (the Latin term for seed) and *sema* (the Greek term for sign) may either be planted productively (within the realm of the father as logos) in order to produce legitimate offspring (speech) or may be scattered on the barren ground outside his presence (writing). As Derrida suggests:

> Writing and speech have thus become two different species, or values, of the trace. One, writing, is a lost trace, a nonviable seed, everything in sperm that overflows wastefully, a force wandering outside the domain of life, incapable of engendering anything, of picking itself up, of regenerating itself. On the opposite side, living speech makes it capital bear fruit and does not divert its seminal potency toward indulgence in pleasures without paternity.

This opposition, however, is destabilized by the disseminating play of writing from which Plato's argument cannot escape. We can trace the effects of this dissemination most obviously in the network of textual referrals between the related concepts of the *pharmakon*, the *pharmakeus* and the *pharmakos* that Plato employs whenever he is forced to confront writing and its

dangerous effects (see UNDECIDABILITY). As Derrida reveals, the disseminating proliferation of these terms within Plato's argument undermines the conceptual systems on which it is based. Thus, the opposition between speech and writing is effectively disabled.

While the notion of dissemination assumes a prominent place within any deconstructive reading, its usefulness is not limited to any one school or critic. By reminding us that every text is characterized by a play of signifiers that no author or reader can control, the term forces us to recognize that no text can ever be reduced to its signified content. As a result, dissemination calls into question the traditional conception of the book as a unified totality by acknowledging a proliferation of meanings waiting to be discovered – but not exhausted – by each new reading. See also DECONSTRUCTION, LOGOCENTRISM, PRESENCE, UNDECIDABILITY.

See M. McQuillan (ed.), *Deconstruction: A Reader* (2000) and N. Royle (ed.), *Deconstructions: A User's Guide* (2000).

JA

Dissociation of sensibility   A term coined by T. S. Eliot in 'The metaphysical poets', originally an anonymous review in *TLS* (1921) of Grierson's anthology, *Metaphysical Lyrics and Poems of the Seventeenth Century*. Its success dates from its reprinting under Eliot's name in 1924. The essay concludes: 'The poets of the seventeenth century...possessed a mechanism of sensibility which could devour any kind of experience. ...[But with Milton and Dryden] a dissociation set in, from which we have never recovered...'. This malady of English poetry allegedly stemmed from a separation of the 'thinking' and 'feeling' parts of the poets' consciousness, an inability to accommodate intellection in the poetic synthesis. Thus thought and emotion in poetry appeared embarrassingly raw. A unified sensibility, such as Donne's, was able, on the other hand, to feel a thought, 'as immediately as the odour of a rose'. The poetry of the 'moderns' was to recapture this unified sensibility: *The Waste Land* is a kind of pattern for the poetic amalgamation of disparate elements. Coleridge's synthesizing IMAGINATION is at the back of this idea, but the terms and concept derive from the French symbolist critic Remy de Gourmont, and Eliot sees in Baudelaire, Laforgue and Corbière a similar unification (which was also present by implication in Pound and Eliot himself). By 1931 Eliot was detecting the dissociation even in Donne, but in his last reference to the problem (in 1947) he reaffirmed the original doctrine, though in more general terms: 'All we can say is, that something like this did happen; that it had something to do with the Civil War... that we must seek the causes in Europe, not in England alone...'. Cleanth Brooks attributed the dissociation to Hobbes and L. C. Knights to Bacon, but Frank Kermode, in a chapter on the doctrine in *Romantic Image* (1957), described the concept as 'quite useless historically'.

FWB

Documentary   See BIOGRAPHY.

Dominant   See POETICS.

Double irony   See IRONY.

Drama   As a form of literature, drama has been studied for centuries – 'a poem written for representation' (Johnson). In other words, it has been judged primarily as a poem, and all that peculiarly belongs to the stage – acting, production, scenery, effects – have been subsumed under the vague term 'representation'. The alternative is to invert that position, and stress the representation before the poem. In the theatre, the poet's art is only one among many, and it is not an essential one: indeed, words at all are not essential. In Greek the term meant simply to act or perform, and the definition is still valid; all others are derivative and of limited historical significance. The dictionary offers 'a set of events... leading to catastrophe or consummation'; but that relates to Victorian theatre and to a Victorian view of Greek tragedy. The dancing and flute playing which Aristotle discussed are not events, and do not lead to catastrophe; nor does the Fool in *Lear*, nor the tramps in *Waiting for Godot*. Beckett's play is constructed against an expectation of consummation, but its positive qualities are vested in the tramps, who are clowns. Their performance derives for us from the circus, or more specifically from Charlie Chaplin, but the association of clown and outcast is ancient, recurrent and common to most societies.

The clown invites our laughter, and through it our derision. The clown's opposite is the heroic actor, who invites admiration (naïvely, emulation or identification), and whose identity is established by: presence on the stage and the physical power to dominate the scene and the audience; but the heroic actor, far more than the clown, depends on words, and can use them. For such an actor (Alleyn), Marlowe created the language of Tamburlaine. Hamlet's language rarely displays such authority, and readers have doubted Ophelia's view of him as a noble mind o'erthrown; Shakespeare sets what the actor *is* (leading actor) against what the actor *says*, and makes that the focus of Hamlet's relation to the player king. A heroic actor relies on projecting the role through his personality, which means that the 'character' presented depends on the actor's own. The clown, on the other hand, like the character actor, appears to be quite other than the actor. But king and clown are equally roles that individuals play (as parents do to their children): the actor's relation to the audience is a double one: the actor must imitate men and women as they appear to be, and must represent our urge to play a role – the paradox that we can only 'be ourselves' when we can find a role to play. For the first, the actor's language must resemble speech, for the second it will not; hence the duality observable even in Aeschylus, where the reader may concentrate on elements of human utterance which the actor will find to be only inflections in a poetry whose general condition is close to recitative. Lear can attack the storm with tremendous rhetoric; his Fool can use snatches of folk song and ballad. The relation of king to fool is profoundly disturbing in *Hamlet*, acutely painful in *Lear*.

The range of a celebrated dramatic text, then, derives from the roles that actors play. The peculiar richness of Shakespeare's drama depends on the derivation of his company from the multiplicity, of talents masquerading in the Middle Ages under the general term of minstrels (and the status of vagabonds). The impoverishment of drama representing upper-middle class drawing rooms did not derive only from its social narrowness, but also from its lack of theatrical range. The problem for Elizabethan dramatists was to unify the diversity at their disposal (dancing and fooling would happen whether it was part of the play or not). Marlowe wrote great poetry only for those moments when it would be needed; for others, only the necessary words for what was largely silent action; for the clowns it seems likely that he provided only a scenario to be fulfilled with improvization. Shakespeare seems always to have provided a fuller text, but in *Romeo and Juliet*, Peter and the musicians must have been relied on to do more than was set down for them; by the time of *Hamlet* he requires even clowns to perform strictly within the 'necessary questions of the play', which have become too consistently intricate for undisciplined expansion.

Drama, then, is not a poem; not even a dramatic poem. But prose is only in special circumstances adequate to its nature. It cannot be defined in literary terms, or if it must be, they take on a different meaning in the theatre. Action in a novel is the journeys and battles in which individuals engage; in drama that is only a secondary sense, action must primarily mean the movement of actors on the stage. It is not enlightening to offer a map of Scotland in an edition of *Macbeth*: he does not travel from Glamis to Forres, but enters and exits on the stage. Drama depends on actors with an audience. Performances, even of the same production with the same cast, will vary, sometimes radically, from night to night; and the variation will primarily depend on the different audiences, and the actors' response to them. There is no such consistent object to abide our criticism as a painting, or a printed poem; nor can there be an 'ideal theatre of the mind'. Actual performance is inherent in drama. So *King Lear* may be one night a rather abstract dissertation on Nature, the next an overwhelming experience whose end is silence. Dramatic criticism has to reckon with this variability and actuality; but it must not be defeated by it; the variables are neither infinite nor arbitrary. *King Lear* is never *Endgame*.

See S. W. Dawson, *Drama and the Dramatic* (1970); Clifford Leech, *The Dramatist's Experience* (1970); Stanley Wells, *Literature and Drama* (1970); Mark Fortier, *Theatre/Theory: An Introduction* (2002).

MSB

Dramatic irony   See IRONY.

E

Ecocriticism The study of literary texts with reference to the interaction between human activity and the vast range of 'natural' or non-human phenomena which bears upon human experience – encompassing (amongst many things) issues concerning fauna, flora, landscape, environment and weather.

Although ecocriticism is principally part of a wider response to a modern environmental crisis, its roots lie in what its adherents perceive to be the 'human-centric' model of history originating with the Greeks. The latter were the first to focus on 'Man Apart' – that is, humankind without reference to the physical environment in which the species subsists, – as merely one element of a complex ecosystem. For ecocritics, history since the Greeks testifies to the triumph of 'Man Apart', and the marginalization of any perspective attempting to re-integrate humankind into the natural environment.

'Man Apart' came into his own with the Age of Enlightenment and the onset of industrialization. The task of science since the eighteenth century has been the domination of nature through the accretions of rational knowledge. During the same period, the industrial imagination roamed unchecked throughout the world, constantly searching (much of the time aided by scientifically derived knowledge) for ways to better exploit the planet's natural resources. Ecocriticism emerged at a time (the latter half of the twentieth century) when, after centuries of systematic exploitation, many of those non-renewable resources were nearing the point of exhaustion. As such, it may be regarded as the literary critical wing of a general 'green' consciousness that has emerged in the developed world since the Second World War.

There are two main impulses or strands to ecocriticism. The first addresses itself to the growing canon of 'ecoliterature' that has emerged in response to the global environmental crisis – imaginative writing which self-consciously engages with 'green' issues. In this respect, it is worth noting the 'literary' air which permeates much ecocritical writing itself; infused with the proselytizing nature of their subject, and naturally indisposed towards received critical discourses (which they perceive to be infected with the scientific spirit), ecocritics have a tendency towards 'purple' prose – writing that is intended to sway the emotions as well as engage the intellect.

The second, more challenging, impulse involves re-reading the existing literary canon in ecocritical terms, that is, the attempt to address 'standard' literary texts in the light of what they reveal about human relations with the non-human world. Because of the extent to which his writing is grounded in a specific determining landscape, a writer, such as Thomas Hardy, for example, lends himself quite easily to this kind of analysis. The typical Hardy narrative (say, *Tess of the D'Urbervilles*) presents a human crisis against a background in which alternative discourses of time (beyond the average human lifespan) and space (varieties of 'natural' as opposed to 'built' environment) are constantly invoked to provide ironic distance upon the action.

The ecocritical task is less easy (although potentially more rewarding) when addressed to material that does not appear to lend itself readily to the task in hand. This is where ecocriticism can come into conflict with a variety of other critical 'isms', upon whose 'natural' territory it may seem to be intruding. Emily Brontë's *Wuthering Heights* (1847), for example, has traditionally been dominated by a variety of humanist, feminist and Marxist analyses, each of which has attempted to interpret the text in terms of their own concerns. An ecocritical analysis would not necessarily reject such interpretations, but would look to integrate them into its own critical system which, to reiterate, addresses the interaction of human and extra-human phenomena, in this case, the Yorkshire landscape, the weather and the ubiquitous animal imagery invoked throughout the text.

In the academic sphere, ecocriticism faces many of the same critiques levelled at its 'green' political counterpart, namely, that it is divisive, that it is ultimately collaborative with that which it ostensibly opposes and that it represents an effete response to a genuine global environmental crisis on the part of professionals-in-search-of-a-career. Ecocritics respond by indicting the inadequacies of present practices in the face of environmental crisis, by pointing out the culpability of traditional critical systems, and by maintaining the absolute priority of ecological issues to all human concerns. See also CYBERCRITICISM.

See Jonathan Bate, *Romantic Ecology: Wordsworth and the Environmental Tradition* (1991); Greg Garrard, *Ecocriticism* (2004); Cheryll Glotfelty and Harold Fromm (eds), *The Ecocriticism Reader* (1996).

GS

Écriture See DECONSTRUCTION.

Effect Concentration of critical attention on the psychological effect of poetry on the reader is attacked by W. K. Wimsatt and Monroe C. Beardsley, in their essay 'The affective fallacy' (*The Verbal Icon*, 1954), as encouraging impressionism and relativism much as the 'Intentional Fallacy' (see INTENTION) encourages biography and relativism. They relate the practice to the nineteenth-century tradition of affective criticism in which critics were concerned to exhibit and record their emotional responses, to catch the intensity of their experience of a work without bothering to investigate the causes of the experience. This habit of regarding poetry as an exclusively emotional affair arises from the Romantic distinction of psychological events into 'thought' and 'feeling', 'reason' and 'emotion': in such a scheme poetry is always the expression of feeling or emotion. I. A. Richards, in *Principles of Literary Criticism* (1924), continued to associate poetry with an 'emotive' as opposed to a 'scientific' use of language, and attempted to apply behavioural psychology to analysis of the effects of poetry. His failure to find terms in which the psychological processes of the reader could be described meant that descriptive criticism had to seek explanations not in psychology but in language. Thus Wimsatt and Beardsley argue that emotive import depends on the descriptive and contextual aspects of a word; it is not something added on but a function of meaning. So for an emotion we have not merely a cause, but an object, a reason – one is angry *because* one thinks a thing is false, insulting or unjust. The emotion aroused by poetry is felt in response to an organization of meaning. The descriptive critic seeks to describe the *reasons* for emotion, the meaning of the poem as a structure of language.

An absurd misunderstanding of this argument concludes that poems have no effect, no emotional quality, are merely objects to be 'objectively' analysed. But the critic could hardly hope to account for an effect that was not experienced. Wimsatt and Beardsley rightly insist that in explaining the reasons for their response to a work – in any case a more complex mental event than a state of 'feeling' – critics must seek terms which relate to the public object, the poem as a pattern of knowledge. See also FEELING, PLEASURE, READER, SINCERITY.

PM

Eiron   See IRONY.

Elegy   Some genres, such as EPIC and SONNET, are fairly unequivocal in classical and/or modern European literature: the first of these two examples is identified by its scale, its subject matter, and its manner of handling that subject matter; the second must obey stringent metrical rules. 'Elegy' illustrates a different type of genre-term: ultimately classical in origin, transplanted into modern European terminology only as a word, without the classical formal basis, unrestricted as to structure (except for the minimal requirement that it be a VERSE composition), overlapping with a number of similarly inexplicit terms (complaint, dirge, lament, monody, threnody), yet conventionally tied to a limited range of subject matters and styles (death and plaintive musing), and readily comprehensible to educated readers. In these respects, a most typical genre-term.

Elegia in Greek and Latin was a type of metre, not a type of poem – a couplet consisting of a dactylic hexameter followed by a pentameter. Since this verse-form was used for all kinds of subjects, the classical ancestry is relevant to modern elegy principally in an etymological way.

From the English Renaissance, 'elegy' or 'elegie' referred to a poem mourning the death of a particular individual.

Spenser's 'Daphnaida' (1591) and 'Astrophel' ('A Pastorall Elegie upon the death of the most noble and valorous Knight, Sir Philip Sidney', 1595) are influential early examples; Donne uses the word in the same sense (e.g. 'A Funerall Elegie' in *An Anatomy of the World*, and the titles of several poems in the collection *Epicedes and Obsequies upon the Deaths of Sundry Personages*); then there are the 'Elegies upon the Author' by several hands appended to the 1633 edition of Donne's poems. But since Donne also uses the word for his collection of twenty 'Elegies', casual, erotic and satirical poems on various topics, the precise 'funeral elegy' sense was obviously not securely established.

Milton's 'Lycidas' mourning the death of Edward King (1637) revives the pastoral form, with its apparatus of shepherds, nymphs and satyrs, and sets the pattern for the modern English elegiac tradition. The best-known poems in this mode are Shelley's 'Adonais' on Keats (1821) and Matthew Arnold's 'Thyrsis' on Clough (1867). (Milton and Arnold refer to their poems as 'monodies', not 'elegies'.) Tennyson's 'In Memoriam' on the death of Arthur Hallam (1833–50) is not pastoral, but introspective and personal.

The language of funeral elegies provided opportunity for plaintive, melancholy generalizations on death or on the state of the world: there are signs of this appropriation of the mode for general complaint already in 'Lycidas', where the author 'by occasion foretells the ruin of our corrupted clergy'. Thomas Gray's 'Elegy Written in a Country Churchyard' (1750) is the archetypal general meditation on the passing of life, unconnected with any particular death. Coleridge departicularized the definition still further when he stated that the elegy 'is the form of poetry natural to the reflective mind' – so elegy came to be a mood, or a style, as well as a poem for a specific dead person. This second, looser, definition of elegy is invoked by literary historians to characterize assorted melancholy poems of any period, for example, the so-called 'Anglo-Saxon elegies' including 'The Wanderer' and 'The Seafarer', both tales of personal deprivation shading into regretful meditations on the mutability of the world and seeking divine consolation.

As long as we are clear that there is a strict and a loose definition of 'elegy', that there is slender classical warrant for the term in either of its two familiar modern senses, and that we perforce apply it to works which were not thought of by their authors as 'elegies' (remember that the paradigm elegy 'Lycidas' is called a 'monody'), we have a useful exploratory genre-term.

See A. F. Potts, *The Elegiac Mode* (1967); Peter M. Sacks, *English Elegy: Studies in the Genre from Spenser to Yeats* (1985); Jahan Ramazani, *Poetry of Mourning: The Modern Elegy from Hardy to Heaney* (1994).

RGF

Emblem   Bacon in 1605, wrote 'Emblem reduceth conceits intellectual to images sensible'. In its fullest development the emblem comprised a symbolic picture plus motto and explanation; familiar moral and religious paradoxes were encoded in popular books like Francis Quarles's *Emblemes* (1635), and poetic emulation of such 'silent parables' (cf. ALLEGORY, CONCEIT) helped stimulate 'concreteness' and palpability in metaphor, and witty, reflexive verbal texture (see J. A. Mazzeo, 'A critique of some modern theories of metaphysical poetry', 1952, reprinted in W. R. Keast (ed.), *17th Century Poetry*, 1962). 'Emblem' or 'Device' came to signify a complex of meaning enacted through analogy (whether in paint or words or spectacle); a compressed poem-within-a-poem, or a central motto or hieroglyphic epitomizing the poem's intention. It might be traditional (the insignia of saints or nations) or bizarrely original, simultaneously announcing and hiding its meaning, assuming the portentousness of a talismanic sign.

More recent use of the term has been vexed by the ambiguous 'concreteness' it implies (see IMAGE); also by the awareness that, no matter how personal its communicative intention, 'emblem' suggests an arrogantly intentionalist aesthetic at odds with modern critical thinking ('A Device' said Puttenham (1589) 'such as a man may put into letters of gold and send to his mistresses for a token'). Postromantic distrust of the 'frigidity' of calculation, combined with the discredit of analogical thinking, inhibited reactions to emblematic techniques. They exist however: in *Coole Park and Ballylee, 1931*, Yeats exclaims 'Another emblem there!' with the assurance that characterizes public and explicit image making.

See Rosemary Freeman, *English Emblem Books* (1948); Erwin Panofsky, *Studies in Iconology* (1962); Edgar Wind, *Pagan Mysteries in the Renaissance* (1958); Michael Bath, John Manning and Alan R. Young (eds), *The Art of the Emblem* (1993); Michael Bath, *Speaking Pictures: English Emblem Books and Renaissance Culture* (1994).

LS

Epic   European literature was described by Samuel Johnson as a series of footnotes to Homer; and Keats's 'On first looking into Chapman's Homer' expresses a delight at Homer in superb translation. The *Iliad* has remained the type of classical epic ever since Aristotle's *Poetics*, and the romantic fascinations of the *Odyssey* have not been exhausted by *Ulysses* and the *Cantos*. Virgil's *Aeneid*, recapitulating the themes of Odyssey and Iliad, consecrated the epic as the supreme literary form of antiquity, and so it remained for Dante and for the Renaissance humanists. The Christian epic *Paradise Lost* was the consummation of Renaissance efforts to soar 'above the Aonian mount'; it was also the last. Dryden and Pope chose to translate rather than to emulate Virgil and Homer; Arnold lectured on the Grand Style.

Victorian definitions of epic spoke of 'national themes' (usually war) and invoked Milton's 'great argument' and 'answerable style'. Classically trained critics, expecting art to see life steadily and see it whole, looked for an idealized realism and debarred folklore and romance elements. W. P. Ker disqualified *Beowulf* because its hero fights monsters and not humans; Tolkien defended it on the same grounds. Bowra (*Heroic Poetry*) held that heroic poetry, for all the power of the gods, is centred on the human level, and that magic should not play a determining role. Twentieth-century advances in the study of non-classical heroic and oral poetry (Chadwick, Bowra, Parry, Lord) illuminated the connection of epic with 'heroic ages' where the warrior-lord of a pastoral society is the shepherd of his people in peace, and in war achieves glory by a life of action. 'Breaker of cities' and 'tamer of horses' are equally complimentary epithets; and death is better than dishonour. So it was with those at Thebes and at Troy; so with Beowulf, with Charlemagne, with Myo Cid; so perhaps with Gilgamesh and with King David. A heroic age lasts very few generations, and is firmly integrated about a few central places and figures.

The stories of these particular heroes are known through writing; the heroes of the Old English *Widsith* remain names. It is only in the mid-twentieth century that the techniques of oral composition were definitively analysed by Milman Parry; his work showed in minute detail how the text of Homer has the same formal characteristics as the improvised oral epics of Yugoslavia; both verbal phrase and type-scene and overall structural patterning are part of a repertoire of stock formulae, a tradition which evolved in response to the conditions of oral improvisation. Parry's methods have been applied to the products of other cultures. But the consequences of his work for the poetics of an epic written in an 'oral' style have to be worked out critically. There is, after all, a qualitative difference between Homer's epic and the Yugoslav *epos*; their compositional mechanics may be the same, but their aesthetic effects differ, at least in degree, and the difference may be due in part to a literate finishing of the *epea pteroenta*, Homer's 'winged words'.

Between Homer and Virgil lies a vast difference, and again between Virgil and Milton; critics speak of primary, secondary and tertiary epic. The verbal art of Virgil refines and transmutes the clear and inevitable directness of Homer into something softer; the laughter of his gods, when heard, is less uncontrollable. For all the sternness of its ethos and beauty of its surface, his world has a fuller moral and psychological dimension, and a more personal reverberation, than Homer's. Milton himself and his concerns as a Renaissance humanist and Protestant are so powerful in *Paradise Lost*, and it contains in baroque form so much of the extravagance of the so-called romantic epics of Ariosto, Tasso and Spenser, that the usefulness of the term 'epic' may be disputed. The epic surely cannot be an individual's personal view of the world?

The point about epic, Northrop Frye argued, is its encyclopaedic scope and its cyclic structure; the anger of Achilles, the journeys of Odysseus and Aeneas – these stories in their resolution recapitulate the life of the individual and of the race. The note of epic is its objectivity:

> It is hardly possible to overestimate the importance for Western literature of the Iliad's demonstration that the fall of an enemy, no less than of a friend or leader, is tragic and not comic. With the *Iliad*, once for all, an objective and disinterested element enters into the poet's vision of human life. With this element, ... poetry acquires the authority that since the *Iliad* it has never lost, an authority based, like the authority of science, on the vision of nature as an impersonal order.

Frye argued well for this pattern and this authority in Virgil and Milton; he also considered the Bible an epic.

It is this objectivity and authority that Joyce sought and Brecht wanted in his 'epic theatre'. The epic qualities achieved by Tolstoy, aimed at by Steinbeck and even by Cecil B. de Mille are based on the idea of epic presenting the whole of the life of a society against a natural background with simplicity, grandeur and authority. The fate of characters is part of the overall pattern. 'The lives of men are like the generations of leaves' or an incident in battle is 'as when a shepherd in the mountains sees a thundercloud (or a wolf)...'. The coherence of the pattern of life is maintained by these traditional epic similes; there is the feeling that the whole is more than the part you are reading, and that you know, in general, what the whole is like. Aristotle remarked that Homer leaves the stage to his characters; this impersonality of narrative technique

stems from the fact that Frye's 'poet's vision' is the traditional vision of a preliterate society. Hence the *aidos* of epic, its respect for the given facts of nature and human life, which it crystallizes into generic type-scenes and verbal formulae; hence its pattern, beauty and authority.

See Erich Auerbach, trans. W. Trask, *Mimesis* (1953); Maurice Bowra, *Heroic Poetry* (1952), *Virgil to Milton* (1945); H. M. and N. K. Chadwick, *The Growth of Literature* (reprinted 1968); Northrop Frye, *Anatomy of Criticism* (1957); W. P. Ker, *Epic and Romance* (1896); G. S. Kirk, *Homer and the Epic* (1965); C. S. Lewis, A *Preface to Paradise Lost* (1942); A. B. Lord, *The Singer of Tales* (1964); Milman Parry, ed. A. Parry, *The Making of Homeric Verse* (1971); Gregory Nagy, *Homeric Responses* (2004).

MJA

Epic theatre   The cardinal concept of the work of Bertolt Brecht (*the* classic MODERNIST, and, after Shakespeare, perhaps the most frequently performed of all dramatists), 'epic theatre' means, simply, a theatre that narrates, rather than represents. Stemming from the period in which Brecht first began to study Marx, with *The Threepenny Opera* of 1928 as its first major exhibit, the theory is grounded in historical and political propositions – in the view, espoused by mentors like the sociologist Fritz Sternberg and the critic Walter Benjamin as well as by Brecht himself, that the workings of modern industrial civilization, and the essentially 'inorganic' cities spawned by it, are too abstract and complex to be visually apprehended, or immanently represented upon the stage. Upon such premises Brecht built a 'scientific' theory of a radical drama in which experimental work upon contemporary society might be carried out through a sober, narrative analysis of its inherent (and frequently comic) contradictions.

Consequently, the theory of the 'epic theatre' emphasizes rationality, and devices calculated to secure a suitable environment for its exercise. Brecht felt that to foster a state of relaxation in the theatre – an atmosphere in which reason and detachment, rather than passion and involvement, were to predominate – was to subvert the established theatre and the bankrupt 'culinary', 'Aristotelian' plays that were performed in it. He had in mind, essentially, the drama of bourgeois realism, with its roots in Lessing's neo-Aristotelian theory, and its aim of achieving empathetic identification between audiences and 'stars' who in turn identify themselves with their roles, and represent individual psychologies in emotionally charged styles of acting. One alternative model was cabaret, where drinks and smokes guarantee a laid-back, critical frame of mind: 'I even maintain' (wrote Brecht in a hyperbolic mood) 'that one man with a cigar in the stalls at a Shakespeare performance could bring about the downfall of western art'. In such an atmosphere, Brecht's plays are commonly introduced by narrators (sometimes cynics, like the comperes of cabarets) who see through social façades and distance themselves from the events they recount; played by actors who do not identify with their roles; and set in remote times and places – Chicago, China, medieval Georgia and Victorian London – with which no spectator can identify.

The ensemble of these measures is to produce the famous *Verfremdungseffekt* or 'alienation effect'. This concept, with its formalist and idealist antecedents (the Russian FORMALIST *ostranenie* or 'making strange', and German Romantic

'romantic irony'), shifts critical attention from 'affekt' to 'effekt', to the perhaps idealized possibility of audience politicization through a process where cool detachment leads to correct and effective judgement and action. 'Alienation means historicizing, means representing persons and actions as historical, and therefore mutable', writes Brecht in the 1929 essay 'On experimental theatre', restating the Marxist equation of scientific and historical consciousness. The attainment of such consciousness means, for Brecht, the 'alienated' awareness that history's outcomes are never inevitable, always amenable to political intervention and transformation.

Consequently, the epic theatre's foregrounding of narratives and narrators does not imply any straightforward, unproblematical unfolding of chronological or other linear sequences. In a continual recapitulation, perhaps, of the frustrations of 1926, when he was forced to abandon plays that foundered upon the invisibility and unrepresentability of processes like the operation of the Chicago Grain Market, the emphasis of Brecht's work is upon discontinuity. No chain of events is held together by a natural or self-evident logic; the spectator is to experience the constant disruption of narrative structure, as one device undercuts another. Actors are continually abandoning speech for song, or taking off masks to become other characters, or to take part in other plays; scenes are shifted abruptly in time and space, with intervening chasms. The epic theatre asserts narrative in an unpropitious time (compare Benjamin's essay 'The Storyteller', on the loss of narrative art), rather than takes it for granted.

Yet, in the history of the reception of Brechtian theory, it may be possible to point to some of its *own* contradictions.

It has created a new aesthetics, perhaps, but not a new politics of art. The ease and ubiquity of its absorption was foreshadowed by the instant worldwide success of *The Threepenny Opera* and 'Mack the Knife', a song whose basic propositions (1. that the equation of businessmen and sharks insults sharks; 2. that the upholders and subverters of bourgeois law are interchangeable) have seemed to offer little resistance to painless consumption. Whether or not Brecht can be held responsible for the dissemination of his work in versions that (to requisition a phrase of Clive James's) often have less of the atmosphere of poisonous old Berlin than of poisonous old Bournemouth, the fact remains that Brechtian techniques have now been universally domesticated on television.

Perceiving such problems, Brecht in his last years began to replace the theory of epic theatre with the theory of dialectical theatre, and to base it on the much more radical practice of the *Lehrstücke* (where the entire distinction between performers and audience was abolished, and the performance itself – with potential Nazi wreckers at the doors – became a political act). In Anglo-American criticism, where the critical working-through of Brechtian theory has been sluggish, such difficulties have surfaced only in recent years, but are thoroughly comprehended in (for instance) Fredric Jameson's 'Afterword' in *Aesthetics and Politics* (1978).

Cf. CONTRADICTION.

See also Walter Benjamin, *Understanding Brecht* (1973); John Willett (ed.), *Brecht on Theatre: The Development of an Aesthetic* (1974); G. Bartram and A. Waine (eds), *Brecht in Perspective* (1982); J. L. Styan, *Modern Drama in Theory and Practice: Expressionism and Epic Theatre* (1983); J. Reinelt, *After Brecht: British Epic Theater* (1996).

MAH

Epistle   See VERSE EPISTLE.

Essay   Both the term and the form were invented by Montaigne (1533–92) and adopted soon afterwards into English by Bacon; literally the try-out in discursive prose of an idea, judgement or experience. Although the essay is by definition informal and even conversational in manner, the persuasive and rhetorical tradition of much Greek and Roman writing was familiar to Bacon and Montaigne and lies behind what they write. We therefore find in all essays a direct and even intimate appeal to the reader; sometimes, as in Swift's 'Modest proposal', this is complex and ambiguous in line with the ironic purpose of engaging the reader in the interpretative process; sometimes, as in George Orwell's most effective essays (e.g. 'Shooting an Elephant'), the rhetoric is all the more influential for being muted and oblique. Usually, though, the essay is a polished and sophisticated form of fireside chat, a smooth way of putting over moral reflections, aphorisms and *obiter dicta* in a less rigorous and rebarbative manner than the treatise or ethical disquisition permits. It must appear relaxed but not flabby, nonchalant but not trivial. In France, Montaigne set the pattern of a fundamentally moral argument based on anecdotes and the lessons to be drawn from them – the gentle art of egotism, in fact, involving autobiography of a sort, if selective and intellectual in style rather than frankly confessional. In England, William Hazlitt, Charles Lamb and others made it more sentimental and whimsical by playing down the serious aspect the French kept to the fore. In America, Washington Irving, Emerson and Thoreau wrote in the genre, and the form flourished, particularly among black writers, such as James Baldwin and Leroy Jones. In all cases, however, there is no formal structure of progression, and little attempt at a final synthesis: the play of the mind in free associations around a given topic is what counts. Essays are therefore not debates, but dialogues with an assumed reader; but in the finest examples, this does not preclude a fruitful and stimulating tension between a frequent high seriousness in the theme and the almost casual informality of the way in which it is handled. An attempt was made by Scholes and Klaus to subdivide the genre according to its analogies with the oration, the poem, the story and the play, but since even they admitted that 'any essay may be a combination of the four basic forms', the most sensible approach is that which views the essay as a minor art-form in its own right.

See Robert Scholes and Carl H. Klaus, *Elements of the Essay* (1969).

JWJF

Essentialism   Associated with the tenets of HUMANISM, essentialism is based on the belief that all individuals, or groups of individuals, possess certain fundamental, innate traits. Thus, essentialism treats identity as fixed, permanent and stable. Essentialists also assume that there are certain basic and unalterable physical and psychological differences between, for instance, men and women, heterosexuals and gays/lesbians and people of different races. To put it most simply, essentialists view identity as the product of biology rather than the construction of culture. In chapter 14 of Charles Dickens's *Bleak House* (1852–3) a character called Mr Turveydrop offers us an easily recognizable example of such views when he exclaims, 'Wooman, lovely Wooman...what a sex you are!' Collapsing GENDER into sex, this comment implies that *all* women (emphasized by the capitalization of 'Wooman') fit neatly into a single, self-evident category determined by shared physiological features. Yet, this 'Wooman' – far from constituting a 'natural' category – refers to a historically specific construction that is intimately bound up with contemporary DISCOURSES of class, gender, nationality and race. Turning from literature to the real world, we might also consider the fate of two individuals: a young black man living in South Africa during the reign of apartheid and a middle-class white man living in the South of England in the twenty-first century. Although each possesses a penis (the definitive marker of sexual DIFFERENCE and, for the essentialists, sexual identity), such superficial similarities mean little when compared to a whole range of other contextual factors that differentiate these men. Both universalizing and transcendent, essentialism is inherently reductive because it ignores the decisive role that factors, such as environment, history, class, education, the family and language itself play in constituting who and what we are.

At certain stages in their development, branches of both feminist and postcolonial theory advocated an essentialist view of gender and race in an attempt to consolidate a more positive and self-determined notion of women and persons of colour. For example, the French feminist Luce Irigaray has argued that experiences specific to women, such as menstruation and childbirth, mean that they are more connected to the material realm than men and therefore hold a different set of ethical values. More recently, however, such methodologies have been called into question, especially by those influenced by POST-STRUCTURALISM which is decidedly anti-essentialist in orientation. It is now widely recognized that any attempt to privilege the differences *between* men and women, or people of different races, minimizes the key differences and diversity *within* such groupings. One of the most important of such critiques of essentialism is that of the American feminist Judith Butler, who argues that femininity is the effect, rather than the cause, of behaviours held by essentialists to be natural and intrinsic to women (see PERFORMATIVITY). Speaking more generally, the essentialist view of the individual has been replaced by the post-structuralist notion of the SUBJECT. Rather than being seen as fixed, stable and permanent, the subject is contingent, multiple, fragmented and always in process. Above all, the subject is a construct subject to external forces and factors over which it has no control. One of the most important of such forces is language itself which, according to post-structuralism, constitutes rather than reflects our identity and the world in which we live.

As we have already seen, essentialism is based on a belief in certain unalterable, fundamental truths about the individual and human nature more generally. Thus, it should come as no surprise that an essentialist reading of a literary text would concentrate on how these universal and immutable values are expressed by the author. Such a reading would, moreover, treat the text as an autonomous entity, divorced from both its context of production and consumption. See also DIFFERENCE, HUMANISM and THE OTHER.

                                                                JA

Ethical criticism   Until the late eighteenth century, it was a commonplace of criticism that literature should promote virtue. From *The Epistles* of the Roman poet Ovid (43 BC–AD 17) to the novels of Samuel Richardson (1689–1761) literature was expected not so much to imitate nature as to improve it by providing examples of good behaviour which readers could emulate. This changed with the advent of romanticism. Literature was now seen as an expression of emotion rather than a guide to ethics. Of course, writers did not cease to be concerned about ethical issues-look, for example, at how the Victorian novelists tried to raise awareness about the plight of the poor, but literature was no longer conceived primarily as a guide to right action. This became even more pronounced at the end of the nineteenth century with the aesthetic movement which promoted the idea of 'art for art's sake': beauty, not morality was to be the new touchstone of literature.

Nor did ethics seem to be a priority of modernist art where the interest was more in the nature of consciousness than in the workings of conscience. Moreover, the nature of modernist art made it difficult to engage with ethical issues. The emphasis on formal experimentation rather than accurate representation made it difficult for the reader to connect any moral matters that might arise in a work with his or her own experience of the world. Ethics is central to the work of F. R. Leavis (1896–1978) but he did not believe that literature should be used as a guide to behaviour. His was a much more subtle conception, one which stressed the power of literature to make us more responsive to the possibilities for growth and development in both ourselves and the society in which we live.

The advent of French critical theory in the 1970s signalled another change in the perception of literature. Thinkers, such as Jacques Derrida (1930–2004), Michel Foucault (1926–84) and Jacques Lacan (1901–81) focussed on the nature of signification while in Britain CULTURAL MATERIALISTS drew attention to the role literature played in legitimizing the social order. One criticism of these developments is that they undermined the idea of individual responsibility, not only by showing that social and economic and even linguistic structures limited the freedom to act, but also by questioning the very idea of the human itself. To be fair, there was something deeply ethical about theory's aim to give a voice to those on the margins but such concerns often seemed lost in the sort of highly abstract, formal analysis that can be found, for example, in the writings of Derrida. It was dissatisfaction with these and other elements of theory that led to a revival of ethical criticism. A key figure in this change was Emmanuel Levinas (1906–95) whose idea that we have an absolute obligation to the other struck a chord in a society where social bonds were disintegrating under the impact of market forces.

There is no one form of ethical criticism. Instead, there are a range of ethical concerns, all of them rooted in the fact that a work of literature presupposes a relation between the author and the audience and is therefore ethical by nature. There is the conventional view that literature is ethical because it enables us to empathize with others. It does this by its special use of language which appeals simultaneously to the intellect, the passions and the affections thereby reminding us that ethics is not a matter of following rules but of balancing all kinds of conflicting claims and then taking responsibility for whatever decision we finally make. Ethical criticism is based on close reading which respects the unique character of the work. It also concerns itself with how a work represents the world, especially if it is based on a true event, and with how a work relates to the writer's or the reader's own life. More broadly, there are debates in ethical criticism about whether we should or should

not try to speak for others as this has the potential to oppress them and whether we should judge an act as good in itself or according to the consequences that follow from it. Finally, there is the question of how ethics relates to literary form: are some forms, such as REALISM, more amenable to the exploration of ethical issues than, say, self-referential works? But there are also more straightforward issues here, such as how clearly writers communicate, or how sincere they may be.

See Todd Davis and Kenneth Womack (eds), *Mapping the Ethical Turn: A Reader in Ethics, Culture and Literary Theory* (2001); Andrew Hadfield (ed.), *The Ethics in Literature* (1999); Dominic Rainsford and Tim Woods (eds), *Critical Ethics: Text, Theory and Responsibility* (1999).

GD

Euphony   See TEXTURE.

Eurocentrism   Put simply, Eurocentrism is a way of thinking that privileges Europe (or, 'the West') as the centre of historical development, and posits European culture as superior to all others. It is, therefore, a species of ethnocentrism; but is also more than that. Whilst ethnocentrism, in the abstract form of believing one's own culture to be better or more satisfying than anyone else's is arguably a feature of all human societies, and is therefore, transhistorical and transcultural, Eurocentrism is a specifically modern construct that has emerged in complex relation to the formation of capitalism and colonialism. This means that prior to the emergence of the modern world and the ideological formations that sustain it (of which Eurocentrism is one, highly important, dimension), European self-centredness was no more than a 'banal provincialism'; afterwards it becomes part of 'a theory of world history and...a global political project' (Amin).

However, this should not be taken to imply that Eurocentrism is a coherent set of ideas that may be located in a series of identifiable texts; rather, its force derives from the way it has embedded itself into the common sense of European discourse. It is not a theory in itself but forms the basis, or framework, for many theories of history, society and humanity and is manifested in day-to-day encounters between individuals, in the media and in political discourse, as well as in the sophisticated formulations of academic specialists. It is, therefore, more than just a prejudice – whether unconscious or not. Rather, its ideological power resides in the way Eurocentric ideas become visible as 'facts' (Blaut). These 'facts' may or may not be true: capitalism *did* emerge in Europe; Europeans are *not* more intelligent than other 'races' etc. However, the force of these 'facts' lies in the manner by which they are explained or interpreted so as to conform to the Eurocentric vision. Eurocentrism can thus appear disinterested and objective and may even refract a discourse that ostensibly challenges European dominance and superiority.

Eurocentrism is both historical and geographical. That is, it assumes certain propositions about both space and time. At its core lies a belief in European exceptionalism that underlines the notion of a 'Europe' that is territorially and civilizationally distinct from the rest of the world. This 'Europe' is a mythical construct that consists of a fabricated genealogy of European civilization that can be traced back through an unbroken historical continuity to classical Greece. In so doing, it erases the marks of classical Greece's emergence within and affiliation to a wider Mediterranean cultural sphere that had its centre of gravity in

what has become known, following the emergence of Eurocentrism itself, as the 'Orient'. This distinction from the 'Orient' (as a marker for all of Europe's Others) is another feature of Eurocentrism, and is most fully developed in the discourse of Orientalism. As a result, historical development moves northwards and westwards, from the eastern and southern half of the great Eurasian land mass to the Atlantic shore. As for those spaces beyond Eurasia, such as the Americas and Africa, these are historically 'empty' until filled by European colonization, which brings them into History.

From the Eurocentric viewpoint, it is only Europe and Europeans that can therefore make History; the Others are either consigned to a fossilized 'past' that has been surpassed by European advance (since it could not be denied that civilizations did exist outside Europe, in west, south and east Asia, some means of accommodating this fact with European exceptionalism and superiority had to be found), or are awaiting the hand of Europe to help them onto the stage of history. Thus, the advances in human history are all reframed and resituated within a narrative that has at its centre a Europe whose development and progressive maturation is its subject. It is not Eurocentric, therefore, to acknowledge that capitalism emerged in Europe; what *is* Eurocentric are those historical narratives that suggest it could not have happened otherwise. In this sense, whilst Eurocentrism is a definitive feature of the ideology of capitalism, it has also historically been part of its critique. Marxism, for instance, is but one of the oppositional discourses to capitalist hegemony that is itself marked by its Eurocentrism.

If Europe represents the highest form of civilization, historical progress involves the progressive diffusion of European civilization from its centre to the outlying peripheries. As such, Eurocentrism is never separable from colonialism, or from the racism which accompanied it. All modern colonial discourse is Eurocentric and, conversely, Eurocentrism is necessarily colonialist in its implications. The end of history, and the future of humanity, is conceptualized in terms of the world's progressive Europeanization, or, in today's language, Westernization. Such ideas have, of course, been consistently challenged but their durability is such that they remain part of the hegemonic structure of the contemporary world. See also ORIENTALISM.

See J. M. Blaut, *The Colonizer's History of the World* (1992); Samir Amin, *Eurocentrism* (1989).

AM

Evaluation   When we engage critically with a literary work, we are not merely describing it, making it accessible to other readers; at the same time we *judge* it, explicitly or by implication. But the 'objectivity' of description is often felt to preclude evaluation, which is suspected of being a subjective, authoritarian action. T. S. Eliot testified to the tension between the descriptive and evaluative roles of criticism by arguing for the primacy of both. In 1918 'Judgement and appreciation are merely tolerable avocations, no part of the critic's serious business' (*The Egoist*, V), while in 1923 the critic is urged to 'the common pursuit of true judgement' ('The function of criticism', *Selected Essays*, p. 25). Eliot's self-contradiction reflected the enduring tendency of criticism to define its ambitions in terms of one or the other of these ideally complementary activities. The alternative emphases produce historically distinct traditions, and propose sharply differentiated programmes.

The evaluative tradition is in England rooted in the neo-classic criticism of Dryden, Pope and Johnson. They saw themselves as arbiters of public taste, interpreting the works of the past and, in their light, judging the work of the present. Their concern was the preservation and assertion of traditional literary and cultural values; the commitment of such criticism to moral and aesthetic standards makes public judgement constantly necessary, and belief in them makes it possible. This tradition of public criticism, mediating between the past and the present, the artists and the public, was continued in the nineteenth century by major critics, such as Matthew Arnold and Henry James, and survived in the twentieth century in the work of Leavis and the *Scrutiny* writers.

The challenge to this tradition, evident in Eliot's 1918 declaration, emerged from the aspirations of many academic disciplines at the beginning of the twentieth century to the attitudes and procedures of the fashionable sciences. The new enthusiasm for objectivity and disinterestedness, for precise analysis and comparison, implied the irrelevance of public critics and their concern for judgement. Leslie Stephen urged that the critic 'should endeavour to classify the phenomena with which he is dealing as calmly as if he were ticketing a fossil in a museum'. The scientific analogies were ultimately false – literature is not fossilized, not so many value-free facts – and in practice the 'objective' criticism of Eliot and I. A. Richards was full of strident value judgements. But the desire for objective procedures led to the development of a descriptive criticism whose end was not judgement but knowledge, which took the value of the works it examined for granted. Descriptive criticism assumed not that judgement is irrelevant but that it is implicit in description and analysis; the analysis of a work is a discovery of form, of order, and is thus a testimony to value. The public critic asserts and defines standards against which any work must be measured, but a descriptive critic like William Empson has declared that 'you must rely on each particular poem to show you the way in which it is trying to be good; if it fails you cannot know its object' (*Seven Types of Ambiguity*, 1930). This lack of interest in 'bad' literature and urbanity about problems of evaluation pointed to the critic's new role in the intellectual and cultural safety of the university, distanced from contemporary culture and the reading public, while the public critic's mantle was assumed by the reviewer.

See W. K. Wimsatt, Jr, 'Explication as criticism' and 'Poetry and morals' in *The Verbal Icon* (1954); Steven Connor, *Theory and Cultural Value* (1992); Patrick McGee, *Telling the Other: Question of Value in Modern and Postcolonial Writing* (1992).

PM

Existentialism Literary and philosophical responses to the experience of nothingness, anomie and absurdity which attempt to discover meaning in and through this experience.

All Existentialist writers begin from a sense that an ontological dimension (Being; the Encompassing; Transcendence; the Thou) has been forced out of consciousness by the institutions and systems of a society which overvalues rationality, will-power, acquisitiveness, productivity and technological skill. Because this essential dimension properly constitutes the substantial unity between person and person, thing and thing, subject and object, past,

present and future, its loss is said to cause individuals to feel that they have been thrown into a world of reified fragments which say nothing, into a world of human beings who talk past each other and into a time-stream of disconnected present moments without past or future (see Heidegger, *Being and Time*, 1927). Thus, human institutions, severed from the generative source, cease to be sign-structures of that source and become factitious structures which engage the surface levels of the personality and provide no home. Even language, the most self-evident institution, is felt to be a complex of cerebralized structures which impede communication and give only limited control over the empirical world. Nietzsche called this total experience of forfeiture 'the death of God', and perhaps K.'s vision of the world in Kafka's *The Castle* (1926) forms its fullest literary expression: long conversations lead nowhere; shambling buildings are inhabited by beings going through meaningless motions like bees in a hive after the removal of the queen; and everything is permeated by a sense of groundlessness, futility and grey opacity. K. is therefore a menace because his wilfulness perpetually threatens to smash this fragile world and precipitate it into the nothingness that underlies almost everything.

At the same time, the *Angst* which haunts the Existentialist world was said – and this paradox is fundamental to Existentialist psychology – to point to the possibility of its own transcendence. Precisely because the individual can experience absurdity so intensely, there must, it is argued, be some inherent human propensity to order and meaning. *Angst*, in other words, is seen as the by-product of the conflict between this propensity and the factitious forms which have been imposed upon it.

Existentialist writers and thinkers did not, however, share a unified understanding of this propensity. Sartre, the most consistently atheistic of the Existentialists, equated it with the human will shorn of all illusions and responsible only to itself. Camus, more of an agnostic, located it below the will, in the spontaneous potential of the personality, but refused to name it, pointing to it through a variety of metaphors. Heidegger, whose thinking is crypto-theistic, referred to it as *Sorge* (care) and Kierkegaard, an avowed Christian, identified it with the soul. Nevertheless, it is this propensity which is said to save individuals from nihilism, despair or escape into the ready-made values of the fallen world.

Furthermore, Existentialist writers and thinkers draw radically different metaphysical conclusions from the existence of this propensity. Although, for Sartre, it points to nothing beyond itself and is not capable of overcoming the *néant* in any final sense, it does permit individuals to live with theor 'unhappy consciousness', to tolerate their own *Angst*. For Camus, however, it enables humanity to find happiness and peace of mind in an absurd universe (Meursault and Sisyphe), engage in collective work against the forces of negation (Rieux and his friends) and, occasionally, to glimpse transcendent powers. For Jaspers, it enables people to alter their 'consciousness of Being' and 'inner attitude towards things' and to listen in an attitude of 'philosophial faith' for the silence of hidden Transcendence as it emanates into experience and overcomes fragmentation, isolation and encrustation (Jaspers, *The Perennial Scope of Philosophy*, 1948). For Buber, the Jewish Existentialist, it indicates the possibility of attunement to and existence according to the timeless moments which are generated when the 'eternal Thou' breaks into time through the 'human Thou' (Buber, *I and Thou*, 1923). For Kierkegaard, a Christian Existentialist, it is the divinely motivated principle of 'subjectivity' which urges the individual to make the 'leap of faith' and discover the task and responsibility for that task which God has laid upon each person even if that task ends in failure and absurdity (Kierkegaard, *Fear and Trembling*, 1843).

Consequently, Sartre's famous dictum 'existence precedes essence' – often considered to be the basic tenet of Existentialism – can mean one of two things. Either that existence is inherently meaningless so that individuals have, by the exercise of the will, to create their own values. Or that, for each individual, there is a hidden meaning embedded in existence which, by the exercise of total personal resources, the individual has to discover and live by.

On the one hand then, theistic and crypto-theistic Existentialism moved towards an inner-worldly mysticism where the experience of the Transcendent is discovered within and not apart from society. On the other hand, agnostic and atheistical Existentialism moved towards an attitude of defiance which can turn into a social or explicitly ideological commitment (Camus's Socialism and Sartre's Marxism).

In all cases then, a radically negative experience was seen by Existentialists to contain the embryo of a positive development – though the psychological and philosophical content of that development is extremely diverse.

See W. Barrett, *Irrational Man* (1961); J. Collins, *The Existentialists* (1977); C. Hanley, *Existentialism and Psychoanalysis* (1979); P. Roubiczek, *Existentialism* (1964); G. Rupp, *Beyond Existentialism and Zen* (1979); Walter

Kaufman (ed.), *Existentialism from Dostoevsky to Sartre* (1977); Mary Warnock, *Existentialism* (1977); David E. Cooper, *Existentialism: A Reconstruction* (1990).

RWS

Explication   See ANALYSIS.

Expressionism   A label applied to the *avant-garde* literature, graphics, architecture and cinema which appeared throughout the German-speaking world, 1910–*c*.1922, and of which Vorticism was the closest equivalent in England. First used of German painting in April 1911, and of literature in July 1911, the term gained rapid currency with reference to the visual arts but was probably established as a literary critical term only as late as mid-1913. Several important early Expressionists died without ever using the term; other important writers reacted negatively to it during the years in question; others denied any validity to it or were unwilling to associate themselves with it.

At the most, Expressionism is a blanket term. It does not characterize a uniform movement propagating a neatly definable set of ideas or working towards well-defined and commonly accepted goals. The product of a generation which had been born into a pre-modern Germany, grown up during twenty-five years of unprecedentedly rapid social change and achieved maturity in a society which was extensively industrialized and urbanized, Expressionism stands between two worlds and is riven by inner conflict, contradiction and paradox. Thus, the classic early Expressionist poem, for example, is marked by a time-sense of imminent crisis, torn between a desire for stillness and an urge to lose itself in chaos, and characterized by a disjunction between a rigid verse form and images of rigidity and

a violence which threatens to explode these. Correspondingly, the syntax of an early Expressionist poem involves a struggle for dominance between noun and verb, and its adjectives are used not to describe the surface of a static noun but to point metaphorically to a hidden dynamism at work below that surface. Expressionism is, however, not just a stylistic phenomenon but, in Bakhtin's sense, a metalinguistic *Problematik* which can be resolved in a variety of ways.

The works of early Expressionism, 1910–14, are, typically, situated on the edge of the specifically modern context, the megalopolis of industrial Capitalism, and present this under two aspects: beneath a rigid artificial, asphalt crust, and controlled by the authoritarian father-figure, chaotic forces, ungovernable by the individual, are destructively active. Furthermore, in the early Expressionist vision, the machine, ostensibly a tool for extending human dominance over Nature, turns back on itself, becoming a Frankenstein monster, a Golem which seeks to devour the beings that made it. Consequently, the inhabitants of the Expressionist city are presented as spectral, puppet-like beings assailed by dark powers over which, despite their assumed and absurd self-confidence, they have no final control.

To this ambiguous and disturbing vision, various responses are possible: withdrawal into nostalgia for pre-modern forms (Ernst Blass's and Georg Trakl's poetry), cosmic pessimism (Georg Heym's poetry), irony (Jakob van Hoddis's and Alfred Lichtenstein's poetry), ecstatic irrationalism (Ernst Stadler's and Ernst Wilhelm Lotz's poetry; Ludwig Rubiner's manifesto *Der Dichter greift in die Politik*) – which may, as with *Ich-Dramen* like Reinhard Sorge's *Der Bettler* and Walter Hasenclever's *Der Sohn*, involve a passionate wish to murder the father – or the Rimbaldian desire to find a saving, spiritual dimension beyond the sterile surface and demonic night-side of the modern city (Georg Heym's *Novellen*; Georg Traki's last poems and Wassily Kandinsky's theoretical work *Über das Geistige in der Kunst*).

The outbreak of war reinforced the early Expressionist vision and gave urgency to some of the possible responses. Thus, the urban landscape seemed to the Expressionists to have prefigured the battlefields of the Great War whose mechanized slaughter was, in turn, seen as a horrendous extension of the Capitalist system of production, with people and material going in at one end and corpses coming out of the other. Correspondingly, although the War was greeted enthusiastically by some Expressionists for a few weeks or months as a means of overcoming everyday boredom and revitalizing a dead Society (Hugo Ball, Rudolf Leonhard, Hans Leyboid, Ernst Wilhelm Lotz), the experience of trench warfare soon made it clear that something more than affective dynamism was necessary for social renewal. This realization accentuated in some Expressionists the temptation to withdraw from the modern world (Gottfried Benn) or surrender to cosmic pessimism (August Stramm).

At the same time, Autumn 1914 saw the emergence of Kurt Hiller's *Aktivismus* – a pacifist neo-humanism, shorn of idealist metaphysics, which attracted considerable support from among the Expressionists and which placed its hopes in the emergence of a new, spiritualized humanity and redeemed society out of the Purgatory of the War. These and similar millenarian aspirations intensified and spread as the War went on, merging by 1918 with a sterile revolutionary rhetoric of which the final scenes of Ernst Toller's *Die Wandlung* (1917–18) are an example and the whole of Toller's *Masse Mensch* (1920–1) a critique. When the German Revolution of 1918–19 failed to produce the hoped-for total revolution, a widespread disillusion set in among surviving Expressionists which frequently ended in suicide, exile, or a 'sell-out' to some totalitarian organization, and which is reflected in the drama of cultural and political despair, such as Georg Kaiser's *Gas trilogy* (1916–19).

Expressionism issued into DADA, the Bauhaus and Constructivism. Where DADA continued the metaphysical investigations of early Expressionism, offering systematic folly and carnivalization both as a means of coming to terms with a many-layered and paradoxical vision of reality and as a political weapon, the Bauhaus and Constructivism, through the medium of architecture, investigated how the utopian neo-humanism of late Expressionism might be realized with the new techniques and materials provided by the twentieth century.

A comprehensive anthology on this subject is Thomas Anz and Michael Stark (eds), *Expressionismus: Manfeste und Dokumente zur deutschen Literatur 1910–1920* (1982). Critical works include: R. F. Allen, *German Expressionist Poetry* (1979); R. S. Furness, *Expressionism* (1973); J. Ritchie, *German Expressionist Drama* (1976); W. H. Sokel, *The Writer in Extremis* (1959); S. Vietta and H.-G. Kemper, *Expressionismus* (1975); J. Willett, *Expressionism* (1970).

RWS

F

Fable A short moral tale, in verse or prose, in which human situations and behaviour are depicted through (chiefly) beasts and birds, or gods or inanimate objects. Human qualities are projected onto animals, according to certain conventions (e.g. malicious craftiness for the fox). Fables are ironic and realistic in tone, often satirical, their themes usually reflecting on the commonsense ethics of ordinary life: they dramatize the futility of relinquishing a small profit for the sake of larger (but hypothetical) future gains, of the weak attempting to take on the powerful on equal terms, the irony of falling into one's own traps, etc. Such themes are close to the advice of proverbs, and the moral point of a fable is usually announced epigrammatically by one of the characters at the end.

The beast fable is extremely ancient, evidenced from Egypt, Greece, India and presumably cognate with the development of a self-conscious folklore in primitive cultures. The Western tradition derives largely from the fables of Aesop, a Greek slave who lived in Asia Minor in the sixth century BC. His work is not known directly, but has been transmitted through elaborations by such writers as Phaedrus and Babrius. Collections were extensively read in medieval schools; the tone of the genre became more frankly humorous. The most famous medieval example is Chaucer's 'Nun's Priest's Tale'. The fable achieved greater sophistication in the hands of Jean de la Fontaine (1621–95), whose verse fables revived the fashion throughout the Europe of the seventeenth and eighteenth centuries. England's representative in this mode was John Gay (1685–1732). In Germany, G. E. Lessing (1729–81) preferred the simpler model of Aesop to the refined modern version.

The fable had twentieth-century practitioners, too. George Orwell's *Animal Farm* (1945), sometimes seen as an allegory, employed the beast fable as the vehicle for an extended SATIRE on the totalitarian state. In America, James Thurber contributed *Fables for our Time* (1940). See Niklas Holsberg, *The Ancient Fable: An Introduction* (2003); Jayne Elizabeth Lewis, *The English Fable: Aesop and Literary Culture, 1651–1740* (1996).

RGF

Fabula See FORMALISM.

Fabulation See FICTION.

Fancy See CONCEIT, IMAGINATION, WIT.

Fantastic Now commonly comprises a variety of fictional works which use the supernatural or apparently supernatural. Examples are found in German Romanticism (e.g. Tieck, Hoffman); in English GOTHIC fiction and ghost stories; in nineteenth-century French literature (e.g. Nodier, the later Maupassant); and in twentieth-century depictions of dream worlds (e.g. Carroll) or seemingly impossible worlds and events (e.g. Kafka, Borges).

Not all works in which the supernatural or eerie appears are classified as *fantastic*, however. Works of *fantasy*, such as Tolkien's fiction and C. S. Lewis's Narnia series, create their own coherently organized worlds and myths. References to familiar everyday activities render these worlds more homely and comprehensible. The everyday details are integrated into the other world, extending its range of reference; the combination of 'real' and 'supernatural' suggests a world of greater opportunity and fullness than one consisting of 'real' elements alone. If the 'real' world is also depicted separately (as in Lewis), movement between the two worlds happens at specific points in the text, so that any character is always in either one world or the other. The reader is invited to feel not bewilderment at but respect for the order of the 'supernatural' world, even awe and wonder.

It is characteristic of the *fantastic* text that the reader is made unsure how to interpret and respond to the events narrated. Critics have stated that the fantastic cannot exist without the notion of a clear dividing line (which the text transgresses) between things possible according to the laws of nature and things supernatural and impossible: for some, what defines the fantastic is a brutal intrusion of the mysterious into real life. But the reader's bewilderment is rarely confined to this shock effect. Are the ghosts in Henry James's *The Turn of the Screw* (1898) hallucinations created by the protagonist's repressed feelings, or are they external to her in some sense – and if so, what sense? Are we to read Kafka's *Metamorphosis* (1916) as a description of mental illness from the inside, a metaphor for some kind of alienation, or a literally true story (the protagonist turns into an insect, but the objective third-person narrative is remarkably matter-of-fact)? Are Poe's stories penetrating studies of human aspirations and limitations, or carefully contrived games which the narrator plays to keep the reader in suspense for as long as possible and maximize mystification and horror?

Frequently, the bewilderment is increased by the text's language. The STYLE is lucid, even crystalline, but poor in undertones, repetitive in its creation of ATMOSPHERE. The lucidity often resides in an overgeneral statement of the narrator's or protagonist's impressions: Poe's reference to 'the thrilling and enthralling eloquence' of Ligeia's 'low musical language' (*Ligeia*, 1838) leaves the reader unsure what kind of speech and auditory sensations to imagine, more aware of the intensity of the narrator's response than its quality. In the work of Cortázar, a lucid, matter-of-fact style conveys bizarre and impossible meanings, the truth of which the narrator takes for granted. Lucidity and intensity, we may reflect, are compatible with some forms of insanity.

The confusion usually focuses on the narrator's or the protagonist's personality. Protagonists are characteristically isolated from interaction and discussion. Family life, a steady career, friendship, even common everyday activities are either meaningless to them or highly problematical: Anselmus in Hoffmann's *Golden Pot* (1815), using a door knocker to gain admittance to a house, sees it turn suddenly into a snake. The protagonists' lack of conventionality and urge towards ideal perfection can take different forms. Frequently in Tieck and Hoffmann, they hold themselves open to the unexpected, aware of both the spiritual opportunity and the spiritual risks of this, whereas in *The Turn of the Screw* and Maupassant's *Le Horla* (1887) attempts are made to create a stable world by leaving out worrying aspects of the self and its environment – repressing them, Freudians would say. The attempt to make life manageable yet satisfying thus becomes an attempt to transcend human limits: Stevenson's *Dr. Jekyll and Mr. Hyde* (1886) tries to resolve his tensions by neatly splitting his personality. But in thus pushing human nature beyond its normal bounds, the protagonist sets up unconscious compensatory mechanisms and becomes decreasingly able to think straight. Rarely, however, are more restrained, socially conventional lifestyles presented favourably; the attempt to exceed one's limits invites in the reader a fascination which makes any condemnation ambiguous.

Modern criticism has stressed links between fantastic texts and the societies in which they appear. In industrial society, 'the individual comes to see himself at the mercy of forces which in fundamental ways elude his understanding' (David Punter, *The Literature of Terror* (1980), p. 128); the fantastic 'characteristically attempts to compensate for a lack resulting from cultural constraints' (Rosemary Jackson, *Fantasy: The Literature of Subversion* (1981), p. 3). Critics thus see their task as a translation of the supernatural terrors of the text into the social ones which underlie it. The fantastic gives indirect expression to doubts about itself which society refuses to entertain if they are directly stated; the protagonist's confusion arises from the urge to express aspects of self which society condemns and accordingly for which no adequate language is available.

See Irene Bessière, *Le Récit fantastique* (1974); David Punter, *The Literature of Terror* (1980); Eric S. Rabkin, *The Fantastic in Literature* (1976); Tzvetan Todorov, *The Fantastic* (English translation 1973); Rosemary Jackson, *Fantasy: the Literature of Subversion* (1981); Lucie Armitt, *Theorising the Fantastic* (1996); Neil Cornwell, *The Literary Fantastic: from Gothic to Postmodernism* (1990).

MHP

Farce   Interpolations in church liturgy; later, that 'forced' between the events of liturgical drama, usually comic. Farce is comedy involving physical humour, stock characters and unrealistic plotting. It combines elements from pantomime, music hall and social comedy into a theatre of sexual innuendo, snobbery and slapstick. English farce is broader and more physical, with dropped trousers and chamber pots predominant. It stays close to circus and music-hall humour. French farce crudifies manner comedy (see MANNERS), balancing sexual suggestiveness and social humour, for example, the plays of Georges Feydeau. More literate and polished, it reflects the elegant vulgarity of the *boulevardier*. English music hall had its counterpart in American vaudeville, but this produced no distinctive American farce tradition. The American contribution is rather to be found in the visual and physical humour of silent films (Chaplin, Keaton) which in their turn provided models for the techniques of ABSURD drama.

Farce seeks to demonstrate the contiguity of the logical and the illogical. It explores a closed world where belief is suspended because nothing has a real cause. Action is self-generated, once the ground rules are accepted. These rules embody a mechanical, deterministic view of life which undermines pretensions to human dignity (free will): all women are predatory, all husbands are fools, all banisters rotten, all doors revelatory. This encapsulated universe encourages a comedy of cruelty since the audience is insulated from feeling by the absence of motive, and by the response being simultaneously more and less aggressive than real-life response, for example, the custard pie routine.

Modern playwrights, such as Joe Orton (*Loot, What the Butler Saw*) revived the farce conventions and used them to force the audience to rethink concepts of the normal and the abnormal. Called 'highcamp' comedy, this type of farce realizes its ideas through discarded fictions, involving its audience in the conscious manipulation of its own response. See also COMEDY.

See M. E. Coindreau, *La Farce est jouée* (1942); Leo Hughes, *A Century of English Farce* (1956); Albert Bernell, *Farce: A History from Aristophanes to Woody Allen* (1990); Jessica Milna Davis, *Farce* (2001).

GG

Feeling   Accounts of how a work of literature is created, or of how it affects the reader, touch on two areas of non-literary investigation. Epistemology, the theory of how we come to know, is an ancient philosophical puzzle. Since the late eighteenth century, psychology has also approached such problems. It is an axiom in epistemology that two processes are involved in knowing: traditionally, *reason* and *feeling*; philosophy has usually concentrated on the former, the latter being left to psychology. The two terms suffer from the imprecision of all traditional labels. *Feeling*, especially, has a wide and confusing range of meanings. It is partly synonymous with 'emotions'. Psychology has a similar axiomatic frame for discussion: the presentation of a mental event in terms of *thought* (cognition), *feeling* (the conscious character of the event) and *will* (conation, which may be conscious or unconscious). *Feeling* is a way of considering the general sensibility of the body.

Aesthetic theory has made use of such philosophical and psychological thought. In reaction to the Western belief that *reason* is dominant, it has been argued that feeling is itself formulation, that is, it prefigures thought or reasoning. Eliseo Vivas argued that literature is 'prior in the order of logic to all knowledge: constitutive of culture' (*Creation and Discovery*, 1955). The *gestalt*-psychologists are of

this view, and some philosophers have followed their lead, arguing that feeling itself participates in knowledge and understanding. Art is the area of creative activity in which organic sensation plays the strongest controlling part. I. A. Richards expounded a variant of this idea in his *Principles of Literary Criticism* (1924). He wanted to restrict feeling to refer to pleasure/un-pleasure, to mean 'not another and vital way of apprehending' but a set of signs of personal attitudes. As well as people who neatly reason things out, there are, he suggests, some who can read these signs (feeling) particularly well, better than most of us. Such people are, when they create something which allows us to read some of the signs better, great artists. Thus for Richards, it is not the *intensity* of the feeling that matters, but the *organization* of its impulses, the quality of the reading of the signs.

Another way in which *feeling* is used in aesthetic theory was illustrated in the work of the philosopher Susanne Langer: see *Philosophy in a New Key* (1942) and *Feeling and Form* (1953). She argued that feeling is expressed by ritual and attitude, which in turn are embodied by the artist in presentational symbolism. Music is the art which fits best with such ideas. Wagner argued that music is the representation and formulation of feeling itself. But literature has moral, social and rational dimensions that interfere with clear exemplification of any feeling-based aesthetic. See also EFFECT, PLEASURE, READER.

See Derek Matravers, *Art and Emotions* (2001); David Punter, *Writing the Passions* (2000).

AMR

Feminist criticism   Developed as part of the discourse of the second wave feminism which emerged in Europe and America in the late 1960s to revive political and social issues associated with turn-of-the-century suffrage debates, and to question again the extent of women's actual participation in Western cultures. Both feminists and feminist literary critics are of course indebted to pre-twentieth-century writers, and to writers of the interwar years, like Virginia Woolf – 'if one is a woman, one is often surprised by a sudden splitting off of consciousness, say in walking down Whitehall, when from being the natural inheritor of that civilization, she becomes on the contrary outside of it, alien and critical' (*A Room of One's Own*, 1929). However, one of the fundamental observations, and difficulties, of feminist criticism has been that the *continuous* traditions (including the anti-traditions) of literary studies have largely obscured women's work and women's perspectives.

> One serious cultural obstacle encountered by any feminist writer is that each feminist work has tended to be received as if it emerged from nowhere.... women's work and thinking has been made to seem sporadic, erratic, orphaned of any tradition of its own.
>
> (Adrienne Rich, *On Lies, Secrets and Silence*, 1979)

Thus, a major effort of feminist criticism has been to recover and reread the work of women writers, as a problematic appendix to the existing corpus of literature, neither exactly 'a tradition of its own', nor yet part of a shared culture. Much of this rewriting of literary history has been pragmatic, scholarly and anti-theoretical in its bias, devoted to rendering women's texts legible without foregrounding methodological issues. The 'feminism' involved sometimes recalls

the late-romantic, vaguely androgynous individualism (intellectual and imaginative life as potentially neutral territory) which characterized Simone de Beauvoir's enormously influential retrospective survey of oppression in *The Second Sex* (1949). However, this has been uneasily combined with the suspicion that, while society remains 'patriarchal' in its division of other kinds of labour, then neither access to, nor interpretation of, literature can be gender-free.

The most identifiable divergences in feminist criticism begin here: between a mainly Anglo-American emphasis on the recovery, reprinting and revaluation of works more-or-less admitted to belong to a minority culture (a defensive or recuperative strategy); and a more aggressive, mainly French stress on literary language (indeed, language itself) as a primary locus of the repression of radically disjunctive female 'otherness'. The thinking of French feminist critics is openly, if ironically, indebted to STRUCTURALISM and POST-STRUCTURALISM, and particularly to the revision of Freudian assumptions about creativity in the work of Lacan and Derrida. Whereas the work of reconstruction seeks to describe plural (if warring) cultures, the advocates of DECONSTRUCTION argue that patriarchal culture continually subsumes 'otherness' by means of linguistic strategies still to be exposed and analysed. In its most extreme form the post-structuralist reading of patriarchy delineates a closed culture: the individual's entry into subjectivity is determined by the symbolic orders of language and family, in which

> the phallus is the privileged signifier (Lacan); intellectual life and the world of letters constitute a hidden homosexual succession, a *logocentric* economy which has suppressed its own

duplicitous origins (patricide) in imposing order and wholeness of meaning on its discourse (Derrida). Deconstruction opening up the relationship between what authors command and do not command of the language they use seeks to demystify the (phallic) Word, and authorise absence, disjunction, *différance*. Moves like these, concerned with subverting the authority of 'classical' traditions of thought and letters, have an obvious attraction for feminist thinkers, not least because they suggest an area of discourse in which 'Woman and artist, the feminine and the *avant-garde*, are elided.... Writing, the production of meaning, becomes the site of both challenge and Otherness; rather than (as in more traditional approaches) simply yielding the themes and representation of female oppression.'

(Mary Jacobus, *Women Writing and Writing about Women*, 1979)

Feminist criticism which adopts such a position scrutinizes its texts for fissures and cracks and signs of heterogeneity, re-examining 'the masculine imaginary, to interpret how it has reduced us to silence, to mutism...to find a possible space for the feminine imaginary' (Luce Irigaray). The 'feminine' is all that is repressed in a patriarchal linguistic structure: for example, the Oedipal phase of rhythmic, onomatopeic sound (unmediated, ecstatic) which precedes the symbolic order (Julia Kristeva).

Some feminist critics have sought for themselves a fluid and problematic language that will harmonize with the Babel/babble of the *avant-garde* (Hélène Cixous, Monique Wittig). Others' procedures have been more traditional in style and method. All, however, subscribe to the thesis of women's continuing exclusion from full participation in culture, while they differ widely on questions of the nature and extent of that exclusion, and on the centrality of 'language' (in the structuralist sense). As well as extending the canon, and rewriting aspects of literary history, feminist criticism has brought new pressure to bear on the analysis of texts at many levels, from the structure of the sentence to the concept of 'character' and the composition of 'I', and has foregrounded certain literary 'kinds' (from diaries and journals to GOTHIC, FANTASTIC and speculative fiction) as specially charged interfaces between masculine culture and female culture.

Post-colonial and lesbian feminists have questioned the category of 'woman' within feminism as a universal, asking whether a predominantly heterosexual white Western movement can represent women from other or minority cultures. Identity aspects, such as class, ethnicity, sexuality and even age striate the notion of similar experience promoted by feminism in the 1970s and 1980s.

See WOMANIST, GENDER.

See Simone de Beauvoir, *The Second Sex* (1949); Mary Ellmann, *Thinking About Women* (1968); Monique Wittig, *Les guérillères* (1969); Kate Millett, *Sexual Politics* (1970); Julia Kristeva, *La revolution du langage poétique* (1974); Hélène Cixous, 'The Character of "Character"', *NLH* 5 (1978); Ellen Moers, *Literary Women* (1977); Elaine Showalter, *A Literature of Their Own: British Women Novelists from Brontë to Lessing* (1977); Angela Carter, *The Sadeian Woman* (1979); Mary Jacobus (ed.), *Women Writing and Writing About Women* (1979); Marks and Courtivron (eds), *New French Feminisms* (1980); G. Spivak, *In Other Worlds* (1987); Rita Felski, *Literature After Feminism* (2003).

LS and LSM

Fiction   A complex term with many overlapping uses. Although often used synonymously with *novel*, it is a more generic and inclusive term. NOVEL has a narrower historical and ideological content than fiction – novels did not exist in Greek or Roman culture, but works of fiction in prose did. Equally, allegories in prose (like *Pilgrim's Progress*) are works of fiction, but not novels. 'Novel' is thus a genre term, while 'fiction' is a generic term. 'Fiction' can more easily designate hybrid forms than 'novel'; it can include artistic intentions and formal characteristics in prose works (structures and devices borrowed from romance or poetry, pastiche or dramatic forms, etc.) which indicate either simple unawareness of novels (e.g. the *Satyricon*) or a deliberate questioning of the assumptions of the novel-genre (e.g. *Tom Jones*). Thus, by virtue of this high level of generality, 'fiction' can be opposed to 'novel' by both writers and critics alike.

The two terms also diverge because 'novel' must refer to the *product* of imaginative activity, whereas 'fiction' can be used to describe the activity itself (it derives from the Latin *fingo*, to fashion or form). Fiction thus has a transitive sense that implies a mental process; we speak of works *of* fiction – an ambiguous phrase which suggests either the category to which they belong or the activity by which they were produced.

There has always existed a moral and intellectual distrust of fiction as a mode of writing which leads people to believe in things which are not 'true' or which do not exist in nature. However hostile to each other's definition of 'nature' (compare Plato's *Republic* with Bentham's *Theory of Fictions*), the perennial opponents of fiction equate it with lies and deception. The maker of literary fictions may be self-deceived, or may intend to deceive others. For a classic (and ironic) account of this attitude, see George Herbert's platonic poem 'Jordan I' (beginning, 'Who says that fictions only and false hair/Become a verse?') and for an explicit defence of fiction against the pressure of utilitarian 'fact', see Dickens's *Hard Times*. Traditional puritanism or moral scepticism is reflected in the pejorative epithet *fictitious* which derives from the sense of fiction as an unnecessary or undesirable deviation from truth; the adjective *fictional* does not normally have the same emotive content. Imaginative literature is of course the primary manifestation of this pernicious tendency, and attacks on fiction are usually attacks on literature, but clearly there is also a wider sense implied of fiction as an element in human thought and action.

A more positive use of *fiction* has recently been revived in literary criticism (see Hans Vaihinger, *The Philosophy of As If*, 1952 and Frank Kermode, *The Sense of an Ending*, 1967) which would appear to make both literature and what the critic wants to say about it more broadly relevant to other ways of writing and thinking and other educational disciplines. The assumption behind this use of the term is that all mental activity is to be construed on the analogy of imaginative creation. A fiction in this sense refers to any 'mental structure' as opposed to the formless flux existing outside our minds, the Pure Contingency which we call nature. Time, for example, is a fiction we impose on nature for the purposes of living. All mental activity, it is claimed, is fictional because it involves shaping material which is inherently shapeless. We can only make sense of things by imposing fictions (shapes or interpretations) on them. 'Fiction' thus becomes a kind of umbrella, sheltering many different kinds of mental activity and cultural institution. The term appears to have become the focus of a valuable relativism, an anti-positivistic, anti-empiricist *caveat*. The justification for such an extension is not so clear; the argument seems flawed and ultimately uninformative. If we can only make sense of things through fictions, how do we know of the existence of that which is non-fictional? By the same argument, the vitally necessary assumption of Pure Contingency is also a fiction. Equally, it is absurd to reduce whatever is true to whatever we cannot make sense of. In addition this extension of the term initiates a set of general conditions for the operation of fictions which makes it either impossible or unnecessary to distinguish between one fiction (say, poetry) and another (say, history).

Another aspect of the extension of this term needs justification. Fictions in general are like legal fictions – suppositions known to be false, but taken as true for the purposes of practical or theoretical convenience. Where this usage extends to a description of mental processes, it overlaps with the preceding sense, but the stricter model gives a more explicit account of the role of belief implied in that sense. It is claimed that fictions are mental structures which we know to be false, but which we accept as true for the purposes of mental coherence and order. Thinking becomes a matter of simultaneous belief and disbelief in the truth of our ideas; we know that our interpretations of things are ultimately false, but we must go on relying at least in part on these fictions because we have no other way of making sense of things. The term seems relativistic because it sensitizes us to the limitations of our own and other people's viewpoints, but it also tends to imply such mental diffidence that it is hard to know how we could take the truth of any idea seriously enough to be sceptical about it.

There is a danger that the unthinking use of the term could lead to a lack of intellectual commitment in criticism, because no fiction will need justification when it implies its own falsehood. On the other hand, the term is not really relativistic at all, if it implies that all our critical interpretations are ultimately invalid in the same way. It then becomes the banner of a naïve and reactionary fundamentalism, which measures the validity of all ideas by a single standard of truth (Pure Contingency or Chaos). Perhaps the most telling objection to the extension of this term is that it adds to our vocabulary without adding to our understanding: except where it can be shown to be false, according to conventional criteria, it makes no difference to an interpretation that we call it a 'fiction'.

Literary fictions may have various degrees of plausibility. The archaic adjective *fictive*, revived by the American poet Wallace Stevens, is used extensively in modern criticism to denote the making of fictions which do not suspend the reader's disbelief, but stimulate it, in order to establish particular kinds of rhetorical effect. Many novelists in the post-war period, such as Barth, Borges, Beckett, Genet and Nabokov, often depended for their effects on a consistent sense of implausibility, and such writers forced critics to distinguish shades of meaning in their terminology to account for varieties of literary self-consciousness. Hence, the use of the cognate terms *fictiveness* and *fictionality*, which differ from *fiction* or *fiction making* by their implication of authorial self-consciousness. Critics have also distinguished between MODERNIST self-consciousness and the POSTMODERNIST degree of self-consciousness in the post-war period which flaunted its own conditions of artiface. Hence, the rise of such terms as *metafiction*, *surfiction* and *fabulation,* which purport to describe the mood of postmodernism. See R. Federman, *Surfiction* (1975); R. Scholes, *Fabulation and Metafiction* (1979); P. Waugh, *Metafiction* (1984). See also LITERATURE.

VS

Figure George Puttenham defines 'figurative speech' as follows:

> a novelty of language evidently (and yet not absurdly) estranged from the ordinary habit and manner of our daily talk and writing, and figure itself is a certain lively or good grace set upon words, speeches, and sentences to some purpose and not in vain, giving them ornament or efficacy by many manner of alterations in shape, in sound, and also in sense, sometime by way of surplusage, sometime by defect, sometime by disorder, or mutation, and also by putting into our speeches more pith and substance, subtlety, quickness, efficacy, or moderation, in this or that sort tuning and tempering them, by amplification, abridgement, opening, closing, enforcing, meekening, or otherwise disposing them to the best purpose.

(*The Art of English Poesie,* 1589)

He then devotes a dozen chapters of his treatise to listing, classifying, defining and exemplifying figures. In this enterprise he follows the venerable tradition of RHETORIC, in which literary composition is thought of as 'invention' (choosing a subject matter) and 'amplification' or as Puttenham calls it, 'exornation', of the subject by a decorous choice from the figures. The hundreds of figures, schemes and tropes available for this purpose were listed in many handbooks designed to help budding and practising authors to regulate their style according to received principles; this tradition of prescriptive rhetoric continued in the school-books long after Puttenham's day. In this, an unrealistic and mechanical theory of composition is implied; and authors within this tradition (e.g. Chaucer) achieved excellence largely in spite of it, or by a self-consciously ironic use of figures. From a critical point of view, very little is to be gained by memorizing lists of names for figures, and much is to be lost in so far as the attitude encourages students to view literature as theme plus ornament. Yet, some terms have remained current and valuable in analysis (e.g. chiasmus, hyperbole, metonymy, synecdoche, etc.). See also RHETORIC, SCHEME.

See Bradford T. Stull, *The Elements of Figurative Language* (2002); Laura Kendrick, *Animating the Letter: The Figurative Embodiment of Writing from Late Antiquity to the Renaissance* (1999).

RGF

Foot See METRE.

Foregrounding (A free translation of the Czech term, *aktualisace.*) It is a concept evolved by the pre-war Prague school of linguistics and poetics, under the influence of Russian formalist doctrines, to represent the abnormal use of a medium, its obtrusion against a background of 'automatic' responses, which is characteristic of much, if not all, artistic expression.

In literature, foregrounding may be most readily identified with linguistic *deviation*: the violation of rules and conventions, by which a poet transcends the normal communicative resources of the language, and awakens readers, by freeing them from the grooves of cliché expression, to a new perceptivity. Poetic metaphor, a type of semantic deviation, is the most important instance of this type of foregrounding.

More generally, foregrounding may include all salient linguistic phenomena which in some way cause the reader's attention to shift from the paraphrasable content of a message ('what is said') to a focus on the message itself ('how it is said'). One may thus subsume under foregrounding the deliberate use of ambiguities (e.g. punning) and, more importantly, parallelism, in its widest sense of patterning over and above the normal degree of patterning which exists in language by virtue of linguistic rules.

Foregrounding is a useful, even crucial, concept in stylistics, providing a bridge between the relative objectivity of linguistic description and the relative subjectivity of literary judgement. It is a criterion by which, from a mass of linguistic detail, those features relevant to literary effect can be selected. It is not, however, an entirely precise criterion: the contrast between foreground and background is a relative one, and only subjective response can ultimately decide what is and what is not foregrounded. Further unclearnesses are: Is the writer's intention a relevant indication of foregrounding? What is the psychological basis of foregrounding? (Foregrounded features can 'work' without coming to one's conscious attention.) Can foregrounding be equated with artistic significance?

The last question can be answered negatively by pointing out two difficulties in the way of any attempt to make foregrounding the basis of a comprehensive theory of literary style. (1) Deviations and parallelisms often seem to have a background rather than a foreground function, and resist critical justification except in terms of vague principles, such as euphony and VARIATION. (2) With prose, a probabilistic approach to style in terms of a 'set' towards certain linguistic choices rather than others is often more

appropriate than an approach via foregrounding, since significance lies not so much in individual exceptional features of language as in the density of some features relative to others. Foregrounding in prose works applies rather at the levels of theme, character, plot, argument, etc. than at the level of linguistic choice. See also FORMALISM.

See V. Erlich, *Russian Formalism* (1965); Jan Mukařovský, 'Standard language and poetic language' in P. L. Garvin (ed.), *A Prague School Reader on Esthetics, Literary Structure and Style* (1964); G. N. Leech, 'Linguistics and the figures of rhetoric' in R. Fowler (ed.), *Essays on Style and Language* (1966).

GNL

Form Often used to refer to literary kinds or genres (e.g. 'the epic form'). But we prefer to take form as what contrasts with 'paraphrasable content', as the *way* something is said in contrast to *what* is said. The word 'paraphrasable' is important since the way of saying affects what is being said – imperceptibly in prose works of information, vitally at the other end of the spectrum in lyric poems. But since authors do in fact often revise their works to improve the STYLE rather than the matter, since synopses are written and found useful, since writers (like Ben Jonson) can turn prose versions of their work into verse, and since it is evident that much the same point may be made in plain or figurative language, simple or complex sentences, it is clear that even though form and content may be inseparable for the 'full meaning' of a work, the paraphrasable content may nevertheless be used to enable the concept of *form* to be discussed (cf. PARAPHRASE).

Form in this sense has traditionally been felt to be either *organic* or *imposed*. Felt, because this is rather a psychological distinction than a technical one. In the one case, manner seems to fit matter like a velvet glove, form seems to spring from content; in the other case, the form seems an iron gauntlet that the content must accommodate itself to. In some short lyric poems where form and content are inseparable anyway, it may be difficult to decide whether, say, apparent oddities of metre and rhyme are flaws in an imposed form or examples of organic fluidity. In most of these cases, however, the difficulty of decision will itself suggest that the decision is irrelevant to a critical judgement. For the modern dogma that organic form is better hardly stands up to examination. All 'given patterns' – such as sonnet, rondeau, ballade – are imposed forms; and while it is true that the content must fit them effortlessly or be faulted, it is also true that the form took precedence. In some cases, too – particularly in large novels dealing with amorphous material – imposed form may seem a beneficial discipline even though the imposition is evident. Moreover, it is easier to encompass aesthetic effects of composition and complementarity (see AESTHETICS) by imposed form than by organic form. Organic form tends to emphasize what is said, imposed form how it is said. So where neither emphasis is evident other approaches to the work will clearly be more profitable.

Whether considered to be organic or imposed, form must be either *structural* or *textural*, the one being large-scale, a matter of arrangement, the other small-scale, a matter of impressionism. *Structure* at its most obvious (plot, story, argument) is the skeleton of a work; *texture* at its most obvious (metre, diction, syntax) is the skin. But certain elements are comparable to muscles. A *motif* for instance is structural in so far as the images making it up are seen as a chain, textural in so far as each is apprehended sensuously as it

comes and contentual, rather than formal, in so far as the chain carries a meaning that one link, an unrepeated image, would not. In the last analysis, structure is a matter of memory, texture of immediacy.

Since structure is a matter of arrangement, it includes the formal ordering of the content in time. *Temporal form* may be *linear* or *fugal*. Linear form is that of traditional literature, in which first things come first, and last last. Fugal form is characteristic of modernist experimental writing, which takes liberties with chronology on the grounds that literature need not present life in a linear form. Linear works, of course, may give more or less reading-time to similar periods of narrative time, but fugal works, in addition, rearrange temporal sequence so that first and last things come not in order but where they will make most impact (usually by standing in juxtaposition). Counterpoint takes over from melody, so to speak. Such structuring used well, gains thematic and aesthetic benefits in return for the sacrifice of traditional storyline and suspense. Such emphasis of temporal form tends to give greater importance to textural quality (since the reader is less distracted by an eagerness to see what happens next).

Works of this kind present themselves more concretely as objects in space than as abstract patterns of cause and effect, and it follows that the reader's attention will be directed towards their textural rather than their structural qualities. The elaboration of texture invariably has the effect of arresting movement – whether of thought or action – and substituting the opaque for the transparent in language. At its furthest extremes such developments lead to CONCRETE POETRY or Euphuistic Prose involving a progressive elimination of meaning, until a point is reached where the textural devices – dependent as they are on the meanings of words – become ineffective. In most works, however, where the marriage of sound and sense is not perfect, compromises are achieved between denotation and connotation, referent and reference. Texture, unlike structure, is an inherent (psychological) property of every part of language, and therefore less under the control of the writer. It follows that part of the author's task consists of eliminating or subduing indeterminate textural elements in the language used. More positively the writer strives to materialize particular meanings, and if language were a more subtle medium, this imitative function could be classified according to the (various) sensory apparatus to which it appealed. As it is, it may be preferable to categorize textural qualities according to the known properties of language. They may be *musical* (onomatopoeia, alliteration, etc.); *lexical* (metaphor, synecdoche, etc.); *syntactic* (chiasmus, antithesis, etc.).

The dominant contemporary view is that form is closely bound up with style and content, and the easy separation of these aspects to the work is largely to be avoided by the critic. See also ORGANIC, STRUCTURE, TEXTURE.

See Wayne C. Booth, *The Rhetoric of Fiction* (1961); Wallace C. Hiddick, *Thirteen Types of Narrative* (1968); Robie Macauley and George Laming, *Technique in Fiction* (1964); J. C. Ransom, *The World's Body* (1938). For further reading, J. L. Calderwood and M. R. Toliver, *Forms of Poetry* (1968); Allan Rodway, *The Truths of Fiction* (1970); Elizabeth Boa and J. H. Reid, *Critical Strategies* (1972); Kenneth Burke, *The Philosophy of Literary Form* (1992).

AER

Formalism A school of literary criticism that grew up in Russia in the experimental 1920s and erected on the foundations laid by the SYMBOLIST movement a critical method that posited the autonomy of the work of art and the discontinuity of the language of literature from other kinds of language. The Formalists outdid in purism the English and American NEW CRITICS, with whom they had much in common.

There were two groups of Formalist critics in the early days: the one in St Petersburg called itself *Opoyaz*, taking its name from the initial letters of the Russian words meaning *Society for the Study of Literary Language*, and was founded in 1916. The other, more linguistically oriented (though both derived their basic techniques from Saussure) was founded in 1915, and called itself the Moscow Linguistic Circle. The Formalists, impatient with the obscurantism that disfigured Symbolist poetics, set about the objective and 'scientific' examination of literary STYLE, defining it in terms of its departure from established norms by means of identifiable and analysable devices. One talented Formalist critic, Victor Shklovsky, in the early essay *Art as Device* (1917), emphasized that the deformation of reality, 'making strange' or 'defamiliarization' (*ostranenie*), was central to all art. He claims that the habitual nature of everyday experience makes perception stale and automatic, but

art exists that one may recover the sensation of life; it exists to make one feel things, to make the stone *stony*. The purpose of art is to impart the sensation of things as they are perceived and not as they are known. The technique of art is to make objects 'unfamiliar', to make forms difficult, to increase the difficulty and length of perception because the process of perception is an aesthetic end in itself and must be prolonged. *Art is a way of experiencing the artfulness of an object; the object is not important.*

Plot in the novel was defined as consisting of the devices which defamiliarize the story, or 'make it strange' (hence the high regard of the Formalists for Sterne's *Tristram Shandy*). The terms *fabula* and *syuzhet* were introduced for, respectively, the raw story-material and the finished plot as presented through the formal devices of construction. An important set of devices drawing attention to the act of narration, the voice of the storyteller and therefore the artificiality of the fiction, are collectively known as *skaz*. In verse theory, one of the best early essays was Osip Brik's *Rhythm and Syntax* (1927), which attempted to describe all the significant linguistic elements in poetry, correcting earlier theorists who had established the primacy of metaphor and image. His concept of *zvukovoy povtor*, sound repetition, was notably fruitful. As the Formalists developed, they grew less iconoclastic, and often managed to assimilate their linguistic techniques to the study of literary history and biography (Eikhenbaum's work on Tolstoy is a notable example): but they took care always to go through the necessary adjustments and manoeuvres in passing from the literary text to its milieu and context. Through the influence in the West of Roman Jakobson, once a member of the Moscow group, Formalist aesthetics exerted a powerful influence on later STRUCTURALIST developments in linguistics and literary criticism. The history of the movement has been admirably described in Victor Erlich's book *Russian Formalism* (1965). See also Tony Bennett, *Formalism and Marxism* (1979); Fredric Jameson, *The Prison-House of Language*

(1972); Ann Jefferson, 'Russian formalism' in Jefferson and David Robey (eds), *Modern Literary Theory* (1982); L. M. O'Toole and Ann Shukman, 'A contextual glossary of formalist terminology', *Russian Poetics in Translation*, 4 (1977). English anthologies of the most important texts are Stephen Bann and John E. Bowlt (eds), *Russian Formalism* (1973); Andrzej Karcz, *The Polish Formalist School and Russian Formalism* (2002). See also LITERATURE, POETICS, STRUCTURALISM.

GMH

Free verse   For many, this is a misnomer not only because most free verse assimilates itself to at least one of the prosodies – syllable-stress (Eliot, 'Prufrock'), quantitative (Pound), pure-stress (Eliot, *Four Quartets*), syllabic (Marianne Moore) – but also because as a term it is dated. But some word is needed to describe speech still deliberate enough to be rhythmic, but not patterned enough to be a metre, to describe a poetry in which utterance is only an intermittent emergence from speech, and whose complexity derives more from multiplicity of tone than from multiplicity of meaning.

The origins of free verse are variously inferred: poetic prose, liberated blank verse (Browning), a specifically free verse tradition (Dryden, Milton, Arnold, Henley). There may be other factors. Versification re-articulates conventional syntax, releases unsuspected expressive dimensions; because we are so accustomed to the writtenness of poetry, typography alone can be relied upon to perform this function (hence a visual prosody). Alternatively, by using dislocated syntax (see OBSCURITY), the poet re-articulates language at the outset and versification is rendered in this sense otiose. And the new apparatus that has facilitated analysis of the recited poem admits the vagaries of personal and regional reading as valid prosodic factors; once these are admitted free verse exists without anyone having to invent it.

The casting off of metres in favour of unopposed rhythms – particularly in the syntax- and cadence-centred prosodies of Whitman and the Imagists – is an attempt to fully develop the expressive function of the latter at the expense of the interpretative (*pace* Pound), discriminatory function of the former. It is also designed to more fully implicate readers in the poem as a psychological or emotional event by withdrawing the substitute sensibility of an accepted prosody and by compelling them to create their own speeds, intonation patterns and emphases. In such verse a prosody is not to be disengaged from the linguistic material; in such verse the line is superseded by the strophe, the line itself (syntactic unit) becoming the measure, and variation in line-length the rhythmic play. What Amy Lowell means by cadence is a retrospectively perceived rhythmic totality, an overall balance rather than the continuously disturbed and restored balance of regular verse.

Ironically the need to do away with rhyme as a worn out convention coincided with the need to retain it as an inherent part of the psychology of creation, the new '*Muse Association-des-Idées*'

(Valéry). Rhyme becomes the crucial ad-libbing mechanism, suited to capturing the miscellaneousness of modernity. The irregular rhyme of free verse is a structuring rather than structural device and is a better guide to the tempo of memory, emotion, etc. than variation in line-length, which has no fixed relation to reading speed. Besides, with rhyme removed, a poem may be deprived of much of its magnetic compulsiveness; because nothing is anticipated, nothing is looked for. Without this inbuilt momentum, the free verse poet has often to fall back on the syntactic momentum of enjambment or the momentum of rhetoric (Whitman, D. H. Lawrence) and the concomitant dangers of overintensification and monotony of tone and intonation; the poet's energies may be too much concentrated on the mere sustaining of impetus, rather than on using language to explore mental states etc. In this sense at least, rhyme is liberating.

See T. S. Eliot, 'Reflections on vers libre' (1917) in *To Criticize the Critic* (1965); G. Hough, 'Free verse' in *Image and Experience* (1960); C. O. Hartman, *Free Verse* (1980); D. Wesling, 'The prosodies of free verse' in R. A. Brower (ed.), *Twentieth Century Literature in Retrospect* (1971); Chris Beyers, *A History of Free Verse* (2001).

CS

G

Gender Frequently still used as a synonym for 'sex', as in: 'she is of the female gender'. The difficulty here is that while gender and sex are most often – though not inevitably – seen as related they are not synonyms or substitutes for each other although, until the interrogations of 'second wave' feminism in the 1970s, they tended to be used as such. In 1974, anthropologist Sherry Ortner published a much-anthologized essay, 'Is Female to Male as Nature is to Culture?' which provided a framework with which to begin to disentangle 'sex' from 'gender'. Ortner investigated the ways in which women's bodies align them with nature ('doomed to mere reproductive life') whereas men, lacking 'natural' creative functions, assert their creativity ' "artificially," through the medium of technology and symbols'. Ortner's hypothesis suggested that gender is to culture as sex is to nature, and that gender is the social expression of, and the roles assigned to, gendered dichotomies of men and women. Thus, it could now be appreciated that the nineteenth-century doctrine of separate spheres for men and women, for instance, was built on constructs of gendered identity rather than any inherent predisposition on the basis of anatomy and capacity for childbearing. The debates relating to women's liberation in the 1960s and 1970s (fuelled by the so-called sexual liberation afforded by the birth-control pill and other reproductive technologies) were also influenced by the work of sexologists, such as Masters and Johnson's (William H. Masters and Virginia E. Johnson) *Human Sexual Response* (1966). Sexologists reported that, far from the female sexual passivity, frigidity or disinclination and inherent monogamy outlined by Freud, women were sexually active, initiatory and multiply orgasmic: 'women's inordinate orgasmic capacity did not evolve for monogamous, sedentary cultures' wrote psychiatrist Mary Jane Sherfey in a 1966 essay on 'The Theory of Female Sexuality'. Thus, the *gender* stereotype which had apparently been predicated on sexual determinants (the body *and* the activity of sex) was thoroughly dismantled and exposed for the vested (largely male) interests it protected and promoted. Now that sex did not necessarily lead to procreation, the notion that female gender identity is always in the thrall of the potential for motherhood (thus, nature not culture) was called into question. Gender was seen to be much more about the reproduction and maintenance of certain societal norms than related to safeguarding the requirements for the reproduction of the species. The rise of sex for pleasure for women has had a dramatic effect on gender, or rather, an effect on the dramatics of gender. Judith Butler's *Gender Trouble: Feminism and the Subversion of Identity*, published in 1990, introduced her now well-known theory of the PERFORMATIVITY of gender. Butler goes further than to say that gender is the performance or expression to which a particular identification gives rise; rather, for her, it is the performance itself that constructs the identification: 'identity is performatively constituted by the very "expressions" that are said to be its results'. Further, Butler believes that, rather than the 'cultural' gender being predicated on the 'natural' sex, it is gender performativity that determines our very apprehension of sexed bodies. Thus, in *Gender Trouble*, Butler elaborates upon Ortner's earlier equation:

> gender is not to culture as sex is to nature; gender is also the discursive/cultural means by which 'sexed nature' or a 'natural sex' is produced and established as 'prediscursive', prior to culture, a politically neutral surface *on which* culture acts. This [is the] construction of sex as the radically unconstructed.

Of course, like other theorists who seek to disrupt the persistent dualism of gender as 'masculine' or 'feminine', Butler attempts to QUEER the binarism of a hegemonic 'compulsory heterosexuality'. Adrienne Rich's essay of 1987, 'Compulsory Heterosexuality and Lesbian Existence', which outlined the notion of a 'continuum' of modes of being in relation to gender – and thus to sex – is an important precursor to Butler's work, as is Monique Wittig's 'One is Not Born a Woman' (1981), in which she claims lesbians refuse not only the 'role' of woman but the whole heterosexual matrix – 'the economic, ideological and political power of man' – by which society operates. Lesbians are thus not women.

See David Glover and Cora Kaplan, *Genders* (2000); Joseph Bristow, *Sexuality* (1997); Shelley Saguaro (ed.), *Psychoanalysis and Woman: A Reader* (2000).

SS

Generative poetics See POETICS.

Genre There is no agreed equivalent for this word in the vocabulary of English criticism. 'Kind', 'type', 'form' and 'genre' are variously used, and this fact alone indicates some of the confusions that surround the development of the theory of genres. The attempt to classify or describe literary works in terms of shared characteristics was begun by Aristotle in the *Poetics*, and the first sentence of his treatise suggests the two main directions genre theory was to follow:

> Our subject being poetry, I propose to speak not only of the art in general, but also of its species and their respective capacities; of the structure of plot required for a good poem; of the number and nature of the constituent parts of a poem; and likewise of any other matters on the same line of enquiry.

Classical genre theory is regulative and prescriptive, and is based on certain fixed assumptions about psychological and social differentiation. Modern genre theory, on the other hand, tends to be purely descriptive and to avoid any overt assumptions about generic hierarchies. In the last century, beginning with such Russian Formalists as Roman Jakobson, there has been a continuing effort to link literary kinds to linguistic structures. Vladimir Propp's seminal study, *Morphology of the Folktale*, written in 1928, was strongly influenced by the Formalists, and he in turn laid some of the groundwork for the genre studies of the later Structuralists in both film and literary criticism. Tzvetan Todorov, however, in his book *The Fantastic: A Structural Approach to a Literary Genre* (1973), takes issue with Propp's attempt to relate the concept of genre to that of 'species' in the natural sciences. Todorov points out that, unlike specimens in the natural world, every true literary work modifies the sum of all possible works, and that we only grant a text literary status insofar as it produces a change in our notion of the canon. If a work fails to achieve this, it is removed to the category of 'mass' or 'formulaic' literature. This assertion inevitably led to debates about the status of 'literature' itself as a genre.

Another significant contribution to genre theory is that of Northrop Frye whose *Anatomy of Criticism* (1957) presents a comprehensive typology of myth and archetype.

The second major distinction is that between genres defined in terms of 'outer form' and 'inner form'. These terms were coined by Rene Wellek and Austin Warren in their *Theory of Literature* (New York, [rev. ed.] 1956), to describe on the one hand specific metres and structures, and on the other, attitude, tone and purpose. They argue that genres ought to be based on both inner and outer forms together, though the ostensible basis may be one or the other (e.g. 'pastoral' or 'satire' for the inner form; 'dipodic verse' or 'Pindaric ode' for the outer). They maintain that it is only by adopting some such complex definition of genre that the confusions of neo-classical criticism can be avoided. In the seventeenth and eighteenth centuries, no attempt was made to discriminate between the quite diverse criteria involved in differentiation by subject matter, structure, language, tone or audience. So not only was it impossible to make useful comparisons between particular works, it was not even possible to say what did or did not constitute a genre. The advantage of Wellek and Warren's definition is that it allows for an important distinction between, for example, novels of *The Oxford Movement*, which do not constitute a genre, and Gothic Novels, which do. See also CHICAGO CRITICS, FORMALISM, POETICS.

See D. Lodge, *The Modes of Modern Writing: Metaphor, Metonymy, and the Typology of Modern Literature* (1977); A. Fowler, *Kinds of Literature: An Introduction to the Theory of Genres and Modes* (1982).

BCL

Globalization   The process whereby individual lives and local communities are affected by economic and cultural forces that operate worldwide. In effect, it is the process of the world becoming a single place. Globalism is the perception of the world as a function or result of the processes of globalization upon local communities.

Part of the complexity of globalism comes from the different ways it is perceived and understood. Some critics embrace it enthusiastically as a positive feature of a changing world in which access to technology, information, services and markets will be of benefit to local communities, where dominant forms of social organization will lead to universal prosperity, peace and freedom, and in which a perception of a global environment will lead to global ecological concern. For this group, globalism is a positive term for an engagement with global issues. Others reject it as a form of domination by 'First World' countries over 'Third World' ones, in which individual distinctions of culture and society become erased by an increasingly homogeneous global culture, and local economies are more firmly incorporated into a system of global capital structured to serve the interests of the wealthiest nations. The chief argument this group raises against globalization is that it does not impact in the same way or equally beneficially upon rich and poor communities.

As a field of study, globalization covers such disciplines as international relations, political geography, economics, sociology, communication studies, agricultural, ecological and cultural studies. Globalization did not simply erupt spontaneously around the world, but has a history embedded in the history of imperialism, in the structure of the world system, and in the origins of a global economy within the ideology of imperial rhetoric. As some recent studies, such as that of Hardt and Negri (2000) have argued, the key to the link between classical imperialism and contemporary globalization in the twentieth century has been the role of the United States and its control of global economic relations. Despite its resolute refusal to perceive itself as 'imperial', and indeed its public stance against the older European doctrines of colonialism up to and after the Second World War, the United States, in its international policies, eagerly espoused the political domination and economic and cultural control associated with imperialism. More importantly, US society during and after this early expansionist phase initiated those features of social life and social relations that today may be considered to characterize the global: mass production, mass communication and mass consumption. During the twentieth century, these have spread transnationally.

That global culture is a continuation of a dynamic of influence, control, dissemination and hegemony that operates according to an already initiated structure of power that emerged in the sixteenth century in the great confluence of imperialism, capitalism and modernity explains why the forces of globalization are still, in some senses, centered in the West (in terms of power and institutional organization), despite their global dissemination. However, how it is engaged by local communities forms the focus of much recent discussion of the phenomenon. In this view the responses of local communities becomes critical. Such critics argue that globalization must now engage everyone whether they oppose or support its forces. Indeed they go further and suggest that the only means of resisting the negative effects of globalization is to engage with and reorganize these forces themselves to a just more and equitable goal (see Hardt and Negri). Since globalization will undoubtedly continue to be a significant feature of the foreseeable future such responses seem likely to produce the most effective form of resistance to the negative impact of globalization and the most hopeful sign that it may yet emerge as the precursor of a more positive global polity.

See M. Albrow, *Globalization: Myths and Realities* (1994); M. Albrow and E. King (eds), *Globalization, Knowledge and Society* (1990); M. Featherstone (ed.), *Global Culture: Nationalism, Globalization and Modernity* (1990); M. Featherstone *et al.*, *Global Modernities* (1995); M. Hardt and A. Negri, *Empire* (2000); A. D. King, *Culture, Globalization and the World System* (1991); E. Kofinan and G. Youngs, *Globalization: Theory and Practice* (1996); R. Robertson, *Globalization: Social Theory and Global Culture* (1992); T. Spybey, *Globalization and World Society* (1996).

GG

Gothic The gothic romance emerged in England when the novel form itself was only a few decades old. Thus, when Horace Walpole published *The Castle of Otranto* in 1764, it was in part a reaction against limitations which the early novelists seemed to have accepted with equanimity. The novel of manners and the novel of didactic sensibility are exposed to the whole sub-world of the unconscious. Sensibility is shown under pressure. Sexuality, elemental passions and fear now moved to the centre of the novelist's stage.

The word 'gothic' initially conjured up visions of a medieval world, of dark passions enacted against the massive and sinister architecture of the gothic castle. By the end of the century it implied the whole paraphernalia of evil forces and ghostly apparitions. The gothic is characterized by a setting which consists of castles, monasteries, ruined houses or suitably picturesque surroundings, by characters who are, or seem to be, the quintessence of good or evil (though innocence often seems to possess a particular menace of its own); sanity and chastity are constantly threatened and over all there looms the suggestion, sometimes finally subverted, that irrational and evil forces threaten both individual integrity and the material order of society.

On one level the gothic novel was an attempt to stimulate jaded sensibilities and as such its descendants are the modern horror film and science fiction fantasy. Yet, as the Marquis de Sade detected at the time and as the surrealists were to assert later, the gothic mode was potentially both socially and artistically revolutionary. The iconography of decay and dissolution which filled such novels clearly has its social dimension (William Godwin in particular drew political morals from his entropic setting) while the assertion of a non-material reality clearly stands as an implicit criticism of the literalism of the conventional novel as it does of the rational confidence of the age itself. The debate between rationalism and the imagination which came to characterize the age is contained within the gothic mode. Horace Walpole was content to leave his terrors irrational and unexplained; Ann Radcliffe, or, in America, Charles Brockden Brown, felt the need to rationalize the ineffable.

The 'classic' gothic novels spanned the years between 1764 and, approximately, 1820, which saw the publication of Maturin's *Melmoth the Wanderer*. Among the best-known examples are: *The Mysteries of Udolpho* by Ann Radcliffe, 1794; *The Adventures of Caleb Williams* by William Godwin, 1794; *The Monk* by M. G. Lewis, 1795; *Frankenstein* by Mary Shelley, 1818. The strain continued in the nineteenth and twentieth centuries both in England (e.g. Iris Murdoch, *The Unicorn*, 1963 and David Storey, *Radcliffe*, 1963) and in America, where it played an important role not merely in the work of such nineteenth-century gothicists as Charles Brockden Brown, Edgar Allan Poe and Ambrose Bierce or, less directly, Hawthorne, Melville and James, but also in the work of authors, such as James Purdy, John Hawkes, Kurt Vonnegut.

The Gothic has developed a strong appeal in fiction and film. Its features can be seen in a range of authors from Angela Carter to Poppy Z. Brite, while writers like Anne Rice have catered for the general cultish vogue for the Gothic in contemporary culture witnessed in the sustained popularity of the Vampire movie.

See Edith Birkhead, *The Tale of Terror* (1921, reprinted 1963); Leslie Fiedler, *Love and Death in the American Novel* (1960); Montague Summers, *The Gothic Quest* (New York, 1964).

See G. St John Barclay, *Anatomy of Horror: The Masters of Occult Fiction* (1978); C. Brooke-Rose, *A Rhetoric of the Unreal* (1981); C. A. Howells, *Love, Mystery, and Misery: Feeling in Gothic Fiction* (1978); R. Jackson, *Fantasy: The Literature of Subversion* (1981); H. Kerr,

J. W. Crowley, and C. L. Crow (eds), *The Haunted Dusk: American Supernatural Fiction, 1820–1920* (1983); P. B. Messent (ed.), *Literature of the Occult* (1981); D. G. Punter, *The Literature of Terror* (1980); Donald Ringe, *American Gothic* (1982); V. Sage, *Horror Fiction in the Protestant Tradition* (1986); T. Todorov, *The Fantastic* (1975); David Punter and Glennis Byron, *The Gothic* (2003); Fred Botting, *Gothic: Critical Concepts in Literary and Cultural Studies* (2004).

CWEB

Grammar   See LANGUAGE, SYNTAX.

Grotesque   The grotesque usually presents the human figure in an exaggerated and distorted way; Bergson's theory of comedy as a whole as a deliberate dehumanization or mechanization of observed behaviour seems too limiting, but offers a stimulating approach to the grotesque. The grotesque exploits similarities between people and animals or things, and vice versa. There is a strong critical tendency to regard the grotesque as in opposition to REALISM. Grotesque art, such arguments run, is failed realism, its failure determined by social or personal inadequacies. Mark Spilka, in *Dickens and Kafka* (1963) put forward the view that the grotesque is conditioned by 'oedipal arrest', an inability to realize the roundedness of personality because of a fixation with the mother; T. A. Jackson, in *Charles Dickens: The Progress of a Radical* (1938), argued that the flatness of Dickens's characters is determined by the dehumanizing forces of the society that Dickens lived in and depicted. But Wolfgang Kayser's book *The Grotesque in Art and Literature* (1963), even if it did little else but dilute the concept of the grotesque to include anything horrific, fantastic or interesting to Kayser, at least stressed the origin of the term in the extravagant, whimsical representations of heads and faces that ornamented classical decorative friezes, rediscovered by Renaissance archaeologists and rapidly imitated by Mannerist artists. A definition of the grotesque that omits its unmotivated playfulness is likely to be unsatisfactory.

The rhetorical strategy of the grotesque in literature is usually deadpan; the reader must not be allowed a perspective that permits explanation of its incongruity or preposterousness. So Kafka's 'Metamorphosis' opens with the matter-of-fact narration of Gregor Samsa's awakening into insecthood. Likewise Pancks's breezy insinuation of grotesque comparison in *Little Dorrit*:

> A person who can't pay, gets another person who can't pay, to guarantee that he can pay. Like a person with two wooden legs getting another person with two wooden legs, to guarantee that he has got two natural ones. It doesn't make either of them able to do a walking match. And four wooden legs are more troublesome to you than two, when you don't want any.

Exaggeration and distortion gain their effect by being passed off in serious and woodenly correct prose.

See Arthur Clayborough, *The Grotesque in English Literature* (1965); Philip Thomson, *The Grotesque* (1972); Anthea Trodd, *Victorian Culture and the Idea of the Grotesque* (1999); Bernard McElroy, *Fiction of the Modern Grotesque* (1989).

MAH

H

Hegemony The term hegemony as defined in conventional discourse signifies simply power. But in contemporary critical discourse it has come to mean power exercised by creating the belief in the majority of people in a society that power is the prerogative of a group or class as a 'natural' or otherwise justified right.

The origins of this contemporary usage can be traced to Marxist theory. Although the term is employed in the late nineteenth century by Russian Marxists, such as Plekhanov, to signify the need to emphasize the leadership of the proletarian class in any successful revolutionary alliance of classes and social groupings, it is to the usage developed by the twentieth-century Italian Marxist, Antonio Gramsci, that the modern importance of the term must be traced. As a Marxist, faced by the rise of fascism in the 1920s, Gramsci's analysis resisted the simple emphasis on economic determinism, which had led to a fatalistic emphasis on the 'inevitability' of the fall of capitalist power. Gramsci emphasized the need to develop the political consciousness of the proletariat to enable its emergence as a 'hegemonic' force in its own right. For Gramsci, the proletariat had to be convinced that it had a 'right to rule'. To achieve this, the existing belief in the 'natural' right to rule of the existing 'ruling class' had to be exposed. The proletariat's cultural forms and ideologies had to be respected and incorporated into the strategy of revolution (even problematic 'popular' concepts, such as nationalism). This meant that new attention had to be paid to cultural forms. As modern modes of mass communication emerged there was an increasing emphasis on ideas of hegemonic control in social critiques.

Even Marxist critics opposed to Gramsci's emphasis on the need for a popular ideological commitment to the revolution based on the humanist idea of the 'winning over' of the proletariat at a conscious level, notably Louis Althusser, who sought vigorously to reconstitute the forces of the state as the primary source for social determinism, recruited to their description of that state not only the coercive forces of the state (police, army, etc.) but its cultural forces (ideological state apparatuses, in Althusser's terms). More positively, we can see the influence of Gramscian ideas of hegemony in Michel Foucault's emphasis on the power of discourse, which, at times, seems to place the cultural, where classic Marxism had placed the economic, as the principal determinant of society. Ideology is crucial as a tool in both levels of analysis, invigorated now as a means of linking the economic and the cultural in a powerful fresh mode of social analysis.

In post-colonial societies where power was often exercised by a small minority over a majority population Gramscian 'hegemony' has been a crucial concept in explaining how such power was successfully exercised. Hegemonic power is always in the last analysis based on force. But the fact that such force need only be used as a last resort indicates how important the exercise of hegemonic control is in maintaining imperial control.

From the point of view of literary and cultural criticism this contemporary usage of 'hegemony' serves to place the production of culture at the heart of the issue of power and social change. It suggests that social texts, literature, film, television, the Internet, etc., may be crucial in allowing a ruling class to exercise power. They may also, of course, be crucial means of resistance to such power by a revolutionary class. So cultural and social texts themselves become a site of struggle of the utmost importance in determining who controls social processes and who exercises power successfully.

The analysis of such texts has been central to the emergence of 'cultural studies' in the academies of Europe and America, leading to significant reassessments of the institutions of literature, and mass media in social analyses of their societies past and present. The emergence of print, the development of literary forms, the development of popular genres and of new modes of providing texts to the masses in new media have all been the subject of extensive analysis as critics engage with the issue of how texts influence, confirm and maintain power.

See Robert Bocock, *Hegemony* (1986); Joseph V. Femia, *Gramsci's Political Thought: Hegemony, Consciousness and the Revolutionary Process* (1981); Antonio Gramsci, *Selections from Political Writings 1921–1926* (1978), *Letters from Prison* (1975); James Joll, *Gramsci* (1977).

GG

Heresy of paraphrase   See PARAPHRASE.

Hermeneutics   Comprises the general theory and practice of interpretation. The term was first specifically applied in the seventeenth century; but hermeneutic practice is as old as the exegesis of texts. Many questions that are still current in contemporary interpretation can be traced through the history of Western hermeneutics, which typically handled two categories of text: Classical and Biblical. Each was obscured by cultural and historical distance, yet, each held a meaning or value that the interpreter tried to reach. In theology, Origen produced a triple explication through grammatical, ethical and allegorical meanings, and Augustine added an 'anagogical' or mystical dimension. The Reformation intensified hermeneutic activity as Protestant theologians tried to form an autonomous interpretation of scripture; and later, Enlightenment rationalism made for codification of interpretive procedures. Early in the nineteenth century, Friedrich Schleiermacher proposed a general hermeneutics that would underlie all specific interpretations and provide them with a system of understanding. This programme has remained a hermeneutic ambition; as Paul Ricoeur points out, it echoes the Enlightenment and the Critical philosophy of Kant, but it also displays a Romantic element. Schleiermacher distinguished between 'grammatical' interpretation, based on the general discourse of a culture, and 'technical' interpretation, based on the individual subjectivity of an author. The interpreter seeks to reconstruct that subjectivity, and may gain a better grasp of it than the author. Here an intuitive psychologism complements the comparatist approach of 'grammatical' method; and intuition is also evident in Schleiermacher's famous legacy, the hermeneutic circle. Trying to understand any hermeneutic object – a sentence, a text – we approach the parts by reference to the whole, yet, cannot grasp the whole without reference to the parts. This 'circular' process also applies in approaching an unfamiliar author or period: some foreknowledge seems essential. For Schleiermacher, the problem was resolved intuitively, by a 'leap' into the circle, like the leap of faith.

This may sound suspiciously unscientific in an age of progress; and by the end of the nineteenth century, Wilhelm Dilthey had to make room for hermeneutics in the face of the huge prestige of the natural sciences and their positive methods. He produced yet another division; between the explanation of external objects in the natural sciences, and the understanding of inner states in the human sciences. Hermeneutics applied to the latter; Dilthey thus follows Schleiermacher in his psychological emphasis. His concern is not so much to understand the text as to reconstruct the lived experience of its author. Such experience, says Dilthey, is intrinsically temporal, and interpretation must therefore itself assume a temporal or historical character. The role of history was to remain important for hermeneutics; and in the 'understanding of spiritual life and of history' Dilthey gave literature an 'immeasurable significance'; for 'in language alone the inner life of man finds its complete, exhaustive and objectively intelligible expression'. Literature is thus a privileged object for hermeneutic study.

Martin Heidegger moved twentieth-century hermeneutics away from psychologism towards ontology: the question of being, and of being in the world, a world whose strangeness demanded interpretation. The philosophical issues will not concern us here; but it is important to note Heidegger's reformulation of the hermeneutic circle, not as a problem to be resolved by an intuitive leap, but in terms of interplay between an interpreter and a tradition which is encountered, understood and remade in an open dialectic. As Fleidegger's pupil Hans-Georg Gadamer describes it, 'There is a polarity of familiarity and strangeness on which hermeneutic work is based . . . that intermediate place between being an historically intended separate object and being

part of a tradition.' This concept of tradition is crucial for Gadamer's dealings with history, and with what he calls an effective consciousness of history. Far from being neutral, the interpreter is always situated in relation to the tradition 'out of which the text speaks'. This situatedness (and its prejudices) must come to consciousness as the interpreter's 'horizon'. The text's horizon is of course different and distant; and though a fusion of horizons is sought, historical distance is not cancelled but recognized as itself productive of meaning. In this sense, and not in Schleiermacher's, the interpreter may understand more than the author.

The open dialectic and evolving tradition of Gadamer's hermeneutics act to prevent closure; meaning is understood but it is never final. A desire to avoid the 'Babel of interpretations' has prompted E. D. Hirsch, Jr to seek a regulative principle for hermeneutics through another reconstruction of the author. He separates 'meaning' and 'significance'; significance is any relationship between meaning and something else – taste, period, and so on. It is thus variable and the concern of criticism. Interpretation, on the other hand, deals with meaning; this does not change because it is intended by an author – though seen not as historically active, nor as unconsciously motivated, but as 'that "part" of the author which specifies or determines verbal meaning'. However, this specifying intention must itself be specified by the interpreter, and so its practical use for validation would seem to involve us in a really vicious circle. But the subsequent controversy in hermeneutics does not stem from Hirsch, who has been subjected to devastating critique (see David Hoy, later). It rather concerns what could be called the optimism of Schleiermacher, Dilthey and Gadamer. Much as these hermeneuts differ, they do share an allegiance to universality, and to a common human nature which suggests a measure of co-operation and of shared discourse in the interpretive dialogue. Hermeneutic objects may differ, but they are credited as truths which await illumination. Ricoeur has distinguished between this 'hermeneutics of belief' and a contrary 'hermeneutics of suspicion' whose exemplary figures are Nietzsche, Marx and Freud. Such figures are concerned not just to clarify but also to demystify; texts may be mistrusted rather than revered, and tradition may be a repository of false consciousness. Such attitudes are linked to oppositional practices for the READER, and to the concept of REFUNCTIONING. One noteworthy debate between belief and suspicion has concerned Gadamer and Jürgen Habermas, whose ideological approach derives from the Frankfurt School. For Habermas, a hermeneutics like Gadamer's offers knowledge which is 'sterilized', clear of the suppressed traces of special interest which critical reflection should uncover. But for Gadamer this task is not invariably necessary or primary; he resists the exclusive equation of understanding and unmasking, and the inevitable opposition of reason and authority.

Dilthey's distinction between natural and human sciences has also been challenged, and with it much arts-versus-science rhetoric. The distinction was still followed by Heidegger and Gadamer, prompting comments on the alienation of the detached scientific observer. But for much modern science the observer is not detached, the object is not passive, and investigation occurs within the horizon of a theoretical paradigm. An historian of science like Stephen Toulmin can now claim: 'Critical judgement in the natural sciences, then, is not geometrical, and critical interpretation in the humanities is not whimsical' ('The Construal of Reality' in W. J. T. Mitchell (ed.), *The Politics of Interpretation*, 1983). Both sides must abjure their myths; hermeneutics is no longer judged and delimited by 'hard' science, and its scope is implicitly increased. An even more far-reaching extension is described by Richard Rorty in *Philosophy and the Mirror of Nature* (1980). Rorty proposes the abandonment of that quest for knowledge which seeks essential principles and tries to posit a meta-discourse that commands all others. He calls this ambition 'epistemology' and suggests hermeneutics as an alternative procedure: 'Hermeneutics...is what we get when we are no longer epistemological.' It is thus a polemical term which seeks to turn human inquiry away from envying some predictive sciences towards a pragmatic anti-essentialism which (following Gadamer in this respect) resists closure. Heidegger's open model of the hermeneutic circle applies, suggesting a 'notion of culture as a conversation rather than as a structure erected upon foundations'. Interpretation becomes a pervasive necessity, when, as Stanley Fish remarked in another context, 'interpretation is the only game in town'.

See Andrew Bowie and Friedrich Schleiermacher (eds), *Hermeneutics and Criticism* (1998); Paul Ricoeur, *Hermeneutics and the Human Sciences*, edited and translated by John B. Thompson (1981); Kurt Mueller-Volimer (ed.), *The Hermeneutics Reader: Texts of the German Tradition from the Enlightenment to the Present* (1986).

EC

Hero   In classical myth heroes had superhuman powers; they conversed with gods (sometimes, like Achilles or Theseus, they were demigods) and their lines were accompanied by prophecies and portents. But when these figures appear in the Homeric epics, their status, as Aristotle showed, is changed – they have become aspects of *literary* structure, and 'Unity of plot does not, as some people think, consist in the unity of the hero' (*Poetics*). Homer's heroes, for Aristotle, are elements in the unity of an action, not its sole origin and end as they had been in the loosely cumulative preliterary legends; in epic or tragedy heroes exist for the sake of the literary whole. But the hero is not easily demoted from his mythic status: Romantic criticism, culminating in A. C. Bradley's *Shakespearean Tragedy* (1904) is now notorious for the fallacy of considering heroes in artificial separation from their dramatic context (see L. C. Knights, *How Many Children had Lady Macbeth?*, 1933). Conversely, the New Critics who de-mythologized the hero stressed 'unity' to the point where plays became ritual re-enactments of order rather than actions. The concept of the hero seems inextricably involved with the discussion of dramatic structure. Though by an illusion they seem so, Shakespeare's heroes are rarely continuous creations. When the hero returns to the scene after an absence we do not take up where we left off, or reconstruct some biographical fiction; we take the hero up from where the *play*, in the language and action of other characters, has got to. This is perhaps the clearest indication of the distinction (and the interaction) between dramatic structure and the structure of the hero's consciousness or career; we may in some works be more aware of one or the other, but neither can dominate without evaporating the drama.

The critical issues raised by the Protean forms of the hero in narrative poetry and novels are more complicated, and have been aired less. *Paradise Lost* provides an example: Milton established

a distinctive 'heroic' diction, but initiated simultaneously a fertile debate about who (if anyone) was the 'hero'. Satan, as Dryden said, was *technically* the hero – but was the concept even relevant to a work claiming truth to universal moral and spiritual experience? Surely, Addison urged, Milton had *no* hero in the classical sense (though if we wanted one, it must be Christ)? When, in the romantic period, Blake and Shelley declared Milton *was* on the Devil's side, very different valuations of the heroic came into the open: on the one side radical individualism (represented diversely by Byron, the Brontës and Carlyle), on the other the communal values of restraint, civilization, maturity, first in Scott and Austen, later in the social novels of Mrs Gaskell and George Eliot. Thackeray, who subtitled Vanity Fair (1847–8) 'A Novel without a Hero', applied in *Henry Esmond* (1852) the searching perspective of domestic realism to the great figures of the past. The eighteenth-century epigram, 'No man is a hero to his valet' encapsulated the kind of scrutiny that cut the hero down to size. Carlyle argued, 'It is not the Hero's blame, but the Valet's: that his soul, namely, is a mean *valet*-soul!' – but his own version of 'the Hero' demonstrates grotesquely the vices of essentialism: 'For at bottom the Great Man, as he comes from the hand of Nature, is ever the same kind of thing: Odin, Luther, Johnson, Burns...'

Getting rid of 'the Hero' seemed a critical necessity: as wielded by Carlyle the concept was unmanageable, a barrier to the understanding of literary structures. Critics preferred the slippery term 'CHARACTER', and analysed social and/or verbal detail; rhetoric, action, conventional motifs and large-scale effects were systematically played down. There were, however, many nineteenth-century novels where this obviously did not work (e.g. Emily Brontë's *Wuthering Heights*, 1847, Meredith's *The Egoist*, 1879) and twentieth-century fictional developments, like the absurd, villainous or insane narrator-heroes of Beckett or Nabokov, have produced the term 'anti-hero' to fill a much-felt gap. The hero has re-emerged, in complicity with the author against the norms of 'the whole', and may be, as in Beckett's title, *The Unnameable* (1953), but this is of course a precise inversion, not a banishment, of the classical archetype. Dickens's *Our Mutual Friend* (1864–5) exemplifies a continuing ambivalence – the sinister yet patronizing attitude of the author introducing 'our hero'. We may agree with T. S. Eliot's debunking of 'Sir Philip Sidney/And other heroes of that kidney' but the concept seems inescapable despite its extra, or anti-literary, overtones. The narrative without a hero remains a critical fiction. See also CHARACTER, EPIC, MYTH.

See Thomas Carlyle, *Heroes and Hero-Worship* (1840); Northrop Frye, *Anatomy of Criticism* (1957); R. W. B. Lewis, *The Picaresque Saint, Representative Figures in Contemporary fiction* (1959); Peter Mercer, 'Othello and heroic tragedy', *Critical Quarterly*, 11 (1969); Mario Praz, *The Hero in Eclipse in Victorian Fiction* (1956); Alex Woloch, *The One Vs the Many: Minor Characters and the Space of the Protagonist in the Novel* (2004).

LS

Heroic couplet   See COUPLET.

Historical novel   A term which refers to novels set in a period of time recognizably 'historical' in relation to the moment of writing. The past tense may be employed in the narration; the account may purport to have been written in that past time, or in some intervening time. The subject matter of the historical novel tends to encompass both public and private events, and the protagonist may be either an actual figure from the past or an invented figure whose destiny is involved with actual events. The major practitioners of this, the 'classic' form of the historical novel in English and American literature, were Sir Walter Scott and James Fenimore Cooper. The historical actions in Scott's 'Waverley' and Cooper's 'Leatherstocking' novels largely concerned social changes of great magnitude – the destruction of the Scottish clans, the impingement of the settlers on the new land and their conflict with Native Americans. The protagonist was often someone of mixed loyalties, whose diverse impinging pressures mirrored in individual struggle the interplay of wider social forces.

In England, Thackeray carried forward the tradition of the genre, but reached back to connect it with the comic novels of Fielding and Smollett. Like Scott, Thackeray communicates a sense of momentous and irretrievable social change, but his dissatisfaction with that which prevailed in any given situation seems stronger than Scott's. On the Continent, the successors to Scott included Manzoni, Pushkin, Gogol, Hugo, Mérimée, Stendhal, Balzac and Tolstoy. Gradually, the interests and techniques of the historical novel began to be applied to contemporary events and the genre merged with, even as it helped create, the great realistic novels of the nineteenth century. A double movement occurred in which the treatment of 'history' in fiction became progressively more exotic and archaeologically accurate – as in Flaubert's *Salammbô* (1862) – while treatment of the present became more 'naturalistic'.

The historical novel merges on one side with the realistic novel, on the other – as the historical substance generalizes – it merges with the national epic, and is perhaps the counter-phenomenon to Fielding's notion of the novel as a *comic prose epic*. The epic model here is Virgil's *Aeneid*, in so far as certain events can be seen as inaugurating and justifying (or failing to justify) the nation state.

The question of historical psychology – of the motives and feelings which can be attributed to people in the past – arises. Some historical novelists have attributed to characters in the past substantially the same inner lives as their contemporaries. This type of anachronism, which can be used to significant and to comic effect, is allied to other 'deteriorated' forms of the historical novel, including the 'historical romance', where only costume and not substance differentiates the period of the fiction from the present. See also ARCHAISM.

A penchant for the historical novel reappeared at the end of the twentieth century. A. S. Byatt, whose work is particularly associated with the reinscription of Victorian Britain in works, such as *Possession* (1990), *Angels and Insects* (1992) and *The Biographer's Tale* (1999), writes in one of her essays:

> I believe that postmodern writers are returning to historical fiction because the idea of writing the Self is felt to be worked out.... We like historical persons because they are unknowable, only partly available to the imagination, and we find this occluded quality attractive.

Byatt is referring to authors writing in a fabulist European tradition, such as Lawrence Norfolk, Penelope Fitzgerald, Peter Ackroyd and Tibor Fischer, but her comments about a return to history apply to a wide range of literary production around the millennium. She notes that in the 1950s the historical novel was frowned on as 'escapist' or pigeonholed as 'pastoral', but that it has proved more durable than the majority of 'urgent fictive confrontations of immediate contemporary reality' despite the more recent tags of 'nostalgic' and 'costume drama'. Byatt notes that this renaissance is at least coincident with, if not in part due to, the reconsideration of history's relation to narrative by historians themselves, from Hayden White to Simon Schama.

See Georg Lukács, trans. Hannah and Stanley Mitchell, *The Historical Novel* (1962); A. S. Byatt, *On Histories and Stories: Selected Essays* (2001).

AMG

Historicism Many branches of literary study involve the use of historical evidence: questions of textual transmission and authenticity, of archaic or obsolete language, of sources and literary borrowing, of relations between an author's life and work, are all in the strict sense 'historical'. But the term 'historicism' is usually reserved for that approach to literature which sets it in the context of the ideas, conventions and attitudes of the period in which it was written. Although good literature is 'not of an age, but for all time', the social and intellectual climate within which every writer has to work, and which his writing reflects in some degree, is subject to change. The uninformed modern reader is therefore likely to bring to the literature of the past assumptions and associations that may be quite alien to the frame of reference from which that literature derives its form and meaning. The aim of historicism is to make works of different periods more accessible to the modern reader by reconstructing the historically appropriate background as it affects an understanding and judgement of the work concerned.

The theory as well as the practice of historicism have not gone unchallenged.

It has been argued, for instance, that a modern reconstruction of the cultural or ideological identity of a past age must still be essentially modern in its point of view. Historicism cannot transform a twentieth-century mind; it may only be transferring modern preconceptions from the critical to the historical plane of thought. Moreover, historicism must inevitably be selective and interpretative in treating what evidence there is concerning standards and habits of mind that differ from our own; it may tend to impose a falsifying uniformity and immobility upon its conception of a literary 'period', and its findings are themselves demonstrably subject to change from generation to generation. Much of the historicism of thirty years ago is now as obsolete as other kinds of literary interpretation which were merely of their age. In addition, there is a tendency in historicism to interpret, and measure the work of great and original imagination by the commonplaces of its time, reducing the uniqueness and subtlety of genius to the lowest common denominator of a reconstructed idea of 'period'. If, for instance, a knowledge of Elizabethan ideas about kingship, or of their dramatic conventions, helps us to understand Shakespeare's history plays, we must still remember that Shakespeare is hardly to be circumscribed by an abstraction of the average mentality of his contemporaries. Conventions that have been obliterated by time may be recovered for us by historicism, but the great writers of the past are more than conventional.

Historicism, therefore, cannot provide us with an absolute or objective measure of literary meaning or value. It is not a substitute for the act of intelligent imagination which we call criticism; but it is, properly used, one of the critic's most valuable tools. Provided its limitations are recognized, it can extend and refine our understanding of the literature we most admire. The validity of historicism rests not upon an antiquarian curiosity about how a writer was influenced or interpreted by the world he lived in, but upon the endeavour to enrich modern sensibilities by comprehending and transmitting those ideas and values which preserve the continuity of our civilization.

New historicism evolved in the 1980s as, in some ways, a reaction to structuralism and formalism. Indebted to political, post-structuralist and reader-response theory, new historicism focusses on the intertexuality of (literary and non-literary) texts and the presence of diverse culturally specific discourses within and around the text under examination. New historicism acknowledges both the radical difference of the past and the impossibility of accessing it free from the critic's own historical moment. Critics seek to be vigilant over both their own preconceptions and the traditional tendency to see historical criticism as objective rather than interpretive. Indebted to Foucault, new historicism has developed in tandem with the new cultural history influenced by the Marxism of the 1970s and the French *Annales* historians. In Britain, new historicist criticism developed under the name CULTURAL MATERIALISM, where a greater debt to the work of Raymond Williams was acknowledged. Cf. MARXIST CRITICISM.

See Helen Gardner, *The Business of Criticism* (1960); René Wellek, *Concepts of Criticism* (1963); W. K. Wimsatt, Jr, *The Verbal Icon* (1954); S. Greenblatt, *Renaissance Self-Fashioning from more to Shakespeare* (1980); H. Aram Veeser (ed.), *The New Historicism Reader* (1993); Paul Hamilton, *Historicism* (2003).

DJP

Homophony   See AMBIGUITY.

Humanism   There are two basic positions regarding humanism. The first is that human beings are self-determining creatures and the second is that their lives are largely determined by forces beyond their control. The irony is that these forces, in the shape of economic and social structures, are ones that they themselves have developed. So, a working definition of humanism is that human beings create their world and are conditioned by it. Once we move beyond this very basic formulation, things become confusing and indeed controversial. For example, how do we differentiate humanism from humanity, or even from the individual human being? These are all closely related but subtly different concepts. Even if we try to define humans as a species we run into trouble. It is not only that many other mammals use tools and communicate with one another but also that we share 98 per cent of our genes with the chimpanzee and something like 67 per cent with a banana. The history of written culture is partly an attempt to distinguish humans from other species, often on the basis of their ostensibly divine origin but, since Darwin, we have become more and more aware of our kinship with the animal kingdom. The point is that if we cannot draw an absolute boundary between ourselves and other species, how can we be clear about humanism? Another problem is that the term humanism has been regarded with suspicion because it glosses over questions of class, ethnicity, gender and sexuality. It also provides a 'justification' for interfering in other cultures where it is felt that 'human nature' is not as developed as it might be and this was one of the justifications of imperialism. On the other hand, the notion of humanism can be used more positively as a means of identifying with others. It is this sense of humanism that is most powerfully at work in our response to literature.

The term itself is a nineteenth-century coinage. It referred primarily to the new conception of 'man' in the Renaissance. A key element of this conception was the idea of the individual. This contrasted with the figure of 'Everyman' who was a common feature of the Medieval period. Standing for all of (hu)mankind this figure had no distinctive characteristics, and was moreover a passive person fought over by a good and bad angel. The discovery of classical writers precipitated a change in this view of the human, which could be seen in works like Giorgio Vasari's *Lives of the Artists* (1550). The stress was now on what made a person different and on how they determined their own existence. Along with these developments was a sense not of 'man' as a fallen creature but as one who could aspire to higher things.

Although the culture of Puritanism, in the seventeenth century, undermined the dignity and self-determining nature of the human with its dark theology of damnation, this was eclipsed in the eighteenth century by a new emphasis on the rational nature of 'man'. In the latter half of the period, this gave way to an appreciation of the emotional nature of 'man' which carried its own sort of truth. This was, in crude form, the philosophy of romanticism and another central feature of this thinking was the idea of human beings as creative individuals. During the course of the nineteenth century, various thinkers, such as Marx, Nietzsche and Freud, began to question the idea of human autonomy and essential goodness that had been prevalent since the Renaissance. Marx showed that humans were conditioned by the class into which they were born,

Nietzsche that they were still in the toils of Christian morality which they needed to transcend and Freud that they were torn between their instincts and their ideals. One of the main ideas of humanism was the importance of learning, manifest in the mastery of language. The work of Ferdinand de Saussure (1857–1913) undermined this assumption with his idea, elaborated in different ways by Michel Foucault (1926–84), Jacques Lacan (1901–81) and Jacques Derrida (1930–2004), that language shaped us more than we shaped language.

In recent years there has been a reaction to the 'anti-humanism' of theory. Since human beings are always changing – the intersection of the human and computer technology is an important factor here – there can be no precise definition of humanism. But from the medieval to the modern period, one thing is constant: the idea that humans are divided and unfulfilled and that they look back to the past or to the future to have a complete view of themselves. It may also be a reason why they write literature, to give themselves a sense of wholeness denied in life.

See Tony Davies, *Humanism* (1997); Martin Halliwell and Andy Mousley, *Critical Humanisms: Humanist/ Anti-Humanist Dialogues* (2003).

GD

Humours In medieval medicine the four humours were the fluids whose dominance determined the nature ('complexion') of men: Blood (sanguine); Phlegm (phlegmatic); Choler (choleric); Black Choler or Bile (melancholic). These are used by Ben Jonson to construct an idea of character obsession. A humour may 'so possess a man, that it doth draw / All his affects, his spirits and his power, / In their confluctions, all to run one way' (Prologue to *Every Man Out of His Humour*, 1600). The obsessional humour riding the character is the source of the 'comedy'. In the early plays the humour is 'spent' in the course of the action, freeing the character, in a literal use of the medical analogy. Later the humours are developed as symbolic stances through which the characters are seen to react to the values of the world they inhabit, rather than as simple flaws or biases in their nature. Thus, Morose's silence (phlegmatic melancholy) is simultaneously a cause and a product of his relationship with his society. This sophistication of the theory culminates in a humour character like Overreach (sanguine/choleric?) where the bias is a complex symbol of the general and social values of the world of the Fair in *Bartholomew Fair* (1614? folio 1631) and people's response to them.

Restoration dramatists continued to insist in their critical responses that humour theory is central to comic effect but in practice the increased interest in the presence or absence of the *acceptable response* by which society judges the wit and worth of its members makes humour characterization seem too inflexible. Attempts have been made to distinguish Affectation, with its conscious, social overtones, from Humour, where the stress is individual and pathological. As Congreve says, 'what is *Humour* in one, may be *Affectation* in another; and nothing is more common, than for some to affect particular ways of saying, and doing things, peculiar to others, whom they admire and imitate' (*Concerning Humour in Comedy*, 1696). But though he seems determined to defend the humour concept he rings its knell when he admits in the same work 'that a continued Affectation may in time become a Habit'. For in the world which he inhabits and describes it becomes impossible effectively to distinguish continued affectation from reality (consider the marriage contract in *The Way of the World*). Humour remained an influence in the figures of the Tunbellys and Clumsys of Restoration plays but they no longer had the distinction of being vessels of disruptive forces who had to be freed if others were to escape the shadow of their obsessions: they became mere butts to provoke the humour of those who had learned the correct manner to suit the mood of the world. See also MANNERS.

See Alain C. Dessen, *Jonson's Moral Comedy* (1971); Paul Lauter, *Theories of Comedy* (1964); Kenneth Muir, *The Comedy of Manners* (1970); A. Johnson, *Ben Jonson* (2003).

GG

Hybridity   The term hybridity emerged within post-colonial studies as a response to static and essentialist notions of identity of race and nation promoted by colonial discourses, and also such anti-colonial discourses as NATIONALISM and NÉGRITUDE. Ironically, however, the term hybridity was itself formerly deployed within colonial discourses on mixed race offspring and thus constituted a central term in discourses of colonial racism. Some critics have warned that the uncritical deployment, or fetishization, of 'hybridity' may in fact ironically reinscribe the very structures of thought and domination that it is intended to deconstruct (Young).

The term has been most extensively articulated and theorized by Homi Bhabha. Bhabha introduces the term first within the colonial arena and he, amongst others, has since transported it to other fields of analysis in post-colonial contexts, where hybridity has now become a central term in discussions of multiculturalism and diaspora. It is, within Bhabha's theoretical lexicon, closely related to terms such as 'mimicry' and 'ambivalence', and is embedded within a wider framework of concern with what Bhabha calls the 'Third Space'. This 'Third Space' allows us to conceive of the identities of cultures in terms that transcend the binary dialectic between 'us/them', 'insider/outsider', 'inclusion/exclusion'. It also enables discussion of cultural difference in terms that do not exoticize it for in such exoticism Bhabha detects an Othering principle that distances difference and disavows the constitution of the Self by the Other.

Bhabha sees this 'Third Space' as having a 'colonial or postcolonial provenance' precisely because hybridity emerges specifically from colonial encounters that have resulted in today's 'multicultural' or diasporic societies. (Bhabha) That is, the legacy of the colonial past echoes in a postcolonial present that has been profoundly shaped by encounters between colonial discourses and cultures deemed 'Other', so that the 'location' of culture in such heterogeneous societies exists in-between, as opposed to 'inside', cultural formations that are ideologically reified and rendered static. This is particularly true of nations and nationalisms, and so Bhabha conceives of the Third Space as '*inter*national'.

Hybridity is often spoken of colloquially in terms of its use within horticulture as the combination of two kinds that produce a third. Such a way of thinking reproduces the essential difference between the 'kinds' involved and so reinforces the notion that each element possesses a self-identity that is sufficient in and of itself. In post-colonial studies, however, the intention is to deconstruct the apparent self-identity of cultures that perceive themselves to be whole but are in fact constituted by a lack that requires supplementation by (an) 'Other(s)'. Thus Bhabha, in his essay 'Of Mimicry and Man', rehearses the dilemma of colonial educators in India who require 'a class of Indians native in blood and colour but English in tastes, in morals, and in intellect' (Macaulay, 1835). Thus, in order to facilitate colonialism, there is a 'desire for a reformed, recognizable Other, *as a subject of difference that is almost the same, but not quite*' (Bhabha). However, in creating this class of 'mimic men' the whole question of 'Englishness' is thrown open to question. Where does 'Englishness' reside? In 'blood and colour' or in 'tastes, in morals, and in intellect'? In acquiring English 'culture', have these Indian mimics become English? If so, what has happened to their Indianness? And what gives the English their identity if *anyone* can become English? The colonial 'mimic men' occupy a hybrid cultural space that is indefinable in static or essentialized terms because they are neither one thing nor the other but something else besides, an excess that cannot be contained within the terms 'English' or 'Indian'. This illustrates an ambivalence within those very terms that renders them uncertain.

Hybridity is thus one of the confluence points between postmodernism and postcolonialism. It has, for this very reason, attracted considerable controversy with critics attacking it for being part of a panoply of ideas that textualize and aestheticize power struggles between unequal forces, peoples and cultures, and which overlook the economic dimensions of colonial and post-colonial modernity. Particular concern has been expressed at the ways in which hybridity privileges culture as the most important field of resistance to domination, and reading as the appropriate form of political practice. Moreover, since hybridity destabilizes all collective identities, its political efficacy has been drawn into question for it undermines not only dominant constructs but subordinate ones as well. Thus, it hampers any mobilization of a collective identity as a basis for political resistance.

It could equally be argued, however, that the cultural frameworks that hybridity seeks to dismantle have material effects in the institutional contexts of power. It seeks to draw into question those very contexts within which political and economic practices take place, contexts which are formed and reformed by culture and ideology. By destabilizing 'pure' cultural identities, and by dismantling the hierarchies between them, concepts, such as hybridity contribute to a reconceptualization of the very basis of what is at stake in political struggle. See also POSTCOLONIALISM; ORIENTALISM; ALTERITY.

See Homi K. Bhabha, *The Location of Culture* (1994); Avtar Brah and Annie Coombes (eds), *Hybridity and its Discontents: Politics, Science, Culture* (2000); Thomas B. Macaulay (1835) 'Minute on Education for India' in Philip D. Curtin (ed.), *Imperialism* (1971); Robert Young, *Colonial Desire: Hybridity in Theory, Culture and Race* (1995).

AM

Hyperbole   See CONCEIT.

I

Ideology Traditionally, the word ideology refers to the system of ideas used by the ruling group in society to justify its dominance. It is closely bound up with the idea of class. The dominant class needs to be able to hold onto its power and it does this ultimately by force but normally by ideology; in particular, it promotes the view that what is good for itself is good for the rest of society. Ideology is not simply imposed on us, for then we would know it was ideology. For it to be effective, we should not know that it is ideology at all. Far better for those in power if we freely agree, for example, with their view that 'the private sector runs things more efficiently than the public sector' than that we should have it forced upon us. In fact, we absorb ideology as soon as we begin to speak because language is shot through with perceptions, assumptions, values and ideas that are constantly reinforced in, for example, schools and the media. Here we start to a move away from the notion of ideology as a set of beliefs that legitimize the power of the ruling group to a view of ideology as a complete way of understanding the world; in other words, ideology is our normal consciousness. We can only become aware of the ideological nature of this consciousness when we reflect on how closely it matches the view of reality constantly portrayed by politicians and big business, or if we go and spend some time in a society whose members do not share our view of the world.

Language is the link between ideology and literature. Indeed, the very word 'literature' can itself be seen as ideological to the extent that it hides the power relations implicit in the term. Who, traditionally, has produced 'literature'? The white middle class. Who has access to literature? Those who have gone onto higher education. Who are the most likely to do that? The white middle class. We can see that the writing and dissemination of literature has been used as a marker of social division but, at the same time, it has been claimed that literature is the expression of the nation and so it has a unifying function. This is a classic example of how ideology can work because it expresses what people have in common while reproducing the divisions that keep them apart. In terms of individual works themselves, ideology can function in two ways. The first occurs when a writer simply wishes to write a poem, play or story in order to promote or criticize a particular ideology, and such works are usually fairly didactic. The second functions even when a writer has no such intention because his or her work is ideological to the extent that readers are moved to identify with precisely those characters who are most consistent with the ideology of the society.

This does not mean that works of literature cannot criticize ideology. They may do so either openly or as a function of the way literary language signifies. An example of the first would be George Orwell's *Animal Farm*. It is harder to offer an example for the second since this is always highly particular to any given work and requires the sort of analysis for which there is no space here. The idea is that literary language so transforms ordinary, ideological language that we are able to see what is either repressed or contradictory about it. In this way, literature, according to the French Marxist, Louis Althusser (1918–90), gives us knowledge of ideology. This insight was systematically developed by Pierre Macherey in his *A Theory of Literary Production* (1978).

Since the late 1970s, there has been a decline in the interest in ideology and its relation to literature. One of the main reasons for this is that the concept of ideology always assumed, at some level, that there was a true and a false version of events. The advent of POST-STRUCTURALISM, with its claim that words constitute the world rather than correspond to it, made questions of truth or falsehood, at least in the conventional sense, irrelevant. But such a view is ideological to the extent that it chimes with the prominence given to image, spin and presentation in post-industrial capitalist society. As long as the class divisions of capitalism persist so will our need to understand and indeed resist its ideology.

See Terry Eagleton, *Ideology: An Introduction* (1991); Terry Eagleton (ed.), *Ideology* (1994); David Hawkes, *Ideology*, 2nd edn (2003).

GD

Illocutionary act   See DISCOURSE.

Image   In the eighteenth century, one theory of 'imagination' was that it was a faculty for visualization, so literature was often regarded as a medium which promoted visual responses in the reader: that is to say, 'images'. Descriptive poetry flourished. One basic meaning for 'image' is provided by that context, but other, looser meanings have accreted: any sensuous effect provoked by literary language; any striking language; metaphor; symbol; any figure. 'Image' and 'imagery' have also come to be vaguely laudatory terms, simply gesturing a taste for concreteness, richness of texture, in verse. Finally, NEW CRITICAL poetics,

encouraging the reader to view poems as virtually concrete artefacts, allows whole poems to be regarded as 'images'.

The great appeal of 'image' is its shifting application: in *Macbeth*, for example, the following might be called 'images' or 'imagery':

1   metaphors, similes, figurative language: 'Pity like a naked newborn babe';
2   Lady Macbeth's children: 'I have given suck';
3   Macduff's son, who is a flesh-and-blood character;
4   The vision 'Who wears upon his baby brow...' whom the witches show to Macbeth.

All of these, as 'iterative imagery', a play-within-the-play where distinctions between language, action and character lapse (see Cleanth Brooks, *The Well Wrought Urn*, 1947, ch. 2).

The point of having one word to do all these jobs is clear: the whole play becomes one symbolic utterance, a 'dramatic poem' (or, of course, an 'image'), its central preoccupations iterated at every level. This New Critical treatment of imagery sought to avoid the damaging assumption that verbal texture was incidental ornament.

The effect of over-reliance on the word image is to encourage a focus on literature which makes syntax, argument, plot, temporal and relational structures recede into invisibility, while description and figurative language become foregrounded to a distorted degree. The whole thus isolated becomes a static 'spatial' experience, imagined as a 'cluster' of 'images'. The very use of the term encourages the critic to make the subjective appear objective. It is easy to move on to assertions that poems are revelatory, symbolic, 'icons', that the process they enshrine is 'miraculism' or 'incarnation', the Word made flesh. What starts as a gesture of respect for the TEXTURE of literature ends by importing a sub- or supra-literary structure. The rejection of the work's overt order (dismissed as abstraction) leads to the search for some more esoteric 'hidden' pattern.

'Image' has not got much to do with verbal analysis, and the most persuasive analysts, for example, Empson, have hardly used it. It has become associated with the demand that we respect what is 'there' in the work, but the connection is tenuous. As Richards has shown, 'image' blurs the verbal facts about metaphor, by obscuring the *relations* that are being made (between 'tenor' and 'vehicle') and suggesting that a free-floating 'emblem' is being offered. The real connection of 'image' is with a group of assumptions which 'place' poetry, more or less frankly, in relation to some 'deeper' structure – depth psychology, Baroque Christianity, etc. In the long run this can impoverish literature, since it substitutes for the diversity and fluidity of the literary medium a shadow-play of 'images' whose resolution lies elsewhere.

See P. N. Furbank, *Reflections on the Word 'Image'* (1970); Frank Kermode, *Romantic Image* (1957); I. A. Richards, *The Philosophy of Rhetoric* (1936); Akhter Ahsen, *New Surrealism: The Liberation of Images in Consciousness (The Literary Image)* (1992).

LS

Imagination   Leads a double life – like 'tragedy'. In common usage it has a very equivocal sense, more often than not trivial, even derogatory – 'it's all in your imagination'. But as soon as it is associated with any form of art it becomes an indication of value. The extremes meet in the distrust of Art as the enemy of common sense, decency, reason, good government or sound business.

This ambivalence is ancient, if not universal. In theory, the Renaissance assigned Reason and Imagination to different faculties, and reason was certainly the higher. Imagination co-ordinated the physical senses on which alone it depended, and was therefore shared by all animals; reason was angelic, free of the body, even godlike and therefore peculiar (beneath the moon) to humanity. Such a simplistic version of experience was not really accepted, but the problems of over-valuing imagination were illuminated by Theseus in *A Midsummer Night's Dream*:

> The lunatic, the lover, and the poet
> Are of imagination all compact.

The same trinity bedevilled William Blake in his espousal of Hell. Behind him was not only the rationalism of the eighteenth century, but also its terror of lunacy. Samuel Johnson knew no difference between 'imagination' and 'fancy' and defined them as the power of representing things absent from oneself or others; but he found no power in either to distinguish the tangibly real from dangerous hallucination. Yet, Johnson also recognized Imagination as one of the three constituents of genius in Pope: 'He had *Imagination*, which strongly impresses on the writer's mind, and enables him to convey to the reader, the various forms of nature, incidents of life, and energies of passion'. Pope had likewise Good Sense, but Johnson did not discover any principle to reconcile the two. Nor did Blake, who found subservience to reason as bad as the belief in general truths, and both hostile to the energy of particular imaginative experience.

Coleridge's early reflections on the problem produced the image of an Aeolian harp: the chance play of the wind over a mechanical device. It was an old idea, and has been revived since. Automatic writing and SURREALIST theory came close to it, but were usually sustained by a Freudian faith in their origins in a subconscious mind which offered a concept, but not an explanation, of ultimate meaning. For Coleridge the image served to relate the internal unity of an individual human mind to the external random collection of objects it perceives; and it made a proper (if disturbing) allowance for chance. But it allowed of only a very limited relation to reason, and none at all to the energy of creative power. His efforts to modify the image in revising the poem only produced confusion, and he moved towards a fresh epistemology assisted by reading German transcendentalists (Kant and others). The eighteenth-century propositions that the mind merely received impressions from objects (Locke), and that objects could not be *known* to exist except when contacted by our senses (Berkeley) gave way to the proposition that perception depends on an active mind perceiving an object which nevertheless exists without us.

The peculiar achievement here is to re-define *all* perception as imaginative, a *creative* act of the subjective self; but simultaneously the sanity of a perception is guaranteed by the reality of the object perceived. Subject and object coalesce; objects are only known subjectively, but equally one's self is only known in objects. A bush may burn in a visionary blaze; but it is not a bear: it is a bush perceived in a certain way dependent on one's imaginative predisposition. The position is reassuring, even if paradoxical. Blake placed less confidence in the solidity of objects, far more in subjective vision: he, too, was sane, and knew that a flower was a flower; but he might, in contemplating it, see an old man or an angel, and the validity of the vision was assured solely by the fact that he *saw* it. For Coleridge, a major difficulty remained in distinguishing art from normal perception, which is presumably what he intended by dividing 'secondary' from 'primary' imagination (although nothing he says about secondary imagination is peculiar to art).

Coleridge effectively reconciled imagination with Reason, without apparently diminishing either. The lighter values of poetry were relegated to 'fancy'; imagination was essential to all knowledge, and poetry therefore became a serious form of knowledge. Matthew Arnold expected it to replace discredited religion. The study of literature eventually became a central discipline in universities. 'Object' was ambiguous: strictly, it meant anything, tangible or intangible, regarded objectively; but Coleridge was deeply involved with Wordsworth's poetry, so that his discussion often seems to imply rocks and stones and trees. IMAGISM was therefore a direct derivative and through that, T. S. Eliot's insistence that emotion in art can only be expressed through objects, the OBJECTIVE CORRELATIVE. Wallace Stevens's poetry could fairly be described as a set of variations on a theme by Coleridge. In Eliot and Stevens the association with reason remained dominant; their sanity was never in doubt. Yeats was far more ambiguous: teasing rationalists by flirting with all forms of the esoteric, yet retaining an ostentatious sanity as well. But Yeats saw imagination as essentially hostile to reason, and their relationship rather as fruitful tension than reconciliation; his study of Blake was early and lasting, and it was supplemented by intense interest in his wife's automatic writing.

The *status* of Imagination as a concept owes far more to Coleridge than to Blake; but its use in the twentieth century often owed more to Blake.

See J. A. Appleyard, *Coleridge's Philosophy of Literature* (1965);

R. L. Brett, *Fancy and Imagination* (1969); C. C. Clarke, *Romantic Paradox* (1962); S. T. Coleridge, *Biographia Literaria* (1817), G. Watson (ed.) (1956); Richard Kearney, *The Wake of the Imagination* (1988).

MSB

Imagism   The term was coined by Ezra Pound to denote the principles agreed on by himself and the other members of a literary group he formed in London in 1912. As a broad movement, Imagism signals the beginning of English and American MODERNISM, and a definite break with the Romantic-Victorian tradition. As a stylistic programme, it manifests the desire of the post-Symbolist, pre-war generation for a harder, more precise and objective medium. As a particular school, *Les Imagistes* are the heirs of T. E. Hulme's 1909 group of Impressionist poets who experimented with brief visual poems in the Oriental manner. Finally, Imagism shares with Gautier and the Parnassians the penchant for sculptural hardness and immaculate craftsmanship; with the SYMBOLISTS – the accent on pure poetry to the exclusion of all extra-poetic content, as well as the practice of irregular, 'free' verse; with REALISM – the resolve to remain close to the outlines of concrete reality. The poem projected by Imagism is a laconic complex in which 'painting or sculpture seems as if it were just coming over into speech'. As a model, Pound chose the 'Oread' by H. D. (Hilda Doolittle), commonly considered the most representative of his group:

> Whirl up, sea –
> whirl your pointed pines,
> splash your great pines
> on our rocks
> hurl your green over us,
> cover us with your pools of fir.

The poetics of Imagism may best be considered as three interlocking entities: Hulme's prognosis of a classical revival, the stylistic or workshop prescriptions formulated by Pound and upheld by the school even after his departure from it, and Pound's full-blown Doctrine of the Image. Hulme's case is argued in the few articles and short pieces published during his lifetime and, more elaborately, in his posthumously published work. It consists of a repudiation of Romanticism and its aesthetics of the Beyond. The new poetry was going to be that of 'small, dry things' conveyed by concrete visual metaphor. Rejecting infinity, mystery and an indulgence in emotions, he called for a poetry of self-imposed limitation, corresponding to a metaphysical attitude which regards man as an 'extraordinarily fixed and limited animal', and reality as something that may only be apprehended in isolated glimpses.

The stylistic canon of Pound's school comprises the three principles agreed on by its three original members, Pound, H. D. and Richard Aldington:

1   Direct treatment of the 'thing' whether subjective or objective.
2   To use absolutely no word that does not contribute to the presentation.
3   As regarding rhythm, to compose in the sequence of the musical phrase, not in sequence of a metronome.

These are augmented by Pound's list of 'Don'ts', chiefly intended for the apprentice poet. They vary in substance from general advice (the avoidance of abstraction, rhetoric and non-functional ornament) to suggestions of a more technical nature (the practice of enjambment to diversify the rhythmical 'waves'). Central is the emphasis on poetry as an acquired art, the acquisiton of which demands the labours of a lifetime. The modern aspect of the programme is reflected in Pound's dictum that 'no good poetry is ever written in a manner twenty years old'. But the Imagist is given a free choice of subject matter, not excluding classical themes, and is counselled to study a vast and disparate 'tradition' so as 'to find out what has been done, once for all, better than it can ever be done again'.

Pound's Doctrine of the Image centres on his successive definitions of the term. His earliest attempt – 'an "Image" is that which presents an intellectual and emotional complex in an instant of time' – yields its full meaning when read in conjunction with later pronouncements in which the Image is described as the poet's 'primary pigment', the hard core of poetry wherein it reveals itself as distinct from, and yet, basically parallel to, other arts. The Image – the 'word beyond formulated language' – may comprise traditional metaphor, when the latter can be said to be 'interpretative' of reality, that is, when it posits a relationship based on inherent, not merely fanciful, qualities. Commonly, however, it connotes in Pound such modern procedures as juxtaposition and superposition. Pound's illustration is his own haiku-like 'In a Station of the Metro':

> The apparition of these faces in the crowd;
> Petals on a wet, black bough.

Here 'one idea is set on top of another' to produce the synthetic complex, also described as language's 'point of maximum energy'. The two (or more) components of the Image remain faithful to objective reality, representing two distinct acts of sense-perceptions, yet, their fusion is expected to form a higher, governing reality, untainted with photographic realism. In actual Imagist writing, stringent conformity is the exception. A shorthand notation of impressionistic glimpses,

concise metaphoric miniatures and 'hard', asymmetrical treatments of Hellenic and other motifs constitutes the bulk of a poetry compatible with, but not necessarily occasioned by, the theory.

Assessments of the significance of Imagism vary greatly. Eliot's opinion was that its accomplishment in verse had been 'critical rather than creative, and as criticism very important'. Leavis, another early critic, considered that 'in itself it amounted to little more than a recognition that something was wrong with poetry'. But the formidable influence Imagism exercised, and continues to exert, suggests that such a judgement is untenable. Other critics consider it of importance chiefly as a stage in Pound's development towards his *Cantos*. Wallace Stevens reproaches Imagism with its belief that all objects are equally suited for poetry, and its equation of meaning with bare surface. As a critical movement, Imagism's main significance probably resides in its revaluation of Romanticism and of the nineteenth century which, with few exceptions, it dismissed as a sentimental, blurry, manneristic period. No less significant was its insistence on the functional, rather than the merely ornamental, potentiality of the poetic image, and the latter's capacity for conveying the concrete and definite. In this, it 'isolated the basic unit of the modern poem', as Stephen Spender suggested. But in overstating its case, it was ignoring other, no less effective, poetic energies, as well as dangerously limiting its own scope.

See D. Davie, *Ezra Pound – Poet as Sculptor* (1965); G. Hough, *Image and Experience* (1960); H. Kenner, *The Poetry of Ezra Pound* (1951); H. Kenner, *The Pound Era* (1972); F. Kermode, *Romantic Image* (1957); C. K. Stead, *The New Poetic* (1964); A. Kingsley Weatherhead, *The Edge of the Image* (1967).

NZ

Imitation   The first recorded use of 'imitation' (*mimesis*) as an aesthetic term is Plato's: in the *Republic* it is a derogatory way of describing the poet's counterfeit 'creations', which reflect and mimic the transient appearances of this world (see PLATONISM). Aristotle in his *Poetics* stretches the term to give it a radically different and more complex application: the poet 'imitates' not the accidental features of character in action, but the universal type, 'clothed with generic attributes' (Coleridge). Aristotle is not arguing for a symbolic or emblematic function for literature (only that would have satisfied Plato) but for a concrete manifestation of the 'natural' order he asserted was present (though obscured) in ordinary experience.

Aristotle's 'imitation' combines a sense of the literary work as the representation of some pre-existent reality, with a sense of the work itself as an object, not merely a reflecting surface. The poet is not subservient to the irrationality of the actual: the play or poem has its own natural form and objective status. In the *Poetics* tragedy is like an organism – it grows, achieves its prime (with Sophocles) and decays. The form has an imperative logic whereby (e.g.) the poet chooses a 'probable impossibility' rather than an event which though possible (even historical) does not follow 'naturally' in context. The poet 'imitates' best by allowing the work to achieve its own fitting formal excellence.

This stress on the imitative function of formal harmony (Aristotle says music is the most 'mimetic' art) connects with the second major use of the term in classical and neo-classical criticism – the 'imitation' of one writer by another (Homer by Virgil, both by Milton, all three by Pope). If Homer's epics are the fullest realization of the laws of epic (and involve therefore the fullest correspondence with the laws of reason and nature) then to imitate heroic action and to imitate the form and style of the *Iliad* is one complex process of mimesis. Hence Pope's snappy line on Virgil:

> Nature and Homer were, he found, the same.

Theoretically there is no conflict between formal imitation and representation, but neither 'nature' nor language stay 'the same', and in practice there is tension, issuing in the characteristic neo-classical forms of MOCK-EPIC and PARODY.

For the concept of imitation to retain its precision and range, social, moral and psychological values must seem self-evident: there has to be consensus about what is 'natural' and 'probable', or at least agreement about the value of such generalizations. In the eighteenth century an anti-theoretical realism, reflecting a more fluid, fragmentary and individual reality (see Ian Watt, *The Rise of the Novel*, 1957; and REALISM) began to erode the assumptions behind imitation. The term lost its great virtue of referring to both form and content and was used almost synonymously with 'representation'. Deliberate efforts to resurrect Aristotelian usage (see CHICAGO CRITICS) foundered in stilted and questionable generalization, while more fluent use of the term (e.g. Auerbach's *Mimesis*) had to accommodate shifting definitions of reality.

See Erich Auerbach, trans. W. Trask, *Mimesis* (1953); S. H. Butcher, *Aristotle's Theory of Poetry and Fine Art* (1907) with an introduction by John Gassner (1951); R. S. Crane (ed.), *Critics and Criticism* (1957); G. F. Else, *Aristotle's 'Poetics': The Argument* (1957); Raymond Williams, *The Long Revolution* (1961).

LS

Implied author   See AUTHOR, PERSONA.

Intention   In their influential essay 'The intentional fallacy' (in *The Verbal Icon*, 1954) W. K. Wimsatt, Jr and

Monroe C. Beardsley argued that the author's intentions were not the proper concern of the critic. Their argument has produced many misconceptions about descriptive criticism – that poems are autonomous, or autotelic, that they are discontinuous from language and each other, that any external evidence is critically inadmissible. Essentially the essay disputed the formulae and terminology of expressive criticism with its Romantic concentration on the inspired utterances of the poet, and asserted the existence of the poem as a fact in the public language. The characteristic vocabulary of expressive or intentionalist criticism, its criteria of sincerity, fidelity, spontaneity, originality, pointed to a misconception about the mode of existence of a literary work. It was not a practical message, a real statement, which could be measured for its sincerity against a known context, but a fictional utterance by a dramatic speaker; so it was more properly judged in terms of coherence, profundity, beauty. Consequently, the essay argued, the meaning of a work was better discovered by attention to 'internal' evidence, the language of the poem, which paradoxically, because it *was* language, was public, than to external evidence – the private disclosures of poets, their friends or biographers. This advice has often been understood to mean the irrelevance to critical enquiry of all information that is not derived from the linguistic characteristics of the text. But Wimsatt and Beardsley do not dispute the usefulness of this other information; the core of their argument is that our ability to *use* this information depends upon our sense of its relevance, and that relevance can be established only in relation to the poem as a fact in language. In proposing that the only public existence a work of literature has is its existence in language, they were stating an axiom of descriptive criticism.

See also ANALYSIS, AUTHOR, DISCOURSE, EFFECT, NEW CRITICISM.

See Patrick Swinden, *Literature and the Philosophy of Intention* (1999).

PM

Interior monologue   See STREAM OF CONSCIOUSNESS.

Interpretant   See SEMIOTICS.

Interpretation   See ANALYSIS, HERMENEUTICS.

Intertextuality   With the identification in STRUCTURALISM of language as a series of interconnections between signs came the recognition of the importance of the relationships between those signs and the ways they interact to produce different meaning-formations. Thinking in POST-STRUCTURALISM subsequently tended to emphasize the ways in which signs, and their more complex relations – texts – depend upon each other for their meaning within the structures and frameworks of GENRE and DISCOURSE. Intertextuality is the name often given to the manner in which texts of all sorts (oral, visual, literary, virtual) contain references to other texts that have, in some way, contributed to their production and signification. The notion was initially introduced by Julia Kristeva who envisaged texts as functioning along two axes: the horizontal axis determines the relationship between the reader and the text whilst the vertical axis contains the complex set of relations of the text to other texts. What coheres these axes is the framework of pre-existing codes that governs and shapes every text and every reading act. In Kristeva's view the importance of a text's structure is matched by its 'structuration', that is, the pattern of interconnected fields within which its meaning is transmitted to the reader through already-known vocabularies of generic and discursive formation. For instance, the reader of a detective novel knows it is such not only because of the conventions of style, action and dénouement, but also because the book is shelved in a specific section of the bookshop and is graced by a suitably mysterious image on its front cover. The reader knows what to expect from the novel precisely because of its similarities (whether direct or indirect) to other texts s/he may have encountered.

Intertextuality, with its endlessly receding network of debts and legacies, disturbs a casual belief in the uniqueness of the text and of the originality of the authorial consciousness. Such beliefs are relatively recent phenomena. Until the Renaissance, it was a widely accepted fact that literary texts were patchworks of existing works either directly appropriated or modified into a new form but in which the identity of the author was of little importance. Even after the Renaissance texts tended to be elaborate, often ostentatious revisionings of prior works and interpreted not as plagiaristic copies but as respectful homages to tradition and to the skill of the source-material. Only with the period of Romanticism (in the late-eighteenth and early-nineteenth centuries) does the notion of authorial originality become an important issue. It is tied to the Romantics' idea of the singularity of the creative consciousness that also evidences a movement towards a modern conception of individualism. The text becomes a product of an autonomously acting mind and something that is as unique as the vision of the individual that inspired it. This idea of authorship was severely challenged by structuralist and post-structuralist theorists who claim supreme importance for the fact that language is a system that is already in place before the speaker makes a communicative act. The pre-existence of linguistic codes and structures means that the subject is always already positioned within

interpretive systems and can therefore only employ those systems available to her/him to describe the experience of reality. When we speak, we are always revisiting what has been previously spoken.

The implication of this circularity of language for creative artists is that their texts become collages of other textual influences from the level of the phrase to the arena of genre. The writer (or speaker) becomes an orchestrator rather than an originator, blending and rearranging material to frame an idiosyncratic view of the world. Critics can explore the range of intertextual reference and the creative engagement with the process of inheritance but they cannot escape the framing that contains their imagination, the media used to express it nor the context within which it is consumed. Postmodern artists have deliberately drawn attention to the self-referential quality of art and overtly exposed the frames of both production and interpretation. In a literary sphere, such subversion is often referred to as metafiction and frequently involves writers writing about the process of writing. Many, accepting the inescapability of the system, revel in self-conscious flirtation with prior texts through parodic reframing and rewriting, drawing the reader's eye not to the 'reality' of the world created but to its artificial constructedness. The knowing distance that is created between the acts of reading and interpretation situates intertextuality as a crucial feature of postmodernism's cynicism towards authority and orthodoxy.

Centring on the imprecise intercourse between author/text/reader, intertextuality tends to privilege the reader as indispensable to the creative process. Because the author's role is to manage the echoes that emanate from her/his particular arrangement of textualized forebears, the reader's decoding of that pattern is of equal importance. The 'meaning' that is derived from any given text (whether it be a novel, a poem, a film, a sitcom, an advertisement) depends upon the reader's prior encountering of the intertexts that are invoked – without the necessary semiotic exposure the reception of the work would inevitably bring forth differing, but equally valid interpretations. This interplay between the reader and the author empowered the Reader Response criticism of the 1970s and 1980s which highlighted the supremacy of readerly interpretation over authorial intention, though some form of middle-ground is now seen as a more productive critical approach. The popularity of intertextuality has seen it become a significant element of popular cultural discourse, so much so in fact, that it can appear any time, any place, anywhere. See also CREATION.

See Roland Barthes, *The death of the Author* (1968), *S/Z* (1973); Jonathan Culler, *Structuralist Poetics: Structuralism, Linguistics and the Study of Literature* (1975); Stanley Fish, *Is there a Text in this Class? The Authority of Interpretive Communities* (1980); Julia Kristeva, *Desire in Language: A Semiotic Approach to Literature and Art* (1980).

DL

Irony A mode of discourse for conveying meanings different from, and usually opposite to, the professed or ostensible ones. There are several kinds of irony, though they fall into two main categories: situational and verbal. All irony, however, depends for its effectiveness on the belief in and exploitation of the difference and distance between words or events and their *contexts*.

Since the contexts of situational irony may be primarily social, moral or metaphysical, irony can be further classified as comic or tragic, though these adjectives are in a sense inaccurate.

In tragic irony the ostensible reasons for the hero's downfall, whether it is the anger of the gods or his own relentless pursuit of an ideal, are undercut by psychological reasons of a more mundane sort. Joseph Conrad's *Lord Jim* provides a good example of this. Comic irony uses similar kinds of juxtaposition to describe and deflate the social aspirations of its protagonists. In both forms the pivotal character tends to be the *eiron* himself; a dissembler who brings two conflicting and contrasting worlds into sharp focus. Examples of such characters are Conrad's Marlow and P. G. Wodehouse's Jeeves. Without such characters, there is a danger that an author's ironies will be completely missed by the reader; for, unlike the satirist, he tends to suppress any direct attitudes to his subject, and to rely upon a shared set of assumptions or prejudices, for the establishment of a context.

It is, however, possible to introduce structural ironies without the use of an *eiron*. Typically, this is the form situational irony takes in plays, where narrators, concealed or otherwise, are more difficult to employ; hence the term *dramatic irony*. Here the *eiron* is replaced by members of the audience who have been apprised of a character's real situation before he knows it himself, and who can therefore anticipate and enjoy the frustration of the ideal by the actual. Sophocles's *Oedipus Rex* uses multiple dramatic ironies to criticize naïve rationalism by reversing all the protagonist's normal expectations. Oedipus in attempting to avoid his fate acts in such a way as to seal it. Within this overarching irony, many others operate both to reinforce Sophocles's view of life and to express it with maximum dramatic force. Dramatic irony can take many forms. For a more extended discussion see W. Empson, *Seven Types of Ambiguity*, (1947) 2nd edn, pp. 38–47.

Verbal irony usually operates by exploiting deviations from syntactic or semantic norms. The ability to recognize such irony depends upon an appreciation of the particular linguistic, or sometimes more general social or moral, context. In speech, it is possible to indicate by tone of voice that the word 'clever' in the sentence 'He's a clever chap' is to be understood to mean 'stupid', but as this cannot be said to be any of the meanings of the word 'clever', the writer has to convey his sense obliquely. Irony is thus an art of juxtaposition and indirection, relying for its success on such techniques as understatement, paradox, puns and other forms of wit in the expression of incongruities. In the following lines from Alexander Pope's *Rape of the Lock* the contrasts between heroic style and banal content reflect the opposition within the lines between the spiritual and the physical:

> Whether the nymph shall break Diana's law,
> Or some frail china jar receive a flaw;
> Or stain her honour, or her new brocade;
> Forget her prayers, or miss a masquerade.

Much modern criticism has seen, in the ambiguities of the ironic mode, a response to experience particularly sympathetic. Like symbolism, allegory and metaphor, irony provides a means for unifying the apparent contradictions of experience, but is also uniquely able to assert the world's diversity. Cleanth Brooks's *The Well Wrought Urn* (1947), is one of the more influential mid-twentieth-century studies that made large claims for the prevalence and persistence of the ironic mode.

More recently, some Deconstructionist critics, following Jacques Derrida, have seen writing as a structure divorced from consciousness as an absolute authority, and agree with his conclusion that the term irony will probably cease to be employed in literary criticism. Paul de Man, on the other hand, in his book, *Blindness and Insight: Essays in the Rhetoric of Contemporary Criticism* (1983), pursues the paradoxical idea that irony is at the same time impossible, yet, inescapable. This debate, which lies at the centre of Deconstructive criticism, about how there can be 'other' or ironical meanings if all we have are texts, is described at length by C. Colebrook in her book *Irony* (2004).

See N. Frye, *Anatomy of Criticism* (1957); A. K. Mellor, *English Romantic Irony* (1980); D. C. Muecke, *Irony and the Ironic* (1983); L. Hutcheon, *Irony's Edge: The Theory and Politics of Irony* (1994).

BCL

K

Katharsis   See CATHARSIS.

Kinetic   See LITERATURE.

L

Lament   See ELEGY.

Language   A concept which was central to one of the major disputes of twentieth-century criticism: does literature consist of language, or is language simply one component of literature? In Aristotle's enumeration of the six parts of tragedy, *lexis* (diction) is merely one component. The CHICAGO CRITICS extended this analysis to poetry, detecting four 'parts' in the lyric, among which 'diction' (= language) was said to be the least important. Elder Olson ('An outline of poetic theory' in R. S. Crane (ed.), *Critics and Criticism*, 1957) speaks of 'such embellishments as rhythm, ornamental language' – other examples of 'ornaments' are masques, pageants, progresses, in drama. Language may be decorative, but it is essentially a means, a medium: 'the words are the least important, in that they are governed and determined by every other element in the poem'.

It is curious that Olson gives unobservable elements, such as 'choice', 'thought' and 'character' priority over language. He does grant that access to these elements is through language, but he seems not to realize the implications of this concession: that apprehension of the abstract structure and meaning of a piece of literature is determined by linguistic arrangements. An intentionalist view of literature might claim that the author's poetic decisions control choice of appropriate language, but this neglects the fact that language, once chosen, is out of the control of the author – it is public property and elicits public responses and perceptions: a word in a poem is not simply the poem's word,

but the language's word also – it imports senses and connotations from contexts external to the poem. Thus, as psycholinguists and semanticists would agree, language controls conceptualization and hence apprehension of poetic structure. This has been the standpoint of the NEW CRITICS: in poetry, 'content' is inaccessible except in the terms laid down by 'form'. And as David Lodge argued (*Language of Fiction*, 1966), there is no good reason to propose a different kind of theory for prose fiction. Language may exercise a particularly stringent control over our responses to lyric poetry because of the FOREGROUNDING of surface structure, but this control, even if less powerful in fiction, cannot be qualitatively different: if language governs meaning, it does so in all its usages.

Although many twentieth-century critics asserted the prime importance of language in literature, they did not wholly agree on this question of different 'uses' of language. I. A. Richards, setting up a Romantic, affective theory of literature, distinguished two uses of language, the 'scientific' or 'referential' versus the 'poetic' or 'emotive'. His claim that only scientific language is used 'for the sake of the *reference*, true or false, that it causes' is an essential preliminary to any theory of the 'fictionality' of literature – truth conditions must be suspended (cf. BELIEF). Another influential literary-theoretical account of 'uses of language' is that propounded by Roman Jakobson. Jakobson distinguishes six uses of language – *emotive* (better, *expressive*), *conative*, *phatic*, *referential*, *metalingual* and *poetic* – according to the degree of importance of different constitutive factors of the communicative event: the referential function, for example, lays stress on the non-linguistic context (the 'world') referred to in communication, minimizing other factors, such as the characteristics of speaker and addressee, and the actual structural form of the utterance. The 'poetic' function, on the other hand, invests attention precisely in the formal linguistic construction; and Jakobson offers a very illuminating formula to explain the structural principle of poetic form. The validity of Jakobson's 'poetic principle' is not at issue here; what is questionable is the classification of 'functions'. A partition of functions of language which sets off the 'poetic' or 'literary' as a separate category can lead to neglect of linguistic features which do not fall under the criterion, and thus to an incomplete apprehension of the literary text (see R. Fowler, *Literature as Social Discourse*, 1981, chs 9 and 10).

Theorists of literature have been increasingly ready to recognize the continuity of linguistic processes within and outside literature. Certainly, there are no *linguistic* criteria for distinguishing literature and non-literature (cf. LITERATURE). The consequence of these decisions – to grant priority to language and to see language in literature as not essentially different from the language of other texts – is that we may feed into literary criticism whatever insights we gain about language at large. Such insights, have been very considerable, resulting in a refined and rich debate over the theory of language; a detailed understanding of the principles of linguistic construction at different levels, particularly syntax and phonology; great strides in empirical knowledge of different languages; significant advances in the understanding of the relations between language and thought, and language and society; and a sophisticated discussion of the relationships between linguistics and adjacent disciplines – education, psychology, sociology, anthropology, politics, artificial intelligence, literary theory, literary criticism. A small selection of good textbooks to give a flavour of various parts of linguistics might include W. Downes, *Language and Society* (1984) and M. A. K. Halliday, *Language as Social Semiotic* (1978).

The linguistic study of literature, known as 'stylistics' or 'linguistic criticism', has advanced in several ways. It built on the work of Mukařovský and of Jakobson to make powerful contributions to literary theory (cf. FORMALISM, STRUCTURALISM). It added substantially to knowledge of some aspects of literary structure which are manifestly linguistic in character (e.g. METAPHOR, METRE); and some less obvious topics, such as SYNTAX, were made more salient to the critic. The best way to sample these diverse contributions would be to browse in some of the collections of specialized papers which have been published, such as R. Carter (ed.), *Language and Literature* (1982).

Linguistic studies have also focussed on specific genres of literary writing. For poetry, see G. N. Leech, *A Linguistic Guide to English Poetry* (1969); M. Riffaterre, *Semiotics of Poetry* (1978). For the novel, see R. Fowler, *Linguistics and the Novel* (2nd edn, 1983); G. N. Leech and M. H. Short, *Style in Fiction* (1981). For drama, see D. Burton, *Dialogue and Discourse* (1980). For a general discussion, see Ronald Carter and Walter Nash, *Seeing Through Language: Guide to Styles of English Writing* (1990).

In the move towards theorizing literature as DISCOURSE language is regarded as far more than formal structure and communicated ideas: it is seen as an interpersonal practice with causes and effects in social structure, and ideological implications. Linguistic criticism on discourse premises is a historically grounded practice of analysis, seeking to interpret texts with reference to their and our cultural contexts and ideological systems. In this approach the analysis of linguistic form, and reference to context, are integrated rather than divorced as in most modern criticism. See R. Fowler, *Literature as Social Discourse* (1981), *Linguistic Criticism* (1986). Also M. L. Pratt, *Toward a Speech Act Theory of Literary Discourse* (1977); A. Easthope, *Poetry as Discourse* (1983); Norman Fairclough, *Language and Power* (1989); Ronald Carter, *Language, Discourse and Literature* (1988); R. L. Trask, *Language: the basics* (2004).

RGF

Lexis   See DICTION, LANGUAGE.

Lisible   See PLEASURE.

Literary mode of production   The concept of a 'literary mode of production' was developed by modern MARXIST CRITICISM to explain the ways in which all literary writings depend upon social institutions and relations. Any form of production draws upon certain material forces (in the case of writing, paper, printing, publishing technology and so on), but these material forces are themselves part of a set of social relations between producers, intermediaries and consumers. The social relations between a tribal bard, chief and audience will differ from those between an eighteenth-century poet, aristocratic patron and readers, and these in turn are contrastable with the often isolated literary producer of our own day, who produces work as a market commodity for a rarely encountered audience. Any society may contain a set of different, even conflicting, literary modes of production: the social relations between the popular modern novelist, publishers and readers contrast with those between the writers, directors, actors and audiences of a regional theatre group. Certain literary modes of production may be merely sub-sectors of what we might term the 'general' mode of economic production in society as a whole: modern-day writing is largely part of the capitalist publishing industry. But other literary modes of production may represent survivals from earlier societies, or may try to prefigure new kinds of social relations in society as a whole.

The concept of a 'literary mode of production' does not merely belong to what is termed the 'sociology of literature'. It is not a purely external fact about literary writing, as the colour of a dustjacket may be. On the contrary, it is part of the critical analysis of literature itself. Every work of literature, in however indirect a fashion, implies how and by whom it was written, and how and by whom it is expected to be read. Every work posits an 'implied author' and an 'implied reader', establishes tacit contracts and alliances between itself and its audience. In order to be accepted as 'literature' at all, the work must be a certain kind of product within certain social institutions; most critics would not regard graffiti, which is indubitably a mode of writing (often of considerable interest and value) produced for an audience, as an acceptable literary topic for academic study. What counts as 'literature', in other words, is already a matter of social (and ideological) definition; a piece of writing may be 'literary' for one age and not for another. 'Non-literary' writing may be treated in a 'literary' way, or *vice versa*.

The very definitions and criteria of 'literature', then, belong to a set of values and ideas embedded in a literary mode of production. In turn, the values and social relations of that mode of production will leave their imprint on the works it produces. It is thus very difficult to distinguish an 'external', historical study of literary works from an 'internal', critical one. See also CREATION, CRITICISM, LITERATURE.

See T. Eagleton, *Criticism and Ideology* (1976); P. Macherey, *A Theory of Literary Production* (1978).

TE

Literature In present times generally taken to be imaginative compositions, mainly printed but earlier (and still, in some cultures) was oral, whether dramatic, metrical or prose in form. This is a relatively recent usage, having general acceptance in the European languages only from the nineteenth century. Earlier senses have been less restricted: for example, the body of writings in a language, artistic or not; and particularly, the *study* of such a corpus of written materials. For an account of the history of the term, see René Wellek, 'The name and nature of comparative literature' in *Discriminations* (1970), especially pp. 3–13.

No 'discovery procedure' is needed for literature. Borderline cases are easier to resolve than at first appears, and their manner of resolution is instructive. William McGonagall may be a bad poet, but he is clearly a poet: there is craftsmanship, a sense of tradition, even if both qualities are precariously fulfilled in his work. (We can say he is a poor artist, but that is not the same as asserting that he is not an artist: EVALUATION is quite independent of identification as literature.) But the telephone book, though highly structured, fails to be literature because it is 'real' – a list of people, addresses, numerical codes for calling these actual people. Contrast Scott Fitzgerald's list of Gatsby's visitors in *The Great Gatsby* (1925),

a parodic manipulation in art of a form from everyday life. So the criteria seem to be of different kinds, some formal and some existential; but they apply fairly clearly in individual cases.

We may seek the characteristics of literature from many points of view, some intrinsic and some extrinsic. Extrinsically, we will certainly want to regard it as a definite cultural institution, an interrelated set of SEMIOTIC systems. We can note the values a society assigns to its literature: these vary from society to society and from age to age, ranging from seriousness and ritual, to frivolity and verbal play (and different GENRES have different expectations). Literature has commonly been distinguished from linguistic ephemera, effort being expended to preserve it in script or oral tradition; it has been regarded as a potent tool in the transmission and preservation of cultural values; it has also often been associated with an elite, either conservative or revolutionary, or with an influential and self-esteeming bourgeoisie. Cultural attitudes towards literature, such as these are empirical: they may be derived from anthropological and sociological observations. A different series of extrinsic criteria involves speculation about the relationship between literature and individuals, society or culture. In relation to authors, works have been claimed to be either *expressive*, gestures from the writer's personal character and perceptions (Longinus, Wordsworth) or, contrariwise, *impersonal*, creations which efface their creators as individuals (Yeats, Eliot, NEW CRITICS). In relation to the reader, literature has been supposed to have many different functions and effects. Theorists who assume impersonality in respect to origin generally assume *stasis* in respect to effect: if the audience is 'moved' by the aesthetic experience, it is not moved to action (so propaganda, PORNOGRAPHY, etc. have not been considered art because they are *kinetic*). On the quality of stasis, the aesthetician would generally concur with the law courts: that which pumps our adrenalin is not art (cf. AUTHOR, READER, ART).

More specific theories of literary EFFECT have been proposed: the various sophistications of a concept of PLEASURE, or I. A. Richards's belief that literature causes stability, harmonization of impulses, in a successful reader (*Principles of Literary Criticism*, 1924), or the doctrine of CATHARSIS, the essentially *harmless release* of emotions. Such theories proliferated in the nineteenth and twentieth centuries: pressed to the extreme, the lead to a belief that literature can cleanse and save society (Arnold, Leavis) – but here the theory undermined itself, since on that interpretation literature hardly differs from propaganda or sermons. If literature is a form of persuasion (as the RHETORICAL tradition claims) there must be supplementary criteria specifying exactly what kind of persuasion it is – for example, persuasion to adopt a certain 'world-view' but not persuasion literally to *fight* to change the world.

Fictionality is one such criterion (see FICTION, IMITATION). Evidently literature 'imitates', 'depicts', 'represents', 'presents', 'embodies' people, objects, societies, ideas: Mr Micawber, Middlemarch, Howards End, Camus's plague. Literature is not alone in this respect – the telephone book, an inventory of the contents of a house, the service manual for a car, are also representational. But if someone's neighbours listed in the directory enjoy spatio-temporal existence, Mr Micawber does not; thus the concept of imitation is different for *David Copperfield* and for the telephone directory. Fiction is *creative*: its creations are felt to be real,

but are actually abstract and therefore cannot be said so easily to impinge on one's worldly experience. Literature is irresponsible in the sense of amoral. Compare Archibald Macleish's dictum that a poem must be 'equal to: not true' (*Ars Poetica*). Considerations of truth and reality are not relevant to literature; but my car handbook *must* be true, since it is designed to guide actions.

On the basis of such observations, literature is traditionally distinguished from science, history, philosophy, etc. Literature is at the same time like the other arts (in terms of FORM or STRUCTURE) and unlike them (in terms of LANGUAGE). Now we appeal to intrinsic criteria, and 'poem' creeps in as the general term, inviting us to substitute a focus on the individual literary construct for the 'extrinsic' focus on literature as a cultural institution or as an influence on the psyche. 'Poem' retains its etymological connotations (Greek *poesis*, 'making') and evokes the literary work as a 'made thing', an artefact, a single, unique, construct; a hard enduring object (and not a pale reflection of something else). As soon as we have achieved a definite conception of the poem as a single, coherent, aesthetic object, we are instantly involved in ontological speculations: what mode of being does a literary work enjoy? Is it, in fact, an independent entity, or is it located in, for example, the writer's or reader's consciousness? (see EFFECT, INTENTION, LANGUAGE). If it has a mode of separate being, what are its 'internal' characteristics? Various styles of criteria have found fashion in attempts at the intrinsic definition of literature or of particular kinds of literature. The CHICAGO CRITICS avoided an overall definition, but erected a scheme of 'parts', abstract structural components (CHARACTER, DICTION, PLOT, etc.); a particular selection from this set of components, in an appropriate order of importance, serving to define the nature of each GENRE. Thus the complete field of literature is, allegedly, mapped out by a set of characterizations of the genres. The intrinsic quality (if it exists) remains undefined. A quite different approach, though dependent on equally abstract notions, results from assuming that any literary work is literary by virtue of possessing certain qualities which are common to the arts as a whole (cf. AESTHETICS, and the recommended reading below): 'balance', 'composition', 'structure' and so on. However, a definition of literature derived from general aesthetics would certainly have to be augmented by criteria which make reference to the linguistic medium.

The search for intrinsic linguistic criteria intensified in Russian, Czech and French Formalism and Structuralism, with writers, such as Jakobson, Mukařovský, Todorov and Culler making illuminating claims. The ideas are dealt with in the articles on FORMALISM, STRUCTURALISM, and particularly POETICS, which also list major titles for further reading.

The majority of contemporary critics are of the opinion that literature as such cannot be adequately defined, though its previous definitions can be analysed in terms of their cultural and ideological assumptions. 'Literature' thus appears more as a descriptive term that refers to texts which are deemed to have certain intrinsic family resemblances that enable them to be discussed for extrinsic purposes under the heading, though 'fictionality' is not a reliable measure with which to decide whether a text will institutionally or more generally be considered to be 'literature'.

For the older traditions, see M. C. Beardsley, *Aesthetics: Problems in the Philosophy of Criticism* (1958);

M. Bradbury and D. J. Palmer (eds), *Contemporary Criticism* (1970); E. Vivas and M. Krieger (eds), *The Problems of Aesthetics* (1953); M. Weitz (ed.), *Problems in Aesthetics* (2nd edn, 1970); R. Wellek and A. Warren, *Theory of Literature* (3rd edn, 1963); W. K. Wimsatt, Jr and C. Brooks, *Literary Criticism: A Short History* (1957); Peter Widdowson, *Literature* (1998).

RGF

Logocentrism According to the deconstructive critic Jacques Derrida, the history of Western thought has always been governed by a belief in certain fundamental and eternal truths. Serving as a ground or foundation, these truths provide the basis for all stable meaning. The term coined by Derrida to designate such a belief is logocentrism. From the ancient Greek, *logos* signifies word, speech and reason but is now understood more broadly to refer to any extra-systemic point of reference that functions as the origin of meaning and truth. Thus, the logos can assume many forms including Reason, God, Self, Being and Truth. Whatever form it takes, its role is always the same: to act as a fixed guarantee of meaning. Consider, for example, the interpretive strategies of traditional literary criticism. Firmly embedded within the history of logocentrism, many readers still see the author as a logos presiding over his or her work. Acting as a centre, or foundation, this author is presumed to be both the starting point and final destination for any reading of the text.

Two of the most important characteristics of the logos are captured within the synonymous phrase 'transcendental signified'. As the term transcendental suggests, the logos exists independently of and outside all of the various systems that govern our thoughts. Above all, the logos exists independently of language. Indeed, according to a logocentric way of thinking, the logos is the one signified (mental concept) that has no need for a signifier (spoken or written word). Both self-sufficient and self-determining, it remains untouched by the play of linguistic DIFFERENCES by which meaning is articulated (see STRUCTURALISM). As a pure signified, the logos is a site of unadulterated PRESENCE. More generally, Western thought is not only logocentric but also phonocentric (phono = voice), consistently privileging speech over writing as a vehicle of truth.

It is important to recognize that the logos has a key role to play in the relationship between language and meaning. Language, according to Derrida, is the product of difference and deferral. If, for example, we consider a dictionary definition of a particular signifier, we find not a final or definitive signified, only more signifiers and signifieds that led, in turn, to others. As this analogy suggests, meaning is constantly deferred and disseminated throughout the language system. Yet, as Derrida suggests in *Of Grammatology* (1976), the role of the logos is to 'place a reassuring end to the reference from sign to sign'. Thus the logos holds out the promise of linguistic stability. It is this promise, the very basis of logocentricism, that has been called into question by DECONSTRUCTION and, more generally, POST-STRUCTURALISM. In one of Derrida's most often quoted statements, he asserts that 'there is no outside-text'. While not denying the concept of reality, he insists that we have no access to it except via language. In other words, all of our thoughts, perceptions and knowledge are filtered through language. Thus nothing, including the logos, escapes the play of differences that disrupts any simple notion of self-present meaning.

Once Derrida has demonstrated that the logos is implicated in the play of differences, that is, language, it is robbed of its transcendental status and can no longer function as the origin and guarantee of meaning. In short, the logos is revealed to be nothing more than an illusion. As a result, we live in a decentred universe, devoid of any authorizing ground or foundation. Within such a universe, Truth is replaced by interpretation and fixed meaning becomes multiple and contingent. Thus, it is hardly surprising that, within the logocentric tradition, the pull of the logos remains powerful and we continue to crave the security it offers. Yet, Derrida and other recent critics suggest that such a development should be viewed positively, not negatively. Rather than being haunted by the loss of the logos and a desire to find a substitute, we should embrace the ensuing play of language and meaning as affirmative. Indeed, one might argue that the logocentric belief in stable meanings and ultimate truths actually limits our interpretations of literary texts by assuming that there is a single meaning waiting to be discovered. In contrast, Derrida's notion of decentring liberates the reader by opening the text up to multiple, diverse and even contradictory readings. See also DECONSTRUCTION and PRESENCE.

See M. McQuillan (ed.), *Deconstruction: A Reader* (2000); N. Royle (ed.), *Deconstructions: A User's Guide* (2000).

JA

Lyric That the lyric was originally a song set to the lyre, and later to other musical instruments, is worth remembering now only because the post-Renaissance lyric, or lyrical passage, though not often intended to be sung, nevertheless tends to be relatively mellifluous in sound and rhythm and to have a flowingly repetitious syntax that lends itself to expansive, often exclamatory, expressions of intense personal joy, sorrow or contemplative insight. A sixteenth-century English example is Thomas Wyatt's 'Fforget not yet', from which these two verses are taken:

> Fforget not yet the gret assays,
> The cruell wrong, the skornfull ways,
> The paynfull pacyence in denays.
> Fforget not yet!
>
> Fforget not yet, forget not thys,
> How long ago hathe ben and ys
> The mynd, that neuer ment amys,
> Fforget not yet.

The lyric poem, usually short, was often constructed on a single mood. But the twentieth-century lyric is frequently more complex, allowing for contrastive themes and for changes, even ambivalences, of attitude, though remaining in an emotional rather than intellectual mode. A contemporary example, by the Irish poet Richard Weber, shows a technical relationship with Wyatt's song but greater complexity:

> As my eyes moved thoughtfully
> Over your face
> And your eyes moved thoughtlessly
> Into place
> I knew that all I could not say
> Had been said before
> And left no trace.

British poetry has on the whole developed in the direction Walter Pater suggested (favourable to lyricism) rather than in that which Matthew Arnold suggested (favourable to the long poem). Life seen as a sequence of intensely felt moments, rather than a structure of interrelated and assessed experiences, tends to encourage the use of the first person, vivid images and 'local life' at the expense of architectonics, anecdotal narrative and intellectual abstraction. The effect on criticism or on poetry (even the longest twentieth-century poems tend to be fragmentary, like 'The Waste Land', or built out of poem-sequences, like Ted Hughes's 'Crow') makes it desirable to redress the balance by suggesting that the pressure of feeling *and* intellect which the long poem accommodates has considerable force due to the fact that, while it can avail itself of all the devices of lyricism, the long poem builds up, in addition, a larger structure of controlling tensions and so may achieve a more inclusive intensity than that afforded by isolated 'peak moments'.

See H. J. C. Grierson, *Lyrical Poetry of the Nineteenth Century* (1929); C. M. Ing, *Elizabethan Lyrics* (1951); J. L. Kinneavy, *A Study of Three Contemporary Theories of Lyric Poetry* (1957); Norman Maclean, 'From action to image: theories of the lyric in the eighteenth century' in R. S. Crane (ed.), *Critics and Criticism* (1952); Edwin Muir, *The Estate of Poetry* (1962); Gilbert Murray, *The Classical Tradition in Poetry* (1930); Roland Arthur Greene, *Post-Petrarchism: Origins and Innovations of the Western Lyric Sequence* (1991).

AAAC

M

Magical (magic) realism The term magical realism (*Magischer Realismus*) had its first use in 1925 in German art critic Franz Roh's attempt to define a return to a more realistic style after the abstraction of EXPRESSIONISM.

The movement against Expressionism also involved the so-called New Objectivity movement (*Neue Sachlichkeit*). Both movements were generated by the urge to revisit the neglected possibilities of realism, obscured or dismissed by movements such as Expressionism. They argued for a sparser, clearer form of representation than Expressionism and so had an influence on the work of politically engaged artists, such as George Grosz. At the same time and entwined with this political engagement was a formalist impulse to use realism to expose the inner strangeness of objects. This latter element of the movement emphasized the alienation at the heart of modern experience, its uncanny quality (or *unheimlichkeit* to use Freud's term). It emphasized the urge to perceive reality as in some sense unreal, and the unreal as in some sense embodying the real.

Roh's foundational essay was translated into Spanish by Ortega y Gasset in 1927 and so the term entered the aesthetic vocabulary of both peninsular Spain and the Latin American and Caribbean diasporas. Latin American narrative already had a long history of engagement with the marvelous and the fabulous in texts through the late nineteenth and early twentieth centuries, well before the emergence of the term onto the wider stage of world criticism with the phenomenal success of the English translation of Columbian novelist Gabriel Garcia Marquez's *One Hundred Years of Solitude* in 1967.

In the Caribbean, too, the work of Haitian writer and critic Jacques Stephen Alexis had been instrumental in introducing the term to the post-colonial task of combining the recording force of realism with a recovery of the central role of the fabulous and mythic in indigenous cultures, dismissed by colonial aesthetic preoccupations. Alexis's essay 'Of the magical realism of the Haitians' (1956) sought to reconcile the arguments of postwar radical intellectuals in the post-colonial world who favoured social realism as a tool of revolutionary social representation with the recognition that in many post-colonial societies a largely pre-industrial, peasant society still had its imaginative life and identity rooted in a living tradition of the mythic and the magical. This was also obviously true for the displaced indigenous populations of settler, colonial societies. Examples of the influence of this concern in fiction include Salman Rushdie's *Midnight's Children* (India), Ben Okri's *The Famished Road* (Nigeria) and Thomas King's *Green Grass, Running Water* (Canada).

In this post-colonial context, the social and political dimension of the use of the mythic is emphasized. For example, the Cuban, Marxist novelist Alejo Carpentier in his definition argues that in South America and the Caribbean, Magical Realism (*Real Maravillos*) reflects the shifting, transformative, ever-changing native world and even its very tropical landscape, which becomes for him a symbol of the power of the colonized and oppressed to act as a revolutionary force and to resist and dismantle the static, fixed and conservative force of European aesthetic and politic force.

Despite these politicized readings of the form of magical realism, following the so-called 'Boom' period of magical realism in the 1960s and the overactive promotion by publishers and distributors of novels which employed the form, some post-colonial critics attacked it as having become a means of reinforcing stereotypes of the post-colonial world as an exoticized Other.

At the same time, and perhaps under the increasing tendency of post-colonial texts to 'write back to the centre', in Salman Rushdie's phrase, European and American writers began to explore the ways in which reality could be opened up and shown to be a gloss on the more complex forces at work in the so-called 'rational' societies of the post-Enlightenment period in their own backyards. Genres, such as the Gothic and Science Fiction had already posed just such a critique of post-enlightenment rationality, as had psychological fiction from a different perspective, but now the concept of 'magical realism' asserted that the interaction of realism and the supra-rational was the mode which might best allow us to explore the complexities and contradictions of all late twentieth-century societies. See also REALISM.

See J. S. Alexis, 'Of the magical realism of the Haitians' in *Présence Africaine* (1956); Maria-Elena Angulo, *Magic Realism, Social Context and Discourse* (1995); Jean-Pierre Durix, *Mimesis, Genres and Post-Colonial Discourse: Deconstructing Magic Realism* (1998); Franz Roh, *Nach-Expressionismus. Magischer Realismus. Probleme der neuesten Europäischen Malerei* (1925); Lois Parkinson Zamora and Wendy B. Faris (eds), *Magical Realism: Theory, History, Community* (1995).

GG

Mannerism Has three different, but related usages: as a fairly narrow stylistic term; as a historical period; as a broad literary mode.

A mannered style is marked by obtrusive 'mannerisms' or peculiarities: often an elaborate syntax and elevated diction, remote from a colloquial register. Since the manner remains the same irrespective of the matter, the twin dangers of monotony and bathos threaten. Mannered writers, such as Sir Thomas Browne or Walter Pater, are better taken in small doses. But a mannered style, in drawing attention to presentation as distinct from representation, may bring aesthetic gains.

By analogy with the mannerist painting of the late-sixteenth and early-seventeenth centuries, mannerism may, as a term for a 'period', designate the transition between Renaissance and Baroque literature. The widespread mannered styles of the period, such as Euphuism and Gongorism, might be called mannerist, rather than just mannered.

As a literary mode rather than a period, mannerism largely overlaps with BAROQUE. Indeed E. R. Curtis substituted mannerism for baroque altogether, but extended its reference to mean the dialectical antithesis of classicism, in whatever period. He defined mode in terms of style. Mannerist style is hermetic and ingenious, full of paradox and puns, asyndeton, hyperbole and pleonasm. For other critics mannerism means, more dubiously, a style reflecting a psychological type or sociological pressures. The mannerist spirit is calculating, yet, passionate, disharmonious and modern. In English literature the METAPHYSICAL poets are the archetypal mannerists and parallels are drawn or denied between seventeenth- and twentieth-century mannerism, as, for example, in Joyce. The term has suffered from the reductive tendency of all such vast generalizations.

See E. R. Curtius, trans. W. Trask, *European Literature and the Latin Middle Ages* (1953); John M. Steadman, *Redefining a Period Style: 'Renaissance', 'Mannerist' and 'Baroque' in Literature* (1991); John Greenwood, *Shifting Perspectives and the Stylish Style: Mannerism in Shakespeare and His Jacobean Contemporaries* (1988).

EJB

Manners   Literature has nearly always sought to define the relationship between character and environment. The social context of behaviour makes visible the inner conflicts of individuals. Thus Hamlet's antic posturing is defined not only against his soliloquizing but also against the *manners* of the court. This becomes of more central importance when the society represented is *aware* of the rules by which it exists; when they have attained the status of social conventions. Societies create patterns of behaviour by which success or failure can be measured, and the writer, too, must react to these either by conforming to them or by attacking and exposing them. These conventions are most revered in periods of high social mobility, when outward behaviour becomes the 'sign' of personal success and social respectability. In such periods literature may become preoccupied with the recording of mannerisms and behaviour patterns, for example, in some Victorian novels, such as those of Mrs Gaskell.

The term *manners* is most frequently employed in the phrase 'comedy of manners', usually referring to Restoration comedy (Etherege, Wycherley, Congreve) and sometimes by analogy to the work of writers like Oscar Wilde. These plays explore a universe where all values are bound up with appearances, where honour is synonymous with reputation and truth identified with a glib tongue and a steady eye. The veil of conventions shields the action from anarchy and despair. By their success or failure at society's intricate play, characters separate into true wits or gulls. They learn to live with the precarious balance of forces which govern the way of their worlds. See also CULTURE, SOCIETY.

GG

Marxist criticism   Is distinguished from all forms of idealist, FORMALIST and aestheticist criticism by its belief that 'Literature' is a social and material practice, related to other social practices, and finally explicable only in these terms. It differs from other historical or sociological approaches to literature mainly in its view of the nature of history itself. For Marxism, 'history' does not form a single category or seamless whole: it is grasped, rather, as a field of conflicting interests and forces (cf. CONTRADICTION). Dominant among those conflicts is the epochal struggle between social classes – between those who, by virtue of controlling a society's economic production, can usually dominate its cultural and intellectual production as well, and those exploited classes whose labour makes this privileged situation possible in the first place.

In such class societies, all intellectual production is likely to bear the indelible print of these fundamental material struggles; and in so far as it does, it can be said to be 'ideological'. 'Literature' is for Marxism a particular kind of signifying practice, which together with other such practices goes to make up what may be termed an ideological formation. Such a formation is always complex and contradictory, but it is never innocent. Its impulse is to stabilize and unify the various meanings, values and representations in which a society lives out its own experience, in ways which help to secure and reproduce the power of its ruling class. 'Literature', then, might be said to represent the class struggle at a specific level; in writing, reading, interpreting and evaluating we are already, consciously or not, engaged in a struggle over linguistic meanings which is intimately related to systems of power.

'Vulgar Marxist' criticism accepted this conclusion with a vengeance, reducing literary texts to a mere reflex or symptom of history, content to determine the political 'tendency' of the work. The major traditions of Marxist criticism, however, while firmly locating literature in its historical context, nevertheless granted it a high degree of 'relative autonomy'. It is never merely a 'reflection' or 'expression' of historical forces, but a specific, highly codified social practice with its own conditions of material production and reception (cf. LITERARY MODE OF PRODUCTION), its own conventions, devices and histories (cf. CREATION). Its ideological significance is to be sought not merely in its abstractable political content, but more rewardingly in its *forms* – in its narrative structures and generic rules, its habits of language and characterization, its modes of imagery and technical mechanisms. 'History' and 'ideology' are not merely the extraneous outworks of a literary text: as the intimately informing pressures at work within its very capacity to signify, they are constitutive of its very being.

Historically speaking, Marxist criticism might be roughly if conveniently divided into two main types. On the one

hand, has been what one might broadly term a *genetic* criticism, concerned to relate the literary work to its historical and ideological conditions of possibility. The scattered literary writings of Marx and Engels themselves, drawing as they do on the aesthetics of Hegel, fall into this category, as do Lenin's well-known articles on Leo Tolstoy, or Trotsky's sensitive accounts of his Russian poetic contemporaries. The eminent Hungarian Marxist critic Georg Lukács also belongs to this lineage: his work aims to identify the complex relations between certain historical epochs and the rise and fall of certain literary forms, such as REALISM. The great bourgeois realists, still able to 'totalize' history into a complex significance by deploying characters and events at once sharply individuated and historically 'typical', give way at a point of political crisis to the disturbed, private, more fragmentary forms of MODERNISM. In the work of Lukács's disciple Lucien Goldmann, Marxist and STRUCTURALIST themes are interwoven to provide a similarly genetic account of the flourishing of French seventeenth-century tragedy.

Lukács and Goldmann inhabit an Hegelian, 'humanistic' current of Marxism for which many of the traditional categories of bourgeois aesthetics (unity, truth, beauty and so on) are still valid. The later work of Louis Althusser, Pierre Macherey and others has interrogated these assumptions, grasping the literary text as divided, uneven and contradictory, forced by its complicities with ideology into certain revealing gaps, silences and absences whereby it 'deconstructs' itself and betrays its ideological hand. Such critics have also been more concerned with literature as a form of analysable 'production' than an author-centred 'creation'.

But for both Lukács and Althusser, 'Literature' itself remains a largely unproblematic term – as it does indeed for the Hegelian Marxists of the German Frankfurt School (notably Theodor Adorno and Herbert Marcuse), who find in the very forms of art a spiritual transcendence of class-bound society. They differ thus from the second major Marxist cultural heritage, which concerns itself less with the genesis of the artwork than with its political uses and effects, less with the literary product itself than with the social relations and cultural institutions from which it emerges. The aim of this tradition is to transform or dismantle the very meaning of the term 'literature' by transforming the material means of cultural production in society as a whole. Prominent among such revolutionary cultural workers were the Bolshevik avant-garde artists (Futurists, Formalists, Constructivists, etc.) of the 1920s, who sought not merely a new meaning in art but a new meaning *of* art, fashioning new social relations between artists and audiences, collapsing the barriers between art and social life, and insisting on new media of cultural communication. Crushed by Stalinism, their great inheritors were the revolutionary artists and critics of Weimar Germany (Erwin Piscator, Bertolt Brecht, Walter Benjamin), and to some degree the Marxist SURREALISTS of France gathered around André Breton.

More recent Marxist criticism has revived or sustained these influences, rejecting some timeless notion of the 'literary' for an insistence that what counts as 'literary' in the first place is always a matter of ideological and institutional definition. The work of Raymond Williams in England has been central in this respect. But other influences have been at work too: PSYCHOANALYSIS (how are readers constituted as collective or individual subjects by the unconscious meanings of literary texts, and in what

political direction?); 'reception theory' in a political context; and SEMIOTICS and sociolinguistics (the understanding of literary works as social codes and DISCOURSES, inseparable from ideological modes of perception). For later Marxist criticism, there is no isolated 'literature' to be ideologically examined; what we have instead is a set of LITERARY MODES OF PRODUCTION, embedded in the dominant social relations of capitalism, which may themselves be transformed by political practice to produce new meanings of 'literature' and new audiences. The literary works of the past must be studied in their historical conditions; but, more importantly, they must be constantly rewritten, in order to be put to different kinds of political use. See IDEOLOGY

See further H. Arvon, *Marxist Esthetics* (1973); L. Baxandall and S. Morawski (eds), *Marx and Engels on Literature and Art* (1973); W. Benjamin, *Illuminations* (1973), *One-Way Street and Other Essays* (1979), *Understanding Brecht* (1973); T. Bennett, *Formalism and Marxism* (1979); P. Demetz, *Marx, Engels and the Poets* (1967); T. Eagleton, *Marxism and Literary Criticism* (1976); F. Jameson, *Marxism and Form* (1971); R. Taylor (ed.), *Aesthetics and Politics* (1977); V. N. Voloshinov, *Marxism and the Philosophy of Language* (1973); R. Williams, *Marxism and Literature* (1977); Gary Day, *Class* (2001); Terry Eagleton, *Marxism and Literary Criticism* (2002).

TE

Mask   See PERSONA.

Metafiction   See FICTION.

Metaphor   Like simile is easier to illustrate than to define. In the phrase

> The barge she sat in, like a burnish'd throne
> Burn'd on the water

as well as much else, there is both a metaphor, 'the barge...burn'd on the water', and a simile, 'the barge...like a burnish'd throne'.

In general, a metaphor ascribes to some thing or action X a property Y which it could not literally possess in that context. Responding to this anomaly, the hearer or reader infers that what is meant is that X is Z, where Z is some property suggested by Y, X or the interaction of the two, that can be literally true of X in some context. A simile, using one of several possible syntactic devices of comparison (...as...as,...like..., etc.) states explicitly that there is a similarity (Z) between X and Y though it usually does not state explicitly what this similarity is, and thus the hearer is likewise forced to infer what Z might be in that context.

The study of metaphor generates a great deal of terminology, often itself metaphorical. The most firmly established terms for describing a metaphor are perhaps those of I. A. Richards (*The Philosophy of Rhetoric*, 1936) and Max Black (*Models and Metaphors*, 1962). Richards describes a metaphor as resulting from the interaction of a 'vehicle' and a 'tenor...the underlying idea or principal subject which the vehicle or figure means'. 'Tenor' seems to be used by Richards (as Black points out) to mean either X, or the proposition that X is Z, while 'vehicle' seems to correspond to Y. Black himself uses 'principal subject' (X) and 'subsidiary subject' (Y), more recently, 'primary' and 'secondary' subject ('More about metaphor', 1979).

Metaphors as elliptical comparisons

There is a tradition, traceable to Aristotle, which maintains that there is no important logical difference between metaphors and similes, and that metaphors can be regarded as either similes or literal comparisons with the explicit comparative particles suppressed. Against this view many people feel that, in the first place, metaphors are usually more effective than similes or comparisons, suggesting that there is a real difference between them (Black, 'More about metaphor'), or further, that there is a distinction to be drawn between them in terms of their truth conditions (and thus a difference of meaning). Thus, J. R. Searle argues that a sentence like 'Richard is a gorilla' might say something true about Richard (namely that he is coarse and brutal) whereas in reality, gorillas could be charming and gentle in their behaviour, making 'Richard resembles a gorilla in his behavior' false (Searle, 'Metaphor').

The paraphrasability of metaphors

We usually find no difficulty in paraphrasing dead metaphors (those which have become wholly or partly lexicalized, like 'tying up a few loose ends' or 'swim like a fish'), but the consensus seems to be that fully satisfactory paraphrase of a live and effective metaphor is not generally possible (see especially Davidson, 'What metaphors mean'). This is often taken to argue against the 'truncated simile' view, and Davidson, in particular, claims that metaphors have not just an elusive or incomplete literal meaning, but no meaning at all, over and above their false or anomalous one. To the extent that this view rests on the difficulty of satisfactory paraphrase, it would, of course, be more convincing if our experience was not that paraphrase of ordinary literal sentences is often difficult to achieve to everyone's satisfaction.

Creativity and interaction

The view that metaphors work by a process of 'interaction' between X and Y is a popular one, and surely true, though the precise nature of this interaction needs further clarification. There is a stronger thesis, argued for by Black, that metaphors are 'creative', by which he means that rather than just drawing our attention to some similarity already existing, they 'create' a new similarity (a possibility which, ironically, his own theory finds it difficult to accommodate; cf. Paul Ricoeur, 'The metaphorical process as cognition, imagination and feeling'). It is certainly the case that people can often find some aspect to the interpretation of a word in a metaphor that they may not be able to find in the word in isolation. But as we have no very good way of delimiting what counts as part of the 'meaning' of a word, it is difficult to know whether this is evidence for the creativity thesis, or for the view that there is no sharp distinction between word meaning and factual belief. This is complicated by the fact that people are inclined to say retrospectively that the aspect of meaning focussed on in the metaphor may well have been an unnoticed regular part of the meaning of the word. If there are cases where the meaning of a metaphor is not derivable from the meanings of the words in it, it may well be that the meaning is derived from the mechanisms of conversational implicature (see H. P. Grice, 'Logic and conversation' in P. Cole and J. L. Morgan (eds), *Syntax and Semantics* Vol. 3, *Speech Acts* (1975)).

The literature on metaphor is massive. T. Hawkes, *Metaphor* (1972), oriented towards literary approaches, is a useful starting point. Alongside Paul Ricoeur *The Rule of Metaphor: The Creation of Meaning in Language* (1986), the books by Richards and by Black cited above are classics, which have each generated a large secondary literature. Useful collections are A. Ortony (ed.), *Metaphor and Thought* (1979) and S. Sacks (ed.), *On Metaphor* (1979). The articles in Ortony

(which has a large bibliography) are views from Anglo-American linguistics, philosophy and psychology; included are the papers by Black and by Searle cited above. Sacks represents a variety of literary and philosophical standpoints, and includes Davidson's and Ricoeur's papers. Though dated, Christine Brooke-Rose, *A Grammar of Metaphor* (1958) is a useful work on the syntax of metaphorical expressions in literature. A helpful primer is Zoltan Kovecses, *Metaphor: A Practical Introduction* (2002). See also SIMILE.

SGP

Metaphysical Dr Johnson's observation in *The Life of Cowley* (1779) that 'about the beginning of the seventeenth century appeared a race of writers that may be termed the metaphysical poets' gave currency to a label that is convenient though imprecise. Before Johnson, Dryden had remarked in 1693 that Donne's love poetry 'affects the metaphysics', and in Donne's own lifetime William Drummond of Hawthornden complained of a new poetical fashion for 'Metaphysical Ideas and Scholastical Quiddities'. The twentieth-century interest in this 'race of writers', which after Donne includes Herbert, Crashaw, Vaughan and Marvell, was promoted chiefly by H. J. C. Grierson's anthology, *Metaphysical Lyrics and Poems of the Seventeenth Century* (1921) and by T. S. Eliot's essay, 'The metaphysical poets', originally a review of that anthology. Modern admiration for the intellectual agility and stylistic complexity of this poetry, for its analytical and ironic modes, makes a curious contrast with the disparaging overtones originally attached to the term 'metaphysical'. But the rediscovery of the metaphysicals was part of a reaction to the Romantic tradition of nineteenth-century poetry, and T. S. Eliot's critical interest was closely related to the 'modern' qualities of his own poetry in that period.

As Grierson pointed out, 'to call these poets "the school of Donne" or "metaphysical" poets may easily mislead if one takes either phrase in too full a sense'. Direct imitation of Donne is not the main feature of most metaphysical poetry, nor is it 'metaphysical' in the sense of being philosophical. It is essentially the poetry of 'wit', in the seventeenth-century sense of wit as the capacity to recognize similarity in disparity, and to combine playfulness with seriousness. Thus, the metaphysical CONCEIT, of which the best-known example is Donne's comparison of two lovers to a pair of compasses (in 'A valediction forbidding mourning') turns upon a surprising and ingenious analogy between apparently unrelated areas of experience. It is produced not by the arbitrariness of free association or the irrational process of the unconscious mind, but by the alertness of a mind accustomed to think in terms of correspondences and to reason by analogy. In this respect the 'metaphysic' underlying metaphysical poetry is a traditional but by then obsolescent conception of an ordered universe in which correspondences were held to exist between all planes of being. The metaphysical conceit, of which Dr Johnson said that 'the most heterogeneous ideas are yoked by violence together', characteristically forms part of an ingeniously paradoxical argument in which immediacy of feeling is apprehended through conceptual analogies rather than in sensory images.

Other notable features of metaphysical poetry include a dramatic sense of situation, a plain rather than ornate diction, an elliptical and condensed syntax, a strong tension between the symmetries of metrical form and the asymmetrical rhythms of speech and thought, and a capacity for abrupt shifts of tone. Not all metaphysical poetry possesses these qualities in the same degree; on the other hand, they are also found in the Jacobean drama, and in the prose of the period. The attempt to produce a consistent or exclusive definition of metaphysical poetry is therefore less profitable than a flexible understanding which obscures neither the distinctions between individual poets nor the properties of 'wit' common to the period as a whole. See also CONCEIT, WIT.

See T. S. Eliot, 'The metaphysical poets' in *Selected Essays* (1961); F. R. Leavis, *Revaluation* (1962); G. Williamson, *The Donne Tradition* (1961); Richard Willmott, *Metaphysical Poetry* (2002); Frances Austin, *The Language of Metaphysical Poets* (1992).

DJP

Metre If we are presented with a sequence of events, we tend to perceive them rhythmically: they seem to fall into patterns, whatever their actual temporal relationships might be. This is true of linguistic experiences. Hearing English sentences, we feel that the most prominent syllables recur at about the same time-interval, regardless of the number of intervening light syllables. VERSE is metered as well as rhythmical: there is a metrical superstructure over the rhythm. An additional level of phonetic organization gathers the rhythmical groups into metrical units-lines. In prose, the rhythm continues sequentially as long as the text lasts, but verse is chopped up into regularly repeated metrical units. (It is a vexing question whether there can be a one-line poem.)

Metre emerges from the numerical control of rhythm: it entails counting. Classical French verse counts syllables;

typically, twelve define the line. Anglo-Saxon counts stresses, four to a line, ignoring the number of light syllables. Modern English measures are based on syllabic *and* stress patterning: the paradigm iambic pentameter has five strong stresses – the even syllables out of a total of ten, with the odd ones light. Classical metres were equally complex – syllables were either long or short, and both were counted. In principle, any phonological feature of a language may provide the basis for metre; but the features available vary from language to language. Length of syllable is phonologically inactive in English, so it makes no sense to talk about long and short syllables in English metres; in fact, conventional prosodic analysis is meaningless in so far as it relies on such terms.

Scansion is analysis of verse lines by stating the distribution of the metrically significant features; it displays the design the poet works to, and a set of idealized expectations by the reader:

x / x / x / x / x /
The Sylphs/thro' mys/tic maz/es, guide! their way.

(Pope)

For a line like this, the reader expects five pairs ('feet') of light and heavy syllables. Actually, the experience is much more complex than this neat up-and-down model suggests. Compare:

Before, behind, between, above, below
(Donne)

Unfolded transitory qualities
(Wordsworth)

both instances of the same verse design, but radically different in texture. In the first, the natural stress-patterns of the words fulfil exactly the reader's prosodic expectations; in the second, the word- and phrase-stresses run against the expected pattern, smoothing out the stress-contrasts of the verse design so that there are only three dominant accents. The Pope line presents a middle stage, a delicate syncopation of the prose rhythm against the verse design. Note the way the words *mystic* and *mazes* run across the foot boundaries, bridging the junctures between the second and third, and third and fourth, feet. The interest of metre, it seems, lies in just this tension of the rhythm of prose played against the more stylized norms of metre. We cannot neglect the normal stress-patterns of speech without destroying meaning; at the same time, we throw our prose experience into fruitful conflict with the regularizing metre. Since the stress-patterns of language are infinitely variable, so is the experience of metrical tension. The complexity of the verse experience demands a proportionately discriminating analytic apparatus. The abstract metrical patterns described and classified by the older historians of metre (G. Sainsbury, *History of English Prosody*, 1906–10; T. S. Osmond, *English Metrists*, 1921) give too little information, failing to capture the intricate interplay between the reader's expectations of verse accents or 'beats' and the linguistic realities of ordinary stress. Very few of the older prosodists managed to convey the 'feel' of verse (Robert Bridges, *Milton's Prosody*, 1921, is a brilliant exception). At the other extreme, pure phonetic expositions of verse performances tell us too much-in the physical detail, we lose the abstract scheme which orders the phonetic facts (see Wilbur Schramm, *Approaches to a Science of Verse*, 1935). Modern techniques of *phonemic* metrical analysis concentrate on a display which seeks to show the tension between prose rhythm and ideal metre. The aim is to present an account of the internal structure of lines as selections from the infinite repertoire of rhythm/verse design juxtapositions which a language affords.

See Seymour Chatman, *A Theory of Meter* (1965); Roger Fowler, ' "Prose rhythm" and metre' in *Essays on Style and Language* (1966); Roger Fowler, 'What is metrical analysis?' in *The Languages of Literature* (1971); Donald C. Freeman (ed.), *Linguistics and Literary Style* (1970) (the last three essays); Morris Halle and Samuel Jay Keyser, *English Stress* (1971); Derek Attridge and Thomas Carper, *Meter and Meaning: Introduction to Rhythm in Poetry* (2003); Jeffrey Wainwright, *Poetry: The Basics* (2004).

RGF

Mimesis See IMITATION, REALISM, TYPICALITY.

Mirror Stage, the In 1936 Jacques Lacan (1901–81) delivered a paper to the International Psychoanalytic Conference at Marienbad which introduced his notion of the mirror phase in the development of the human subject: 'The Mirror Stage in the Formative Function of the I'. The paper was revised in 1949 and later published in the collection, *Écrits* in 1966. The mirror stage (sometimes called 'the mirror phase') occurs between 6 and 18 months, when the infant is still in the neonatal state of dependency, awkward and uncoordinated and without structured language. From this realm, with its instinctual drives and diffuse desires (Lacan calls this the Imaginary), the infant sees itself reflected in 'the mirror' and with delight, recognizes itself; 'this jubilant assumption of the specular image by the child at the *infans* stage [...] would seem to exhibit in an exemplary situation the symbolic matrix in which the *I* is precipitated

in a primordial form', claims Lacan. The polished, objectified reflection of a mirror image is crucial as a symbol or emblem of this stage and its effects, although Lacan is also careful to caution that one should not be too reductive: 'the idea of the mirror should be understood as an object which reflects – not just the visible, but also what is heard, touched and willed by the child'. For Lacan, the stage is the first point at which the subject *misrecognizes itself* as a unified, separate and autonomous individual; the polished surface and the insecure child's anxious projections together present a fiction of the self, to which fallacy, with its inevitable fragmentation, lack and obscurity (to itself as much as to others) it is always striving. Lacan is building on Freud's theories of the unconscious and his tripartite model of the mind (id, ego and super-ego) with its desires, conflicts and repressions. He is also elaborating Freud's theories from a perspective informed by structural linguistics, and, in particular, by Ferdinand de Saussure (1857–1913). Thus, one of Lacan's best known and persistently puzzling pronouncements is that 'the unconscious is structured like a language'.

Above all, however, Lacan was at pains to show that the consoling notion that language was a proficiency acquired and at the service of the will of the individual was just as fictive as the unity of the specular image of the self. Rather, says Lacan, the subject is inserted into a language system and is then spoken from it and by it – at the level of the unconscious and by virtue of lack and desire. Freud's castration and oedipal theories are also revised as Lacan outlines the child's relation to language as part of the complex. As the child moves from the symbiotic closeness with the mother s/he perceives that the mother who had been believed to have/be everything, in fact lacks – and in this lack desires the father (what the father has). It is this apprehension of the complexity of separation, threatened castration (or for the girl, the condition of 'castration'), lack and desire that positions the child in the Symbolic order of language and other conventional, socializing systems. Saussure's influence, particularly his work on semiotics and the linguistic sign (comprised of signifier and signified), can be seen in Lacan's papers 'The function and field of speech and language in psychoanalysis' (1953) and 'The agency of the letter in the unconscious or reason since freud' (1957), as in his work on the Phallus as the Transcendental Signifier in the Symbolic order. See also PHALLOGOCENTRISM.

See Malcolm Bowie, *Lacan* (1991); Elizabeth Grosz, *Jacques Lacan: A Feminist Introduction* (1990); Juliet Mitchell and Jacqueline Rose (eds), *Feminine Sexuality: Jacques Lacan and the École Freudienne* (1985).

SS

Mock-epic In heroic epic, the extraordinary and the trivial can coexist and can be respected as part of one another; the trivial has a reassuring, integrative, anchoring function. However, in mock-epic (e.g. Butler's *Hudibras*, 1662–78; Boileau's *Le Lutrin*, 1674; Pope's *Dunciad*, 1728; Zachariae's *Der Renommist*, 1744) the poet is less interested in an open-minded and discursive treatment than in the delights of intellectual penetration and dismissive speed; the even-paced equanimity of epic narration is leavened with the unmerciful self-assurance of personal satire. In the society the poet portrays, the trivial attempts to usurp the position of the extraordinary but manages only to make its pretensions and unrelieved concern with itself extraordinary;

in mock-epic the ritualistic becomes the fussy, dignity becomes pomposity and respect turns out to be veiled but exasperated familiarity.

Groups are parodied by mock-epic because they suffer from that immaturity and falsity which come from self-satisfaction and from the use of criteria of evaluation peculiar to an essentially parochial society; an obsession with behavioural patterns comes to predominate over any broader, more humane understanding of social activity. The characters are not enlarged by encountering resistance to their wishes – actions have the ease and versatility of game and the gods, unlike Homer's, connive with humanity to the point of subservience (see especially Pope's *The Rape of the Lock*, 1712 and 1714). But in the poet's attitude, too, the satirist's contempt gives way to the virtuoso's unfailingly apt and delightfully varied development of an initial stance; the subject, while never ceasing to be a target, is exploited as an instrument of a self-consciously formal and decorative achievement which, through its own game-like quality, its refusal to impoverish a spade by calling it a spade, becomes itself increasingly exhilarating and life-affirming. Mock-epic is a developed form not so much of sarcasm as of euphemism: it has a paradoxical willingness to 'extract from contemporary life its epic dimension, showing us … how grand and poetic we are in our cravats and highly-polished boots' (Baudelaire).

More recently, mock-epic has functioned less as a generical concept and has instead been limited to the area of language, where it covers most grandiloquent modes. Here it is a *defensive* posture and a necessary guarantee of the poet's desire to establish a plausible relationship between language and a contemporary environment; the image is no longer enhanced by being embedded in a rhetorical syntax allegedly equal to it, but rather is given 'epic' finality by being set against voracious and self-perpetuating dictions. This may account for a cyclical mock-epic like Ted Hughes's *Crow* (1970), a mock-epic of short and complete utterances.

See R. P. Bond, *English Burlesque Poetry, 1700–50* (1932); J. Dixon Hunt (ed.), *Pope – The Rape of the Lock* (1968); Ian Jack, *Augustan Satire* (1952); Gregory G. Colomb, *Designs on Truth: Poetics of Augustan Mock-epic* (1992).

MHP and CS

Modernism Modernist art is, in most critical usage, reckoned to be the art of what Harold Rosenburg calls 'the tradition of the new'. It is experimental, formally complex, elliptical, contains elements of decreation as well as creation, and tends to associate notions of the artist's freedom from realism, materialism, traditional genre and form, with notions of cultural apocalypse and disaster. Its social content is characteristically *avant-garde* or bohemian; hence, specialized. Its notion of the artist is of a futurist, not the conserver of culture but its onward creator; its notion of the audience is that it is foolish if potentially redeemable: 'Artists are the antennae of the race, but the bullet-headed many will never learn to trust their great artists' is Ezra Pound's definition. Beyond art's specialized enclave, conditions of crisis are evident: language awry, cultural cohesion lost, perception pluralized.

Further than this, there are several modernisms: an intensifying sequence of movements from Symbolism on (Post-impressionism, Expressionism, Futurism, Imagism, Vorticism, Dadaism, Surrealism) often radically at odds, and sharp differences of cultural interpretation coming from writers apparently stylistically analogous (e.g. T. S. Eliot and William Carlos Williams). A like technique can be very differently used (e.g. the use of STREAM OF CONSCIOUSNESS in Virginia Woolf, James Joyce and William Faulkner) according to different notions of underlying order in life or art. The post-symbolist stress on the 'hard' or impersonal image (see IMAGISM) can dissolve into the fluidity of Dada or Surrealism or into romantic personalization: while the famous 'classical' element in modernism, emanating particularly from Eliot, its stress on the luminous symbol outside time, can be qualified by a wide variety of political attitudes and forms of historicism.

Modernism means the ruffling of the realistic surface of literature by underlying forces; the disturbance may arise, though, from logics solely aesthetic or highly social. Hence, modernism still remains a loose label. We can dispute about when it starts (French symbolism; decadence; the break-up of naturalism) and when it ends (Kermode distinguishes 'paleo-modernism' and 'neo-modernism' and hence a degree of continuity through to postwar art). We can regard it as a timebound concept (say 1890–1930) or a timeless one (including Sterne, Donne, Villon, Ronsard). The best focus remains a body of major writers (James, Conrad, Proust, Mann, Gide, Kafka, Svevo, Joyce, Musil, Faulkner in fiction; Strindberg, Pirandello, Wedekind, Brecht in drama; Mallarmé, Yeats, Eliot, Pound, Rilke, Apollinaire, Stevens in poetry) whose works are aesthetically radical, contain striking technical innovation, emphasize spatial or 'fugal' as opposed to chronological form, tend towards ironic modes, and involve a certain 'dehumanization of art' (Ortega y Gasset). See also CLASSICISM, DADA, EXPRESSIONISM, IMAGISM, SYMBOL, SURREALISM.

See M. Bradbury and J. Macfarlane (eds), *Modernism* (1976); D. Lodge, *The Modes of Modern Writing* (1977); P. Childs, *Modernism* (2000); J. Goldman, *Modernism, 1910–45* (2004).

MSB

Monody See ELEGY.

Motif See FORM, THEME.

Myth Myths are stories of unascertainable origin or authorship accompanying or helping to explain religious beliefs. Often (though not necessarily) their subject is the exploits of a god or hero, which may be of a fabulous or superhuman nature, and which may have instituted a change in the workings of the universe or in the conditions of social life. Critics value myth positively because of its apparent spontaneity and collectivity, expressing some lastingly and generally satisfying account of human experience. Equally attractive is the apparent universality and timelessness of myth. The tantalizing recurrence of mythic heroes and their exploits, or of natural or animal motifs (the moon or water or serpents or horses) have activated many 'Keys to All Mythologies', of which Frazer's and Jung's gained most favour with literary critics. The work of Northrop Frye, for instance, reflected the influence of Frazer's attempt to explain myths by reference to rituals designed to ensure the continuing fertility of animal and vegetable life; Frye assigned all myths to an appropriate place in the cycle of seasons, with their alternation of barrenness, growth and fruitfulness. Their ubiquitous hero is the corn-god, who passes through stages of growth, decline and death in harmony with the turning year. Literature derives from myth, and literary history recapitulates the process, as it moves through a seasonal cycle in which

appropriate modes and genres are dominant – comedy belongs to summer, tragedy to autumn, and so on.

Frazer's beliefs that 'primitive' societies have literal faith in the efficacy of magic, or adopt totems because they regard themselves as blood relations of the totemic animal, or are ignorant of the connection between sexual relations and birth (wittily exploded by Edmund Leach), are checked by ethnographic work. Frazer's ethnocentrism is paralleled by Frye's; his cyclical system to contain all myths and all literary works as a simultaneous order of the mind projects proclivities for autonomy and timelessness derived from SYMBOLISM or perhaps, in their enthusiastic embrace of universal identical duplication, from the optimism of capitalist technology.

The work of Lévi-Strauss and its approach to mythic universals is more fruitful than Jung's theories in accounting for differences as well as for similarities; STRUCTURALISM does not seek a constant significance for the same motif, but rather a variable meaning dependent on its relation to other symbolic elements within a mythology.

The assumption operating here is that myth is a language designed to communicate thought, amenable to a reconverted form of linguistic analysis; the properties common to all myths are not to be sought at the level of content but at the level of a structure necessary to all forms of communication. Mythic thought is about insoluble paradoxes of experience, which appear as 'gaps' the elements of a mythic message are so arranged as to attempt to mediate the gaps. The essential gap is between nature and culture – nature felt as an undifferentiated continuity and culture as the institution of difference upon which communication (which utilizes it to construct binary pairs) rests; the project of myth is therefore an impossibility. The primary mythic theme is thus a Rousseauistic version of the Fall.

Myth as a language, an abstract, 'contentless' systems of signs, thus becomes closer to literature in a different way; in the words of Geoffrey Hartman, 'literature and myth are both mediators rather than media', presupposing an *absence* – nature, reality, God, eternity. The structuralist approach to myth gives strong impetus to fresh thought about the relations between language and 'the thing itself' in imaginative writing. Myth thus may usefully be approached as an *absence* in literature, all the more potent for being so; Romanticism in particular thrives on making poetry out of the longed-for return of the lost gods and myths of the childhood of the race or the childhood of the individual (the poetry of Hölderlin is its major expression). Joyce's *Ulysses*, Eliot's 'The waste land' and similar works of the same generation also exploit (in a different spirit) the gap between primeval myth and its contemporary parodies and urge a more complex approach than the critical tendency to see the presence of a myth as a sign of its reincarnation, regardless of context.

The structural approach to myth as a form of language also makes manageable the analysis of secular myth – about 'race' or otherness – as a schematic ordering of otherwise unintelligible experience similar in its functioning to language. See also SEMIOTICS, STRUCTURALISM.

See J. G. Frazer, *The Golden Bough* (1923); Northrop Frye, *Anatomy of Criticism* (1957); Geoffrey Hartman, 'Structuralism: the Anglo-American adventure' in Jacques Ehrmann (ed.), *Structuralism* (1970), 137–58; E. Nelson Haves and Tanya Hayes (eds), *Claude Lévi-Strauss. The Anthropologist as Hero* (1970); C. G. Jung, *Archetypes of the Collective Unconscious* (1934; trans. R. F. C. Hull, 1959); Claude Lévi-Strauss, *The Savage Mind* (1966), *The Raw and the Cooked* (1970); Octavio Paz, *Claude Lévi-Strauss* (1971); K. K. Ruthven, *Myth* (1976); Bruce Lincoln, *Theorizing Myth: Narrative, Ideology, and Scholarship* (2000).

MAH

Mythos   See PLOT.

N

Narrative The recounting of a series of facts or events and the establishing of some connection between them. The word is commonly restricted to fiction, ancient epics and romances or modern novels and short stories. In imaginative literature the nature of the link between the reader and the text is crucial, and here the *narrator* becomes important. This may be the author speaking in the author's 'own voice'; the author adopting some role towards the reader, such as an honest friend, a joking companion or a contemptuous enemy; or a 'character' or 'characters' introduced to 'tell the story'. Narrative thus has two overlapping aspects. One is a question of content, the assemblage of material, the nature of the connections implied. The other is rhetorical, how the narrative is presented to the audience. Such questions are in literary criticism apt to be considered exclusively in terms of 'imaginative' literature, but an examination of some non-fictional narratives illuminate the profound and far-reaching power of narrative. The word is used in Scots law for the recital of facts at the beginning of a deed or agreement. The connection between them is their relevance to some declaration of intent. There are no complex rhetorical considerations apart from the legal solemnity of the document which claims demonstrable truth for some state of affairs. Similar kinds of narrative, in which convention suppresses the power of the narrator, are found in accounts of scientific experiments or in do-it-yourself books. When we come to 'scientific' eyewitness reports of journeys or travels, the narrator becomes of great importance, a fact recognized by early travel writers like Captain Dampier who commonly establish their credentials in an Introduction. This key role of the travel narrator has been exploited by satirists and expert rhetorical writers like Lucian, or Swift in *Gulliver's Travels*. Narrative is also of crucial importance in the writing of history: the selection of incidents for recording, the treatment of time and its effects, and the kind of connection which the historian establishes between events. The latter is a mark of the cultural context of the writer and is to a degree outside of conscious control.

All historical narrative seems to take up some position at a point in the scale between the demonstration of limited relationships between discrete events, and the implication of some vast, non-human design. Psychological determinism and Marxist apocalypse are only two of the many narrative styles. The rhetorical aspect of historical narrative is important, for instance the epigrammatic fastidiousness of Tacitus:

> *Ubi solitudinem faciunt, pacem appellant*:
> When they make a desert, they call it peace:

or Churchill's flourishes. In English literature, one of the most fascinating instances of historical narrative, in its content, selection, discussion of time and rhetorical skill, is Gibbon's *Decline and Fall of the Roman Empire* (1776–88). Perhaps the particular characteristic of the mid-eighteenth-century world is the chaotic flux of time and experience. In Gibbon's vast panorama of fifteen centuries, the most lasting imaginative effect on the reader is a sense of the way in which the historian's own mind imposes a pattern on the bewildering uncertainties of events. Poets and writers of fiction have long exploited these characteristics of narrative. A sophisticated example of such expertise, pre-dating the novel, is found at the beginning of Chaucer's 'Troilus and Criseyde':

> For I, that god of Loves servaunts serve,
> Ne dar to Love, for myn unlyklinesse,
> Preyen for speed, al sholde I therefor
> sterve...[*help...even if...I die*]

If this poem was read out by Chaucer to a courtly audience, the distinction between the poet, an individual of worldly accomplishment, and this narrator who does not 'dar to Love' must have been a witty gesture, and of importance to the narrative. There is an added complication in the tone, since Chaucer ironically makes the narrative voice describe itself in the same terms as the Pope did in a papal bull, 'the servant of the servants of God'. Defoe's *Robinson Crusoe* (1719) is archetypal both in the fictional development of the narrative, and in the rhetoric of the employment of a narrator, Crusoe himself. A shadowy 'editor' appears in the introduction, and the book is thus an early example of the framework of 'journals' found in drawers and desks, a popular 'realistic' device in the next century. As far as *Moll Flanders* (1722) is concerned, controversy has long raged about whether the moral doctrine, which Moll as narrator expounds, is ironically intended or whether Defoe is actually speaking through his character. Richardson's novels are rhetorically more complex. The employment of a series of 'narrators' in letters to rehearse accounts of the same events from different points of view enriches Richardson's embodiment of

moral imagination, and intensifies the reader's appreciation of the force and ubiquity of obsessional states. Sterne's *Tristram Shandy* (1760–7) questions the nature of the assumed connections between narrated events. Our assumptions about cause and effect, or the relation between thought and action, are attacked. Sterne explores another feature of narrative, the fact that there is a timescale of events and a time-scheme of narration itself, which are not the same. Each of the characters has an interior cinematograph of events and 'explanations' for the connection between them. Tristram Shandy himself, the narrator, has a more complicated picture, but still presents an 'omniscient' view,

The narrator or narrators in a novel may be made puzzled, unreliable or misleading. The early years of the twentieth century, in the work of Freud and others, saw the swift development of certain lines of speculation about the self which fragmented irretrievably the certainty which had prevailed that human perceptions were pretty much the same everywhere. Novelists like Conrad, Ford Madox Ford, Virginia Woolf, Joyce and Faulkner strained the rhetorical technique of fiction to present a refracted picture of experience in all its complexity as unique mental pictures. Readers were increasingly required to interpret a difficult text, to inspect their own responses as they read. See also CHARACTER, NARRATIVE STRUCTURE, STRUCTURALISM.

See Erich Auerbach, trans. W. Trask, *Mimesis* (1953) which gives one kind of analysis of narrative; Wayne C. Booth, *The Rhetoric of Fiction* (1961) provides an exhaustive discussion of modes of narration. See also Robert Scholes and Robert Kellogg, *The Nature of Narrative* (1966); Michael J. Toolan, *Narrative: A Critical Linguistic*

Introduction (2001); J. Hillis Miller, *Reading Narrative* (1998); H. Porter Abbott, *The Cambridge Introduction to Narrative* (2002); Martin McQuillan (ed.), *The Narrative Reader* (2000).

AMR

Narrative structure Refers most simply to the shape of a story's trajectory. Every story is projected from a state of rest by a force of some kind in an arc of rising tension until it reaches the apogee where it begins to fall towards a point of impact. This trajectory represents the 'unity of action' proclaimed by Aristotle to be the essential principle of tragedy, but also applicable to related genres, such as the epic.

Poeticians and students of dramatic and narrative forms have tended to take for granted Aristotle's division of the action into 'complication' and 'denouement' (or 'unravelling') around a central 'peripeteia' or turning point. Modern literary theorists, strongly influenced by Russian Formalism, have often ignored this unifying structural principle, either following Propp in focussing on the mere chaining of narrative functions, or distinguishing (after Shklovsky) between the underlying material of the story, *fabula*, and its compositional form, *syuzhet* or 'plot'. This distinction usually only highlights the sequential relations between episodes and neglects the essential relations of 'complication' and 'denouement', such as their mirror-like opposition in intensity and result, a patterning which is preserved in the traditional 'trajectory' metaphor.

The central point around which the narrative structure pivots is the *peripeteia*, and the nature, placing and stylistic marking of this turning-point determines the nature of the conflict, whether on a physical, psychological or moral level. As Petrovsky showed in 1925, the central phases of narrative structure are normally framed by elements of 'prologue' and 'epilogue', both of these having a general phase (i.e. the total social scene out of which the world of the story arises and to which it reverts) and a specific phase (i.e. essential prior and subsequent information about the lives of the main protagonists).

Most models of narrative structure start by assuming a previous state of rest or equilibrium or normality which is disturbed by an outside force of some kind. The condition initiated by this force gets worse until it reaches an extreme degree. At this point another force comes to bear which reverses the process and allows for the gradual resumption of normality or the establishment of a new equilibrium. This homeostatic pattern may have either a social or a psychological function, or both. MYTHS in both primitive and modern societies tend to come into being as highly formalized, even formulaic, structures which resolve the society's deepest tensions. These may concern social conflicts, ritual taboos or humanity's struggle to come to terms with its physical environment. The narrative structure of the myth allows the real conflict to be projected in dramatized form and resolved via the *peripeteia* and *dénouement*, thus providing both a ritual enactment and a magical relief for the society in question. On the individual level a similar process may be at work: tensions are produced by narrative in the reader/listener which will match in their variety and diffusion his residual psychological tensions, but which are specific enough to be resolved within the context of the art experience, thus channelling the residual tensions into a manageable framework and allowing for their vicarious relief.

Whatever the social or psychological functions of narrative structure, it must be accorded a major role in establishing the aesthetic unity which creates pleasure through the contemplation and enjoyment of purely formal patterning in narrative art. See also DÉNOUEMENT, FORMALISM, MYTH, NARRATIVE, PLOT, STRUCTURALISM.

See G. F. Else, *Aristotle's 'Poetics': The Argument* (1957); L. M. O'Toole, *Style, Structure and Interpretation in the Russian Short Story* (1982); M. Petrovsky, 'Morphology of the novella', *Russian Poetics in Translation*, 10 (1983).

MO'T

Narratology Concerns the study of narrative and proposes the isolation of characteristics common to all narratives whether they be literary, filmic, musical or painterly. It is a theory that seeks to locate the qualities of narrative that underlie all stories and that enables us to recognize modal similarities and distinguish between different registers of presentation and content. It concerns itself less with the detail of the narrative than with the typological building blocks that make the conveyance of that narrative possible. A starting point for understanding narratology is the recognition that many acts of human communication, in a variety of media, contain elements of constructive form that coalesce and interact in broadly similar ways to make a story sensible to the observer/reader. And, because these stories can be transposed between modes of presentation (say in the adaptation of a novel for the screen), they must contain components that are specific to narrative and are sustained regardless of the form within which they are consumed.

The programmatic analysis of narrative developed, perhaps unsurprisingly, out of Russian Formalist and Structuralist schools of linguistic theory. Their attention to the intrinsic literary qualities of a text, divorced from its originating context of production, followed the conviction that human action and communication are governed by preset rules that abide by self-regulating discursive practices and can therefore be isolated and examined as formal elements of operative systems of meaning. Within any story, a narratologist seeks the identifying typological characteristics that correspond to a canon of predetermined laws. Though the events of any given narrative can be presented in a number of ways (as they occur; in direct or indirect recollection; in a deliberate disorder for instance) the narratologist locates what is being narrated independent of the way in which it is told and of the narrating consciousness. By isolating the core narrated story s/he can dispense with the discursive baggage of presentation and the specific vagaries of narratorial control and concentrate purely on the events that underpin the story. This is not primarily a vehicle for interpretational explication, indeed the categorical dismemberment of the text to reveal, as it were, its moving parts, functions less as a determinant of meaning and more as an indicator of the ways that texts are endowed with meaning in general.

Two significant figures within the field of narratology have been Vladimir Propp and Gérard Genette. Propp's *Morphology of the Folktale* (1928) explored the Russian fairy story for typological consistencies and detected over thirty recurrent motifs that invariably appear in a particular order. He also isolated specific character-types who fulfil important roles within the narratives. These are: the hero, the villain, the princess, her father, the dispatcher, the donor, the helper and the false hero.

The identification of these constants established an orderliness to narrative that implied an underlying logic to the stories human tell about themselves and about the world around them. Not all critics agreed with the pre-eminent status of the narrated, however. Influentially, Genette stressed the importance of the way in which the events of a story are unfolded. For him, the attention on the narrated tended to marginalize intriguing variations in the process of recounting and unveiling those narrated components. His method of analysis focussed more closely on the relationship between the text and the story that it contained and, in particular, on the devices brought to bear on the telling to elucidate, obfuscate or problematize the process of revelation. This line of narratological criticism locates and interlinks specific instances of prolepsis, analepsis, ellipsis, summary, repetition and others as a framework of structural embedding that bears a productive relation to the material that constitutes the narrated story.

The most illuminating branch of narratology is that which considers the equal importance of the narrated and the discursive manner of narration. This allows readers to establish distinctions between narrative genera through the identification of consistent features whilst also taking account of the formal and contextual networks within which the narrative as a whole operates. In this way, it is possible to draw connections between the interpretive freight of a text and its stylistic and formal qualities in a manner that is neither reductively mechanical nor vaguely impressionistic.

See Roland Barthes, *Image, Music, Text* (1977); Gérard Genette, *Narrative Discourse* (1972); Claude Lévi-Strauss, *Structural Anthropology* (1958); Gerald Prince, *Narratology: The Form and Functioning of Narrative* (1982); Vladimir Propp, *Morphology of the Folktale* (1928).

DL

Nationalism and ethnicity studies

To some it may seem unnecessary to develop a field of study into nations and nationalism. Nations present themselves as immemorial communities, their histories arching back into the mists of time; they represent the natural divisions of humankind. To study them would perhaps involve nothing more than delineating the distinctive features of that community, or assembling its folklore; for such people – nationalists – there is no need, however, for analysis or explication. And yet, despite their best efforts, nationalists have failed convincingly to present nationhood as a self-evident truth that requires no further explanation. The phenomenon of nations and nationalism has attracted considerable scholarly and critical interest, particularly, in the latter decades of the twentieth century.

Contrary to the nationalists' claims, it is observable that nations represent a historical innovation in the organization of human social life. All critical studies of nationalism, beginning in the nineteenth century with the philosopher Ernest Renan and the historian Lord Acton, have sought to analyse and explain the emergence of nations *historically*, which is to say, as the product of historical forces that determined them, not as the expression of some 'essence'. Renan, in fact, prefigures, albeit it hesitantly, some of the features of nationalism studies that have emerged in the wake of post-structuralism and other advances in cultural theory that propose nations to be cultural constructs that narrativize themselves into being. In particular, his notion of the nation being the product of a daily plebiscite which entails a selective organization of the community's collective memory foreshadows, in some general respects, Benedict Anderson's pathbreaking conceptualization of nations as 'imagined communities'.

There is a loose but nevertheless solid consensus amongst scholars that nations are modern phenomena but there is strong disagreement concerning the nature of their emergence and development. Two broad groups can be identified: those who believe that nations constitute some form of continuity from prior ethnic groups (ethnicists), and those who believe that nations are entirely new formations, fashioned out of scraps of existing cultural material, but nevertheless, constituting a decisive break with older forms of community (modernists).

One of the foremost ethnicists is Anthony Smith, who argues that nations are anchored in pre-existing cultural communities called *ethnies*. These are more or less culturally homogeneous, consisting of a 'myth-symbol complex' that forms a fund of shared historical meanings to which every person in the *ethnie* has access, which bonds 'a people' together, and which ties that people to a 'historical territory or homeland' (Smith 1991: 10–15). The *ethnie* thus places limits on the scope and nature of the transformations that convert premodern communities into modern nations. In particular, the nation is seen as modern mainly inasmuch as 'the era of nationalism succeeded in uniting the community on a new, political basis' (Hutchinson).

The modernists, on the other hand, are sceptical of the bonds between modern national cultures and those premodern elements that can be detected in them. They take a more instrumentalist attitude to the formation of national identity, arguing that nationalists refashion 'culture' as a response in the cultural field to the new socio-political problems posed by the transformation of social reality in modernity. The strongest advocate of this position has been Ernest Gellner. For him, nations are sociologically necessary correlates to objective macroscopic transformations in social life. In modernity, society is mobile – both socially and geographically – and constantly so; this requires the development of a standardized means of communication, that is, 'context-free' since contexts are constantly changing in a mobile society; a centralized education system results and institutionalizes a vernacular language. The result is 'social entropy', or cultural homogenization, and nationalism is an expression of this phenomenon. This sociological determinism is attenuated somewhat in the work of other modernists, in particular Benedict Anderson, the force of whose contribution was to reframe the discussion in terms of ideology and consciousness. In suggesting that nations are 'imagined', he draws attention not only to the idea that 'nation-ness, as well as nationalism, are cultural artefacts of a particular kind', but also to the role of culture in politics because, to be more precise, a nation is an 'imagined *political* community' (Anderson).

Both ethnicists and modernists concur that culture is a vital aspect of nationalism and nationhood. Indeed, this reflects both the fact that nationalism is perhaps one of the earliest forms of cultural politics, and that in modernity the question of identity has emerged as a key site of social and political contestation and negotiation. It is not surprising, therefore, that studies of 'ethnicity' – the signifier of a cultural identity distinct from 'race' on the one hand, and nation on the other – have emerged in the context of the visible heterogenization of nations following large-scale postwar immigrations from the Third World. Ethnicity figures as part of the debates over multiculturalism, debates which take place in a political arena in which the nation-state remains dominant but where the mask of a homogeneous national culture has slipped. See also NÉGRITUDE, POSTCOLONIALISM, HYBRIDITY.

See Benedict Anderson, *Imagined Communities: Reflections on the Origin and Spread of Nationalism* (1983); Ernest Gellner, *Nations and Nationalism* (1983); John Hutchinson, *Modern Nationalism* (1994); Anthony Smith, *Theories of Nationalism* (1971), *National Identity* (1991).

AM

Naturalism   See REALISM.

Négritude   A theory of the uniquely valuable potential of black African peoples and cultures and was, for a period after the Second World War, very influential amongst black intellectuals, artists, activists and politicians who were conducting anti-colonial or anti-racist struggles. It is today most closely identified with two African statesmen-intellectuals, Aimé Césaire and Leopold Senghor, who met as students in Paris in the 1930s and, in response to the racism they encountered, began to formulate and disseminate ideas that celebrated black culture and personalities. This was in opposition to the dominant colonial discourses that perceived Africa as lacking in civilization and culture, and of Africans as primitive savages.

As can be inferred from the different backgrounds of its two principal proponents (Césaire was from the French Caribbean colony of Martinique, whilst Senghor was from the African colony of Senegal), it was from the outset a pannational movement, and though it identified itself closely with Africa, its message was directed to all peoples of the African diaspora, whether in Africa, the Caribbean, America or Europe. Indeed, négritude had been influenced heavily by transatlantic currents that had made an impact in prewar Paris, such as the Harlem Renaissance, and earlier American race activists and thinkers, such as W. E. DuBois. In turn, négritude became popular in America and the Caribbean as well as in Africa and Europe so the movement's trajectory illuminates the diasporic circulation of ideas and cultures theorized by Paul Gilroy as 'the Black Atlantic'. Nevertheless, it also had a profound impact on nationalist struggles in Africa. If this seems somewhat paradoxical, it can be added that this was due to the fact that négritude mobilized many of the discursive tropes and structures of nationalist discourse, particularly essentialism and nativism.

Put simply, the discourse of négritude celebrates what European colonial discourses of race had identified with Africa and Africans only in terms of a lack. Africans lacked civilization and culture; they lacked intelligence; they lacked sensibility and so on. At the heart of négritude is, therefore, a concern with 'race', but its distinctiveness lay in the ways in which this racial foundation was extended and developed to encompass an entire 'way of life' – intellectual, cultural, emotional, physical – that all black peoples shared. This is the essentialist aspect of négritude. Black people, argued Senghor, looked at and behaved in the world in a different way to non-Africans: their relationship to the world around them was unique and this uniqueness should be celebrated on its own terms, not in relation to European and white values and mores. Négritude, like other nativist and essentialist theories of identity, is therefore relativist in its outlook. No one standard of judgement exists by which different cultures and peoples can be measured.

From this theoretical foundation, the discourse of négritude develops through a series of binary comparisons between 'Africans' and (white) Europeans. Instead of 'civilization', Senghor validates the African proximity to 'nature'; instead of promoting intellect, he espouses the African's intuitiveness; instead of advocating abstract rationalism he indicates the more immediate sensuousness of the African's physical experience of life. Ironically, these merely invert the terms of colonial discourse while keeping its structure intact: it was part of the common sense of European racism that Africans were 'closer to nature'; that they were 'physical' (and over-sexual); that they were intuitive (read: irrational); and that they were not capable of intellectual pursuits. All of these constituted the basis for European claims that Africans were 'savages'. Thus, rather than challenging this claim, Senghor's definition of négritude may in fact have reinforced it.

It is only fair to add that Césaire's vision of négritude differed somewhat from Senghor's; probably because of his location away from Africa. His was an imaginative rather than a concrete, lived relationship to Africa and so he was more ambivalent in his espousal of essentialism. Césaire grounded his discourse in the historically shared black experience of suffering, whether in Africa, the Caribbean, America or in Europe. His négritude, whilst still deploying the binaries of racial thought, is less clear-cut, more nuanced, more problematic.

Indeed, this binarism was one of the reasons that négritude was so spectacularly successful and is now out of favour. It encouraged and fed the black separatist movements in America, but also unhinged its own desire for a *pan-national* identification across national and cultural boundaries because it embedded an inclusion/exclusion logic in the very heart of its thinking. This separatism has proved less than successful historically, and given Senghor's and Césaire's humanist and universalist aspirations that négritude would be the first step in the emancipation of all peoples, has also proved something of a failure on its own terms. See also NATIONALISM AND ETHNICITY STUDIES, ORIENTALISM.

See B. E. Jack, *Négritude and Literary Criticism: The History and Theory of 'Negro-African' Literature in French* (1996); Paul Gilroy, *The Black Atlantic: Modernity and Double Consciousness* (1993); Rana Kabbani, *Europe's Myths of Orient* (1986).

AM

Neo-Aristotelianism   See   CHICAGO CRITICS.

Neo-classicism   See CLASSIC, DECORUM, IMITATION.

Neo-Platonism   See PLATONISM.

New criticism   The term *new criticism*, originally coined by J. E. Spingarn in 1910 in protest against the pedantry of the American academic scene (see *Creative Criticism*, 1917) is now used to refer specifically to the work of the American critics associated with the programme announced in John Crowe Ransom's book *The New Criticism* (1941), notably Cleanth Brooks (*The Well Wrought Urn*, 1947), R. P. Blackmur (*Language as Gesture*, 1952), Allen Tate (*Collected Essays*, 1959) and Robert Penn Warren (*Selected Essays*, 1964). Ransom discovered the stimulus for this movement in T. S. Eliot's urging of a new spirit of objectivity in criticism, and in I. A. Richards's attempt to provide a scientific terminology for describing poetic effect. The fundamental effort was to free criticism from the impressionism and emotionalism of the amateur tradition and the intentionalism of literary-historical scholarship (see EFFECT and INTENTION), and to propose an aesthetic that would consider poetry 'primarily as poetry and not another thing' (Eliot). Richards's development of Romantic theories of form as the systemization and harmonizing of elements in poetry, with its idea of the poem as a complex activity of meaning, inspired many of the key terms and concepts of the new criticism: ambiguity, irony, paradox, tension, gesture, etc. However, Richards's attempt to locate this complexity in the psychological *effects* of poetry, rather than in the linguistic structure of the work, had failed to produce immediately useful descriptive attitudes and terminology. The major stimulus here probably came from his pupil William Empson, whose determination to prove poetry capable of explanation led to a brilliantly imaginative account of its verbal complexity (see ANALYSIS). His demonstration that poetic effect often arose from a rich exploitation of the references and relationships inherent in language stood behind the new critical disposition to regard all literary works as structures of language, and to be relatively indifferent to concepts like GENRE, CHARACTER or PLOT.

However, much of the American new criticism took its ideas about language not from Empson but from the semantic work of Richards himself. His identification of poetry as an example of the emotive use of language, in contrast to the *scientific* use, perpetuated Romantic thought/feeling dualisms, and encouraged 'new critics' to conceive of poetry as a special *kind* of language. This fallacy, attacked by the CHICAGO CRITICS, often led to a narrowly prescriptive view of poetic form – such as Brooks's *paradox* – and a concentration on the rhetorical features of certain kinds of complex, highly concentrated poetry. One consequence was a rewriting of literary history; the poetry of the early-seventeenth century replaced that of the nineteenth in critical popularity. Another was a narrowing of descriptive procedures; the axiom that the poem as an organization of language was the only determinant of the critical relevance of external evidence was sometimes modified into meaningless assertions of the 'autonomy' of poems, their explicability without any external reference or knowledge.

The larger tradition of descriptive criticism in England and America derived its assumptions about language in literature from the later Richards of *Philosophy of Rhetoric* (1936), and Empson. It identified poetry not as a kind of language but as a *use* of language, and therefore declared its essential continuity with all language and with culture; it rejected distinctions of language function along emotive/descriptive lines, and asserted a concept of 'meaning' as the result of the total linguistic activity of words in a context (see ANALYSIS). And it rested on the conviction that true descriptive criticism must be ultimately a criticism of literature as organized language, because it is only as language that the work has an objective existence at all.

See Roger Fowler and Peter Mercer, 'Criticism and the language of literature', *Style 3* (1969), 45–72; reprinted in Fowler, *The Languages of Literature* (1971); Stanley Edgar Hyman, *The Armed Vision* (1947, rev. edn 1955); Murray Krieger, *The New Apologists for Poetry* (1956); Brian Lee, 'The New Criticism and the language of poetry' in Roger Fowler (ed.), *Essays on Style and*

Language (1966); Walter Gutton, *Modern American Criticism* (1963); W. K. Wimsatt, Jr and Cleanth Brooks, *Literary Criticism, A Short History* (1957); D. Robey, 'Anglo-American New Criticism' in A. Jefferson and D. Robey (eds), *Modern Literary Theory* (1982); T. Eagleton, *Literary Theory: An Introduction* (1983); Mark Jancovich, *The Cultural Politics of the New Criticism* (1993); A. Walton Litz, Louis Menand and Lawrence Rainey (eds), *The Cambridge History of Literary Criticism: Modernism and New Criticism* (2000).

PM

Novel Of the three main kinds of literature (poetry, drama, novel), the novel is the last to evolve and the hardest to define, for reasons suggested in the name. 'A fiction in prose of a certain extent': this economical definition by a French critic begs more questions than it answers. There are many such fictions predating the emergence of the species as a recognizable type: usually dated from *Don Quixote* (1605–15), and in England from either the seventeenth century (Aphra Behn) or the early-eighteenth century (Defoe, Richardson, Fielding, Sterne), and associated with the rise of prose as an empirical, sceptical instrument for probing familiar environments. This links the novel with realism and a-genericism; Fielding set it up as a mock-species in calling it a 'comic epic poem in prose', intending to suggest its low (or else mock-heroic) style, its width of social range and bagginess of structure, its contingency and episodic design. The self-sceptical element is reinforced by Fielding's willingness to parody Richardson, and then Sterne's to flout the emergent conventions of the species in *Tristram Shandy* (1760–7), which mocks beginnings, middles and ends; chronicity

and reliable narrators. The circumstantial and specific elements, and the engrained scepticism (Ian Watt's 'realism of presentation' and 'realism of assessment', *The Rise of the Novel*, 1957), easily merge here into self-conscious fictiveness, constituents of the novel ever since. Though touching on reportage and history at one extreme, taking structure from non-fictional prose forms (journalism, history, sociology), the novel touches on formalism at its other extreme, taking structure from myth, and symbolic or linguistic coherence. Many classic debates about fiction (novel versus romance in the nineteenth century; life-novel versus art-novel at the turn of the century; 'journalistic' versus 'crystalline' in the mid-twentieth century) cover this spectrum. So does every individual novel. Lacking the metrical-typographical and generic conventions of most poetry, and the theatre-audience presentation of most drama, and using the most familiar, open and deconventionalized form of written language, prose novels are open to a wide variety of registers, structures, typologies. This range an adequate critical definition must cover too.

The fascination of the novel is that, because of its representational dimension, it raises the problem of the nature of a fiction at a point very near to familiar, *un*fictionalized versions of reality. The propensity of novels towards 'giving to the imaginary the formal guarantee of the real', their dependence on recognition and their relative formal contingency, are essential features; though clearly 'reality' is not a stable object. These features have often led critics to see it as a basically referential or mimetic species. Its social density and range, its following of loose and lifelike sequences, are valid objects of critical attention, so long as we remember that realism is an imaginative creation and that the term itself encourages confusion (cf. REALISM). One consequence of the term was the growth of a critical method based on 'plot', 'character', 'description', etc. (i.e. mimetic assumptions); against this, there developed a critical tradition of post-Jamesian fictional theory, stressing other essential structuring features: 'point of view', 'paradox', 'symbol', 'tension', and what Mark Schorer calls 'technique as discovery', a poetic emphasizing means of presentation rather than objects of imitation. What seems apparent is that, though both approaches stress primary features of novels, each often best serves discussion of the kind of fiction contemporary with it: the former tends to get us closer to nineteenth-century realistic fiction, the latter to twentieth-century neo-symbolist fiction. The latter is the more sophisticated, reminding us that all fictions are makings, verbal constructs; its weakness is that it tends to ascribe all primary structure in fiction to rhetorical and linguistic features, rather than to the unfolding of orders perceived in psychology, experience or society (cf. STRUCTURE).

The novel, being an 'institution' of modern society particularly exposed to the contingency of life and prevailing structures of perception (Harry Levin, *The Gates of Horn*, 1963), has passed through marked stages of development; this has encouraged historicist criticism. It has been called the 'burgher epic'; identified with the social eminence of its main reading public, the bourgeoisie; seen as a manifestation of its perception of reality, the secular, material but moralized reality of a particular class; linked with its view of the rounded, individuated human character in sequential moral growth; tied in with particular notions of cause-and-effect and chronological sequence in character and society, a

'progressive' view of self and history. Such criticism tends to assume that MODERNISM constitutes a crisis of the species; hence, it often concludes in prophecies of the imminent death of the novel. This helps demonstrate that versions of reality change over time, and helps explain certain features of novel-development: the dominance of the form at its most realistic in the nineteenth century, and the later emergence of naturalism, certain types of fictional modernism, the anti-novel. It tends, however, to encourage the view that the novel of morals-and-manners (see Lionel Trilling, 'Manners, morals, and the novel', *The Liberal imagination*, 1961) is the prototypical novel, hardly accurate if we take a broad international perspective; to see 'fabulation' as either aberrant or a crisis-symptom (cf. FICTION); often to undervalue contemporary production. Reminding us that realism is a convention, it gives that convention a historic-cultural rather than a creative explanation. Like much stylistic history, it assumes inevitability and undervalues the startling plurality of the novel-form, its remarkable endurance in many different cultural circumstances. A recent trend in novel-criticism has seen its development alongside that of colonialism, beginning with the period of imperial incursions and reaching its apogee at the imperial zenuth of the late nineteenth century.

See also CHARACTER, FICTION, NARRATIVE, PLOT.

See Miriam Allott (ed.), *Novelists on the Novel* (1959); Erich Auerbach, trans. W. Trask, *Mimesis* (1953); Wayne C. Booth, *The Rhetoric of Fiction* (1961); Malcolm Bradbury, *What is a Novel?* (1969); Henry James in R. P. Blackmur (ed.), *The Art of the Novel* (1934); David Lodge, *Language of Fiction* (1966); Ian Watt, *The Rise of the Novel* (1957);

R. Scholes and R. Kellogg, *The Nature of Narrative* (1966); Terry Eagleton, *The English Novel: An Intro-duction* (2004); Jesse Matz, *The Modern Novel* (2004); Malcolm Bradbury, *The Modern British Novel* (2001); Dorothy Hale (ed.), *An Anthology of Criticism and Theory 1900–2000: The Novel* (2004).

Theoretical discussions of various aspects of the novel are plentiful. See, for example, M. Bloomfield (ed.), *The Interpretation of Narrative* (1970); D. Cohn, *Transparent Minds: Narrative Modes for Presenting Consciousness in Fiction* (1978); U. Eco, *The Role of the Reader* (1979); G. Genette, *Narrative Discourse* (1980); W. Iser, *The Implied Reader* (1974), *The Act of Reading* (1978); F. Jameson, *The Political Unconscious: Narrative as a Socially Symbolic Act* (1981); G. Prince, *Narratology: The Form and Functioning of Narrative* (1982); H. Ruthrof, *The Reader's Construction of Narrative* (1981); Firdous Azim, *The Colonial Rise of the Novel* (1993).

MSB

O

Objective correlative   Popularized by
T. S. Eliot (who later admitted his aston-
ishment at its success) in 1919 to explain
his dissatisfaction with *Hamlet*:

> The only way of expressing emotion
> in the form of art is by finding an
> 'objective correlative'; in other words,
> a set of objects, a situation, a chain of
> events which shall be the formula of
> that *particular* emotion; such that
> when the external facts...are given,
> the emotion is immediately evoked.

The application to *Hamlet* now seems
fanciful, but as the technical procedure in
'pure poetry' the general formula is plausible. The most serious omission is the
creative contribution of the unconscious
mind. Eliseo Vivas criticized the concept
in detail in *Creation and Discovery*
(1955), arguing that a writer only discovers a particular emotion to express in
the act of composition. See T. S. Eliot,
Hamlet (1919) in *Selected Essays*
(3rd edn, 1951), p. 145.

Obscurity   A charge levelled at much
experimental twentieth-century poetry,
and some prose. It is perhaps most profitable to think of obscurity as a term
descriptive of a modern poetic rhetoric of
ellipsis, metaphor, typographic enterprise, as a convention for accuracy and
authenticity; not a classical accuracy
derived from a constant correction and
reapplication of ready-authenticated
material, but an accuracy of the unimagin-
able, authentic because unchallengeable;
not 'nobody else has thought this therefore
I must have thought it' but 'nobody else
could have thought this therefore I must

have thought it'. For two comprehensive
and opposing views of the problem see:
J. Press, *The Chequer'd Shade* (1958);
J. Sparrow, *Sense and Poetry* (1934); see
also G. Steiner, 'On difficulty' in his *On
Difficulty and Other Essays* (1978); Allon
White, *Uses of Obscurity: Fiction of Early
Modernism* (1981).

CS

Ode   In English, a much-practised form
of lyric poetry from the time of Ben
Jonson to that of Tennyson, with sporadic
modern revivals. The most elevated and
complicated species of lyric, the ode was
often written to celebrate notable public
occasions or universal themes. It attracted
an exalted diction and free metrical
experimentation, highly formalized
stanza-types rather removed from the
main currents of English versification.
The exponents of this genre were usually
explicitly conscious of their classical
models, hence, the strangeness of the
verse forms: many poets attempted to
render in English metrical patterns
which were natural only in terms of the
sound-structure of Greek.

The classical models are Pindar
(522–442? BC) in Greek and Horace
(65–8 BC) in Latin. Although Horace was
much more familiar to the English, the
Pindaric ode interested poets more,
because it was metrically highly distinctive. Pindar's odes (derived from choral
lyrics in drama) were composed to be
chanted to music by a dancing chorus.
The demands of music and dance resulted
in a highly elaborate stanzaic structure:
this type of ode was built on a sequence of
sections called *strophe*, *antistrophe* and

epode, the sections constructed from lines of varying length. Such a complicated verse-form provided a stimulating challenge to English metrists. The Pindaric ode was 'occasional', that is to say, composed for a specific and important public event (e.g. to honour the victors in Greek athletic games). The Horatian ode, though sometimes public, was frequently personal and reflective. It shared the solemnity and dignity of the Pindaric ode, but was less of a metrist's virtuoso-piece. Its contribution to English poetry was a matter of tone and feeling, rather than of technical design.

The English ode begins with Ben Jonson and rises in esteem through the period of neo-classicism, culminating in some of the more exalted poems of the Romantics and then surviving in public Victorian verse. In 1629 appeared Jonson's 'Ode to Sir Lucius Cary and Sir H. Morison', a conscious attempt to provide an exact English equivalent for the complicated stanza forms of Pindar; Milton's 'On the morning of Christ's nativity', written in the same year, though not Pindaric in the same way, exercises an extremely complex metrical pattern. The Horatian model is represented in the 'Horatian Ode upon Cromwell's Return from Ireland' by Milton's younger contemporary Andrew Marvell. In 1656, Abraham Cowley's collection *Miscellanies* made available a number of adaptations as well as imitations of Pindar, and set a fashion for a type of free Pindaric ode which was to become popular with the Augustans. Three odes of Dryden were also influential: two of them, odes for St Cecilia's Day (1687 and 1697, the second entitled 'Alexander's feast'), honoured the patron saint of music and returned to Pindar at the same time, for they were designed to be set to music. William Collins (1721–59) and Thomas

Gray (1716–71) continued the Pindaric fashion; William Cowper (1731–1800) favoured the less spectacular, more quietly serious, Horatian manner. Towards the end of the eighteenth century, burlesques of the ode began to appear, but the genre was taken over by the Romantics and employed in several notable lyric poems on political, emotional and aesthetic themes: Wordsworth's elaborate ode, 'Intimations of Immortality' (1803, published 1807) and the odes of Keats published in 1820 ('Nightingale', 'Psyche', 'Grecian Urn', 'Autumn', 'Melancholy') are the best-remembered examples in this period, highly philosophical, intense, yet controlled. Coleridge ('France', 'Dejection') and Shelley ('West Wind', 'Liberty', 'Naples' – the last employing an extraordinarily complicated metrical arrangement with some claims to Greek heritage) also practised the form.

Although exceptionally diverse in its structural patterns, the ode was sustained as a poetic ideal for over two centuries of English verse. Its dignity, classical pedigree and technical potentialities endeared it to the Augustans; its intensity and philosophical pretensions made it suitable for the most exalted Romantic verse. Since the Romantic era it has declined in fortune, become the prerogative of poets laureate and of other writers given to ceremonious public utterance. It used to be the mode for metrical experimentation (the classical models warranting departure from established English prosodies) but the radical experimentalism of Europe and America in the twentieth century had no need for such an outmoded basis for metrical licence.

See John Heath-Stubbs, *The Ode* (1969); Norman Maclean, 'From action to image: theories of the lyric in the eighteenth century' in R. S. Crane, *Critics and Criticism* (1952); Carol Maddison, *Apollo and the Nine, A History of the*

Ode (1960); Robert Shafter, *The English Ode to 1660* (1918); George N. Shuster, *The English Ode from Milton to Keats* (1940, reprinted 1964); Paul H. Fry, *The Poet's Calling in the English Ode* (1980).

RGF

Onomatopoeia   See TEXTURE.

Oral composition   See EPIC.

Organic   The notion of organic form in literature (bequeathed to Modern Anglo-American criticism by Coleridge, who referred to it constantly) appealed to a biological analogy which can be mislead-ing as well as revealing. Its revealing aspect was the emphasis it placed on the overall structure of the work and, conse-quently, on the *relationship* of the parts and aspects to each other and to the whole. The whole was thought of as being 'more than the sum of its parts' in the sense that the whole provides impressions which cannot be traced back to the parts in isolation. The validity of this notion, as applied to the non-biological world of art, receives support from perceptual psychol-ogy. Visual impressions of length, colour, texture, prominence and so forth can be altered not by altering the parts that appear to produce them, but merely the context in which those parts function.

A distinct use of 'organic form' opposed organic (irregular, unique) forms to inorganic (regular, traditional) forms. This generally involved an evaluative preference for organic (living, natural) as against inorganic (mechanical, artificial), the central assumption being that organic forms grow from the meaning and embody it while inorganic forms pre-exist and therefore act as a straitjacket to mean-ings. This use of the term ignored the fact that both 'organic' and 'inorganic' forms can be relevantly or irrelevantly used. The term was largely eclipsed by the more

neutral term 'structure' which has all the advantages and none of the disadvantages of the older, Romantic term. See also FORM, LANGUAGE, STRUCTURE.

See George Rousseau, *Organic Form* (1972); Gary Day, *Re-reading Leavis: 'Culture' and Literary Criticism* (1996). On organic doctrine in criticism, see Murray Krieger, *The New Apologists for Poetry* (1956). See also Anne Cluysenaar, *Introduction to Literary Stylistics* (1976); Q. S. Tong, *Reconstructing Romanticism: Organic Theory Revisited* (1997).

AAAC

Orientalism   In modern critical theory, the term Orientalism was popularized by Edward Said's book of the same name, which has subsequently been cited as one of the formative moments in the develop-ment of post-colonial studies. Said draws on Foucault's conceptualization of dis-course as a semantic field which struc-tures and limits what is thinkable and sayable about a particular object. In Said's case, that object is the 'Orient'. It is the discourse about the Orient that constructs its meaning and so what is important for Said is not the 'truth' of the discourse in some correspondence with an actual Orient but rather the internal consistency of the discourse of Orientalism. It is in this sense that Orientalism 'produces' the Orient. The basic structuring principle of Orientalism is 'an ontological and epi-stemological distinction made between "the Orient" and (most of the time) "the Occident"' (Said). Related to this primary binary are a series of subsequent binary divisions that adhere to one term or the other. Thus, whilst rational thought is asso-ciated – whether explicitly or indirectly – with 'the Occident', its opposite is seen as characteristic of 'the Orient'; whilst the Occident is seen as masculine, the Orient is feminized and so on. Consequently,

Orientalism is a discourse that produces the 'Orient' as Europe's Other and in so doing enables Europe to fashion a sense of its own identity. Orientalism therefore not only produces 'the Orient' but also 'Europe' too.

Orientalism sets a limit on European thinking about the 'Orient' because it constitutes the sum of possibilities open to any European thinking about 'the Orient'. The Orient exists as a set of already available and already spoken ideas that permeate through civil society in a wide range of texts – novels, plays, economic theorems, political treatises, scholarly monographs, travel diaries, administrative manuals, and so on – and the institutions that produce them. This archive of knowledge is available to all European – and in due course, non-European – writers, philosophers, administrators, politicians and suchlike, and sets their thinking about the Orient along certain paths that achieve coherence in the context of the discourse as a whole. This is what Said means when he talks about Orientalism involving a 'textual attitude' to the world. For even those with first-hand experience of the Orient, their experiences will in some measure be filtered through what they read about it – and what they read will inevitably be shaped by Orientalist discourse. The implication of this is that every European text that deals with the Orient – whether directly or indirectly, consciously or unconsciously – will be implicated in Orientalism.

The other side of Said's theorization of Orientalism is its link to colonialism. Orientalism, as a body of ideas about an 'Orient', is, he argues, put into the service of power and gives rise to a hegemony that both produces and in turn justifies European supremacy. Here he rejects one of the existing definitions of the term 'orientalism', which referred to specialized scholarship on 'the Orient' that professes to be objective and disinterested. Said attacks such claims as symptomatic of the collusion of such scholarship in the material processes of colonial power and its justification. Knowledge is not conceived as existing in a rarefied world of ideas but rather is profoundly implicated in a complex network of worldly affiliations that serve the interests of colonial and imperial powers. Here Said draws not only on Foucault but also Antonio Gramsci, whose conceptualization of hegemony has shaped much critical thinking on the relationship of culture to power. Gramsci's ideas helped Said to demonstrate how colonial power is justified and maintained not only by raw power and naked aggression based on technological superiority and military might but also by the 'soft' power of ideology. This power is both material and visible on the one hand, and invisible and unconscious on the other; its efficacy lies in what Ngugi wa Thiongo calls 'colonizing the mind' so that both colonizer and colonized think of the assumptions encoded in Orientalism as natural, inevitable and uncontestable (Ngugi).

Said has, however, been criticized by many for appearing to suggest Orientalism is a homogenous and monolithic discourse within which there is no room for agency, difference or dissent. Like Foucault, he has been charged with disabling those who wish to contest existing power structures. Nevertheless, postcolonial studies have developed, refined and nuanced his arguments rather than rejected them. Their value persists in the present as global politics continues to be shaped by talk of a 'clash of civilizations' between 'the West' and 'Islam'. As such, Orientalism remains one of the pivotal conceptual terms in modern critical theory. See also POSTCOLONIALISM, DISCOURSE, EUROCENTRISM.

See Ngugi wa Thiongo, *De-colonising the Mind: The Politics of Language in African Literature* (1981); Edward Said, *Orientalism* (1978); Ziauddin Sardar, *Orientalism* (1999).

AM

Originality

An *Original* may be said to be of a vegetable nature; it rises spontaneously from the vital root of Genius; it grows, it is not made: Imitations are often a sort of *Manufacture* wrought up by those *Mechanics, Art* and *Labour*, out of pre-existent materials not their own.
(Edward Young)

The eighteenth-century notion of originality rests on an analogy between artistic and natural creation, on a cult of individualism and self-expression and, later, a realization that nature, indeed all creativity, is evolutionary. Three distinct, though often conflated, senses of 'originality' are discernible: a psychological theory about the creative act; a theory concerning the proper function of art in society; an aesthetic theory.

The third, aesthetic, sense of originality was the most important for twentieth-century critics. If an original work is so because each aspect contributes to the internal economy of the whole and is not there only for external reasons, then 'original' is virtually synonymous with 'good'. Such a work is original irrespective of whether it is conventional or not. If, however, a work is original because it breaks with convention or, more radically, with tradition, originality in this sense is not an evaluative but a descriptive term. See also AUTHOR, CREATION.

See Ezra Pound, *Make It New* (1934); Edward Young, *Conjectures of Original Composition* (1759, reprinted 1966); Francois Meltzer, *Hot Property: The Stakes and Claims of Literary Originality* (1994).

EJB

Ostranenie   See FORMALISM.

Other, the   In its everyday usage, the term 'other' is seemingly unproblematic. We use it to designate that which is different – other than – ourselves or the myriad of established norms and practices that govern our lives. Yet, in acknowledging the interdependence of self and other, norm and deviation, the preceding sentence already begins to hint at the underlying complexity of this concept and the impossibility of offering a stable definition that does not evoke its antithesis. It is important to recognize, however, that the other is not, in any simple way, the direct opposite of the self. Rather, the two exist in a complex relation that undermines any simplistic conception of self/other, inside/outside or centre/margin. Nor is the other a stable or unchanging entity. Rather, it is best thought of as a site or location upon which we project all the qualities that we – as individual subjects, social groups or even nations – most fear, or dislike, about ourselves. In other words, the other is a construct. It is, moreover, a historically and culturally specific construction that is determined by the discursive practices that shape us into what we are (see DISCOURSE). Thus, rather than representing the real and diverse qualities of any given group or entity, such constructions reflect the values and norms of the individual or group that constructs it.

As the locus of qualities that threaten our sense of who we are, the concept of the other plays a key role in the formation of our identity, or subjectivity. In part, we consolidate our sense of self by distinguishing ourselves from those that are different, or other than, ourselves. In other words, the concept of 'me' is predicated upon what is 'not-me'. Daphne Du Maurier's *Rebecca* (1938) offers us a clear example of how this process works. In this novel, the unnamed narrator (her lack of a proper name immediately signals the lack of a self-sufficient identity) constructs a sense of self by opposing herself to the eponymous Rebecca. Effectively, she seems to say to herself: 'I am what I am because I am not she'. Both feared and admired, Rebecca is clearly constructed as the other of the nameless protagonist. Yet, through a process of imaginative identification, the boundaries between self and other begin to blur until this protagonist, at least temporarily, becomes Rebecca. As this example suggests, the relationship between self and other is complex, paradoxical and contradictory. If the self is predicated on the existence of an other, this other can no longer be conceived as simply external or marginal. Thus, while delineating the boundaries of selfhood, the notion of the other simultaneously destabilizes them.

This complex relationship between self and other lies at the heart of much psychoanalytic theory, including that of Sigmund Freud and the French post-structuralist psychoanalyst, Jacques Lacan. According to Freud, each of us is dominated by an unconscious that we can never know or control. This unconscious is, precisely, the other of consciousness and rational thought; every self is thus already inhabited by an other. When this other within the self makes itself heard or felt, the boundaries of coherent selfhood are called into question. Such destabilizing moments are felt to provoke feelings of the UNCANNY. Offering a more

radical re-interpretation of Freud, Lacan argues that the self is not simply divided by the presence of an other but actually *is* an other. According to Lacan, the child first begins to see itself as an autonomous being during the MIRROR STAGE when it encounters an image of wholeness and coherence reflected back to itself from a mirror or the people around it. Yet, while this identification with what is both 'me' and 'not-me' lends the child an illusory sense of self, it also explodes any simple notion of an autonomous, self-same identity.

In the same way that individual subjects are defined through their relationship to their others, so too are social groups, gender, race and nation. In this respect, it is essential to recognize that the 'opposition' between self and other is never neutral but always hierarchical. In other words, the self – whether it is conceived as male, white, European or heterosexual – is constructed as the positive term. Conversely, the other – be it female, black, non-European or homosexual – is constructed as its negative reflection. This reflection, in turn, helps to consolidate the (superior) identity of those responsible for its construction (see ORIENTALISM). Moreover, such constructions are intimately bound up with questions of power. Once the other has been constructed as inferior, this construction may be used, not only to justify certain material practices (colonization, sexual inequality, 'queer bashing', etc.) but also to naturalize them. For this reason, the concept of the other assumes a prominent place within feminist, post-colonial and queer theories. See also ALTERITY, FEMINISM, DIFFERENCE and ESSENTIALISM.

JA

P

Paradox An apparently self-contradictory statement, though one which is essentially true. Two examples of paradox may help to demonstrate its special significance in modern thought (Schopenhauer, Shaw):

The more unintelligent a man is, the less mysterious existence seems to him. The man who listens to reason is lost: reason enslaves all whose minds are not strong enough to master her.

The movement of twentieth-century philosophy away from causal modes of thought towards an acceptance of contrarieties and oppositions, seems to be reflected accurately in the present critical preoccupation with paradox in literature. An acceptance of the radical discontinuity between thought and existence prompts both Shaw and Schopenhauer to point to the futility of searching for solutions within the unity of thought. Modern criticism, beginning with the rehabilitation of the Metaphysical poets and continuing with the rediscovery of the Augustans, gradually progressed from the exploration of simple intellectual paradox associated with irony and satire, to a discovery of the paradox of wonder in the existential poetry of the Romantics. As Cleanth Brooks has shown (*The Well Wrought Urn*, 1947) the paradoxes upon which such poems as Wordsworth's 'Immortality Ode' are built represent the basic structure of Romantic thought and are far removed from a trivial verbal exercise.

BCL

Paraphrase Depends on the possibility of *synonymy*: the availability of more than one expression for the same meaning. The theory of STYLE seems to demand belief in the possibility of paraphrase, and consequently in a model of language which distinguishes form and content, expression and meaning.

These assumptions were vigorously challenged by neo-Romantic critics, taking as their battle cry Shelley's assault on 'the vanity of translation' and drawing support from the many linguists and linguistic philosophers who have denied the existence of synonyms or asserted that a word in context has a unique and unmatchable meaning. The most vocal advocate for the inseparability of form and content was Cleanth Brooks, who attacked what he called 'The heresy of paraphrase' (*The Well Wrought Urn*, ch. 11): 'the imagery and the rhythm are not merely the instruments by which this fancied core-of-meaning-which-can-be-expressed-in-a-paraphrase is directly rendered'. The alleged heresy is a belief that a poem reduces to an arbitrary conjunction of a 'meaning' (statement, theme, etc.) and a decorative surface. Brooks asserted that the surface is not merely decorative: we apprehend meaning by way of the 'words on the page', and changing the words may change our conception of the poem. Paraphrase is, willy-nilly, part of the critic's normal procedure. See also CONTENT, FORM, STYLE, TEXTURE.

See David Lodge, *Language of Fiction* (1966), 18–26, which rehearses some of the literary arguments on this issue.

RGF

Parody One of the most calculated and analytic literary techniques: it searches out, by means of subversive mimicry, any weakness, pretension or lack of self-awareness in its original. This 'original' may be another work, or the collective style of a group of writers, but although parody is often talked of as a very clever and inbred literary joke, any distinctive and artful use of language – by, for example, journalists, politicians or priests – is susceptible of parodic impersonation. Although it is often deflationary and comic, its distinguishing characteristic is not deflation, but analytic mimicry. The systematic appropriation of the form and imagery of secular love poetry by the sacred lyric is an example of parody in this basic sense. It is one of the ways for a writer to explore and identify available techniques, and may focus on their unused potentialities as well as their limitations. As an internal check that literature keeps on itself, parody may be considered parasitic or creative, and is often both. Perhaps because parodic works are themselves highly critical, they are more frequently annotated than analysed; sometimes parodists are so self-conscious that they pre-empt their would-be critic, providing their own footnotes and explanatory comments (like Vladimir Nabokov in *Pale Fire*, 1962). The parodist addresses a highly 'knowing' and literate audience, for whom criticism is merely a part of literature, not a separate industry. The parodist is often an ironist, affecting admiration of the style borrowed and distorted (Pope 'compliments' Milton in this way in *The Dunciad*, 1728); sometimes explicitly and systematically undermining a rival mode (as Jane Austen does with the Gothic novel in *Northanger Abbey*, 1818); impersonation of the alien style is always the basic technique. In various periods, particularly in the eighteenth century, attempts were made to distinguish different kinds of parodic

appropriation: 'burlesque' was said to be the kind where some new 'low' subject was treated incongruously in an old 'high' style, and 'travesty' the opposite (with Juno using the language of a fishwife). Such distinctions can seldom in practice be sustained, since one parodic work habitually exploits a whole range of incongruous juxtapositions, and the categories obscure the complex intermingling of parodic effects. Both terms, however, are useful to indicate the kind of response a work appeals to: 'travesty' (as in its popular use) implies something savagely reductive, and 'burlesque' the comic immediacy of a theatrical 'spoof'. A distinction can be made, however, between all forms of parodic imitation and 'caricature': the analogy between caricature in painting and parody in writing (established by Fielding in his parodic novel *Joseph Andrews*, 1742) is misleading. Parody attacks its butt indirectly, through style; it 'quotes' from and alludes to its original, abridging and inverting its characteristic devices. The caricaturist's 'original' is not some other already existent style or work, whereas parody is a mirror of a mirror, a critique of a view of life already articulated in art. Parody is so common an element in literature precisely because it adds this extra level of critical comment which is lacking from caricature. See also PASTICHE, SATIRE.

See S. Dentith, *Parody* (2000); Linda Hutcheon, *Theory of Parody* (2000).

LS

Pastiche Whether applied to part of a work, or to the whole, implies that it is made up largely of phrases, motifs, images, episodes, etc. borrowed more or less unchanged from the work(s) of other author(s). The term is often used in a loosely derogatory way to describe the kind of helpless borrowing that makes an immature or unoriginal work read like a mosaic of quotations. More precisely, it has two main meanings, corresponding to two different *deliberate* uses of pastiche as a technique. There is a kind of pastiche which seeks to recreate in a more extreme and accessible form the manner of major writers. It tends to eliminate tensions, to produce a more highly coloured and polished effect, picking out and reiterating favourite stylistic mannerisms, and welding them into a new whole which has a superficial coherence and order. Unlike plagiarism, pastiche of this kind is not intended to deceive: it is literature frankly inspired by literature (as in Akenside's poem 'The pleasures of imagination', 1744). The second main use of pastiche is not reverential and appreciative, but disrespectful and sometimes deflationary. Instead of ironing out ambiguities in its source(s) it highlights them. It cannot be distinguished absolutely from PARODY, but whereas the parodist need only allude to the original intermittently, the writer of pastiche industriously recreates it, often concocting a medley of borrowed styles like Flann O'Brien in *At Swim-Two-Birds* (1939). A closely synonymous term, nearly obsolete, 'cento' or 'centonism', is relevant here: in its original Latin form it meant a garment of patchwork and, applied to literature, a poem made up by joining scraps from various authors. Many of the specialized uses of pastiche are reminiscent of this literary game: it may give encyclopaedic scope to a work, including all previous styles (Joyce's *Ulysses*); it is used by writers who wish to exemplify their ironic sense that language comes to them secondhand and stylized (George Herbert's 'Jordan I'). And a general *air* of pastiche is created by many writers who, for various reasons, refuse to evolve a style of their own, and who (like John Barth) employ other's cast-off phrases with conscious scepticism.

Fredric Jameson argues that parody has been replaced by pastiche in postmodernism, where all the cultural styles of the past are open to cannibalization and appropriation: 'Pastiche is, like parody, the imitation of a peculiar or unique, idiosyncratic style, the wearing of a linguistic mask, speech in a dead language. But it is a neutral practice of such mimicry, without any of parody's ulterior motives, amputated of the satiric impulse, devoid of laughter'.

See Barbara Barber, *Pastiche* (1997); Ingeborg Hoesterey, *Pastiche: Cultural Memory in Art, Film, Literature* (2001); Fredric Jameson, *Postmodernism: Or, the Cultural Logic of Late Capitalism* (1992).

LS

Pastoral   In classical and neo-classical definitions pastoral is a mode with conventional prescriptions about setting, characters and diction. In drama, poetry or prose it employs stylized properties and idealized Arcadian situations from rural life – 'purling streams', 'embowering shades'; singing contests, mourning processions – as a deliberate disguise for the preoccupations of urban, sophisticated people. Pastoral focusses on the contrast between the lives of the people who write it and read it, and the lives of those country people it portrays (both ends of society often appear, as in Shakespearean comedy). It relies on conventions shared with the audience – traditional names (Corydon, Thyrsis, Adonais), inherited motifs (the flower catalogue), plots based on transparent disguises. It may be idyllic, but is more often (as in Spenser's 'Shepheardes Calender' or Milton's 'Lycidas') tinged with melancholy and satire; because of its dimension of reference to contemporary society, pastoral invites allegory and symbolism. The proliferation of stock features made it, in

Greece, Augustan Rome and Renaissance Europe, an extremely precise medium for exploring the attitudes (rural nostalgia, narcissism, self-doubt) of consciously civilized and cultured people – poets particularly (N. B. the heightened self-consciousness of the pastoral ELEGY for a dead fellow-poet).

The artificiality of pastoral is not an evasion of realism: its rural setting is metaphorical, a means rather than an end. Like other conventions, it decays when the means cease to be viable, not because it is false (since it was never true). Many uses of the term are distorted by criteria adopted from realistic fiction. Documentary 'truth to the object' is irrelevant in pastoral, which is a mirror reflecting back its audience and writer rather than a transparent window. Pastoral is a product of pre- or anti-realistic worldviews which stress imaginative projection (e.g. the PATHETIC FALLACY) rather than passive perception. Thus, it lost its credibility with the rise of empiricism (and of the novel) during the eighteenth century, and was partially reinstated in the twentieth by writers like the American poet Wallace Stevens who argued that 'Life consists/Of propositions about life'. 'Failed realism', and 'anything depicting country life' are both uses of 'pastoral' based on unexamined realist assumptions.

Exploratory twentieth-century use of the term dated from William Empson's *Some Versions of Pastoral* (1935). He pointed out that pastoral was not a bundle of conventional properties, but a particular structural relationship ('putting the complex into the simple') which survived and extended beyond the limits of the formal mode. Empson's best example was *Alice in Wonderland*, where the heroine, like the 'shepherd of sixteenth century pastoral, explores the anxieties and complacencies of her society'. While retaining its function as a label, 'pastoral' acquired an extended application which relates to the search for literary MYTHS and archetypes.

See Terry Gifford, *Pastoral* (1999).

LS

Pathetic fallacy Ruskin introduced this notion (*Modern Painters*, vol. 3, 1856) to account for the attribution to inanimate nature of animate, even human, characteristics. He gives 'the cruel, crawling foam' as an example. People, he claims, fall into four categories: those who see nature clearly because their emotions are too dull to interfere (non-poets), those whose emotions are too strong for their intellect (second-order poets), those who, having strong intellect and passions, achieve a balance between the two (first-order poets) and finally those who perceive realities too great for humanity to bear and who revert to expressions which reason no longer controls (prophets). The second and last make use of the pathetic fallacy, but only the former do so through weakness. Ruskin argues, moreover, that the poet who sees nature as having 'an animation and pathos of its own' (rather than borrowed from culture) does not commit the fallacy, but merely shows 'an instinctive sense...of the Divine presence'. What constitutes a 'pathetic fallacy' must therefore vary with the dominant idea of the time: many have seen in such an 'instinctive sense' a fallacy rather than the perception of a truth.

AAAC

Performativity As understood and used in current critical studies, the theory of *performativity* was introduced by Judith Butler (1956–) in *Gender Trouble: Feminism and the Subversion of Identity* (1990). In this book she argued that gender is performative, a mime of dominant characteristics conventionally attributed to gender, and related to the categorization of two different sexes. However, as Butler explains, even if one allows, for the sake of argument, that sexed bodies fall into two categories, 'it does not follow that the construction of "men" will accrue exclusively to the bodies of males or that of "women" will interpret only female bodies'. Following the argument and method of the French philosopher, Michel Foucault (1926–84), Butler adopts a 'genealogical critique' of gender which investigates 'the political stakes in designating as an origin and cause those identity categories that are in fact the *effects* of institutions, practices and discourses with multiple and diffuse points of origin'. However, the discussion of performativity in *Gender Trouble* has sometimes been misunderstood. It has been seen as the recommendation for the deliberate subversion of gender by performative acts, such as drag, for instance, which Butler had used in *Gender Trouble* as an example of perfomativity. As Butler explained in an important interview, published in the journal *Radical Philosophy* in 1994, drag is an example of, but not a paradigm for, performativity. While her thesis is that gender is culturally performed, and thus, a performance, performance is not the same as performativity. Performativity is not about voluntary or deliberate acts of performance and subversion – such as drag – but is rather, the analysis of 'that aspect of discourse that has the capacity to produce what it names' through repetition and recitation. Performance always 'presumes a subject' whereas performativity contests the very notion of a subject able to volunteer to act outside its own instalment by virtue of performativity, which is 'the discursive mode through which ontological effects are installed'. Further, subversion cannot be so deliberate or have such calculable effects. What is

recommended, however, is the sustained interrogation of the discursive and institutional conditions by which these cultural effects are taken as norms (the 'historicity of norms'), constructing as they do, even the apprehension of material bodies. This Butler aimed to clarify in her next book, *Bodies that Matter: On the Discursive Limits of Sex* (1994). Here she returns to reconsider the category of sex (occluded to a large extent by her prior focus on gender) and the materiality of bodies. She questions the way in which certain biological differences, such as pregnancy, which will only ever constitute a relatively small portion of any woman's life, have become the salient characteristics of sex and have been central to the reductive, binary sexing of the body. As she described in her *Radical Philosophy* interview in 1994, she 'wanted to work out how a norm actually materializes a body, how we might understand the materiality of the body to be not only invested with a norm, but in some sense animated by a norm, or contoured by a norm'.

See, Sara Salih, *Judith Butler* (2002); Joan Riviere, 'Womanliness as Masquerade' in Shelley Saguaro (ed.), *Psychoanalysis and Woman: A Reader* (2000); Teresa de Lauretis, *Technologies of Gender: Essays on Theory, Film and Fiction* (1989).

SS

Peripeteia   See NARRATIVE STRUCTURE.

Persona   Originally used to denote the acting masks of classic Greek theatre, the term 'persona' developed extensive critical connotations. It has been commonly used to indicate the difference between the person who sits down to write and the 'author' as realized in and through the words on the page. This persona, or 'second self' of the author has to be distinguished from the narrator even in first-person narration. The degree of correspondence between narrator and persona may vary greatly. In Fielding's *Tom Jones* (1749), for instance, the narrator shares many qualities with the persona – tolerance, humour, wide understanding of human behaviour and humanistic learning. But in the case of Swift's *A Modest Proposal* (1729), to assume continuity between narrator and persona would be disastrous. The narrator deliberately heightens and distorts the view Swift seeks to expose. The distortion establishes the tone which makes us aware of Swift's *voice* in the prose. The persona clearly recommends the very opposite view, the amelioration of conditions and the implementation of social remedies, *not* the breeding of children for food, etc.

Wayne C. Booth argued in *The Rhetoric of Fiction* (1961) that the complex problem of reliable and unreliable narrators involves the persona or, as he called it, the implied author. Thus, 'I have called a narrator *reliable* when he speaks for or acts in accordance with the norms of the work (which is to say, the implied author's norms), *unreliable* when he does not.' Recognizing the persona is therefore central to the act of effective reading, since the persona represents the sum of all the author's conscious choices in a realized and more complete self as 'artist'.

This idea of persona as 'second self' incorporates the metaphorical roots of the 'mask' concept, implying the total being presented to the audience, outside and beyond the actor who assumes it. This, in turn, is rooted in magic ritual where 'masks' are independent beings who *possess* the individual who assumes them. Metaphorically, mask belongs to the group of concepts which imply that artists discover a more fully integrated vision than exists in 'reality'. It implies, too, a way out of the closed world of the ego into an objective vision communicable to others. Late Romantics, like Yeats, turn to the 'mask' concept to express a longing for an art which permits the artist to objectify personal experience and free it from mere subjectivity. See also NARRATIVE.

GG

Phallologocentrism A portmanteau word combining phallocentrism with LOGOCENTRISM. Whereas logocentrism, according to Jacques Derrida, is bound up in the drive to find stability, presence and meaning in objective concepts which are really linguistic effects, phallologocentrism acknowledges the masculine orientation both of this drive and of systems that privilege the (concept of the) phallus as the signifying source of power. Femininity is thus the 'Other', most obviously and essentially of phallologocentrism, but conventionally, of logocentrism too, which has privileged masculine reason over feminine emotion, male culture over female nature, the phallus-bearing body over the body of the woman. As a deconstructive critic, Derrida criticized the dominance of logocentrism in Western thought; in 'Structure, sign and play in the discourse of the human sciences' (1966), for instance, he noted the way in which logocentrism is predicated on and made secure by binary oppositions: presence/absence; male/female; order/chaos; reason/unreason; unity/multiplicity. Building on – in part to dismantle – the claim by Swiss philologist and linguist Ferdinand de Saussure (1857–1913) that language is an arbitrary but conventional system of 'differences without positive terms', Derrida chose instead a strategy that looks to defer meaning rather than to identify stable differences of meaning. Thus, in a feat of linguistic play for which he and other poststructuralists are known, Derrida coined the term DIFFÉRANCE (in French sounding the same as *difference*) to indicate the combination of the verbs to differ and to defer in his theory of meaning. New French Feminists borrowed from Derrida and Jacques Lacan (1901–81) to develop their own analysis of the 'phallacy' of phallologocentrism. Hélène Cixous (1937–) further notes that binary oppositionalism, on which 'every theory of culture, every theory of society' is based – 'everything that's organised as discourse, art, religion, the family, language, everything that seizes us, everything that acts on us' – is always hierarchical and is inevitably related to a primary dualism: Man/Woman ('Castration and Decapitation', English translation: 1981; see also 'Sorties', 1986). In Lacan's return to Freud through structuralism and linguistics, the Phallus is indeed a privileged signifier, the transcendental signifier, but it has little to do with the frail corporeal penis. The Phallus, as the originary and constellating term in the Symbolic language system known as the Law of the Father, always denotes lack in all its human subjects, regardless of anatomical differences. Feminist critics, such as Elizabeth Grosz, in *Jacques Lacan: A Feminist Introduction* (1990), discerned that if all human subjects lack in relation to the Phallus, then women, whose sex is considered an absence, even lack such lack. In 'The meaning of the Phallus' (1958), Lacan insists on the Phallus as an arbitrary signifier divorced from the penis and yet uses a sexual/anatomical analogy in his rationale:

> this signifier is chosen as what stands out as most easily seized upon in the real of sexual copulation [...] by virtue of its turgidity [which the penis, of course, cannot sustain], it is the image of the vital flow as it is transmitted in generation.

Cixous and Luce Irigaray (1930–) in her punningly titled essay 'This sex which is not one' (1977; trans. 1985), for example, exult in the female body and the *jouissance* (orgasmic, sensuous, generous, disinterested, expansive, fluctuating) of its libidinal economy (as opposed to the masculine calculating conservatism). They exhort women to 'write the body' (*écriture féminine*), a fluency that can be criticized for being essentialist and conforming to rather than overthrowing the stereotypes of the madwoman, witch and hysteric. Others, particularly feminist scholars and theorists in the 1970s and 1980s, found the exuberant combination of theory and practice, in terms of writing, at least, to be very inspiring. Also see DECONSTRUCTION, FEMINISM and LOGOCENTRISM.

See Isabelle de Courtivron and Elaine Marks (eds), *New French Feminisms: An Anthology* (1981) and Shelley Saguaro (ed.), *Psychoanalysis and Woman: A Reader* (2000).

SS

Phenomenology At its simplest, phenomenology is the attempt to describe whatever we perceive exactly as it appears to us. This does not make it sound very exciting, and yet, phenomenology has been an important part of philosophical thought for the last hundred years. Although he was not the first to use the term – that distinction went to one Johann Heinrich Lambert (1728–77) – Edmund Husserl (1859–1938) was certainly the first to turn it into a philosophical movement. Lambert used the term to signify the process whereby we move from appearance to truth and this was how it was generally used in the eighteenth century. Immanuel Kant (1728–1804), for instance, probably the most significant thinker of the period, employed the term to refer to the science of how things appear to us. Husserl's main influence, though, was the now largely forgotten Franz Brentano (1838–1917) who regarded philosophy as a description of phenomena not an explanation of them. However, in order to describe phenomena properly, a vital part of which is how they appear to consciousness, it is necessary to suspend all those things, such as tradition, science and common sense, which distort perception. Husserl called this process 'reduction'. Only by reducing the role of habit in our perception can we see phenomena in their purity. It is important to stress that Husserl is not saying that we will see things as they really are, but only as they appear to consciousness.

Husserl influenced a number of thinkers including Martin Heidegger (1889–1976), Hans-Georg Gadamer (1900–2002), Emmanuel Levinas (1906–95), Jean-Paul Sartre (1905–80), Maurice Merleau-Ponty (1908–61) and Jacques Derrida (1930–2004), all of who differed from him in a number of ways. Heidegger, for example, thought Husserl took too little account of the context in which we view phenomena and he also disagreed with the claim that we could describe phenomena as they really appear to us, arguing that all description involves an element of interpretation. Derrida goes even further declaring that it is impossible for us ever to have to have a clear view of the contents of our consciousness because they always come to us contaminated by language. Since we can never escape language, we can never see phenomena in their true light; we can only experience them through words which prevent us from experiencing them in their immediacy. Other criticisms of phenomenology include that is 'pseudo-mysticism', that it is too focussed on the individual and that it puts too much trust in the evidence of consciousness, forgetting that much of our so-called conscious experience is shaped by unconscious forces. Despite this, the main contribution of phenomenology to twentieth and perhaps twenty-first century philosophy remains its insistence on the importance of subjectivity in any account of knowledge.

It is the concern with the subjective nature of experience that links phenomenology with literature since we view poems, novels and plays as in some sense an expression of the author's view of the world. Having said that, there has not been a marked tradition of phenomenological criticism, at least in England, where commentary tends to be either pragmatic or political. Nevertheless, there is a general relationship between phenomenology and criticism. For example, the demand that we try to reduce the role of habit and custom in order to see things afresh is very close to the Russian FORMALIST demand that art should 'make strange'. Moreover, both phenomenology and literature share a commitment to describing lived experience and the fact that some phenomenologists, such as Levinas, are interested in ethics, posits another possible relation between the two activities. And then there are the observations on art by individual phenomenologists. Heidegger argued that art did not represent the world rather it created a new one which disclosed the possibilities for change in the old order. Gadamer discussed the problem of interpretation – which he called hermeneutics – for example, the need to be attentive to what a work actually says rather than impose our own view upon it. But he also said that we are unlikely ever to be able to recover the original intention behind the work of art, for our understanding of it is a fusion of what we want from the work now and what it meant in the past.

Its interest in the subjective experience makes phenomenology a form of romantic criticism but there is little of that philosophy in the work of British romantics, with the exception perhaps of Coleridge. There are, however, pronounced phenomenological themes in the work of F. R. Leavis, although he does not use the term. His concern with perception and the concrete, and his commitment to becoming more conscious in our response to literature certainly chimes with the writings of the major thinkers in this tradition.

See Michael Bell, *F. R. Leavis* (1988); Dermot Moran, *Introduction to Phenomenology* (2000).

GD

Picaresque   A kind of realistic fiction which originated in Spain with the anonymous *Lazarillo de Tonnes* (1554) and the more influential novel by Mateo Alemán, *Guzmán de Alfarache* (1559 and 1604), which was widely translated. Other important novels in this genre include in German, Grimmeishausen's *Simplicissirnus* (1669), and in French, Le Sage's *Gil Bias* (1715–35). The Spanish *picaro* or *picarón*, the anti-hero of such a novel, was translated into English as the *picaroon*; a scoundrel of low birth and evil life, at war with society. The form of the novel is commonly an autobiographical account of the picaroon's fortunes, misfortunes, punishments and opportunism. The tales are episodic, frequently arranged as journeys. The endings are abrupt, either as the picaroon sets off for America for a 'new life', or for the galleys. This allows a sequel to be added; but the mode is not formless. The pessimistic judgement of life does not allow a neat dénouement. Life is just more of the same. The stories inflict physical damage on their characters, and the damage is a sign of experience. Experience, however, is only more instances for picaroons of their irrepressible independence and society's

unalterable hostility. The novels allow a statement of the individual's freedom and independence but invoke the counter-balancing, restraining oppression of society. All picaroons have a series of tyrannical masters, and the servile relationship which demands abasement and allows cheating is a microcosm of the human state.

Picaresque is a term that must refer to the nature of the subject matter as well as to the superficial autobiographical and episodic features of the fiction. Unfortunately, in English it is the accidental arrangements that are usually indicated by *picaresque*: a low-life narrator, a rambling tale. There was plenty of rogue literature in England from Nashe's *Unfortunate Traveller* (1594) onwards. Obviously Defoe in *Moll Flanders* (1722) has some affinity with the picaresque. The novel is episodic; it has an autobiographical narrator and it is realistic. Moll, though, does not seem to be a real *picaro*. She is that peculiarly English figure, a temporary *déclassé(e)*. Smollett's *Roderick Random* (1748) is similar. Random is only temporarily of low estate; he ends by being restored to his own level. He is really a master, not a servant. The same author's *The Adventures of Ferdinand Count Fathom* (1753) is more nearly a real picaresque. Various features of the picaresque are found in different English novels: *Tom Jones* is organized along a journey; Dickens's *Nicholas Nickleby* allows realistic description of scenes of real life; Joyce Cary's *The Horse's Mouth* presents physical decay as the sign of experience, and Gully Jimson enjoys the 'free life'.

See Robert Alter, *Rogue's Progress: Studies in the Picaresque Novel* (1964); A. A. Parker, *Literature and the Delinquent: A Study of the Picaresque Novel* (1947); Giancarlo Maiorino (ed.),

The Picaresque: Tradition and Displacement (1996); Ulrich Wicks, *Picaresque Narrative, Picaresque Fictions: A Theory and Research Guide* (1989).

AMR

Plagiarism   See PASTICHE.

Platonism   In his utopian *Republic* (written *c.*380 BC) Plato banished the artists, having diagnosed the arts as indulgent imitations of a perceptible universe which was itself a misleading shadow of the eternal Ideas. He allowed only propagandist myths ('noble lies') as a concession to the irrationality of the majority, and suggested ironically that the arts were lower than practical crafts – better make a chair than a painting of one.

But Plato's own highly fictionalized method; his use of dialogue and of myth (the Cave, the Spindle of Necessity) undermined his attack on the arts. Plotinus (AD 204–70), founder of neo-Platonism, reinterpreted Plato in the direction of subjective mysticism (stressing the visionary elements in Book 6 of the *Republic*, and the *Symposium*) and his version of Plato the myth-maker and *vates*, mingling with the more practical original, became the source of the most far-reaching claims *for* the arts in Western culture.

The Platonic artist, whether renaissance or romantic, is a philosopher, who aspires to change the world by changing people's attitudes and values. The 'poem' may be an institution or an epic and it is not the work itself that makes the Platonic artist but the 'idea or fore-conceit of the work' (Sidney, *Defence of Poesie*, 1595). 'Imitation' in Platonic terminology can be misleading – theoretically at least the poet will 'to imitate borrow nothing of what is, hath been or shall be' (Sidney). Platonism does not distinguish the arts by media: metaphors from statecraft are used about poetry – 'Poets are the unacknowledged legislators of the world' (Shelley, *Defence of Poetry*, 1821) – and metaphors from poetics about politics or music.

It follows that Platonic criticism avoids classification of genres or of rhetorical figures; the Platonist's interest in language and form is compounded of miraculism and frustration: on the one hand the aspiration towards a fixed, innocent, 'golden' language, in which metre, image and syntax will embody that essential harmony towards which creation strives; on the other a profound scepticism which pushes language to its limits, destroys and impoverishes it as if to prove its eternal enmity to the ideal. The Platonic theorist is always likely to dismiss the product – the words, the rhythms – as 'a feeble shadow of the original conceptions of the poet' (Shelley). This pressure on the medium unites with the idealist yearning towards the one to produce hybrid forms (allegorical epics, lyrical dramas). Again, this is paradoxical: Platonism produces a subversive multiplication of forms in the strife for order.

In literary history, too, the idealist pressures proved liberating. Shelley's reading of Milton (like Blake's) is characteristically Platonic:

> He mingled...the elements of human nature as colours upon asingle pallet, and arranged them...according to the laws of epic truth, that is, according to the laws of that principle by which a series of actions of the external universe and of intelligent and ethical beings is calculated to excite the sympathies of succeeding generations of mankind.

Platonic literary history is repetitious or circular (Yeats), a continual return to mythic figures and structures only incidentally clothed in the trappings of a particular culture.

Platonism is the poets' poetics; more than any other theory it has been responsible for poetic self-consciousness (Collins's *Ode on the Poetical Character* (1746), Stevens's *Notes towards a Supreme Fiction* (1942)). This fact alone indicates its particular freedoms and limitations: it may set the poet squarely at the centre of the world but it undermines the world's reality and solidity. The result is that the processes of creativity become what the work itself is about. See also IMITATION.

See W. H. Auden, 'The poet and the city' in *The Dyer's Hand* (1962); Christopher Butler, *Number Symbolism* (1970); R. S. Crane (ed.), *Critics and Criticism* (1957); Wallace Stevens, *The Necessary Angel* (1951); Anna Baldwin and Sarah Hutton (eds), *Platonism and the English Imagination* (1994).

LS

Pleasure Some texts stimulate rather than satisfy, and indeed Novalis cultivated the fragment as a genre with this intention. But for many Neoclassicists (e.g. Kant), art is made pleasurable by its satisfying harmony of design: once we have discovered a work's central theme, all other features (such as versification or plot) can be seen as closely related to it, creating a complex yet powerfully unified effect. Nevertheless, the problems of applying this view to the disturbing, fearful events in TRAGEDY led Kant and others to postulate a radically different pleasure, aroused by the 'sublime' rather than the 'beautiful': the audience thrills to see tragic heroes rise above adversity and their self-preservation instinct because it feels itself participating in and aspiring towards the potential indomitability of the human spirit. By accepting guilt and the destruction of his achievements, Oedipus transcends them. Note that both 'beautiful'

and 'sublime' pleasure require distance: Oedipus and Lear do not enjoy their tragic experiences as their audiences may, and what distinguishes aesthetic enjoyment of form from a factory owner's admiration of a complex machine or a lecher's of a beautiful body is its disinterestedness: we seek satisfaction neither of self-interest nor of aroused desire, experiencing pleasure in our temporary freedom from such feelings.

Totally unenjoyable literature would probably cease to be published. Yet pleasure, especially if distanced or restful, is often considered suspect and self-indulgent. If we find Diderot's *The Nun* a good read, rather than feeling indignation at the heroine's suffering, we perversely refuse to be disturbed by how human beings can treat one another in society.

Roland Barthes detects insufficiently challenging pleasure in almost all pre-Modernist literature. He too postulates two radically different kinds of pleasure. He argues that we interpret what we read (as also our other experience) by applying already familiar conventions: our previous novel-reading and acquaintance with social assumptions create a large yet finite set of expectations, activated when we tackle another novel. A text might work totally within these limits, avoiding surprise and confirming our cultural expectations: Balzac, despite his complexity, can be seen as very readable (*lisible*), offering pleasure in reassuring recognition of the familiar. But the ideal text is for Barthes totally plural, in the sense that it refuses to imprison its readers within conventions or compel any particular interpretation: such a text he calls *scriptible*. For example, as we read Joyce's *Finnegans Wake* (1939) or Philippe Sollers's *Paradis* (1981), small segments of text, at first apparently disconnected, can be related in innumerable different ways. This experience, in which each reader 'writes' or constructs their own text, Barthes sees as liberating.

Although such works may indeed be used by the patient and inventive for individualistic self-expression, Barthes implies a heedlessly optimistic view of the reader. Faced with segments which can mean almost anything and an absence of authorial direction, readers will imagine and impose interpretations deriving from their previous habits of sense-making and thus from their acquired conventions: supposedly liberated reading becomes indistinguishable from uninventive, self-indulgent mental drift. A more useful approach to pleasure's origins is to analyse the experience of having expectations sometimes confirmed, sometimes surprised by a text (impossible if it is totally plural). At a first reading, there is delight in a release from and expansion of our limited consciousness as we compare our responses with the text's; at a later reading, the no less pleasurable realization that our perceptions of it have altered and that therefore our relation with it remains productive. See also AESTHETICS, READER.

See Roland Barthes, *The Pleasure of the Text* (trans. 1976), *S/Z* (trans. 1975); Donald W. Crawford, *Kant's Aesthetic Theory* (1974); William Wordsworth, 'Preface' (1802 version) to *Lyrical Ballads*.

MHP

Plot A term of highly varied status. It can mean just the paraphrasable story of a work – the simple narrative line which we can then flesh out by considering character and description, tone and texture, pattern and myth; E. M. Forster's 'low', 'atavistic' story-telling. So creative writing courses offer compendia of plots; so many works (lyric poems, modernist novels) can be 'without' it. The usage is partly derived from Aristotle's word *mythos* in the *Poetics*, commonly translated as 'plot'; and for a richer sense of the term it is worth recalling what he said. Aristotle's plot was the mimesis (i.e. the analogous *making*) of an action. He distinguished six parts in his exemplary species, tragedy, but did not reduce them to equivalence: plot constitutes the dynamic whole to which the other parts relate, the necessary order as opposed to the enabling features of development. It is the distilling centre of the choices available to the author; having determined a medium (stage, book) and a mode (lyric, dramatic), the author must also choose other essential principles of coherence. The plot must have a shape (e.g. a rise in the hero's fortune followed by a descent); it must have a sequence or order determining the kind and degree of effort at particular points (beginning, middle, end); it must have a size (magnitude, duration) which will help determine that shape and sequence. It must have agents and a society: for these there must be a language, appropriate not only to them but also to the other elements of the structure. It must have a developing psychology culminating internally in good tragedy in the protagonist and externally in an effect on the audience (CATHARSIS); and it must accord with and seek out general human experience (universality). Aristotle's *mythos* is close to Henry James's assumptions in his preface to *The Portrait of a Lady*, when he distinguishes a *donnée* and then sees certain elements as being of the essence and others of the provision. This adds what is perhaps implicit in Aristotle; that there is play in writing for *continuous* choice; plot is *emergent* from the selective logic of the writerly act.

Few twentieth-century critics took up this complex usage, viewing plot as a necessary order of a fiction. An exception were the Chicago Aristotelians (see CHICAGO CRITICS), who spoke persuasively of its value as a means of distinguishing the determining order of a work. (The Russian FORMALIST critics also usefully explored the concept.) What (here to adapt Aristotle considerably) seems apparent is that the 'deep' definition of plot approximates to the difficulties of the writing process before and during composition: it involves recognizing an essential relationship, familiar to writers if not always to critics, between 'plot' in its simple story sense and other elements much more complicated than is usually understood – characters, local linguistic devices ('speeches', 'descriptions'), general linguistic devices (rhetorical strategies, pervasive symbols), generative sequence in actions at narrative and tonal levels, starts and finishes.

Plot is a compositional whole. Even then, it *can* seem a deterministic grid, making the writer of a fiction a God-figure whose command over characters is absolute. (This analogue – character as liberal, plot as determinist – has often been a theme in fiction: Muriel Spark's *The Driver's Seat*, 1970 is a clear example.) This is a possible derivative of the concept of plot, and suggests its coherent wholeness. See also CHARACTER, NARRATIVE STRUCTURE, STRUCTURALISM, STRUCTURE.

See Aristotle, trans. I. Bywater, *Poetics* (1909); R. S. Crane, 'The concept of plot and the plot of *Tom Jones*' in Crane (ed.), *Critics and Criticism* (1957); E. M. Forster, *Aspects of the Novel* (1927); Henry James, 'The art of fiction' (1888), reprinted in Morris Roberts (ed.), *The Art of Fiction and Other Essays by Henry James* (1948); N. J. Lowe, *The Classical Plot and the Invention of Western Narrative* (2004). For the Formalist/Structuralist tradition, see Lee

T. Lemon and Marion J. Reis (trans.), *Russian Formalist criticism: Four Essays* (1965); *Russian Poetics in Translation, Vol. 4, Formalist Theory* (1977); Tzvetan Todorov, *The Poetics of Prose* (trans. 1977); Seymour Chatman, *Story and Discourse* (1978).

MSB

Pluralism   See CHICAGO CRITICS.

Poetic diction   See DICTION, POETRY.

Poetic licence   It has sometimes been argued that, because of the difficulty of satisfying the additional voluntary restrictions of poetic form, the poet has a 'licence' to relax some of the normal restrictions of the language-system. The most thorough attempt to find a justification for this was made by the Russian Formalist and Prague Structuralist critical schools. According to Shklovsky, people living by the sea grow impervious to the sound of the waves.

> By the same token, we scarcely ever hear the words which we utter.... We look at each other, but we do not see each other any more. Our perception of the world has withered away, what has remained is mere recognition.

By disturbing language, and therefore the view of reality which we receive through language, the poet refreshes perception and replaces recognition by an impression of novelty. Or, as Roman Jakobson has put it, 'The function of poetry is to point out that the sign is not identical with its referent.' On this view, the kind of 'licence' we ought to grant should cover neither technical incompetence nor novelty for its own sake, but only deviations which bring about a new sense of inner and outer realities. Many writers, even prose-writers, have agreed. Conrad, for example, wrote that 'the development of ... phrases from their (so-called) natural order is luminous for the mind'. See also FOREGROUNDING, FORMALISM, ORIGINALITY.

See Victor Erlich, *Russian Formalism* (1965) for a general discussion of the topic and for the quotations from Shklovsky and Jakobson above.

AAAC

Poetics   In modern usage poetics is not the study of, or the techniques of, poetry (verse), but the general theory of literature. From the Russian FORMALISTS, Prague School and French STRUCTURALISTS to structuralist and POST-STRUCTURALIST writers there has been an appeal for a science of literature which should be devoted not to the piecemeal criticism or interpretation of specific literary texts, but to identifying the general properties which make literature possible: one should study 'literariness' rather than existing works of 'literature'. The search was, then, for general laws underlying particular texts: for an 'essence' to literature. For a clear programmatic statement, see T. Todorov, 'Poétique' in O. Ducrot *et al.*, *Qu'est-ce que le structuralisme?* (1968).

Universals of literature might seem an over-abstract and overambitious goal, given the great formal diversity of poems, plays, novels, oral stories, etc., and most work in poetics has consisted of descriptive studies of specific kinds or genres of texts. Narrative genres from the oral anecdote and fairy tale to the epic and novel have been analysed in terms of claimed universal elements, such as 'functions' of characters and the relations between them in fable, plot or narrative structure, or the relations between these internal elements and relationships and the position of the narrator or reader (see Shlomith Rimmon-Kenan, *Narrative Fiction: Contemporary Poetics*, 1983). Dramatic genres involve the same elements and

relationships with the additional modalities of character/actor and stage/audience relations (see Keir Elam, *The Semiotics of Theatre and Drama*, 1980). Poetic genres have been studied in terms of the formal patterning of sounds (assonance, alliteration, rhymes); rhythms (metre, phrase- and sentence-rhythm), relations of lines, stanzas, sections, syntax, point of view, etc. (the verse analyses of Roman Jakobson have been an important model and focus for controversy). Poetics does not aim, however, to study these 'devices' piecemeal, but seeks the determining patterns of literary structure, such as the relationship between automatism and FOREGROUNDING and the master device of the 'dominant' (Jakobson), that component of a work which sets in motion and determines the relations between all other components.

Theory and description in twentieth-century poetics was much influenced by the analogies provided by the 'generative' linguistics of Noam Chomsky (cf. LANGUAGE): hence generative poetics. Chomsky proposed that mature native speakers possess 'linguistic competence', based on universal properties of language, which allows them to produce and comprehend an unlimited number of new sentences; a grammar of a language captures this linguistic competence and assigns structural descriptions to sentences of the language. Such a grammar is said to 'generate all and only the grammatical sentences of the language'. Analogously, argued the poeticians, experienced readers of literature possess 'literary competence', a knowledge of the essential universal properties of literature which gives them access to the significance of specific literary texts: just as we know the grammar of our own language, we may in some sense know the 'grammar' of (e.g.) story construction, and even a naïve reader or listener senses when a story is deviant, if it is incomplete, if events seem to be in the wrong order or if causal and sequential connections between elements are inconsistent or suppressed.

Although, as suggested above, universal literary competence is implausible, competence in particular genres with which the reader is familiar is reasonable, and grammars of genres of the kind suggested by Todorov could be regarded as accounting for such competence. At this point the linguistic analogy can be brought closer: the particular technical concepts which linguists use for describing sentences (e.g. deep structure, transformation, embedding, semantic feature, lexical item, etc.) can be applied to the larger unit, text, on the SEMIOTIC assumption that texts are structured analogously to sentences. A strictly generative poetics involves the analogic use of linguistic concepts in accounting for a text as derived from underlying abstract units of significance. We may distinguish between *syntactic* and *semantic* approaches to the generation of literary texts. Working with syntactic analogies, Todorov and Kristeva in France applied traditional grammatical terms to the analysis of narrative structures: 'proper name' represents character; 'adjective' represents properties of or states experienced by the characters; 'verb' represents actions by the characters that modify situations or affect the characters. See T. Todorov, 'The grammar of narrative' and 'Narrative transformations' in *The Poetics of Prose* (trans. 1977); J. Kristeva, *Le texte du roman* (1970). In America, the syntactic transformations of Chomsky's grammar have been applied to the ordering of narrative functions analysed by Propp in his *Morphology of the Folk-Tale* (1928, trans. rev. edn, 1968): a story consists of 'moves' or

sequences of actions, and it is these, not individual verbs, which may be reordered, inverted or embedded (three typical transformations). Moreover, there is a semantic congruence between key sequences, such as the hero's struggle to solve a riddle set by the donor of a magic aid and his struggle to overcome the villain and thus achieve victory and rewards. A similar exploration of narrative transformations which underlie the shifting roles of characters was attempted by Todorov in his analysis of the novel *Les liaisons dangereuses* (see *Littérature et signification*, 1967).

Two Russian poeticians, Zholkovsky and Scheglov, took a more radically semantic line: literary *texts* are generated from *themes* (the object of search in traditional literary analysis and interpretation). The entire literary work is an expansion of a basic theme, and our ability to move to and fro between text and theme must depend on some rather consistent psychological mechanisms ('expressiveness devices') whereby simple meanings are 'processed' into more complex meanings. The number of such mechanisms is probably quite small, but it must include 'concretization', 'multiple realization', 'augmentation', 'contrast', 'antecedence', 'reversal' and 'ellipsis'. These may operate at any level of structure and at any phase in the generation of the text, so that their operation is not confined to specific sentence-like structures and sequences, as with the syntactic generative models. This model provides a set of procedures whereby we can trace the derivation of a literary text from its deep theme while making explicit at every stage our interpretative and analytical processes. See Yu. K. Scheglov and A. K. Zholkovsky, 'Towards a "theme-(expression devices)-text" model of literary structure' in G*enerating the Literary Text*, *Russian Poetics in Translation*, I (1975);

L. M. O'Toole, 'Analytic and synthetic approaches to narrative structure: Sherlock Holmes and "The Sussex Vampire"' in R. Fowler (ed.), *Style and Structure in Literature* (1975).

Although founded on the generative model of linguistic competence, this generative poetics does not confine itself to studying the sequential arrangement of quasi-grammatical elements, but focusses on the specific mechanisms of literary competence. For other questions which are traditional concerns of poetics, see LITERATURE.

See also J. Culler, *Structuralist Poetics* (1975); V. Erlich, *Russian Formalism: History, Doctrine* (1965); R. Fowler, *Literature as Social Discourse* (1981), chs 9 and 10; R. Jakobson, 'Linguistics and poetics' in T. A. Sebeok (ed.), *Style in Language* (1960). Relevant journals include *Communications, Journal of Literary Semantics, Poetics, Poetics Today* (formerly *Poetics and the Theory of Literature*), *Poétique, Russian Poetics in Translation*.

MO'T

Poetry The terms 'poem', 'poetry', 'poetic' and 'poetics' seem to be necessarily frequent in critical writing but various in their senses. The commonest use of 'poem' is 'any composition in verse': VERSE referring to a set of technical conventions for regulating a composition by line-length, for making the *line* part of the expressive form, and 'poem' claiming to be a genre-term subsuming any production which utilizes that convention. There is some redundancy here, if poetry is equated with verse, but perhaps we need the term, for we have no other word, parallel to, say, NOVEL in PROSE, for a complete set of verses. However, poetry is also commonly *contrasted* with verse, both in a quantitative way, as using more

tropes, more linguistic reverberations, and in a qualitative way, as using them more productively. Verse may also be considered 'prosy', that is, mechanically correct but uninspired: this characterization merges with the pre-twentieth-century idea of poetry as a metaphysical quality, an intangible, romantic, virtue. So the technical, descriptive, distinction between prose and verse is blurred: verse may be poetic or prosaic, prose may be poetic or not. The overtly evaluative 'poetic' hazardously transcends formal categories, except in such usages as 'poetic diction' by which is meant the artificial vocabulary conventions obeyed in, say, Anglo-Saxon or Augustan verse: *purling streams, finny tribes* and the like.

The technical imprecision of 'poem' and its derivatives is allowed by its etymology: Greek *poesis*, meaning a 'making', in verse or not. The contrast invoked is between that which is *constructed* and that which is natural. Traditionally 'poetry' has narrowed to the sense of a *verbal* making (as opposed to *poesis* in the other art media), but is still more general than 'verse', so again obscuring the distinction between metred and unmetred language which common usage supports. So 'poetics' comes to mean the general aesthetics of literature-as-opposed-to-other arts and, more particularly, literature-seen-as-verbal-construct. The latter, more restricted, usage derives from the extension of NEW CRITICAL doctrine, which stipulates that the method of analysis must be basically verbal (see David Lodge, *Language of Fiction*, 1966, and articles by various authors in early issues of the new periodical *Novel*); critics can thus discuss 'the poetics of fiction', considering the novel as a fundamentally verbal construct and its peculiar inner 'world' as ultimately linguistically created. So a novel can in this sense be (akin to) a 'poem', and again the verse criterion for poetry arguably disappears.

See Jon Cook (ed.), *Poetry in Theory* (2004); David Buchbinder, *Contemporary Literary Theory and the Reading of Poetry* (1991); Jeffrey Wainwright, *Poetry: The Basics* (2004).

RGF and AER

Point of view   A term used in twentieth-century theory and criticism of FICTION to designate the position from which a story is told. Although a large number of these have been distinguished by some critics, only two are common: first-person and third-person narration (few authors attempt the second-person: John Fowles, Lewis Grassic Gibbon, Michel Butor). Narration from the first-person point of view has some obvious advantages in that it enables the author, without artificiality, to enter the intimacy of the protagonist's mind, in a STREAM OF CONSCIOUSNESS manner or otherwise. But there are also limitations to this form of narration: if access to the hero is privileged and extensive, by the same token, since we are not able to read the minds of other people, the thoughts and feelings of the other characters remain a matter of conjecture to hero, author and reader alike. Needless to say, some novelists turn this opaqueness to good ironic account (cf. *The Outsider* by Albert Camus (1942) which relies heavily on the inscrutability of others). Traditionally, the third person is, however, the more widespread mode of narration, and most novelists have assumed it grants them licence to virtual omniscience. In a famous essay Jean-Paul Sartre pilloried François Mauriac for usurping wisdom reserved only to God, who – Sartre concluded with cutting emphasis – is no artist, 'any more than Mr Mauriac is'. As if to forestall this sort of broadside, some novelists have followed the example of Flaubert in *Madame Bovary* (1857) and used omniscience with such discretion that it passes virtually unnoticed. Others, again, have adopted Dickens's practice in *Bleak House* (1852–3) (intercalating Esther's narrative with omniscient narrative, and allowing Esther occasionally to narrate things not observed by her but reported to her by others), or have imitated the manner in which Conrad, in *Under Western Eyes* (1911), employs an intelligent first-person narrator having privileged access to the mind of another through the perusal of a private diary or correspondence. Henry James is the novelist usually most associated with detailed exploration of point of view, but some experimental novelists like Alain Robbe-Grillet transcend the issue altogether by abrupt and unsignposted shifts from one point of view to another, in line with a systematic undermining of the entire traditional notion of consistency, and produce works which read as William Faulkner's *The Sound and the Fury* (1929) would, if all its paragraphs were placed in a hat and pulled out in random order. See also NARRATIVE.

See Norman Friedman, 'Point of view in fiction', *PMLA*, 70 (1955), 1160–84, updated by Wayne C. Booth, *The Rhetoric of Fiction* (1961); G. Genette, *Narrative Discourse* (1980); S. S. Lanser, *The Narrative Act: Point of View in Prose Fiction* (1981); F. Stanzel, *Narrative Situations in the Novel* (1969); B. Uspensky, *A Poetics of Composition* (trans. 1973); Paul Simpson, *Language, Ideology and Point of View* (1993).

JWJF

Polyphony   See DIALOGIC STRUCTURE.

Polysemy   See AMBIGUITY.

Pornography   Classified by the Library of Congress as 'Literature, immoral', has evaded definitions by critics and courts alike precisely because of the difficulty of establishing the exact relationship between literature and morality. Lawyers have tended to describe it in terms of its effects – the pornographic is that which tends to deprave or corrupt – while recognizing that the pursuit of literary or scientific objectives may be held to justify even the potentially corrupting.

Pornography cannot simply be equated with eroticism, although the word originally signified accounts concerned with prostitutes. Lawrence, for example, saw eroticism as an essential element in human relations and as a reassuring contrast to the sterility of the modern environment; the SURREALISTS discovered in the erotic evidence of the central role of intuition and evidence of that reconciliation of opposites which was their chief aim. In other words eroticism has been seen as an essential aspect of the battle between humanity and its social determinants, as a key to mystical experience and a salutary reminder of a non-rational dimension to existence. Pornography, on the other hand, has no aim beyond sexual stimulation. As Lawrence suggested, pornography is a result of the separation of sexuality from a notion of the whole person; it stems, at least in part, from a refusal, for religious, moral or aesthetic reasons, to admit in a public way to the centrality or the detailed reality of the sexual impulse. By this argument pornography is the inevitable by-product of prudery, and it is scarcely surprising, therefore, to discover the extent of pornography during the Victorian years: see Stephen Marcus, *The Other Victorians* (1966).

Pornography may constitute a conscious defiance of conventional standards of taste and propriety; it is thus potentially a subversive, even a revolutionary,

force. It appears to push sensibility to its limit and to stand as an implicit criticism of a society intent on denying freedom of thought and expression. It is perhaps significant that pornography was permitted for a brief period during the French Revolution. Yet, if it is subversive in its appeal to anarchic impulses it is cathartic in its purgation of such impulses. Finally, therefore, pornography is perhaps little more than the perfect consumer product, simultaneously creating and doing its best to satisfy a specific need. Twentieth-century feminist critics have argued for and against poetry: a critic like Andrea Dworkin sees in it exclusively masculine constructions of a passive female sexuality open to abuse, while a writer, such as Angela Carter has argued for its liberatory, Marcusian potential. The ICA volume *Pieces of Flesh* (2001), edited by Zadie Smith, is an attempt at writing stories with a twenty-first century sensibility more at ease with the commercialism of the porn industry.

See Anon, *The Obscenity Laws* (1969); Norman St John Stevas, *Obscenity and the Law* (1956); Peter Michelson, *Speaking the Unspeakable: Poetics of Obscenity* (1992); Bradford K. Mudge, *The Whore's Story: Women, Pornography and the British Novel, 1684–1830* (2000).

CWEB

Postcolonialism Emerged out of developments within literary studies in the late 1970s as the revolution in 'theory' was extended to encompass the cultural, political and economic legacy of empire and its aftermath. For many, the pivotal moment in the development of postcolonialism came with the publication of Edward Said's path-breaking book ORIENTALISM in 1978. Here, Said linked the cultural and intellectual discourse of 'the West' with the material practices of colonialism. This concern with the relationship between culture and power is the dominant feature of postcolonialism, which has broadened into a disciplinary sub-field in its own right. Nevertheless, it is also a highly contested and, to a great extent, controversial area of study and this is reflected in diasgreements over the term itself.

The term 'postcolonialism' has emerged from these controversies as a way of marking the existence of a field of discourse rather than a particular theoretical concept – the absence of the hyphen indicating perhaps the lack of substantive content within the term. However, this is not to imply the field is therefore theoretically empty. On the contrary, it is distinguished, if not fraught, by theoretical complexity and richness; indeed, for some it is overly theoretical and this in itself is reason to suspect that far from increasing our understanding, postcolonialism tends to obfuscate the urgent political, economic and social crises that have been brought about and intensified during and after colonialism. Many critics charge it with concentrating too much on culture at the expense of a genuinely radical critique of the materialities of power and inequality in a post-colonial age.

The absence of the hyphen is perhaps indicative of the indeterminacy of what exactly is meant by 'post-colonial' (i.e. with a hyphen). The 'post' clearly refers to and implies a period 'after' colonialism and in this strict literal sense the object of postcolonial studies is the historical period of the late twentieth century as the European empires of the nineteenth and early twentieth centuries broke up and former colonies achieved their political independence. However, this is unsatisfactory because to suggest that colonialism has ended is to overlook the fact that

the configurations of power in the colonial world have remained largely intact in the post-colonial period. That is, far from achieving independence, the former colonies have now succumbed to more subtle forms of domination. Analysis of neo-colonialism and the structures of domination and subordination in the post-colonial period is one of the key features of postcolonialism and so the hyphen seems misplaced from that perspective.

It has been suggested that the 'post' refers to everything that happens after the colonial intervention so that historically postcolonialism encompasses the colonial period as well as its aftermath. This is one reason why 'colonial discourse analysis' is also one of the key sub-fields of postcolonialism. In examining the production and reproduction of discourses produced by and for colonialism, in deconstructing their rationales and habits of mind, in analysing colonial representations of the subjugated peoples, colonial discourse analysis seeks to lay bare the processes through which colonialism was practised culturally as well as materially, and how ideologies justifying colonialism were disseminated and embedded into consciousness. Colonial discourse analysis adopts Foucauldian concepts of discourse that conceive of culture as a material practice, and rejects criticism of discourse analysis as thereby privileging cultural critique over material analysis.

Others, however, have criticized postcolonialism for privileging the colonial encounter as *the* central fact in the histories of colonized peoples. This takes for granted the centrality of European experience and posits the experience of the colonized as an adjunct to that. It thereby replicates at the level of analysis precisely that kind of dependency that remains a feature of contemporary neo-colonialism, leading some critics to suggest that postcolonialism is the 'cultural logic' of neo-colonialism writ small in the language of the metropolitan academy. Certainly, the theoretical sophistication of post-colonial theory, and its sometimes difficult and opaque language, extends itself to criticism that postcolonialism is an over-elaborate, abstracted and self-indulgent form of cultural analysis that does little to address the politically urgent problems of the formerly colonized world. The writings of Gayatri Spivak and Homi Bhabha, who, along with Said have been characterized as the 'holy trinity' of postcolonial theory, raise objections because of their dense style. Yet, particularly in the case of Spivak, this may be seen as a postcolonial strategy of 'deforming' the discourse of European knowledge, a discourse that Said has shown to be deeply implicated in colonialism itself.

Ambiguity concerning the *temporal* scope of postcolonialism is offset by a fair degree of consensus concerning its geographical provenance. Postcolonialism sees modern colonialism as having been global in scope and so it concerns itself with a global agenda, concentrating as much on the former European (or Western) 'centre' as the colonial 'peripheries'. It has extended its concern into debates concerning multiculturalism, diaspora, racism and ethnicity as the mass migrations in the postwar period by formerly colonized peoples have radically transformed the cultures and societies of their erstwhile masters. In addition, a generation of feminist scholars have examined the intersections of gender and sexuality with colonial and post-colonial discourses on race, ethnicity and nation. See also ORIENTALISM, SUBALTERN, HYBRIDITY, NÉGRITUDE.

See Aijaz Ahmad, *In Theory: Nations, Classes, Literatures* (1992); Homi K. Bhabha, *The Location of Culture* (1994); Edward Said, *Orientalism* (1978), *Culture and Imperialism* (1993); Gayatri Chakravorty Spivak, *The Spivak Reader* (1996); Bart Moore-Gilbert, *Postcolonial Theory: Contexts, Practices, Politics* (1997).

AM

Postmodernism A philosophical response to the fragmentation of MODERNISM in the post-1945 period, postmodernism's influence on intellectual debates about the production, valorization and interpretation of cultural production has been enormous. Its principal theoretical tenets have been hotly disputed since the appellation was first used in 1947 to describe a mode of architectural style, but in broad terms postmodernism refers to three key areas of socio-cultural interaction. First, it describes a period after modernism though this has always been a contentious and rather arbitrary distinction as, for some critics, the technical and formalistic experiments of postmodernism are little more than extensions of modernist engagements with form and language. Certainly the two major artistic movements of the twentieth century differ less than some critics would contend, but equally both would resist the cohering framework of the term 'movement' as each seeks to break from the suffocating uniformity of conservative aesthetics. The term 'postmodern' began to be used during the 1960s as a means of distinguishing the subversive fiction of writers, such as John Barth, Donald Barthelme, Samuel Beckett and Jorge Luis Borges from the experimental works of high modernism composed during the 1920s and 1930s. The playful, irreverent liberties taken with language, narrative structure, typology and the reader/text interface by these novelists suggested an exhaustion with the modes of traditional expression and championed an artistic freedom that allowed the celebration of non-literary media derived particularly from popular culture within the text. The modernist notion of the artist alienated from the mundane irrelevances of daily life forging an ethereal connection with an other world of art was gradually being replaced by an artist that revelled in the visceral contemporaneity of the everyday, moulding out of the maelstrom of mass culture an aesthetics of ephemerality.

The second key feature of postmodernism is its deeply ambiguous political character. Where modernist art scorned the insubstantiality of the political realm, claiming that it reflected only a temporary and localized example of human praxis, postmodern culture centred itself on the inherently political qualities of art. From this can be inferred the strong links between postmodernism and Marxism, a legacy deriving in no small measure from the Leftist political persuasions of many of the academic proponents of the field. The rise of postmodernism as a philosophical discourse during the 1960s and 1970s was matched by the emergence of literary theory, and in particular linguistic and discourse analysis. The work of Roland Barthes, Jacques Derrida, Michel Foucault and Julia Kristeva quickly became associated with the theoretical principles underpinning postmodernism and whilst they tacitly acknowledged the economic enchainment of the work of art, they moved the agenda of the Left onto fresh territory by insisting that all cultural practices were imbued with oppressive undertones and therefore offered sites of productive political struggle. That any communicational act was conceived, made and interpreted within ideology and thereby excluded competing ideological formations became a defining intellectual reference point for postmodernism and,

allied to significant socio-economic shifts in the Western world, encouraged the formation of emancipatory movements dedicated to the vocalization of previously marginalized politics. Tied to this vision of an ideological equivalence is the third principal arena of postmodernism's impact.

In 1979, Jean-François Lyotard published *The Postmodern Condition: A Report on Knowledge*. In it he argued that the postmodern condition was characterized by a deeply felt scepticism towards metanarratives (discursive formations promising a totalized account of knowledge). For Lyotard the traditional pivots of human belief (whether they be religion, philosophy or science) could no longer be sustained for each reveals its domineering ideological insistence in its intolerance of competing voices. The totalizing imperative of the metanarrative obscures and denigrates the claims of Others and, in so doing, according to Lyotard, it invalidates itself. The freedom that this anti-establishmentarianism extended was grasped by a host of liberation movements (such as feminism, gay rights and the racially and religiously dispossessed) as a vindication of their rights. Not all critics agreed with Lyotard's egalitarianism: Jürgen Habermas and Fredric Jameson in particular attacked the lack of distinction between an ideological free-for-all and the monolithic state bureaucracies that hold sway in the West. The dominance of late-capitalism means, for Jameson, that there is no distance between postmodern art and the society that created it, thereby rendering the act of critical judgement impractical – one is ultimately always judging postmodernism from within postmodernism and therefore merely ordering a procession of self-referential landmarks.

The 1980s saw attempts to formalize postmodernism's stylistic characteristics with particular attention to the recycling, often parodically, of existing images, forms and cultural codes. By focussing on the pre-inscribed status of artefacts from across a high/low cultural divide, producers celebrated the circularities of artistic creation, vaunting the impossibility of originality by reappropriating conventionalized forms to pastiche and ironize their ideological 'sincerity'. Ultimately this self-reflexive wit became ubiquitously employed to refer to any radicalization of the aesthetic act and casual invocations of postmodernism were used to identify a return to a form of conservatism (such as in the worst excesses of post-feminist chauvinism). That such a traduction is consistent with postmodernism's own cultural relativism is itself ironic, but it is appropriate that a philosophical movement dedicated to the politics of consumption should ultimately eat itself.

See Jean Baudrillard, *Simulacra and Simulations* (1980); Jürgen Habermas, *The Philosophical Discourse of Modernity* (1985); Linda Hutcheon, *A Poetics of Postmodernism: History, Theory, Fiction* (1988); Fredric Jameson, *Postmodernism, or The Cultural Logic of Late Capitalism* (1991); Jean-François Lyotard, *The Postmodern Condition: A Report on Knowledge* (1979).

DL

Post-structuralism As a general term for developments in literary theory and criticism, especially the 'linguistic turn', became common in the 1970s. Like all such compounds, it is ambiguous. Is the relation to STRUCTURALISM one of succession or supercession? – that is, do we see post-structuralism as simply later than its predecessor, or is it in some sense a development? Both usages can be found; and post-structuralism covers so many practices that it is difficult to define. But

it can be approached as a working through, in various fields of inquiry, of some implications of DECONSTRUCTION. Derrida's influential lecture on 'Structure, sign and play in the discourse of the human sciences' (*Writing and Difference*, 1967, trans. 1978) proposed a disruption in the very concept of structure as a stable system, mischievously quoting Lévi-Strauss against himself. The effects of deconstruction, though, were not confined to a critique of structuralism. They rather emphasized a methodological shift, a move away from explanation by origin, order by opposition, fixed or closed signification and the person as a unified subject. Recent PSYCHOANALYSIS, notably that of Jacques Lacan, encouraged the latter move, and much recent psychoanalytic criticism is one variety of post-structuralism. It can also be traced in cultural and ideological analysis like that of Michel Foucault or Gilles Deleuze, and in the feminism of Hélène Cixous or Luce Irigaray. Divergent accounts of the READER, like Bloom's 'misreading', can be cited; so, of course, can the literary studies listed under DECONSTRUCTION. Roland Barthes's career shows the post-structural shift with particular emphasis, as in the sardonic opening of *S/Z* (1970, trans. 1974): 'There are said to be certain Buddhists whose ascetic practices enable them to see a whole landscape in a bean.' Such tidy encapsulation had been Barthes's own ambition in the mid-1960s, and it is precisely what post-structuralism rejects.

See Catherine Belsey, *Post-structuralism: A Very Short Introduction* (2002) and Mark Poster, *Critical Theory and Post-structuralism: In Search of a Context* (1989). Two useful anthologies: *Textual Strategies: Perspectives in Post-Structuralist Criticism*, edited by Josué V. Harari (1979); and *Untying the Text: a Post-Structuralist Reader*, edited by

Robert Young (1981). *The Oxford Literary Review* and *Diacritics* publish relevant articles.

EC

Practical criticism   See ANALYSIS, CRITICISM, NEW CRITICISM, READER.

Presence   To begin, three examples: Rene Descartes's famous pronouncement 'I think therefore I am'; the signature that binds us to a contract; and the proverb 'The letter killeth but the spirit giveth life'. What links these seemingly disparate phenomena is that each is based on a certain conception of presence as a source of authenticity and guarantee of meaning. Thus, the stability of Descartes's 'I' is supposedly underwritten by the fact that this thinking subject is present to itself within consciousness. Following the same logic, a signature is meant to testify to the present intentions of its bearer at the moment of signing. The proverb, finally, effectively privileges the spirit – an internal essence associated with the ultimate presence of God – over the destructive powers of writing. This valorization of presence as a site of truth and authentic meaning is ubiquitous throughout the Western world and dominates all aspects of our thought. As Jonathan Culler suggests in *On Deconstruction* (1982):

> Among the familiar concepts that depend on the value of presence are: the immediacy of sensation, the presence of ultimate truths to a divine consciousness, the effective presence of an origin in a historical development, a spontaneous or unmediated intuition, the transumption of thesis and antithesis in a dialectical synthesis, the presence in speech of logical and grammatical structures, truth as what subsists behind appearances, and the effective presence of a goal in the

steps that lead to it. The authority of presence, its power of valorization, structures all our thinking.

Speaking more specifically, this valorization of presence is part and parcel of the logocentric history of the West, of its desire for a stable ground or foundation (the logos). However the logos is conceived – Being, Essence, Origin, Truth, etc. – its role is always the same: to anchor and fix meaning. Its ability to do so is, in turn, based on the assumption that the logos is a site of unmediated presence. Escaping the play of differences by which meaning is articulated, the logos constitutes a pure and self-present signified.

This logocentric emphasis on presence is seen most obviously in its privileging of speech over writing. From Plato to the present day, the history of Western thought has consistently considered speech to have a privileged relationship to truth. When we speak, we seem to have direct access to our thoughts. The voice that is always present to the speaker at the very moment it issues forth, is inextricably linked to understanding. At the same time, the spoken signifiers seem to fall away – to efface themselves – in order to reveal an unmediated and transparent meaning. Speech is therefore the sign of truth located within the realm of the logos that guarantees its authenticity. Writing, on the other hand, is held to be incapable of bypassing speech and is thus construed as the mere sign of a sign: the written signifier of the spoken word. Its written signifiers, moreover, introduce a material barrier between meaning and its communication. As a result, writing has traditionally been treated as a medium divorced from truth. In this sense, writing is like an illegitimate or orphaned child. Without a father (speaker or logos) to control it, writing can slip out of our control and become subject to misinterpretation. Moreover, defined broadly as a system of differences where meaning is never self-present but is, instead, produced through difference and deferral, writing disrupts and threatens the very notion of presence and all its associated values. For example, the privileged status of speech is overthrown by the recognition that all signs – spoken or written – function only in relationship with other signs and thus the presence of a speaker can never anchor the meaning of his or her words.

Precisely because writing represents such a profound threat, the logocentric tradition has always done its best to exclude and repress this destabilizing force as external, secondary and derivative. Yet, as the deconstructive critic Jacques Derrida has demonstrated, the effects of writing cannot be contained. As a system of differences, writing exceeds and contains the concept of presence and, indeed, constitutes its non-originary origin. As Derrida asserts in his essay '*Différance*' (1982): 'An interval must separate the present from what it is not, in order for the present to be itself, but this interval that constitutes it as present must, by the same token, divide the present in and of itself'. Inhabited by the trace of an absence that is never simply present, it is no longer possible to think of presence as originary or as the source and guarantee of meaning. See also DECONSTRUCTION, DISSEMINATION AND LOGOCENTRISM.

See M. McQuillan (ed.), *Deconstruction: A Reader* (2000); N. Royle (ed.), *Deconstructions: A User's Guide* (2000).

JA

Prose Though apparently the antithesis or sibling of verse, prose suffers from a lack of the precise definition which more readily delimits its formal counterpart.

From its 'different' look on the page, verse at first glance announces itself as something formed, pretentious, arresting; the claim to coherence, the inescapable frequency of line-endings, the alternate acceptance of and resistance to the potentially monolithic control of metre, gives verse a tenseness which may render it inadequate to explore modes of experience which are untense, only partially coherent, not attainable except by free-and-easy groping, such as that of Montaigne. But theories of prose are heavily outnumbered by those of POETRY, many of which, willingly blinded by the partially incidental etymological relationship between 'prose' and 'prosaic', are liable to stigmatize prose as irredeemably more ordinary, diffuse, unrefined, straightforward, and thereby to assume an often unexplained superiority for extraordinariness, compression and refined obscurity.

Prose, like the Homeric epic, becomes formulaic if it aims at fixity and crystallization. Flaubert, for example, in attempting to refine it, eventually subjects it to a near-monolithic discipline, an impoverishment of language to a finite, recurring range of devices, not unrelated perhaps to the formulaic meagreness of memoranda and scientific discourses. His prose can often be read only one way: many of his ternary sentences are so clear in structure and cadence, so controlled in meaning, that the alert reader's initial experience of them can scarcely avoid being total; this excludes any search for alternative groupings of word or idea, and presents us with a bareness where language, thought and character lie unrelievedly open to our merciless gaze. Indeed, one resource of prose, which makes it an eminently suitable vehicle for REALISM, is the relative looseness of its context, its refusal to presuppose the inevitability of complex pattern, its ability to acknowledge the right of something to exist as itself and not some other thing, as a self-sufficient detail which may be absorbed only slowly into an organized perception.

Stanzas, by their visual shape, announce their separateness and monumentality; the appearance of the most frequent prose forms (ESSAY, NOVEL, SHORT FICTION) asserts an often-reassuring substantiality and continuity. A danger, yet also a resource of longer forms, is repetition: the early pages of Dostoevsky's *Crime and Punishment* (1866), for instance, make much use of adjectives, such as 'petty', 'disgusting', 'filthy', 'loathsome', 'ill-tempered', 'weary', which come increasingly to share each other's overtones, so that the qualitative unvariedness of Raskolnikov's perceptions is rendered, as well as the ebb and flow of their intensity. Frequently a variety of strands are sustained and repeated during a prose work: throughout *Mutmassungen über Jakob* (1959), Uwe Johnson sustains various possible interpretations of the central character's death; none is a full interpretation, but no satisfactory unified view emerges either, the various strands attempting to fuse but partly failing to do so: the book's continuing hesitation between them generates a highly complex view of an insoluble riddle, while also conveying a view of East German life as paralysingly slow. Slowness, as prose has perhaps realized better than the verse paragraph, is no barrier to complexity; the groping centrifugal incompleteness of a vision (e.g. in Proust) is no barrier to intensity.

The reassuring substantiality of prose, its ability to exist at low tension (enhanced in some authors by a casual colloquial tone approaching everyday speech, or other temporary or permanent withdrawals from a consciously literary mode of narration) makes it easier for prose to establish clear hierarchies of significance than for verse: some parts of an essay or novel may be less important without being unimportant. Prose can without mockery admit and accept that something plays a minor role; it can if it wishes avoid being cleverer than life, whereas verse, with its evidently deliberate patterns, imposes an air of absoluteness on its material. See also VERSE.

See Robert Adolphe, *The Rise of Modern Prose Style* (1968); Ian A. Gordon, *The Movement of English Prose* (1966); George Levine and William Madden (eds), *The Art of Victorian Prose* (1968); Tzvetan Todorov, *The Poetics of Prose* (1971, trans. 1977).

MHP

Protagonist   See CHARACTER, HERO, PLOT.

Psychogogia   See CATHARSIS.

Psychology and psychoanalysis   The connection between literature and psychology is an ancient one. The classic locus is Aristotle's series of attempts to account for the effects of tragedy and his deployment of the term CATHARSIS. Such a play as *Hamlet* has traditionally been seen as an account of the psychological consequences of chronic circumstantial dilemma. With the rise of the novel, a new dimension of psychological intensity comes on to the literary agenda; Pamela, in the eponymous Richardson novel, supplies us with a set of insights into a mind; but a mind which demands to be read simultaneously as typical of a particular historical moment, the rise of individualism as an accompaniment to the social transition to capitalism. In the eighteenth century in the West, the whole structure of the mind's relation to society and nature becomes the problematic site on which the literary is constructed.

With the arrival in England of ROMAN-TICISM, we see a shift of attention onto the creativity act itself. Following on from Kant's classifications of mental activity, and from Schelling's delineation of an aesthetic philosophy, Coleridge provides another crucial locus in *Biographia Literaria* (1817). His principal contributions are in giving an account of the kind of activity in which the poet engages, and in fitting this into a hierarchy of mental activities. The central term is IMAGINATION; Coleridge conceives of this semi-theologically, comparing the task of the poet with the divine creative task, but his attempts to differentiate between imagination, reason and understanding nevertheless constitute an early psychology of creativity. It was also Coleridge who provided the first useful coinings of the word 'unconscious', paralleling Hegel's efforts to detect the mind's mode of recapitulating past history. This interest in the creative urge continues through Shelley, and is later given an added twist by Darwin's problematic assertion of human kinship with the animals: problematic because it implies the possible operation within the mind of forces beyond individual or species control.

Psychological speculation in English criticism continues through the 'appreciative' but subtle essays of Swinburne and Pater, and into T. S. Eliot's major work on the relations between the writing of poetry and the presence of the TRADITION. But all of this was largely overtaken by the work of Freud, whose evolution of psychoanalysis as a technique which eventually generated a 'metapsychology' fundamentally altered the field of speculation. The most basic of Freud's discoveries was that there does exist a large part of the psyche which is not under the direct control of the individual. In referring to this as the unconscious, Freud generated a paradox: how can we know of the existence of the unknowable?

We know of it, Freud contends, in three ways: through dreams; through parapraxes, principally slips of the tongue; and through the technique of analysis and its main tool, free association. These phenomena demonstrate that memory is merely a filtering mechanism, and that a large part of what we apparently forget is in fact stored. A major image for this occurs in his late work *Civilisation and its Discontents* (1930), where he compares the unconscious to an ancient city, but one where all the preceding versions of that city continue to exist, superimposed one upon another: from the unconscious nothing ever goes away. The terms in which we become aware of these suppressed areas of the psyche are linguistic, for language, according to Freud, is a double structure: while we think we speak what we mean, something else is always speaking through us (see, e.g. *Jokes and Their Relation to the Unconscious*, 1905). Literature is deeply implicated in this double structuring: Freud says that much of what he has discovered was already known to us in the works of Goethe and the great German writers, because the artist has privileged access to otherwise unknown realms.

The techniques of psychoanalysis are essentially the techniques of close reading, and the posture of the analyst is that of the disinterested but observant interpreter of a text, seeking to discern the unconscious level which can be sensed beneath, or within, the everyday chains of discourse. But that relationship is always complicated: in dreamwork – our attempted recollections of dream – we are always performing an act of naturalization, trying to represent our inadmissible wishes in forms which will not severely dislocate cultural conventions. This activity relies on certain crucial devices, principally condensation and displacement, which have since been assimilated to the structuralist categories of metaphor and metonymy.

Freud's dissident disciple Jung concentrated on the transindividual, collective unconscious; and his involvement with the arts has generated a set of readings in which the main focus is on the discernment of specific 'universal' symbols or archetypes. Jung moves further back into the realm of biologism, asserting that the central shapes of the organism are responsible for the structuring of works of art. This approach has proved more fruitful in the visual arts; where writing has been concerned, some post-Freudian developments have been more concerned with the relation between the instincts and socio-historical change. Herbert Marcuse, for instance, working both with psychoanalysis and with a version of Marxism mediated through the Frankfurt School, suggests that different 'instinctive' shapes emerge in response to different social conditions (e.g. the 'performance' principle within capitalism; the necessity of an element of 'surplus repression' to the smooth running of the State). His claims for literature, and particularly for the more surrealist kinds of lyric poetry, are high; he regards them as ways of uttering the otherwise unutterable, as modes of escape from the bondage of ideology (see Marcuse, *One Dimensional Man*, 1964 and *Eros and Civilisation*, 1966).

More recent post-Freudian developments have moved into a different area, taking on board the concepts of STRUCTURALISM and POST-STRUCTURALISM, and offering new ways of describing the displacement of the subject. One of the most prominent thinkers has been Jacques Lacan, who has fashioned a remarkable discourse from Lévi-Straussian anthropology, linguistics, recent French philosophy

and his own clinical experience. His central ideas can be found in *Écrits* (1977) and *The Four Fundamental Concepts of Psycho-analysis* (1977). Language, he claims, is the major force through which the human individual is constituted as a structured, gendered subject; the entry upon language is a simultaneous submission to social authority, in which the individual passes under the 'name of the Father' and is coloured with patriarchy at the very moment of emergence from undifferentiation. Lacan's discovery of the 'mirror-phase' and his less well-known work on psychopathology offer versions of the construction of the subject which have proved congenial to literary and other critics searching for explanations of the constitutive power of language and image (see, e.g. *Yale French Studies*, 1977: *Literature and Psychoanalysis*).

This work has been followed to fascinating if complex conclusions by Gilles Deleuze and Félix Guattari (see *Anti-Oedipus: Capitalism and Schizophrenia*, 1977 and *A Thousand Plateaus*, 1988); it has also been taken up in FEMINIST CRITICISM. The writings of Juliet Mitchell, Jacqueline Rose, Julia Kristeva, Hélène Cixous, Luce Irigaray and others offer variously deconstructive approaches to Freud's evidently inadequate accounts of female sexuality; principally, and especially in the French context, mediated through Lacan, they seek to establish a specifically female location in relation to language, and to prescribe a practice of writing. Some feminist approaches define grammar itself as a form of patriarchal power, while seeking to avoid a logocentric prescription of a utopian alternative. In the work of Hélène Cixous we see the opposition male/female modulated into other categories: single/collective; quasi-permanent/recognizedly transitory (see Kristeva, *Strangers to Ourselves*, 1991; *The Cixous Reader*, Susan Sellers (ed.), 1994; Irigaray, *This Sex which is not One*, 1985; *Feminism and Psychoanalysis*, Elizabeth Wright (ed.), 1992). Other recent work in feminist psychoanalysis, notably by Nancy Chodhorow, suggests a whole new pattern in which female skills in nurturing are seen as having been systematically downgraded in the interchange between the generations in favour of the phallocentric, and feminist critics have discerned this power structure in particular literary works (see Mitchell, *Psychoanalysis and Feminism*, 1974; Marks and de Courtivron (eds), *New French Feminisms*, 1980).

There are several further contemporary developments worth pointing to. The work of Melanie Klein on young infants, and her descriptions of familially induced psychosis, are now being seen as capable of generating accounts of the origins of creativity and symbolism in early infancy; Klein also presents a version of what it is like to be human which has a revisionary relationship to the now conventional theorizing of sexual difference. Her work is sometimes referred to as 'object-relations psychology'; referred to under the same heading, although it has significant differences, is the work of such analysts as D. W. Winnicott. From Freud and Klein have come the attempts to read a whole culture and its myths suggested by the group relations practice of Wilfred Bion and pioneered by the Tavistock Institute, a project of cultural analysis which is convergent with Foucault's institutional histories. It should also be noted that one of the great charges levelled against Freud was that he had prevented the world from ever again indulging in the primal innocence implied in fantasies of the free individual; certainly this development now finds an echo in the work of a large number of creative writers – Thomas Pynchon, J. G. Ballard, William Gibson, Don DeLillo – where the complexity of subject construction which Freud originally proposed is increasingly being taken as an alternative to traditional notions of character autonomy, a development which itself follows from earlier twentieth-century writers of the bureaucratic State – Chekhov, Kafka, Lu Xun – and their perceptions of the intense relationship between the psyche and the external forces which condition its development and shape.

Perhaps the most significant immediate development in psychoanalysis, the implications of which for literature and literary criticism are still being worked through, lies in the work of Jean Laplanche, and especially his book *Essays on Otherness* (1999). Here he essentially replaces the structuralist Lacanian categories with a new repertoire of interpretative tools, centred on the enigma and the message. Lacan's revelation was to tell us in what ways the unconscious is 'structured like a language'; Laplanche comes to demonstrate how it is not structured like a language, and indeed not 'structured' at all in any meaningful sense of the term, thus situating the tasks of the psychoanalyst and the literary critic against a very different and more challenging backdrop.

See also Freud, *The Interpretation of Dreams* (1900) and *Introductory Lectures on Psycho-Analysis* (1916–17). A useful anthology of Jung is Anthony Storr (ed.), *Selected writings* (1983). On object-relations psychology, see Michael Rustin, 'A socialist consideration of Kleinian psychoanalysis', *New Left Review* (1982). The best general accounts are Maud Ellmann, *Psychoanalytic Literary Criticism* (1994) and Elizabeth Wright, *Psychoanalytic Criticism* (2nd edn, 1998). See also D. W. Winnicott, *Playing and Reality* (1974); Joseph H. Smith (ed.), *The Literary Freud* (1980); Peter Fuller, *Art and Psychoanalysis* (1980); Samuel Weber, *The Legend of Freud* (1982); Ned Lukacher, *Primal Scenes: Literature, Philosophy, Psychoanalysis* (1986); Adam Phillips, *Promises,* *Promises*: *Essays on Literature and Psychoanalysis* (2000); David Punter, *Writing the Passions* (2001); Canham and Satyamurti (eds), *Acquainted with the Night: Psychoanalysis and the Poetic Imagination* (2003).

DGP

Q

Queer theory Until the 1990s, 'queer' was commonly a slang word, usually derisory, used to mean 'homosexual'. Since the 1990s, 'Queer theory' and 'Queer studies' have been legitimate theoretical approaches engaged with in University departments, as 'Gay and Lesbian Studies' had been somewhat earlier. Queer Theory was also given popular impetus by the activist group Queer Nation, who were frustrated with the constraining and often prescriptive 'identity politics' of lesbians and gay men. Even though 'queerness' is most often associated with lesbian and gay subjects, being queer is to resist any models of sexual stability and static identification, albeit with an overarching resistance to 'heterosexual hegemony'. Rather, explains Annamarie Jagose in *Queer Theory* (1996), queer theory's 'analytic framework also includes such topics as cross-dressing, hermaphroditism, gender ambiguity and gender-corrective surgery'. There are several generally acknowledged pioneers of queer theory and Michel Foucault (1926–84) is invariably numbered among them. His three volumes *The History of Sexuality* (1976–86) is particularly influential in this regard. Two other books, both of which appeared in 1990 and had their roots in Foucauldian thought, also made a formative contribution: *Gender Trouble: Feminism and the Subversion of Identity* by Judith Butler and *Epistemology of the Closet* by Eve Kosofsky Sedgwick. However, Judith Butler has also described, in a 1994 interview, how she was unaware of her own status in Queer Theory circles until after it had been well established. To her mind, the catalyst had been Teresa de Lauretis's special issue, 'Queer theory: lesbian and gay sexualities' in *Differences: A Journal of Feminist Cultural Studies* in 1991. Nonetheless, Judith Butler's work is profoundly influential in Queer Theory. For instance, when Dennis Halperin, author of *Saint Foucault: Towards a Gay Hagiography* (1995), claims that 'queer is by definition whatever is at odds with the normal, the legitimate, the dominant. There is nothing in particular to which it necessarily refers. It is an identity without an essence', he unmistakably draws on Butler's theories of gender PERFORMATIVITY and on the discursive effects on sex that masquerade as material origins or causes. Her 1994 book, *Bodies that Matter: On the Discursive Limits of Sex*, contains a significant chapter entitled 'Critically queer' in which she asks some challenging questions of a theoretical approach which has 'refunctioned' as new and affirmative, a term that once 'signalled degradation': 'Is this a reversal that retains and reiterates the abjected history of the term?'; 'Does the reversal reiterate the logic of repudiation by which it was spawned?'; 'Can the term overcome its constitutive history of injury?' Other reservations about queer theory note the way in which 'queer chic' has been hijacked by postmodern visual culture, so that rather than being subversive, queerness is just the latest commercial novelty. While 'queer' is so visible, so aesthetically permissible, so 'heterosexually camp', its loses its radical political force.

See Andy Medhurst and Sally R. Munt (eds), *Lesbian and Gay Studies: A Critical Introduction* (1997); Donald E. Hall, *Queer Theories* (2002); Annamarie Jagose, *Queer Theory: An Introduction* (1996).

SS

R

Reader Classical theory, seeing literature as an affective medium, necessarily assumed a reader to be affected, but did not emphasize the reader as such. Horace, in his *Art of Poetry*, says that the poet's aim is either to profit or to please – but readers are dismissed with the casual comment that elders prefer profit and youngsters pleasure. To cite 'the poet's aim' as Horace does is to shift from affect to intention, a typical move in author-centred criticism. Neoclassical discussions of taste suggest attention to what in the twentieth century was called the reader's competence. Eighteenth-century fictional practice goes further, enacting the dynamics of reading: an inscribed reader for Fielding or Sterne is functionally engaged in a temporal process of challenge and response. Nineteenth-century novelists often imply a social dimension for readers, including them by address in some actual or imagined community; but twentieth-century didactic criticism usually glossed this by a return to authorial intention. As usual, it is Henry James who offers crucial insights into the question of author versus reader. An early formulation suggests that the balance of power is on the author's side: 'the writer makes the reader, very much as he makes his characters'. But James described his own reading practice in terms of 'reconstruction', and his emphasis is increasingly on the reader as an active figure rather than a mere affective target for experience or instruction.

One influential twentieth-century study of reading was the 'practical criticism' of I. A. Richards, which used empirical accounts by actual readers. It was not, however, pure empiricism, since it was informed by a motive: the production of a totally unified reading, in which all inconsistencies are resolved. And this totalization in turn produced a supposed psychological result of synthesis and harmony. Reading was thus seen as therapeutic, in a tradition that goes back to Aristotle. Unified readings were also the concern of Anglo-American NEW CRITICISM; in the famous article on 'The affective fallacy' by Wimsatt and Beardsley (*The Verbal Icon*, 1954), affect was ruled out as a confusion between the poem and its results. To see the work as autonomous is to forbid specific attention to readers. Reaction against new critical autonomy prompted studies of readers and their responses which tended to use a dynamic rather than an affective orientation. It is important to note that reader study is *only* an orientation, not a method. It is indeed possible to convert any formal description into a 'readerly' account simply by changing terms, so that a reader instead of a critic discovers formal distinctions. Theories that try to go further than this can be categorized in terms of the methods that they seek to appropriate. Similar appropriations do not necessarily produce similar results. Thus, Norman Holland and Harold Bloom, both studied reading through psychology or psychoanalysis; but while Holland used the reader's 'identity theme' to produce unified, convergent readings, Bloom staged an Oedipal conflict which prompts *mis*readings that diverge from the authority of their predecessors. This split between convergence and divergence, or between total and plural readings, can also be found in appropriations of SEMIOTICS. It can be seen from my discussion under that heading that Riffaterre's reader, transforming the essential 'matrix' of a text, is a supreme exemplar of convergent activity; while Umberto Eco's work seems to offer both convergent and divergent emphases. In so far as he attempts a systematic account of how readers extend their codes, he seems to offer a positive, total study. But in so far as he follows Peirce on the unlimited nature of semiotic process, any such account must be provisional, one of many plural readings. Plurality or divergence are emphasized in borrowings from SEMIOTICS that have felt the impact of DECONSTRUCTION; the later work of Roland Barthes is a case in point. *S/Z* (1970, trans. 1974) studies reading through the interplay of semiotic codes, yet, refuses to codify that interplay. Where Eco offers diagrams, Barthes prefers the undecidable model of an interwoven textile. Barthes's presuppositions are also evident in his hedonism. *The Pleasure of the Text* (1975) may recall Horace by its title, but the Barthesian reader thrills to the decidedly unHoratian qualities of transgression, discord and excess.

Reader studies from the University of Constance offered a more sober set of appropriations. H. R. Jauss's approach derived from sociology and HERMENEUTICS. His 'reception aesthetics' moved away from intrinsic accounts of an individual reader's response to consider the communal 'horizon of expectations' against which any work is received. These horizons are historically generalized as 'paradigms', following Thomas Kuhn's work in the history of science. In his earlier writing, Jauss betrayed a modernist bias in his emphasis on innovation, evaluating works by their degree of distance from the horizon against which they appeared.

And though he went on to repudiate it, Jauss was by no means alone in this approach. Theorists as different as Barthes, Iser and Fish have concentrated on the change or frustration of a reader's expectations; change is always seen as somehow salutary, a variety of Horatian 'profit'. Jauss's colleague Wolfgang Iser built on the phenomenology of Roman Ingarden. They considered the reader's activity in 'actualizing' what is only potential in any text. Iser attempted a compromise in the balance of power between text and reader. The text offers a 'structure of appeal' which calls for its 'implied' reader; their interaction creates the aesthetic object, as the reader works through gaps and indeterminacies in the text, through shifts of vantage point, through distinctions of theme and horizon. This process, though idealized, is one of the most intimate accounts of reading yet produced; but it was fundamentally challenged by Stanley Fish. Fish's approach derived in part from linguistics and stylistics, but his writing is both eclectic and variable. Instead of implying a reader, the text becomes itself a product of the reader, in that its significant structures are not given but ascertained by prior interpretive procedures that are always already in place. 'Strictly speaking,' says Fish, 'getting "back-to-the-text" is not a move one can perform'. To get rid of the text as an autonomous authority might seem to open the way for the most widely divergent readings, but Fish differed from Barthes or Bloom in preserving a convergent factor. Reading is not a radically private affair. It always takes place within an 'interpretive community', social or institutional or both. Though communities and their memberships change, there is always a set of normative procedures available – if only for challenge – at any given time.

Though Fish himself did not pursue the point, to speak of communal constraints is to suggest a politics of reading. Barthes's apparent perversity, for example, is politicized by his claim that power is inscribed in the language itself. He thus produces a rhetoric of contestation which, in different forms, is echoed by a range of oppositional reading practices that seek not simply to actualize the meaning of a text but to call it into question. This activity is especially strong in FEMINIST CRITICISM, and it is neatly characterized in the title of a book by Judith Fetterley: *The Resisting Reader* (1979).

See Umberto Eco, *The Role of the Reader* (1979); Elizabeth Freund, *The Return of the Reader* (1987); Gerry Brenner, *Performative Criticism: Experiments in Reader Response* (2004). Two useful anthologies are edited by Jane P. Tompkins, *Reader-Response Criticism: from Formalism to Post-Structuralism* (1980); and by Susan R. Suleiman and Inge Crosman, *The Reader in the Text: Essays in Audience and Interpretation* (1980). The Constance School is described in Robert C. Holub, *Reception Theory: A Critical Introduction* (1984). William Ray, *Literary Meaning: From Phenomenology to Deconstruction* (1984) covers the major theorists.

EC

Realism   In literary history, realism is usually associated with the effort of the NOVEL in the nineteenth century, particularly in France, to establish itself as a major literary genre. The realism of Balzac and the Goncourt brothers was essentially an assertion that, far from being escapist and unreal, the novel was uniquely capable of revealing the truth of contemporary life in society. Baizac, in *La Comédie Humaine*, saw himself as a scientific historian, recording and classifying the social life of France in all its aspects. The adoption of this role led to detailed reportage of the physical minutiae of everyday life – clothes, furniture, food, etc. – the cataloguing of people into social types or species and radical analyses of the economic basis of society. The virtues pursued were accuracy and completeness of description. At its extreme the realistic programme runs into two difficulties. Technically, it becomes obsessed with physical detail and topographical accuracy for its own, or history's sake, and so novels may amount to little more than guidebooks or social documents. Second, it becomes confused about the distinction between art and history or sociology: the novelist is only metaphorically and incidentally a historian; whatever the relations of writing with the 'realities' of society, the novelist is finally involved in the making of fictions, and has responsibilities to FORM that the historian or sociologist does not.

The failure to acknowledge this crucial distinction is evident in the development of realistic theory into *Naturalism*, whose claim for an even greater accuracy and inclusiveness rested on an analogy with scientific method. Naturalism, notably in the theories of Emile Zola, borrowed its terms from post-Darwinian biology and asserted the wholly *determined* both individual and society. Since humans were simply higher animals, their nature was controlled by the regular forces of heredity and environment. So the novelist as social historian now appeared as the taxonomic biologist, displaying a scientific objectivity in elaborate documentation and unwonted frankness in regard to bodily functions. Fortunately, many of Zola's novels, at least, managed to survive their methodology.

The theory of realism in England was much less coherent and scientific. Until the 1880s, when the debate on realism and naturalism was imported from France, critics and novelists tended to talk rather of the novel's duty to be true to 'life'. The central concern in this injunction was not the representation of material reality but the investigation of the moral behaviour of people in society. The mechanistic and deterministic elements of realism were alien to the temper of Victorian novelists and their critics. But the concern for truth, for morality and for an accurate and unromanticized description of contemporary society, defined an unmistakably realistic concept of the novel. Of course, such demands implied a general agreement about the nature of reality, about certain self-evident truths concerning the individual and society, for without these there could be no way of identifying the abnormal, the deviant, the novels that were untrue to life. At the worst, this critical demand could narrow to a prescription for a conformist fiction of the commonplace, novels for Mrs Grundy. Dickens, George Eliot and Henry James, all major realists in different ways, found it necessary to assert a larger idea of realism that might answer to more complex views of the possibilities of life.

All theories of realism, however sophisticated, rest on the assumption that the novel imitates reality, and that that reality is more or less stable and commonly accessible. But it is possible to conceive of the relationship between art and reality in terms of imaginative creation rather than imitation. The writer may be said to imagine, to invent a fictional world which is more than a copy of the real one. Such a shift in conceptual metaphors produces attitudes to the novel, and perhaps even novels, with quite different priorities from those of the realist tradition. The emphasis moves from accuracy of representation to aspects of

form – narrative structuring, symbolic patterning, linguistic complexity and so on. Much of the major modernist fiction of this century – the later James, Conrad, Joyce, Woolf – and most postmodernist novels, seem to exist in terms of this alternative poetic; they advertise their fictionality. Arguably all novels relate in some way to the general complex of realism, but relatively few can be fully understood in the terms of the specific theory of realism.

This is why attempts to use 'realism' as a critical term to define the core aspect of the novel, rather than as a label for a diverse but identifiable tradition, prove unsatisfactory, if initially attractive. Ian Watt, in *The Rise of the Novel*, points out that we find in nearly all novels, in comparison to other genres, an accentuation of the temporal and spatial dimensions. Novels give us a sense of people existing in continuous time, and locate them in a physical world more specifically than any other kind of literature. In *this* sense *Ulysses* is the supreme realist novel. The difficulty arises when Watt goes on to specify, as a defining element of realism, 'the adaptation of prose style to give an air of complete authenticity', and takes, as models of authentic report, the novels of Defoe and Richardson. The implication is that the novelist attempts to divert attention from the fictionality of the text by avoiding all eloquent and figurative language. Novelists write the neutral prose of the dispassionate reporter so that reality, or their image of reality, may seem more purely itself. On this view of realism the ideal novel would be a flawless mirror to the world; but since language is never neutral, such a novel is impossible. More importantly, it is doubtful whether many novels, even within the realist tradition, have any such ambitions for linguistic transparency. Perhaps Arnold Bennett, Sinclair Lewis or Theodore Dreiser longed for the anonymity of reportage, but there is nothing self-effacing about the language of Flaubert, Dickens or James.

Hence as a critical term, 'realism' identifies some important characteristics of the novel form, but fails to define it. Most novels are too complex to be accounted for in terms of their representational authenticity, and the languages of the novel are too various to be subsumed under the model of direct report. The art of the novel is rhetorical as well as representational; 'realism' gives us an account of only one of its dimensions. See also FICTION, IMITATION, NOVEL.

Emile Benveniste posited in *Problems in General Linguistics* that narration operates in two different ways. When narration calls attention to its act of narration as presuming both a speaker and a listener, with the speaker seeking to affect the listener in some way, it appears as *discourse*. By contrast, when 'events that took place at a certain moment of time are presented without any intervention of the speaker', the narration appears as *histoire*. Catherine Belsey in *Critical Practice* refers to this distinction between 'discourse' and 'histoire' to point out how in classic realist fiction 'the events seem to narrate themselves', whereas discourse assumes a speaker and a listener. Accordingly, the 'authority' of classic realism's impersonal narration stems from its effacement of its own status as discourse. Consequently, in late twentieth-century criticism, realism was frequently discussed in terms of a hierarchy of discourse, with the narrator occupying a discursive position above the characters and standing between them and the reader.

See Harry Levin, *The Gates of Horn a Study of Five French Realists* (1963); R. Stang, *The Theory of the Novel in*

England, 1850–1870 (1961); Ian Watt, *The Rise of the Novel* (1957); René Wellek, 'The concept of realism in literary scholarship', *Neophilologus* 44 (1960), 1–20, reprinted in *Concepts of Criticism* (1963); D. Grant, *Realism* (1970); G. Lukács, *Studies in European Realism* (1950); C. Belsey, *Critical Practice* (1980); Dario Villanueva, *Theories of Literary Realism* (1997); Pam Morris, *Realism* (2003).

PM

Reason　See FEELING, IMAGINATION, SENSIBILITY.

Reception　See READER.

Refrain　A refrain is a line, or a group of lines, of verse, repeated in its totality so regularly or in such a specific pattern as to become a controlling (ballad) or defining (fixed forms) structural factor.

In the BALLAD, much of the effect of a refrain depends on the narrative not at first comprehending it: each goes its own way. But as the poem proceeds, the narrative increasingly invests the refrain with circumstance and an awful aptness, while the refrain makes of the narrative something pre-ordained and lyrically self-engrossed. Ultimately, the poet may anticipate the refrain and explore the various opportunities it offers (e.g. Poe's *The Raven*). For an exceptional reversal of refrain's irreversibility, see Pound's *Threnos*, in which the refrain – 'Lo the fair dead!' – is finally ingested into the body of the verse, parenthesized by brackets and surmounted by the word 'Tintagoel', which *resurrects* the lovers, Tristram and Iseult, even as it identifies them.

In ballads in lighter or coarser vein, the refrain may act as a verbal substitute for knowing laughter, in patriotic ballads (e.g. *The 'George Aloe'*), as a mark of steadfastness in vicissitude and insolent complacency in victory. The nonsense refrain – 'Heigh ho! says Rowley', 'Ay lally, o lilly lally' – seems to be a way of expressing a complete acquiescence in the mood of the poem without interfering with its meaning, a way even of momentarily backing away from the meaning of a song in order to capture its feeling nearer to its pre-verbal inarticulacy.

In many ballads and rhymes, the refrain enjoys a typographical separation which points to its origin in a dialogue, between the poet and chorus. But in many of the fixed forms (rondel, triolet, rondeau) the refrain has been absorbed into the poem and thus emerges only gradually from it; indeed, it may appear to betray the poem by becoming at once the poem's subject and limitation, formally beautifying but intellectually stultifying. The alternating refrains of the villanelle, in particular, suggest a choking process; the peculiar anguish of those villanelles devoted to the theme of time (e.g. Dobson's *Tu ne quaesieris*, Henley's *Where's the use of sighing*, Auden's *If I could tell you*), derives from the continual notation of passing time within a structure that wastes time and condemns the poet to contemplative immobility. But the fixed form may equally struggle against its refrain, not allow it to settle into a repressive role; it may outwit it with an indefatigable novelty or humanity, it may make it an instrument of novelty itself, or it may re-integrate the refrain by making its lyric intentions unknown to itself, dependent on the fancy of the 'common' lines.

CS

Refunctioning A translation of the German term *Umfunktionierung*, which was used by certain left-wing German writers and critics of the 1930s (Bertolt Brecht and Walter Benjamin, in particular)

to suggest the way in which works of art and literature could be constantly put to diverse uses. Such writers rejected the view that literary works were 'timeless', stressing the historical conditions of their production and reception; but they also dismissed the notion that literary works belonged only to their historical moment, and that their meaning was 'exhausted' by what they meant to their contemporaries. On the contrary, works of literature could be given new meanings by successive generations, turned to social uses unthinkable for their authors and so ceaselessly reinterpreted and 'rewritten'. For such a theory, the 'meaning' of a literary text does not reside within it like the core within a fruit; it is the sum-total of the history of uses to which the text is put. Such uses will naturally be constrained by the nature of the literary work itself: it is not possible to put any work to any kind of use. But it is equally impossible to read off from a literary work the various interpretations which it may validly receive in different historical contexts.

For writers like Brecht and Benjamin, the most significant meanings of a literary work are always determined by one's present situation. Though it is often enough to establish what a work 'originally' meant, we can, of course, only establish this within the limits of our own discourses, which may be quite alien to the discourse of the work itself. The German critical traditions of HERMENEUTICS and reception theory (cf. READER) ponder the interpretative problems involved in this encounter between our own social world of meaning, and that of a literary work produced in different conditions. But whereas HERMENEUTICS is on the whole concerned with the problem of how we can recapture, as faithful as possible, a sense of what the work originally meant, the exponents of 'refunctioning' were more concerned with lending the work a new, contemporary set of meanings, if necessary by deliberately 'misreading' it. (For certain critics, in particular, the American Harold Bloom, all readings of literary texts are 'misreadings'; other, DECONSTRUCTIVE, critics, having rejected the notion of a 'correct' reading, deny the distinction between 'true' and 'false' readings.)

Refunctioning, then, is a deliberate using or appropriation of an artefact. But it would insist, against those who would regard this as scandalous or unethical, that all criticism is, inescapably, a form of use of the text: there is in this sense no disinterested criticism. The difference is between those schools of criticism which frankly admit that they are using the work – often for political ends – and those which do not. The criticism of Coleridge or T. S. Eliot would in this view be quite as 'ideological', and ultimately political, as that of a Marxist writer; it is just that the latter makes his or her position plain.

An example of refunctioning would be Brecht's attempt to produce Shakespeare's politically conservative *Coriolanus* for socialist audiences and socialist political ends. Such an attempt, of course, may fail: it may be that changed historical conditions result in people's ceasing to extract any significant meaning from a work of the past, even a highly valued one. (It may also be that if we discovered more about the original meanings of certain past works – say, Greek tragedy – we might cease to value them as highly as we do.) If, on account of a deep historical transformation, people ceased to find relevance in the works of Shakespeare, it would be interesting to ask in what sense, if any, those works were still 'valuable'.

See T. Eagleton, *Walter Benjamin, or Towards a Revolutionary criticism* (1981); P. Widdowson (ed.), *Re-Reading English* (1982); J. Willett (ed.), *Brecht on Theatre* (1964), *The New Sobriety: Art and Politics in the Weimar Republic* (1978).

TE

Representation　See DECONSTRUCTION, DRAMA, IMITATION, REALISM, TYPICALITY.

Response　See EFFECT, READER.

Revisionary writing　Draws together theoretical developments in the fields of sociology and cultural studies but particularly, historiography and postmodernist literary criticism. Commencing from the post-structuralist recognition that all acts of communicative interchange involve a speaker, a hearer and a message, that each participant transmits or receives from a position of ideological partiality and that the message is equally contained by the ideological framework of discourse, revisionary critics (and writers) seek the tensions and discontinuities in this clashing of world views. Working with the concept of HEGEMONY, as formulated by Antonio Gramsci, these critics examine the textual products of a given society for the ways in which the political and cultural assumptions that those texts make about their society reflect (or possibly resist) the dominant forces that give shape to the experience of living. Because the hegemonic network of power relations that operates in any given society through the auspices of culture necessarily privileges voices that reinforce the stability of the ruling elite and maintain the political status quo, so certain subaltern voices are marginalized. Post-structuralism's attention to discursive practices of unconscious empowerment and postmodernism's interest in the contestation of totalizing ideas of truth enables critics to imagine other possible world formations by highlighting the narratives of the repressed communities.

Revisionary writing, or Revisionism as it is sometimes termed in academic circles, gained significant popularity during the 1970s and 1980s in the field of historiography. The work of Stephen Greenblatt, Louis Mink and, in particular, Hayden White, explores the structural and ideological parameters of historical writing to destabilize the claims to privileged status that the discipline has enjoyed since the mid-eighteenth century. White, in his celebrated books *Metahistory* (1973) and *Tropics of Discourse* (1978), studied the ways in which historiographical writing tended to mimic literary forms and tropes as rhetorical means for establishing a persuasive case for a specific reading of historical events. By employing the frameworks of fiction in the representation of supposedly 'truthful' and factual incidents, historians create, so White argued, certain well-defined and recognizable trajectories that may enable a satisfying narrative of cause and effect, but that indicate the containment of history within certain political, ethical and ideological boundaries. History's claim to 'truth-telling' was seriously undermined by the New Historicist movement (as it became known) and though extreme diagnoses that 'history is fiction' have been gradually tempered over time, the impact of the metahistorical turn has been significant far beyond the field of historiography.

If History, or for that matter Literature, is an ideological state apparatus designed to promote and preserve a particular hegemonic balance, then counter-histories resist the consensual imperative of that hegemony by demanding acknowledgement of their validity. This has been seen most strikingly in the field of literary studies where the traditional canon of English Literature (established in the early part of the twentieth century and heavily influenced by F. R. Leavis's notion of the

'Great Tradition') has had to be rethought in order to accommodate the claims of those previously excluded. Feminist, queer and postcolonial writing has sought the revision of the concept of Literature by revealing the exclusionary politics of a canon that tended to be built around dead, white, European men. Writers, such as J. M. Coetzee, have taken their own transgressive stance by literally revisioning classic texts: in *Foe* (1986) he takes an icon of protestant bourgeois culture, *Robinson Crusoe* (1720), and rewrites it from the perspective of a woman. In Angela Carter's *The Bloody Chamber and Other Stories* (1979) and Jeanette Winterson's *Oranges Are Not The Only Fruit* (1985) the fairy story is disarticulated to reveal the implicit sexism and disempowerment of women that the form enshrines. Such revisions expose the inherent assumptions of a particular kind of text, but for some critics the indoctrinating impact of ideology manifests itself at the level of the word that needs to be depoliticized before a literature of genuine self-expression can be conceived. In the popular imagination, this sensitivity is often derided as political correctness but the repositioning of a grammatical imbalance is an important facet in an inclusive revisioning of power relations between individuals, groups and global communities.

Also of importance is Adrienne Rich's essay, 'When we dead awaken: writing as re-vision', where Rich argues that 'Revision – the act of looking back, of seeing with fresh eyes, of entering an old text from a new critical direction – is for women more than a chapter in cultural history: it is an act of survival.... how our language has trapped as well as liberated us, how the very act of naming has been till now a male prerogative'. See also POSTMODERNISM and POST-STRUCTURALISM.

See Antonio Gramsci, *Selections from the Prison Notebooks* (1971); Stephen Greenblatt, *Renaissance Self-Fashioning: From More to Shakespeare* (1980); Christian Moraru, *Rewriting* (2001); Hayden White, *Metahistory* (1973), *Tropics of Discourse* (1978); Adrienne Rich, *On Lies, Secrets, and Silence: Selected Prose 1966–78* (1979).

DL

Rhetoric   Traditionally, the art of putting a thought over in a particular manner; command of a number of artfully different manners of expression or persuasion. As a result of the diversity of its products, there is and has been no certain orthodoxy in its doctrines. On the other hand, in spite of the discord which has characterized it both as a subject and as a discipline, rhetoric probably does have a boundary or two and, within each of its schisms, a surprising amount of homogeneity and tradition. There is not all that much difference, for example, between two textbooks of English composition, say A. M. Tibbett's *The Strategies of Rhetoric* (1969) and Kane and Peter's *A Practical Rhetoric of Expository Prose* (1966). Nor are these two texts entirely unrelated to Irving Rein's *The Relevant Rhetoric* (1969), although the latter work is concerned with teaching speakers rather than writers. And in a broader sense, all three of these books are recognizable descendants of such Sophistic handbooks as the *Rhetorica, ad Alexandrum* and the *Rhetorica ad Herennium*. They share a considerable amount of subject matter and a few attributes with even such famous philosophic rhetorics as Aristotle's or Campbell's or a respectable writer's in this vein, Perelman's *The New Rhetoric, a Treatise on Argumentation* (1969): a concern for grammar, figures, argumentative devices and forms, how authors present their credentials, relates to their audience, attempt to persuade – even a few pieties about ethical and intellectual truth. At the same time, no student who pays a moment's attention to epistemology, ontology or intellectual history is likely to confuse Rein with Aristotle, a composition handbook with a formal theory of discourse or, for that matter, fail to discover that Campbell's beliefs very often contradict Aristotle's, that neither writer's first principles would be at ease with the reformed positivism of Perelman.

This inordinately broad range of opinion as to what constitutes rhetoric, from a concern with the grammatical or inflectional efforts of novices to the search for the mainsprings of rational discourse, is further complicated by the fact that from classical times onwards the majority of writers on the subject, despite their own particular allegiances, have dealt with rhetoric as something akin to mathematics, a more or less universally applicable tool. That it may profitably be viewed as such is perhaps so, but this bias has more often led generations of rhetoricians into a marked fondness for eccentric eclecticism, vague key terms, untenable and extreme generalizations and a naïve enthusiasm for instant social and language reform.

The temptation to consider rhetoric as an all-embracing compositional and critical discipline, panacea and touchstone for human motivation has also occasionally led scholars to conclude that all writers in all times have succumbed to it, that its universality is chronological as well as conceptual. Charles O. McDonald, to cite one case, argues in his *Rhetoric of Tragedy: Form in Stuart Drama* (1966), that English dramatists from Shakespeare to John Ford were thoroughly infected by an 'antilogistic' 'Sophistic' 'habit of mind', caught, allegedly, from a somewhat too free association with the two thousand years of rhetorical tradition which he outlines in a hundred pages of prefatory material. We are left with the provocative if eristic implication that Gorgias of Leontini made a demonstrable and significant contribution to *Hamlet*.

All of this is not to say that the 'garden of eloquence' is naught but a jungle of verbiage, nor to disparage the occasional fine flowerings in the pioneer work of such twentieth-century writers as Father Ong, Wayne C. Booth, Richard McKeon and Kenneth Burke. A fair case could even be made out to show that the infinite variety and lack of cohesion in rhetoric and rhetorical studies is favourable to independent thought, original research and heuristic scholarship. And certainly the long and complex history of the influence of rhetoric on Western thought is too important a subject to be ignored by serious investigators into language and literature. Yet the fact remains that the resurgence in the twentieth century of scholarly interest in rhetoric did not produce a substantial body of important thought or impressive research. There is not a single well-regarded general history of the subject, there are surprisingly few careful studies of the theories held in various periods, and there is a marked paucity of modern theoretical treatises which will withstand more than a few minutes' critical scrutiny. And beyond that, the relationships of rhetoric to history, literature, linguistics, homiletics, law and philosophy have seldom been investigated in any detail, let alone understood on more than a superficial level.

Looked at from a constructive point of view these all too obvious gaps and shortcomings in rhetorical studies constitute the one major advantage which rhetoric has over many of its academic neighbours: it

has yet to be exploited to the point where its body of knowledge is inevitably repetitious, replete with miniscule observations and haunted by portents of collision with dead ends.

Cf. STYLE, a term with a similar basic meaning and a similar wide range of connotations and thus power to evoke contention. Both 'style' and 'rhetoric' signify systems of conventional (hence, variously prescriptively teachable) verbal devices for the 'ornamentation' of a discourse. If style often suggests artificiality, self-indulgence or preciousness, rhetoric, because it is initially a verbal art for persuasion often connotes design, insincerity, even lies. Alternatively, the availability of hundreds of rhetorical handbooks – lists and examples of figures and schemes – produced over the last two thousand years may suggest a mechanical shallowness of linguistic technique. Attempts to make the term exploratory and critical rather than normative and technical (e.g. I. A. Richards, *Philosophy of Rhetoric*, 1936; Wayne C. Booth, *The Rhetoric of Fiction*, 1961) play down the evaluative dimension and the sinister side of 'persuasion'. Booth's book also shows that it is, unfortunately, all too easy to neglect the linguistic aspects of persuasion; here 'rhetoric' is being used in an essentially untraditional sense.

Wimsatt and Beardsley's *Literary Criticism, A Short History* (1957) provides an elementary account of the classical and medieval tradition.

TGW

Rhizome The term 'rhizome' was first used by the French writing/thinking team of Gilles Deleuze (1925–95) and Félix Guattari (1930–92) in 1976, although its currency as a theoretical concept derives from the introduction to *A Thousand Plateaus: Capitalism and*

Schizophrenia (1980), and its subsequent 'application' throughout that text. Botanists use the term to differentiate between the diffused underground growth systems of certain kinds of plant (such as couch-grass) and those with a dominant or radicle/radical root system (such as the carrot). In the adaptation of Deleuze and Guattari, rhizome refers to a non-hierarchical network in which established practices of logic, causation, filiation, etc. (including the practice which would look to oppose rhizome and root) cannot function.

Derrida and Foucault notwithstanding, Deleuze and Guattari are perhaps the most mutinous of a generation of revolutionary French thinkers. Although trained as philosopher and psychiatrist, respectively, both rejected the notion of (the) intellectual discipline because of what they understood to be its inherent collusion with the bourgeois capitalist state. The work produced during their twenty-year partnership was dedicated to the unmasking of this collusion, and to the advancement of an anti-disciplinary counter-tradition derived from a variety of brilliant (some would say hopelessly egotistical) intellectual figures, including Baruch Spinoza (1632–77) and Friedrich Nietzsche (1844–1900).

The rhizome is one of the most audacious rhetorical figures developed by Deleuze and Guattari. In the introductory essay to *A Thousand Plateaus* they describe it with reference to a number of characteristic 'principles', including connection, heterogeneity, multiplicity and rupture. As a metaphor for the organization of human experience, the rhizome is explicitly cast against another botanical organism – the tree – which, with its connotations of solidity, hierarchy, longevity and totality, has been central to the development of established forms of knowledge. Rhizomatic thought is anti-systematic,

contingent and improvisatory; it does not follow established narrative principles, it does not proceed ineluctably along pre-established lines towards predetermined goals. Instead, it proceeds by way of leaps between different, seemingly incommensurable, parts of the system; it is chaotic and metamorphic, forging temporary links between different languages and different categories only for them to disintegrate as new pathways are mapped and new connections forged. Above all, the rhizome is always and everywhere opposed to binary thought which, even when it opposes the Multiple to the One, is still mortgaged to the One – which is to say, to an ordered, hierarchical model of reality in which everything is (and can only ever be) itself.

Although Deleuze and Guattari begin *A Thousand Plateaus* by outlining 'the book' as an example of the rhizome, the application of their anti-disciplinary thought to the discipline of literature would be difficult to assess; yet, their focus on the rhizomatic nature of desire (which, they claim, Freud recognized but then eschewed so as to preserve the integrity of psychoanalysis) has proved influential in some literary analyses. The idea of 'literature' itself – a vast interconnecting web of narratives and characters which may be entered or exited at any point, and in which critical tweakings at one point will set off vibrations throughout the web – is also a potentially fruitful idea. With its incalculable army of users deploying the technology to communicate in a seemingly endless variety of official and unofficial ways, some have claimed that the Internet is the rhizomatic system *par excellence*.

It is unlikely if those with an intellectual and/or material investment in the tradition of rational thought descended from the Greek philosophers are about to welcome the rhizome with open arms (or open minds). By the same token, most 'oppositionalist' critics (feminists and post-colonialists, for example) have enough on their hands trying to deal with (what they perceive to be) the abuses of power facilitated by rationalist thought over the years; attempting to 'unthink' the whole system of discursive exchange could rob them of the grounds for resistance, and thus deny them an identity. It is in this context that Deleuze and Guattari have often been accused of bad faith: only those possessed of a deep familiarity with the workings of an established system could advocate its terrorization in such an apparently blasé manner. The mercurial Frenchmen reply that the system cannot be changed from within; a true revolution can be effected not (as advocated by generations of revolutionary thinkers) by 'radical' thought which always remains demonstrably in thrall to that which it opposes, but by 'rhizomatic' thought which, lacking a visible (and thus always vulnerable) front, constitutes a kind of guerrilla assault upon the established power/knowledge complex – irregular, erratic, always just about to cause trouble somewhere else.

See Roland Bogue, *Deleuze and Guattari* (1989); Gilles Deleuze and Felix Guattari, *A Thousand Plateaus: Capitalism and Schizophrenia* (1987); Paul Patton (ed.), *Deleuze: A Critical Reader* (1996).

GS

Rhyme A word in a line and a word in a scheme of things that transcends the line; and it is by virtue of this duality that it can at once act as the line's ticket to membership of a larger poetic community and counterpoint the line by suggesting with its rhyme-partner meanings extremer than or contradictory to the line's meaning.

Rhyme is also the music that thought and feeling are capable of: thought when it is so just as to delight the ear as well as the mind, feeling when the consonance it achieves testifies to its participation in a principle greater than itself. In the service of rhetoric, rhyme is an insidious substitute for causality. In a rhyme like *play*: *stray*, to take a simple example, the poet can play on the knowledge that the reader, attempting to rationalize the phenomenon of near-homonymity, will see lightheartedness as the necessary source and necessary outcome of vagabondage; as Daniel so succinctly puts it: 'Whilest seeking to please our ear, we enthrall our judgment' (*A Defence of Rhyme*).

Rhymes in dramatic, and particularly tragic, verse, encode patterns of predestination; they are recurrent moments of irrevocability; the rhyme-words fit much too snugly for characters to be able to go back on them (*name: shame, cast: waste, success: distress*). It is also probable that in the course of a play, the audience will become familiar with rhyme-groups in their entirety; in other words rhymes act as gravitational centres for dramatic syndromes and create, ironically, a sense of freedom which, however, is at best limited and in the very act of rhyming shown to be illusory. The group '*cacher: chercher: attacher: approcher: reprocher: toucher*', for example, which we find in Racinian drama, covers a whole behaviour pattern, and of the possible combinations most involve contradiction or duplicity.

It is rhyme that has allowed, encouraged the diversification of strophic forms, the rhythmic organization of lines. Rhyme schemes, even in the abstract, execute meaningful gestures. *Abab* describes the thrust and parry, give-and-take of leisurely discursive development; *abba* describes, apart from its self-stabilizing chiastic structure, an aggressive movement in which the *aa* pair outflanks and envelops the *bb* couplet, so that the *bb* couplet is ever in danger of becoming a mere parenthetic insertion.

See Philip Hobsbaum, *Metre, Rhythm and Verse Form* (1995); Jeffrey Wainwright, *Poetry: The Basics* (2004).

CS

Rhythm   See METRE.

Ritual   See MYTH.

Romance   A term which can encompass the medieval narrative poem, Spenser's *Faerie Queene*, gothic horrors and Mills and Boon is bound to be difficult to define. The linguistic history of the word (the romance, a romance, romance) reflects a movement from the definite to the indefinite which illustrates the necessary diffusion which must accompany such linguistic longevity and plasticity. As Gillian Beer points out (*The Romance*, 1970), the 'term "romance" in the early Middle Ages meant the new vernacular languages derived from Latin, in contradistinction to the learned language, Latin itself'. *Enromancier, romancar, romanz* meant to translate or compose books in the vernacular. The book itself was then called *Romanz, roman, romanzo*. The word became associated with the content of these diverse works – usually non-didactic narratives of ideal love and chivalric adventures, such as *Sir Gawain and the Green Knight* or Chrétien de Troyes's *Le Chevalier de la Charete*. Then these medieval romances, which took both poetic and prose form and which continued to influence the Elizabethan romance, tended to be regarded with some suspicion and even contempt by the classically oriented writers of the seventeenth and eighteenth centuries (see Arthur Johnston, *Enchanted Ground: The Study of Medieval Romance in the Eighteenth Century*, 1964).

The romance is usually concerned with an avowedly fictive world, though the medieval romance was more directly rooted in contemporary fact than might seem apparent from our perspective. At the same time it could be viewed increasingly as an imaginative and psychological projection of the 'real' world. In the nineteenth century, renewed interest in things medieval (cf. GOTHIC), together with a growing respect for the power of the imagination and the intangible truth of the inner world, gave new life to a form which tended now to be counterposed to the apparent facticity of the novel (cf. NOVEL, REALISM). In many mid-nineteenth-century works, such as *Jane Eyre, Dombey and Son* and *Silas Marner*, many of the qualities of romance and realism appear alongside each other in the narrative. Hawthorne saw the essential difference between the two as lying in the imaginative freedom granted to writers of romance which enabled them to pursue psychological and mythical truth more single-mindedly.

The main criticism of the romance, from Cervantes to Dr Johnson and Jane Austen, has been a moral one. The reader, it is argued, is seduced into applying its values, appropriate enough to the artificial world treated by the writer, to a real world in which pain has a genuine sharpness and the romantic pose is little more than a pallid gesture. This sense is retained in modern practice: sentimental ideals are presented in the knowledge that their power lies simultaneously in their apparent reality and actual ideality.

See J. M. Nosworthy, *Introduction to Cymbeline* (1955); E. H. Pettet, *Shakespeare and the Romance Tradition* (1949); Ad Putter and Jane Gilbert, *The Spirit of Medieval Popular Romance: A Historical Introduction* (2000); Janice Radway, *Reading the Romance* (1991).

CWEB

Romanticism The confusion surrounding the term 'Romanticism' seems only to be deepened by further attempts at definition. A. O. Lovejoy's famous essay 'On the discrimination of romanticisms' insisted on the need for discrimination between the meanings of the term at various times and in various countries. The danger perceived by Lovejoy was that the word loses *all* meaning unless we insist on defining our references. Other critics, René Wellek and Northrop Frye, argued that Romanticism is not essentially an idea but 'an historic centre of gravity, which falls somewhere around the 1790–1830 period' (Frye). They accused Lovejoy of attempting to break this historic characteristic into its component parts and of trying to insist on a romantic period or character wherever any of these components appear. This 'fallacy of timeless characterization' of Romanticism they saw as destructive of the specific quality of the historic romantic period. They attempted to define the romantic event from a more isolatedly critical context. Whereas Lovejoy saw Romanticism as the general term for a range of related ideas, poetic, philosophic and social, his refuters lay more stress on the characteristic images which haunt the romantic imagination. The central distinctive feature of the romantic mode was said to be the search for a reconciliation between the inner vision and the outer experience expressed through 'a creative power greater than his own because it includes his own' (Frye); or the synthetic IMAGINATION which performs this reconciliation and the vision it produces of a life drawing upon 'a sense of the continuity between man and nature and the presence of God' (Wellek).

The central feature of these attempts to define a Romantic entity is the development of romantic theories of the imagination.

M. H. Abrams provided an indispensable account of the origin and development of romantic theories of perception and imagination in *The Mirror and the Lamp* (1953). Underlying these theories, from the end of the eighteenth century and for the next hundred years or more, is the sense that humanity has become separated from nature, which leads to a false characterization of external nature as 'fixed and dead'. The romantic poet seeks a way to reactivate the world by discovering the creative perceptiveness which will allow the writer to draw aside the veils which modern living has laid across the senses and seek a perception where the false separation of Nature (fixed, external objects) and nature (the living being of the perceiver) can be reconciled: a new synthesizing vision. The romantic thinker often feels that such a faculty is not an invention, but a rediscovery of the truth about the way we perceive and create which has been lost in the development of more complicated social forms and the growth of rational and self-conscious theories of human thought. This belief leads to a marked historicism, to an increased interest in primitivist theories of culture: to a persistent strain of historical reconstruction in romantic writing, a medieval element in poetry and the novel, and an idealized resurrection of ballad and folk-song.

This attempt to revitalize the perceptive process is also bound up with the desire to rediscover a 'living language'. The search in ballads and in everyday language (Wordsworth) is only a side-issue. At root the romantic is trying to find a way back – or forward – to the Word, the Logos which is the act it describes. The romantic thinkers are finally baffled by their loyalty to the traditional concept of art as an embodiment or vitalized representation of a separate perceptive act in the 'real' world. But their struggles with this problem prepare the way for the more total concepts of the post-romantic artists, the SYMBOLISTS and IMAGISTS who force romantic aesthetics to its logical conclusion by identifying a desire for complete reconciliation between perception and art: 'How can we know the dancer from the dance?' (Yeats) Romantic artists suffer an agonizing struggle to grasp and express what they perceive; they are continually aware that they cannot objectively 'trust' what they see since they are involved in *creating* what they see. They are barred from the convenient symbolic systems available in existing mythic patterns because such public symbols falsify the truth of personal feeling. On the one hand lies the quagmire of personal mythology with its resulting lack of communicative power (Blake), on the other the terrible isolation of the specific and actual: 'the weary weight of all this unintelligible world' (Wordsworth).

The artist feels isolated, unable to discover what must exist, some objective form or Form to embody the sense of continuity between the imagination and the visible world, and is drawn towards those experiences which offer a blurred version of the separation of ego and event, drug hallucination or the radical innocence of childhood perceptions. But such experiences are special and not typical, and they are also transient, Thus Wordsworth, looking back at the apparent directness of childhood, sees it slipping away as 'shades of the prison house' close round him.

Coleridge argued that 'we receive but what we give' ('Dejection Ode'), but his poem celebrates this realization in the context of the inevitable pressures of time and decay. At the heart of the romantic dilemma is the agony of the disappearing dream. Life in nature is life in *our* nature, and that is subject to decay. With the romantic thinkers and poets, with Wordsworth's lost 'splendour in the grass', Keats's and Coleridge's 'fragments' ('The Fall of Hyperion', 'Kubla Khan') we have begun the artistic dilemma which leads to Yeats's desire for the immutable permanence of the golden bird of Byzantium and the modern, post-Symbolist search for unchanging form in the heart of chaos itself.

During the 1970s Harold Bloom, Paul de Man and other Yale critics, all distinguished Romantic scholars, concerned themselves with Romanticism in the light of the work of Derrida, initiating a major reformulation of Romantic writing through deconstruction. Paul de Man, for example, argued that the romantic historical consciousness had been a powerful influence on the modern development of a historical identity. Their work has been enormously influential on subsequent studies of the subject.

See M. H. Abrams (ed.), *English Romantic Poetry* (1960) (includes Lovejoy's essay cited above); M. H. Abrams, *The Mirror and the Lamp* (1953); D. Aers, J. Cook and D. Punter, *Romanticism and Ideology* (1981); M. Butler, *Romantics, Rebels and Reactionaries* (1981); Paul De Man, *The Rhetoric of Romanticism* (1984); F. Kermode, *Romantic Image* (1957); J. J. McGann, *The Romantic Ideology* (1983); Duncan Wu (ed.), *A Companion to Romanticism* (1999); Paul de Man et al., *Romanticism and Contemporary Criticism* (1993); Kathleen Wheeler, *Romanticism, Pragmatism and Deconstruction* (1993); Harold Bloom (ed.), *English Romantic Poetry* (2004); David stevens, *Romaticism* (2004).

GG

S

Satire   A genre defined primarily, but not exclusively, in terms of its inner form (see GENRE). In it, the author attacks some object, using as his means wit or humour that is either fantastic or absurd. Denunciation itself is not satire, nor, of course, is grotesque humour, but the genre allows for a considerable preponderance of either one or the other. What distinguishes satire from comedy is its lack of tolerance for folly or human imperfection. Its attempt to juxtapose the actual with the ideal lifts it above mere invective.

From this need to project a double vision of the world satire derives most of its formal characteristics. IRONY, which exploits the relation between appearance and reality, is its chief device, but as Northrop Frye points out in his essay on satire and irony (*Anatomy of Criticism*, Princeton, New Jersey, Princeton University Press, 1957, pp. 223–39) it is irony of a militant kind, 'Irony is consistent both with complete realism of content and with the suppression of attitude on the part of the author. Satire demands at least a token fantasy, a content which the reader recognises as grotesque, and at least an implicit moral standard.'

Frye goes on to describe three phases of satire which correspond roughly to the traditional classification of Horatian, Menippean and Juvenalian satire. The first of these, low-norm satire, takes for granted a world full of anomalies, follies and crimes, and employs a plain, common sense, conventional *eiron* to stand against the various *alazons* who represent aspects of the unjust, ruling society. The theme of the second phase of satire is 'the setting of ideas and generalizations and theories and dogmas over against the life they are supposed to explain'. It employs Menippean cynicism to attack systems of reasoning and their social effects. The third phase, or satire of the high norm, abandons common sense pragmatism itself, and by a slight shift of vision and perspective, presents the world, stripped of its social conventions, as a locus of 'filth and ferocity'.

In the last of these phases the moral standard referred to by Frye is often only discernible in the satirist's tone of indignation; and in those forms which effectively deny the author any tone of voice, satire has to be achieved differently. For example, much critical discussion of Restoration Comedy has fruitlessly pursued the question of the dramatists' attitudes towards their subjects. Where an author is forced to efface himself from his creation, or chooses to mask his own attitude, as Swift does in *A Modest Proposal* (1729), he must rely on the reader to make the necessary comparison between the grotesque fantasy he creates and the moral norms or ideals by which it is to be judged. The best clue to the intentions and the achievements of the Restoration dramatists lies in the techniques of distortion they employ – or fail to employ – in the creation of a fantasy world.

In some satires distortion takes the form of displacement: the substitution of an animal world for the human in Swift's *Gulliver's Travels* (1726), or George Orwell's *Animal Farm* (1945). In others, inverted values serve to distort reality. This technique makes possible the subgenre of MOCK-EPIC. Yet again, writers may use a variety of devices: caricature, exaggeration, parallelism or parody, to achieve similar ends.

See R. C. Elliott, *The Power of Satire: Magic, Ritual, Art* (1960); R. Paulson (ed.), *Satire: Modern Essays in Criticism* (1971); C. Rawson (ed.), *English Satire and the Satiric Tradition* (1984).

BCL

Scansion See METRE.

Scheme Redefined by classical rhetoricians and grammarians until its meaning became indeterminate, 'scheme' in the sixteenth and seventeenth centuries was enormously popular in the vocabulary of literary and rhetorical theorists who, exploiting their new methods, managed to repeat the process. Any reasonably accurate reading of the versatile definitions and usages of the term in such works as Richard Sherry's *Treatise of Schemes and Tropes* (1550), Henry Peacham's *Garden of Eloquence* (1577) or John Prideaux's *Sacred Eloquence* (1659) will arm the critic with sufficient authority to explain and defend as 'schemes' all known figures and tropes in English and Mandarin Chinese, the 'conceits' of seventeenth-century poetry, the rhetorical strategies of Robespierre, and the designs, foils, plots and prosody of Vladimir Nabokov. Or, conversely 'scheme' has been dealt with as a special kind of FIGURE: an 'easy' one, a 'figure of sound' or, more simply, as a hazy synonym for 'trope'. To support such interpretations of Renaissance thought and practice requires the suppression of a considerable amount of evidence, not only because of the extreme scope of the viewpoint in the original texts, but also because 'figure', in Renaissance terms, is habitually referred to as a subordinate component of 'scheme'. Cf. FIGURE.

TGW

Scriptible See PLEASURE.

Semiotics Deals with the study of signs: their production and communication, their systematic grouping in languages or codes, their social function. It is doubly relevant to the study of literature, for literature uses language, the primary sign system in human culture, and is further organized through various subsidiary codes, such as generic conventions.

Semiotics has an odd history. Various Western thinkers – the Stoics and Saint Augustine, Locke and Husserl – have treated signs and sign-functions, without quite constituting a separate study. Other disciplines can be seen, retrospectively, as crypto-semiotic; thus Tzvetan Todorov has discussed rhetoric from a semiotic point of view (*Theories of the Symbol*, 1977, trans. 1982). It is probable that any study as ambitiously inclusive as semiotics will always be plagued by problems of cohesion and demarcation. These problems are reflected in the double founding of modern semiotics from within different disciplines, by the American philosopher Charles Sanders Peirce (1839–1914) and by the Swiss linguist Ferdinand de Saussure (1857–1915).

Saussure's reorientation of linguistics from a diachronic to a synchronic approach, from the study of historical change to the systemization of a given state of language, conditions his treatment of the sign. 'Language is a system of signs that express ideas', and the interrelationship of signs thus determines meaning. The expressive function of the sign is achieved through its components of signifier (as image or form) and signified (as concept or idea); their linkage, with minor exceptions, is seen as arbitrary and unmotivated. Similarly, the system of signs that comprises a language expresses no given or predetermined meanings;

these arise from the interrelations of the system: 'in language there are only differences *without positive terms*'. And since language is only one among sign systems (Saussure mentions writing, military signals, polite formulas) it is possible to envisage a future 'science that studies the life of signs within society', which Saussure calls 'semiology' – a term common in French discussions, but elsewhere yielding to 'semiotics'.

While Saussure envisages an extension to the science of signs, Peirce begins with a generalized system, which he sees as a branch of logic. And while Saussure works with binaristic, dyadic relations, Peirce puts everything in threes, even coining the term 'triadomany' for his obsession. The triads make for a certain dynamism in Peirce's account; he is interested in semiosis, the act of signifying, and the triadic description of this act presents it as a mediation between two terms by a third. 'A *sign* is anything which is related to a Second thing, its Object... in such a way as to bring a Third thing, its *Interpretant*, into relation to the same Object'; the interpretant is itself a sign, so the process recurs. Peirce offers an exhaustive and exhausting taxonomy of all aspects of semiosis, but most of his terms are now neglected except those describing the relation between the sign and its object; Peirce differs from Saussure in allowing a greater role for motivated linkage. Besides the arbitrary 'symbol', he describes the 'icon' (linked through resemblance) and the 'index' (with an existential or causal linkage). These terms are now often applied to the signifier/signified pair.

Although Peirce may offer more scope as a critical tool, Saussure has exercised the greater influence. While Peirce's logic was neglected, Saussure's linguistics flourished, and drew his semiotics

along with it. A crucial factor was the rise of STRUCTURALISM, in which the role of linguistics as a systematic model – either directly, or through its adaptation in anthropology – was paramount. Structuralism and semiotics, as they impinged on literary studies, were often indistinguishable, especially when semiotics concentrated on the production of meaning rather than its communication. And they raised similar problems for critics. Could the individual text be analysed as a sign-system? If not, of what system was it an instance? Was it justified to accord any privilege or particularity to literary language as an aesthetic code?

Semiotics should arguably be self-critical, and the fashionable structuralist semiotics of the 1960s did sometimes reflect on its procedures; thus Roland Barthes's *Elements of Semiology* (1964, trans. 1967) extends the Saussurean base, gives a greater role to motivation, and expresses doubts about binarism. But any expressed doubt in this period was counterbalanced by a surge of scientist optimism about the development of what was seen as a rigorously objective and comprehensive study – especially when contrasted with impressionistic literary criticism. And there were undeniable advances; for example, in describing the signifying systems of NARRATIVE. But 1970s and 1980s saw extensive 'poststructuralist' criticism of this semiotic enterprise. The positivist ideal of a closed and total structuration is itself subject to the metaphysical critique of DECONSTRUCTION. More particularly, the idealization of systems can lead to neglect of the dynamics of signification and a reductive account of the agents involved. To combat this reductionism, Julia Kristeva uses psychoanalysis to enlarge the notion of the speaking subject in semiotics; and the later work of Roland Barthes persistently strives to extend and to de-formalize the role of the reader. Umberto Eco's *Theory of Semiotics* (1976) actualizes the potential dynamism of Peirce and the social hints of Saussure. It emphasizes process through what Eco calls 'the mobility of semantic space'. Codes are subject to change in use: through undercoding, the simplification of alien systems, and through overcoding, the addition of extra signifying rules that are crucial in stylistic or ideological elaboration. And the 'unlimited semiosis' promised by Peirce's interpretant that is itself a sign means that for Eco any determinate meaning is replaced by something transitory, the provisional semantic stability of a given culture or subculture.

This is not to suggest that all semiotics has abjured determinate signification. A contrary example is Michael Riffaterre's *Semiotics of Poetry* (1978), which describes the reading of poems in terms of a 'semiotic transfer' between two systems. The first system is mimetic: for Riffaterre, prior readings are unpoetically referential. They suggest difficulties or 'ungrammaticalities' (predictably, as Riffaterre's examples are Symbolist and Surrealist), which are resolved by code-switching from mimesis to poetic semiosis proper. In the latter system all relationships are finally motivated, it is produced by transforming the 'matrix', a unifying node of significance which is variously encoded in text or intertext. The essentialist and organicist bias of Riffaterre's theory has been sharply questioned.

The study of culture itself as a semiotic phenomenon was initiated by the work of Jan Mukařovský and the Prague school, which began in the 1930s. And the most ambitious approach to a semiotics of culture also came from Eastern Europe, in the work of Jurij Lotman and the Moscow-Tartu school of semiotics. In 1971, Lotman produced one of the most thorough accounts of structuralist semiotics as applied to literature: *The Structure of the Artistic Text* (trans. 1977). This, predictably, uses a synchronic approach; but Lotman's cultural studies also encompass diachrony. In the first place, he makes typological distinctions between the semiotic practices of historical cultures: thus medievalism is marked by 'high semioticity', which 'proceeds from the assumption that everything is significant' (there is an overlap here with the work of Michel Foucault); whereas enlightenment culture sees the world of natural objects as real, so that 'signs become the symbols of falsehood'. Second, Lotman studies diachronic change by describing the interplay between culture as patterned information and an unpatterned 'non-culture', or by describing cultural 'translation' in which communicative needs encourage a creative recoding.

See John Fiske, *Introduction to Communication Studies* (1982) ch. 3; R. W. Bailey, L. Matejka and P. Steiner (eds), *The Sign: Semiotics Around the World* (1978); M. E. Blanchard, *Description: Sign, Self, Desire; Critical Theory in the Wake of Semiotics* (1980); Terence Hawkes, *Structuralism and Semiotics* (1977); Jonathan Culler, *Structuralist Poetics* (1975).

EC

Sensibility The prestige of mathematical reasoning in seventeenth-century Europe was immense, and the end of the century might in England be called the Age of Reason. To some thinkers, it looked as if having accomplished so much in interpreting the natural world, reason could go on to solve problems hitherto left to less clear and distinct methods of investigation – matters of values and morals. But poets and critics in England never accepted the total primacy of reason, and they were very willing to take over a moral and aesthetic doctrine which was in reaction against a too great demand on reason. Such a doctrine existed: the elaboration of a notion of a personal, inner faculty, an emotional consciousness which came to be called *sensibility*. The doctrine assumed great importance in English thought in the eighteenth century, so much so that after mid-century, the Age of Sensibility would be a better label for the critical context of English literature. The book that crystallized this idea was the Earl of Shaftesbury's *Characteristics of Men, Manners, Opinions, Times* (1708–11). Shaftesbury develops a not very clear neo-Platonic argument and an ethic, based on this inner aesthetic sense, 'to learn what is *just* in Society and *beautiful* in Nature, and the Order of the World'. The natural moral sense is also the *individual* taste, though Shaftesbury did not abandon all traditional restrictions on its free workings.

It is too neat to see the development of the powerful idea of sensibility only as a reaction to prevalent philosophical doctrine, or as a component in the history of Western empiricism. Northrop Frye, in a valuable article 'Towards defining an age of feeling' (reprinted in J. L. Clifford (ed.), *Eighteenth-Century English Literature*, 1959) suggests that there are two polar views of literature. One is an aesthetic, Aristotelian view that considers works of literature as 'products', that seeks to distance the audience. The other view is psychological, seeing the creation of literature as a 'process', and seeking to involve the audience in this. Longinus's treatise *On the Sublime* is the classical Greek statement of the latter, and Longinus is an important source for

eighteenth-century aesthetic theory. Sensibility is the important constituent in the eighteenth-century form of the second view. There had been a shift in critical interest from the late seventeenth century onwards, away from categorizing works of literature to investigating the psychological processes involved in creating and responding to art. 'Genius' is the fascinating concept in discussions of the artist, 'sensibility' both in discussing the artist and analysing the audience's response. Since 'process' is also to be seen in history and in nature, sensibility involves a sense of the past and is frequently the informing principle of reflective 'nature' poems like Thomson's *Seasons* (1726–30). Shaftesbury held that 'the *Beautiful*, the *Fair*, the Comely were never in the Matter, but in the *Art* and *Design*: never in Body it-self, but in the *Form* and *forming Power*'.

Wordsworth and Coleridge developed this idea of the 'aesthetic imagination', which leads to the Coleridgean 'primary imagination' where sensibility, human perception, is 'a repetition in the finite mind of the eternal act of creation in the infinite I AM'. Shaftesbury's 'sensibility' was a little more modest than that, but it had an all-important moral side. This was later developed by Adam Smith in his *Theory of Moral Sentiment* (1759), which had great influence on critics in later discussions of sensibility. Smith added a related doctrine: the power of sympathy. Sympathy powered the benevolence that Shaftesbury advocated, and Shakespeare, it was agreed, had it to a sublime degree. A poet to be truly great also needed a concomitant of sensibility, the 'enthusiastic delight' of imagination. Sensibility was the particular faculty that responded to the greatest imaginative power, the *sublime*, another important part of the later eighteenth-century critical picture. This whole aesthetic was audience-based. Sensibility, though instinctive, could be cultivated, and the whole psychological theory gave greater and greater prominence to education, a 'sentimental education'. Obviously, sensibility and sentiment could become a cult. It did, giving rise to a good deal of attitudinizing. It is the cult of 'sensibility' taken beyond the bounds of reason and common sense that Jane Austen portrays in *Sense and Sensibility* (1811), in the character of Marianne Dashwood, whose selfish concentration on her own feelings is contrasted with the self-control and consideration for other people's feelings shown by her 'sensible' sister, Elinor. See also IMAGINATION.

See Jerome J. McGann, *The Poetics of Sensibility: A Revolution in Literary Style* (1998); Markman Ellis, *The Politics of Sensibility: Race, Gender and Commerce in the Sentimental Novel* (2004).

AMR

Sexuality   Generally taken to be related to sex; that is, to the characteristics of sexed bodies, and to sexual desires, fantasies and acts – most often with the aim of orgasm – 'the quality of being sexual or having sex' (OED). The term first came into common usage in the late-eighteenth and early-nineteenth centuries. As Joseph Bristow notes in *Sexuality* (1997), a book devoted to answering his opening question 'What is sexuality?', 'psychoanalysis was the first body of theory to produce a detailed account of why sexuality must be understood separately from reproduction'. However, Freud's essay of 1931, 'Female Sexuality' is preoccupied with the 'normal' heterosexual development from infant to adult sexuality. To resist the normative is to suffer trauma and repression. For the woman, it is to be an hysteric, in the grip of 'a masculinity complex', suffering from 'penis envy' and refusing to acquiesce to the passivity of an adult, vaginal-oriented female sexuality (as opposed to the infantile clitoral activity). The word 'homosexual' is also a relative latecomer to Euro-American cultural discourse, appearing, according to Eve Kosofsky Sedgwick in *Epistemology of the Closet* (1990), during the last third of the nineteenth century. As Kososfsky Sedgwick observes, it is not that a wide range of sexual behaviours or 'sexual clusters' did not exist before nineteenth century, but rather that a range of 'new, institutionalized taxonomic discourses – medical, legal, literary, psychological – centering on homo/heterosexual definition proliferated and crystallized with exceptional rapidity' at this time. There has been a move to see sexuality as more individual – just as there is a sense that there is a greater freedom to express 'who we really are' and to ask for 'what we really want' sexually. Thus, although many would claim that there is undoubtedly still the persistent assumption that most people are innately heterosexual, there is also broader acknowledgment that a wide range of sexual behaviour (homosexual, bisexual, QUEER, transgender, transsexual) is not pathological or perverse. However, the fundamental notion that sexuality is inherent or latent, something to be uncovered and then expressed, is controversial. According to Michel Foucault (1926–84), in volume one of *The History of Sexuality* (1976), the notion that we are freer to profess and act out our sexual preferences is a myth. Rather, in Foucault's terms, the very premises of sexuality and sexual behaviour have been constructed by the prevailing cultural discourse which creates, institutionalizes and protects the interests of power. Sexuality tends to be seen as something natural that was formerly subdued by powerful institutions, such as the church, but which has now been liberated. However, Foucault refutes this. His point is, not just that 'sexuality' is historically contingent, but rather, that just where Western society now feels itself to be most free, it is being most disciplined, most policed. As a society we have seen 'sexuality' become a category to be obsessively scrutinized and discussed, its subjects compelled to 'confess' their sexuality in infinite detail. For Foucault, this bringing of sex under the microscope is part of the science of sexuality (*scienta sexualis*), with psychoanalysis becoming the new confessional. The increasing distinction between sex as the means for procreation (and a societal duty to protect this) and of sex for pleasure/recreation, has been instrumental in the discursive construction of the category of 'sexuality'.

See Andy Medhurst and Sally R. Munt (eds), *Lesbian and Gay Studies: A Critical Introduction* (1997); Joseph Bristow, *Sexuality* (1997).

SS

Short fiction Probably the most ancient of all literary forms; the term covers everything from the fable, folktale or fairy-story, to such sophisticated and highly developed structures as the German *Novelle*, via the stories of the *Decameron*, and Cervantes's *Exemplary Tales*. Like the EPIC, short fiction goes back in time far beyond the art of writing, and it was not until relatively recently in the history of literature that stories arose from anything but a common stock; praise went to the art of the teller rather than the originality of his material. It was only at the beginning of the nineteenth century that short fiction, because of the requirements of magazines of everwidening circulation, came into its own and attracted notable writers to practise it, like Pushkin, Edgar Allan Poe, Henry James, Anton Chekhov, James

Joyce, Thomas Mann, Franz Kafka and D. H. Lawrence, as well as those like Maupassant and Katherine Mansfield who excelled in this particular genre.

Perhaps because of its diversity short fiction has given rise to surprisingly little, theoretical criticism. One of the earliest, and best attempts to define the genre was Poe's, in two reviews (1842 and 1847) of Nathaniel Hawthorne's tales: 'short prose narrative, requiring from a half-hour to one or two hours in its perusal', working towards a 'single effect' created by incidents chosen with economy and a rigorous sense of necessity in the design. Other critics (most of them in fact themselves practitioners of the art, such as H. E. Bates, Sean O'Faolain and V. S. Pritchett) have stressed the fact that short fiction must be exemplary and representative, a world in brief compass; that it establishes unity of impression and a feeling of totality, by concentrating on a single character, event or emotion, and by compression and the avoidance of digression or repetition; that it satisfies our craving for paradox and shape, our longing to perceive a dramatic pattern and significance in experience, even if this means sacrificing plausibility to effect (as sometimes in Pushkin and Maupassant, not to mention Poe). Truman Capote goes so far as to assert that 'a story can be wrecked by a faulty rhythm in a sentence – especially if it occurs towards the end – or a mistake in paragraphing, even punctuation'; James, he says, 'is the maestro of the semicolon', and Hemingway 'a first-rate paragrapher'. O'Faolain argues similarly that the language of short fiction should be 'spare', and that realistic detail is only a 'bore' if it simply seeks 'idle verisimilitude' rather than 'general revelation by suggestion'. All these theorists insist on meaningful openings (not of the anecdotal 'by the way' kind), and natural yet appropriate endings, either the 'whimper' sort as in Chekhov, or the 'whip-crack' variety practised by Maupassant. The sonorous last phrase of Joyce's closing story in *Dubliners*, for instance ('upon all the living and the dead'), is effective because it has been prepared for throughout by gradual and almost imperceptible shifts of tone from the breezy opening onwards ('Lily, the caretaker's daughter, was literally run off her feet'). In this story, as in other masterpieces of the genre like Pushkin's 'Queen of spades' or Kafka's 'Metamorphosis', a central, controlling image maintains an essential unity which transcends as it complements the unity guaranteed by the more obvious devices catalogued by Poe and others.

Short fiction is less diffuse than the NOVEL, just as the short story proper differs from the folk tale of the *Thousand and One Nights* variety in that it does not easily tolerate loosely connected episodes, digressions and moral or bawdy commentary; but the closest analogy for short fiction probably lies outside literature proper. As Bates saw, the film and the short story are expressions of the same art, that of telling stories by a series of gestures, shots and suggestions, with little elaboration or explanation. It is certainly no coincidence that some of the most effective films are adaptations of short fiction.

See Caroline Gordon and Allen Tate, *The House of Fiction* (1960); Eugene Current-Garcia and Walton R. Patrick, *What is the Short Story?* (1961); Sean O'Faolain, *The Short Story* (1948, reprinted 1964); H. Bonheim, *The Narrative Modes: Techniques of the Short Story* (1982); Dominic Head, *The Modernist Short Story* (1992); Susan Lohafer, *Reading for Storyness* (2003).

JWJF

Sign See SEMIOTICS.

Simile While METAPHOR is a dramatic, absolute and intuited identification of two phenomena, simile is a comparison, discursive, tentative, in which the 'like' or 'as . . . as' suggests, from the viewpoint of reason, separateness of the compared items (Marston, *Antonio* and *Mellida*):

> and thou and I will live –
> Let's think like what – and thou and I
> will live
> Like unmatch'd mirrors of calamity.

Because simile is usually a pointedly rationalized perception, it has none of the revelatory suddenness of metaphor nor expresses and demands the same degree of mental commitment to the image. Instead it presents itself as a provisional, even optional, aid whose function is explanatory or illustrative. Simile appeals to what we already know about things, metaphor invites the imagination to break new ground; for this reason we can pass an evaluative judgement on simile, whereas we must either take or leave a metaphor. The temporariness of simile underlines, in the work of a Baudelaire or a Rilke, the fact that the universal analogy is only glimpsed, only fragments vouchsafed. And because simile is temporary, it and the totality of experience it promises are infinitely renewable. Simile is a figure with much stamina.

Because simile does not upset reality, but merely inflects our perception of it, keeping different phenomena discrete, it can be used with some irresponsibility. On the one hand, this means it can play an important alleviatory role, letting air and whimsy into involved narrative or analysis (Proust) and on the other, that poets not prepared to envisage the chaos of metaphor can use simile as the repository for their inventive boldnesses and keep their metaphors conventional (early Hugo, George).

The position of the 'like' phrase is significant. When it succeeds the justificatory adjective or verb ('thy beauty... stings like an adder' – Swinburne), we are given a metaphor defused; the figurative dimension of 'stings' is superseded by its literal dimension. When it precedes (*'Mon coeur, comme un oiseau, voltigeait...*' – Baudelaire), the relationship between phenomena is more complete; here the 'like' phrase not so much explains away the verb as supposes other verbs.

In calling simile provisional, we mean that the comparability is provisional, its appositeness dependent on a particular confluence of circumstances, and this has made simile a natural vehicle for a relativistic view of the world (Proust); the world of simile is a world of passing acquaintances, incessant sensory flirtation with objects never finally known. But within these limitations the simile, by using or implying the present tense, can lift an action or perception out of the fleeting and exceptional and install it in the constant and familiar. (As A *does* B, so X *did* Y.) This is a main function of the epic simile, where often a noble or complex sentiment is made accessible to the reader through being linked with a familiar external state of affairs. The same expository function is performed by those fantastic Renaissance conceits which take the form of similes. These two notorious stanzas from Donne's 'Valediction: forbidding mourning', for instance, externalize, in an exploratory fashion, a spiritual and emotional state which might be impenetrable without the similes:

Our two soules therefore, which are one
Though I must goe, endure not yet
A breach, but an expansion
Like gold to ayery thinnesse beate.

If they be two, they are two so
As stiffe twin compasses are two,
Thy soule the fixt foot, makes no show
To move, but doth, if th'other doe.

CS

Sincerity Prior to the eighteenth century, a term of little significance in criticism: the absence or otherwise of dissimulation on the part of a writer (though not necessarily of a fictional character, such as Iago in *Othello*) was neither questioned nor thought worthy of comment. But in the late 1760s, Jean-Jacques Rousseau's *Confessions*, an unprecedentedly frank, if subtly edited, autobiography, projected a persona of the author which the reader was beguiled or bludgeoned into taking at face value. Soon after this, Goethe, in his early novel *The Sorrows of Young Werther* (1774), attacked calm rationalism and exalted instead sensibility and passionate feelings, all in the name of sincerity. Both these works were to prove of seminal importance in the Romantic movement, which arose in the late eighteenth century and lasted well into the nineteenth. During this period writers popularized the image of poets suffering intense emotions of grief and joy which they then proceeded to enshrine directly and 'sincerely' in their works. But with E. T. A. Hoffmann's allegorical fairy-story *The Golden Pot* (1813), Byron's epic satire *Don Juan* (1819–24) and Baudelaire's figure of the poet as dandy (analysed in his essay *The Painter of Modern Life*, 1863) a new note is struck: the idea of pose, show, even outright duplicity begins to creep in. In the 1880s Nietzsche perceptively noted that 'every profound spirit needs a mask'. This tendency culminated in the life and art of such *fin-de-siècle* 'decadents' as J. K. Huysmans, the creator in *Against*

Nature (1884) of the character Des Esseintes, whose neurasthenic extravagances fascinated Oscar Wilde and his contemporaries. It was Wilde who enunciated the pithiest of anti-sincerity paradoxes when he wrote that 'the first duty in life is to be as *artificial* as possible'. Around the same time the discrepancy between what people may say or do in public and what they really think (betrayed through dreams or by involuntary slips of the tongue) attracted Sigmund Freud's scientific curiosity, and led to the publication of such studies as *The Psychopathology of Everyday Life* in 1914 (see PSYCHOLOGY). After Freud it was no longer possible to take an innocent attitude towards the issue of sincerity, and this deepened awareness of complexity in matters hitherto thought relatively simple was reflected in the work of modernist novelists. The nocturnal persona of Molly Bloom, the speaker of the closing monologue in James Joyce's *Ulysses* (1922), is clearly more sincere, or at least more authentic, than her everyday self. Similarly, in bringing the titanic clashes of ancient tragedy into the demure and sedate drawing rooms of her characters, Ivy Compton-Burnett (1892–1969) called into question the 'sincerity' of much that passes for polite conversation. Her French disciple Nathalie Sarraute (b. 1902) concentrated on the phenomenon of 'sub-conversation', or the level of social intercourse which is never heard aloud but conveys unavowed animosities, conflicts and resentments, in fact all the unseemly deceptions hidden beneath urbane surfaces.

The evolution of attitudes towards insincerity in art and life is thus a complex one, and examination of it is not assisted by imprecision in the term 'sincerity' itself. All the intellectual historian can say with any assurance is that 'at a certain point in its history the moral life of Europe added to itself a new element, the state or quality of the self which we call sincerity' (Lionel Trilling); and that this point occurred somewhere around the middle of the eighteenth century. Trilling defines the meaning of the term as 'congruence between avowal and actual feeling'. In this sense it tends, in discussions about literature, to become the amateur's panacea, used as a means of explaining or isolating literary excellence; in such naïve exercises in evaluation it serves as a loose form of approbation (cf. 'genuineness' or 'authenticity'). On examination the most apparently 'sincere' works usually turn out to have reached their final form long after the original emotions which gave rise to them, and should ultimately be seen to have more in common with a literary tradition than with the feelings of a particular individual. Leo Tolstoy, himself an almost archetypally sincere writer, put it succinctly when he saw 'poetry in the fact of not lying', by which he meant that the work of art has its own truthfulness, which has little or nothing to do with the honest transcription of feeling. Sincerity as usually understood is therefore not a very helpful word in the literary critic's vocabulary and should be sparingly employed. As Oscar Wilde discerned with his usual acuteness, 'Man is least himself when he talks in his own person. Give him a mask and he will tell you the truth.' See also PERSONA.

See I. A. Richards, *Principles of Literary Criticism* (1924), chs 23 and 34; Henri Peyre, *Literature and Sincerity* (1963); Lionel Trilling, *Sincerity and Authenticity* (1972).

JWJF

Skaz   See FORMALISM.

Society   In critical usage, a term with two main senses: (1) the 'society' of a novel, play or poem, a social world created or imitated within the work, (2) the 'society' of literature's creation and consumption, the world of customs, values, institutions and language-habits in which the work is created, published and read, the culture in its broadest definition (cf. CULTURE). In autotelic theories of literature (those which assume that literary works are self-sustaining, coherent structures) the two usages are commonly held distinct. In realistic theories of literature (those which assume that literary works in some sense copy life) they blur. In historicist theories of literature (those which assume that the literary work is an instance of contemporary discourses) they become virtually indistinguishable.

Critics from Plato and Aristotle on have known that literature is essentially 'social' – has social causes, contents and effects. The question is how valuable that insight is. With the personalization of romantic art, and the self-subsistence of symbolist art, the tendency to stress the distinctiveness of literary expression grew, reacting against deterministic social accounts of literature: those which saw it as a social mirror, a social product (e.g. Tame), a social criticism (e.g. naturalism) or an ideological instrument (e.g. some Marxist critics). Criticism tended to substitute median terms: 'culture' for the milieu, 'icon' for the work. But the final decades of the twentieth century saw new interest in the complex transactions existing between 'literature' (meaning either the single text, or the entire corpus) and 'society' (meaning a particular community or the large-scale social metastructure). There are various reasons for this: the growth of sociology, linguistics and structuralism; an increasing critical stress on fiction as opposed to poetry; a general tendency towards the politicalization of thought.

What is clear is that the term 'society' invites or reveals critical confusion, since it refers to something that can be thought of as primarily inside or outside the work. The society of, say, a Jane Austen novel can be thought of primarily as a fiction (a deliberately selective, conventionalized milieu which is an aspect of the composition) or a structure from outside 'reported' or analysed. Beyond this are larger issues. We can see literary works as social products and agents, and society as an envelope around literature, analysable in terms of reading publics, authors' *Weltanschauungen*, content-analysis, linguistics and ideologies. Or we can see them as creative centres lying outside such determinisms, though perhaps as potential powers *in* society. 'Society' raises all the problems of the territorial boundary separating 'art' from 'reality'; for that reason it will always constitute a critical crux, and remain a centre of attention for critics interested in the complex relationships between the fictional and formal and the world we observe round us. See also CULTURE.

See Malcolm Bradbury, *The Social Context of Modern English Literature* (1971); Alan Sinfield, *Society and Literature 1945–70* (1983); Raymond Williams, *Culture and Society 1780–1950* (1961).

MSB

Soliloquy   A formal device by which a dramatic character, alone on the stage, reveals feelings, thoughts and motives in speech to the audience. In its simplest form, as often in the Elizabethan drama before Shakespeare, it can be merely a means of directly communicating information that has not emerged in the course of the action or dialogue; for unskilful playwrights, therefore, it may be no more than a substitute for fully dramatic writing.

The typical soliloquy is either a passionate speech giving vent to the immediate pressure of feeling at a point of crisis, or a deliberative speech in which a particular dilemma or choice of action is debated and resolved or, since one may lead naturally to the other, a combination of both. Thus, the most effective soliloquies are introduced at moments of urgency for the character concerned, particularly, when there is a reason for privacy and secrecy rather than public display of passion or reasoning. Sometimes, however, the soliloquy may be spoken directly to the audience by characters who wish to take them into their confidence. Clowns and villains are inclined to this mode of address: the clowns because they often stand on the periphery of the plot and so invite the audience to join them in ridiculing situations in which they are not directly involved, and the villains (like Shakespeare's Richard III and Iago) because their awareness of the audience's presence adds to their stature as clever rogues in charge of events.

When the audience is eavesdropping on a meditative or impassioned soliloquy, the dramatist has the opportunity to internalize the presentation of character and to trace the dynamics of thought and feeling even beyond the level of the character's own awareness. In Shakespeare's subtlest soliloquies (those of Hamlet and Macbeth, for instance) the audience is made to recognize ironies and ambiguities in what the character says, but of which the character is unaware. Thus, the actor is given the opportunity not only for a virtuoso performance of a set speech, but also for suggesting either the involuntary direction the character's thoughts and feelings move in, or the painful effort to articulate what lies almost out of reach of the character's words. In both cases the language and style of these great soliloquies do not describe the character's state of mind, they act it out.

See W. Clemen, *English Tragedy Before Shakespeare* (1961); Farleigh Dickinson, *Shakespeare and the History of Soliloquies* (2003).

DJP

Sonnet   Technically the sonnet is easy to identify: fourteen lines divided (usually) by rhyme and argument into units of eight lines (octave) and six (sestet). The metre is normally the prevalent metre of the language – in English the iambic pentameter, in French the alexandrine and in Italian (the original language of the *sonetto*, 'little song') the hendecasyllable. Petrarch (1304–74) was the first major sonneteer: his *Rime* to 'Laura' established the essential form and matter – a record of the intense and hazardous service of a lover, a service offering precarious local triumphs and the certainty of final defeat. Petrarch's rhyme-scheme (abba, abba, cde, cde, *or* cdc, dcd) was significantly different from Shakespeare's (abab, cdcd, efef, gg) which had more ironic possibilities. But the point of the proliferating formal rules which characterize the sonnet convention often gets lost in cataloguing variations: *every* sonnet is a 'variation' on the norm. What the convention means to the poet is a specialized 'vocabulary' of formal devices in addition to the normal rules of the language (cf. METRE), and the voluntary subjection to this discipline produces (hopefully) a high precision of utterance, a new and paradoxical freedom: 'rhyme is no impediment to his conceit, but rather gives him wings to mount and carries him, not out of his course, but as it were beyond his power to a far happier flight' (Samuel Daniel, *Defence of Rhyme*, 1603). The over-running of grammatical logic in the sonnet is analysed in Robert Graves and Laura Riding,

A Survey of Modernist Poetry (1928) and William Empson, *Seven Types of Ambiguity* (1930), ch. 2; the development of a sustained metaphoric argument, in Winifred Nowottny, *The Language Poets Use* (1962).

It is clear that sonnets are often technical 'exercises', but it by no means follows that they are therefore insincere. In exploring the medium, poets are exploring their own capacities to feel and think: Sidney's declaration *Astrophel* and *Stella*, *c.*1583), 'I am no pick-purse of another's wit' has an ironic edge, but is justified in the emotional thoroughness of his expropriations. Conventionality can be misunderstood and overstressed; it is perfectly possible to write insincere sonnets – to be facile, self-deceived, inexperienced or gross (Ben Jonson, 'An Elegie'):

Such songsters there are store of;
    witness he
That chanced the lace, laid on a
    smock, to see,
And straightway spent a sonnet

The fragile idealism of the convention invited parody and self-parody (as in Shakespeare's *Love's Labour's Lost*), but proved inseparable from its ability to endure through time and change. Donne's famous lines form 'The Canonisation' catch both the permanence and the fragility:

We'll build in sonnets pretty rooms;
As well a well wrought urn becomes
The greatest ashes, as half-acre tombs

In the sonnet the individual poet may find a fullness and spaciousness of meaning that could not be attained in isolation: 'The true father or shaping spirit of the poem is the form of the poem itself, and this form is a manifestation of the spirit of poetry, the "onlie begetter" of Shakespeare's sonnets who was not Shakespeare himself, much less that depressing ghost Mr W. H., but Shakespeare's subject, the master-mistress of his passion' (Northrop Frye, *Anatomy of criticism*, 1957). The uncompromising technical discipline of the sonnet combined with the logical and emotional intensity available has preserved its fascination for many poets right down to the present day.

See J. W. Lever, *The Elizabethan Love Sonnet* (1956); Hallett Smith, *Elizabethan Poetry* (1952); Antony Easthope, *Poetry as Discourse* (1983).

LS

Sound According to Mallarmé, versification (and therefore poetry) exists whenever a writer attempts STYLE, giving equal prominence to sonority and to clarity of linguistic performance: '*Toutes les fois qu'il y a effort au style il y a versification*'. But sound is a primary aspect of poetry rather than of prose, and Mallarmé's dictum that the aesthetic impulse, the '*effort au style*', renders prose and poetry indistinguishable visual vehicles of versification, fails to convince: prose is a most unsatisfactory medium for writers concerned with sound (and for some poets, poetic writing is little better). The writer of prose can only control sound and attempt to indicate subtleties of sound, by means of punctuation.

A reviewer of essays by Robert Creeley, a poet obsessed with sound, was moved to comment, 'One is puzzled by the exotic syntax'. The writer of poetry cannot only produce exotic syntax, but can also counterpoint punctuation spatially with line endings; the pause at the end of the line offers an additional means of scoring sound to the comma, the semicolon, etc. Spatial 'punctuation', and typographical variation – innovated by Mallarmé in his '*Un Coup de Des...*' (1897), and simplified yet more radically by Raoul Hausmann's *Optophonic Poems* of 1918 – increased the poet's grammatical/ spatial/typographical syntax, and partially solved the problems of scoring sound. Such problems are usually restricted to the work of poets for whom sound is of the same importance as meaning; work where variations of sound result from idiosyncrasies of the specific poet's voice and speech patterns, rather than being sonic variations within the confines of some pre-established communal verse structure, such as the sonnet or the haiku, or variants within some similarly pre-established line/rhyme convention.

Whilst such conventions appeal to the collective 'mind's ear', their very visual nature – the fact that such stereotyped symmetrical structures can be charted diagrammatically – suggests that the poetry of such conventions subordinates sound to visual semantics; the extreme product of this tendency being 'CONCRETE' POETRY, a purely visual poetry of silent, spatially punctuated semantics.

It is thus essential that the visual experience of reading poetry motivated by both sonic and semantic considerations be complemented by the audial experience of the poet's voice. Clearly it is impossible to totally appreciate unrecorded poetry of the past, though phonetic reconstructions of such works as *Beowulf*, and reconstructed 'period' readings, such as Basil Bunting's approximations of Wordsworth's accent, may offer valuable insights into the sonic values of past works. Whilst it is incontestable that poetry exists whenever there is effort towards sonic or semantic style, the ear should not be neglected, for poetry aurally experienced may well transcend prose, verse and book.

See Nicholas Zurbrugg (ed.), *Stereo Headphones*, 4 (1971), 'Futurism and after: Marinetti, Boccioni, and electroacoustic literature', *Comparative Criticism*, 4 (1982); Roland Barthes, 'The grain of the voice', in *Image-Music-Text* (trans. 1977); Richard Swigg, *Look with the Ears* (2002).

NCPZ

Speech   See DECONSTRUCTION.

Speech act   See AUTHOR, DISCOURSE.

Stasis   See LITERATURE.

Story   See MYTH, NARRATIVE, NARRATIVE STRUCTURE, PICARESQUE, PLOT.

Stream of consciousness   A technique which seeks to record the flow of impressions passing through a character's mind. The best-known English exponents are Dorothy Richardson, Virginia Woolf and James Joyce. Later novelists have often employed the technique, though rarely with such thoroughness as its early proponents. For them it was a fresh weapon in the struggle against intrusive narration. By recording the actual flow of thought with its paradoxes and irrelevancies they sought to avoid the over-insistent authorial rhetoric of Edwardian novels. They felt that the traditional techniques could not meet the social pressures of the new age; believing that, in Virginia Woolf's words, 'human nature had changed...in or about December 1910', they rejected the socio-descriptive novel in favour of a novel centring on 'the character itself'. Inner thoughts and feelings now occupied the foreground of attention.

Theoretically, the aim is inclusiveness: 'No perception comes amiss' (Woolf). But, in practice, each novelist developed selective principles and personal structural procedures. Joyce and Woolf use the technique in quite different ways. Woolf's style is leisurely and repetitive, returning constantly to dominant images (e.g. the chimes of Big Ben in *Mrs Dalloway*, 1925).

These images have no significance outside the novel: Woolf alone makes their meaning by the patterning she creates in the flow of recorded experience. Disconnected association is heightened and ordered by the passionate yet rational mind which conceives and controls it. Joyce's work, with its mastery of the abrupt shift from reflection to reflection, approaches the theory more nearly: 'Not there. In the trousers I left off. Must get it. Potato I have. Creaky wardrobe...'. But he, too, inevitably imposes structures on the random. In *Ulysses* (1922), the ultimate order and meaning of events is related to those primary images which span human culture; each event is continuous with all other such events in human history, refracted through language into its radical meaning: Bloom/Stephen are Ulysses/Telemachus, as they are the eternal type of Father/Son.

Each writer seeks a different way of organizing, and so communicating, the arbitrary, and each finally gestures towards the inability of any single device to render fully the processes of thought.

See Leon Edel, *The Modern Psychological Novel* (rev. edn, 1964); Melvin J. Friedman, *Stream of Consciousness: A Study of Literary Method* (1955); Robert Humphrey, *Stream of Consciousness in the Modern Novel* (1954); Dorrit Cohn, *Transparent Minds: Narrative Modes for Presenting Consciousness in Fiction* (1978); David Dowling, *'Mrs Dalloway': Mapping Streams of Consciousness* (1991).

GG

Stress   See METRE.

Structuralism   To be understood at two levels of generality: first, as a broad intellectual movement, one of the most significant ways of theorizing in the human sciences in the twentieth century; second, as a particular set of approaches to literature (and other arts and aspects of culture) flourishing especially in France in the 1960s but with older roots and continuing repercussions.

The basic premiss of structuralism is that human activity and its products, even perception and thought itself, are *constructed* and not *natural*. Structure is the principle of construction and the object of analysis, to be understood by its intimate reference to the concepts of *system* and *value* as defined in SEMIOTICS. A structure – for example, the conventional sequencing of episodes in fairy stories, the geometry of perspective in post-medieval art or something as apparently mundane as our arrangements for what, when and how we eat – is not merely an insignificantly mechanical ordering. Each element in the structure, whether 'unit' or 'transformation' or whatever, has meaning in the Saussurean sense of 'value' because it has been selected from a system of options and is therefore defined against the background of other possibilities. This is a radical view of meaning in its proposal that meanings do not come from nature or God, but are arbitrary, manmade. Clearly these assumptions encourage ANALYSIS and CRITIQUE and therefore disturb the complacency of traditional human inquiries.

Structuralist students of literature linked semiotic assumptions with ideas from other sources, principally Russian FORMALISM; Prague School structuralism (cf. FOREGROUNDING); the narrative analysis of Vladimir Propp; structuralist anthropology as blended from linguistics and Propp in the cooking-pot of Claude Lévi-Strauss; the new generative linguistics of Chomsky. Their activities and publications were too vast and diverse to summarize here, but I can mention the three most important, paradigmatic, models of analysis.

First, is the theory of literature and the attempt to formulate general rules to distinguish literary from non-literary discourse: see POETICS. 'Poetics' is the theory of 'literariness' rather than the description of individual literary works. The late Roman Jakobson was the key figure in this ambitious enterprise: his seminal paper 'Linguistics and poetics' (1960) proposed what would in Chomskyan terms constitute a set of 'substantive universals' to characterize the essence of literature, based on processes of repetition, parallelism and equivalence. Another version of poetic theory follows the lead of Chomsky and relocates literariness: it is said to be not an objective property of texts but a faculty of (some) readers who are said to possess a 'literary competence' in addition to and analogous to the universal 'linguistic competence' postulated by Chomsky. See J. Culler, *Structuralist Poetics* (1975). Neither of these proposals seems very plausible; for a critique, see Fowler, 'Linguistics and, and versus, Poetics', reprinted in *Literature as Social Discourse* (1981). However, if the writing of generative rules for all and only those texts constituting Literature seems an impossible project, the more modest programme of generative grammars for specific *genres* has seemed a feasible enterprise, and this has been attempted by Tzvetan Todorov in a number of studies: see his *Grammaire du Décaméron* (1969) and *The Fantastic* (1973).

Second, is the analysis of verse where the reference-text here is the analysis by Jakobson and Lévi-Strauss of Baudelaire's 'Les chats' (translated in the DeGeorge and Lane anthologies). The analysts sift the poem for all kinds of linguistic symmetries, from rhyme to syntactic minutiae,

such as tense and number, and thus rework it into an intensely patterned formal object, static and impersonal and remote from the communicative and interpersonal practices which language ordinarily serves. This analysis has been taken as an example of the application of linguistics to literary analysis, fabricating 'poetic' structures which the reader does not perceive: see M. Riffaterre, 'Describing poetic structures' (1966), reprinted in Ehrmann; Fowler, 'Language and the reader' in *Style and Structure in Literature* (1975). Aspects of Jakobson's theory provided illumination in verse analysis, as Riffaterre's own later work demonstrates: see his *Semiotics of Poetry* (1978).

Third, has been the more successful *analysis of narrative structure*. The inspiration came from Vladimir Propp's *Morphology of the Folk-Tale* (1928), which appeared in French translation in 1957 and in English in 1958. Propp noted that, though the individual characters in Russian tales were very diverse, their *functions* (villain, helper, etc.) could be described in a limited number of terms (he suggested thirty-one, falling into seven superordinate categories). By reference to these elements, the narrative ordering of any tale could be analysed as a sequence of 'functions of the *dramatis personae*' and associated actions. This is in fact a generative grammar of narrative: a finite system (paradigm) of abstract units generates an infinite set of narrative sequences (syntagms). The linguistic analogy was seized on by Lévi-Strauss and made explicit by A. J. Greimas (*Sémantique Structurale*, 1966), who provided a sophisticated reinterpretation of Propp's analysis in semantic terms. It became a standard assumption in narratology that the structure of a story was homologous with the structure of a sentence; this assumption allowed the apparatus of sentence-linguistics to be applied to the development of a metalanguage for describing narrative structure. The work of Roland Barthes, Tzvetan Todorov and Gerard Genette are particularly important in this development. See *Communications* 8 (1966): the contribution of Barthes is translated as 'Introduction to the structural analysis of narratives' in his *Image–Music–Text* (1977); this model was applied to a story from Joyce's *Dubliners* by Seymour Chatman in 'New ways of analyzing narrative structure', *Language and Style*, 2 (1969). Chatman's *Story and Discourse* (1978) applies many ideas from the French structural analysis of narrative in an English context. See also Fowler, *Linguistics and the Novel* (2nd edn, 1983). An informative general account of French structural narratology is Shlomith Rimmon-Kenan, *Narrative Fiction: Contemporary Poetics* (1983).

Anglo-Saxon reaction to structuralism was in many ways hostile, deploring its mechanistic and reductive style. Fortunately, the response in France was more subtle and more positively critical, confronting problems of what is neglected in the structuralist approach: reader, author, discourse as communicative practice and as ideology. See AUTHOR, DECONSTRUCTION, DISCOURSE, POST-STRUCTURALISM, PSYCHOLOGY AND PSYCHOANALYSIS, READER, SEMIOTICS.

For an account of structuralism in the broader sense see Jean Piaget, *Structuralism* (1971). David Robey's *Structuralism: An Introduction* (1973) reprints a series of accessible lectures on structuralism in a variety of disciplines. Structuralism in literary studies is the subject of Jonathan Culler, *Structuralist Poetics* (1975); Terence Hawkes, *Structuralism and Semiotics* (1977); John Sturrock, *Structuralism* (2002); Ann Jefferson, 'Structuralism and post-structuralism' in Jefferson and Robey (eds), *Modern Literary Theory* (1982). Anthologies of structuralist writings include R. T. and M. DeGeorge, *The Structuralists. From Marx to Lévi-Strauss* (1972); R. Macksey and E. Donato (eds), *The Structuralist Controversy* (1972); J. Ehrmann (ed.), *Structuralism* (1970); M. Lane (ed.), *Structuralism, A Reader* (1970).

RGF

Structure All critical theories have some notion of structure but the terms in which organization is discussed will vary: pattern, plot, story, form, argument, language, rhetoric, paradox, metaphor, myth. Starting from these dispositions, the term 'structure' then becomes an enabling reference; the reader is advised to consult potentially parallel entries (e.g. FORM, where structure is distinguished from texture, both being aspects of form) to see how this can be. The proposition is reversed here: such features are typologies of structure, organizational means for arriving at hypotheses about the principles of coherence in a given work. There are many such means, but they fall into two main categories: those derived from internal means and emphasizing features likely to be found especially in literature, and those derived from applying general principles of structure found in language, or the psychology of individuals or communities, or in social structure, to works of literature for typological purposes.

Criticism can generalize features like genre, rhetoric, motif and language into recurrent types in order to come to perceptions about what is distinctively literary. But developing order in fictions has analogues, deliberate or attributable, in order outside fiction. Thus, while many typologies of order will concern what is distinctive about literary presentation, they are also likely to extend to structures in writings not fictional: to those in language in general; then to those in forms of expression or consciousness; and then in a society at large. These things open literature to analogical explanation and to linguistic, psychological, sociological and ideological study; and they may creatively suggest the recurrence of structure analogously through all culture (cf. STRUCTRUALISM). The main danger here is that of applying methods of structural analysis assumed to be 'objective' because scientific, and derived in the first instance for other purposes, to literary works: an interesting case of the application of structural fictions to structural fictions.

See Kenneth Burke, *The Philosophy of Literary Form* (1957); R. S. Crane, *The Languages of Criticism and the Structure of Poetry* (1953); Northrop Frye, *Anatomy of Criticism* (1957); Frank Kermode, *The Sense of an Ending* (1967).

MSB

Style   One of the oldest and most tormented terms in literary criticism; its meaning is controversial, its relevance disputed. One usage can be discarded at once: criticism is not concerned with the belief that some authors or books have style (are 'stylish') whereas others do not. We must assume that all texts manifest style, for style is a standard feature of all language, not something peculiar to literature or just to some literature.

A style is a manner of expression, describable in linguistic terms, justifiable and valuable in respect of non-linguistic factors. The concept 'manner of expression' is controversial (see below), but the other two parts of the definition seem not to be: that it is a facet of language; and that it is given significance by personal or cultural, rather than verbal, qualities.

From 'style', 'stylistics' is derived as a branch of literary study. Some historians of criticism have called any approach to literature which pays close attention to aspects of language (imagery, sound-structure, syntax, etc.) 'stylistics'. This can be misleading, since stylistics is a historical division of criticism with its own principles and methods. Stylistics is less diffuse, more single-minded, more mechanical, than criticism in general. Similarly, the word 'style' itself has relatively technical connotations; those not involved in (strict) stylistics have tended to speak of 'tone' or, often, 'rhetoric'.

Linguistic form is not absolutely controlled by the concepts we want to express. There are alternative ways of putting messages into words, and the choice among alternatives is exercised along non-linguistic principles. Whether I say 'Shut the door!' or 'I wonder if you would mind closing the door, please?' is determined by a whole complex of personal, cultural and situational facts structuring the communicative event of which the sentence is a part. Stylistics posits that these extra-textual influences on the form of communication are organized systematically, and that the system brings about orderings of linguistic form which are themselves systematic and, more important, *characteristic*, that is, symptomatic of one particular set of extra-verbal factors. This determination of style by context works outside literature as well as within it (see D. Crystal and D. Davy, *Investigating English Style*, 1969). Thus styles may be seen as characteristic of an author, of a period, of a particular kind of persuasion (rhetoric), or a genre. Literary stylisticians have generally been concerned to test such hypotheses as these: authors' styles – 'linguistic fingerprints', allegedly – have been one focus; we also find such generalizations as 'Ciceronian',

'Senecan', 'Attic', 'baroque', 'mannered', 'grand', 'middle', 'low', 'terse', 'expansive', 'florid', 'periodic', etc. These labels indicate that stylistics is a *classificatory* mode of literary study, generating categories of text arrived at on the basis of many different kinds of taxonomic criteria, generally a mixture of linguistic/formal and extra-linguistic/situational.

Style depends on a FOREGROUNDING of some selected feature, or set of features, of linguistic surface structure. A particular diction may be prominent, or a persistent rhythm, or a certain reiterated syntactic organization. This density in one part of the language may not catch our conscious attention, but it causes a certain stylistic impression in us: we feel that the text belongs to a familiar authorial or cultural milieu. 'Density' suggests counting, and indeed stylistics (unlike linguistics) is implicitly quantitative, and is sometimes explicitly so. Extreme instances of quantitative stylistics would be G. U. Yule's statistical work on literary vocabulary, and the more recent computer-assisted studies in authorship-detection. Here counting is directed to discovery; usually we count to confirm hypotheses – that there *is* a syntactic or lexical tendency which explains our perception of a peculiar period-style, for instance.

The idea of style involves an idea of choice among equivalent ways of expressing the same thought. Such a proposal was anathema to the NEW CRITICS (cf. PARAPHRASE), for whom a change in wording was inevitably a change in meaning. The New Critical attitude relied on a false use of 'meaning'. Sentences may have the same propositional content (be synonymous) but express it in different ways so that the reader's *mode of apprehending* meaning is distinctively determined. Richard Ohmann has suggested that this distinction – between

semantic *content* and stylistic or rhetorical *form* – is explained by the division between deep and surface structure found in generative linguistics. See Ohmann's 'Generative grammars and the concept of literary style' in D. C. Freeman (ed.), *Linguistics and Literary Style* (1970). Stylistics as an academic subject was born at the time of the birth of modern linguistics, and has continued to use some of the techniques of linguistics. Charles B. ally, an eminent French stylistician, was a student of Saussure's; Leo Spitzer developed his methods in an attempt to bridge a gap between linguistics and literary history; and Stephen Ullmann, besides being an influential stylistician of French fiction, was also an expert on semantics.

The term 'stylistics' or 'linguistic stylistics' has come to designate any analytic study of literature which uses the concepts and techniques of modern linguistics, for example, in the title of Anne Cluysenaar's excellent book *Introduction to Literary Stylistics* (1976) which is not a study of style as such but an introduction to practical textual criticism refined by linguistic ideas. It is preferable to restrict the term to the linguistic study of style in the sense indicated above, devising appropriate terms for other literary applications of linguistics. See LANGUAGE for discussion and references. Cf. POST-STRUCTURALISM.

See R. W. Bailey and D. M. Burton, *English Stylistics: A Bibliography* (1968); M. W. Croll and J. Max Patrick (eds), *Style, Rhetoric and Rhythm* (1966); H. Hatzfeld, *A Critical Bibliography of the New Stylistics, Applied to the Romance Languages, 1900–1952* (1953); Graham Hough, *Style and Stylistics* (1969); Josephine Miles, *Style and Proportion: The Language of Prose and Poetry* (1967); *Lance St John Butler, Registering the*

Difference (1999). Relevant journals include *Style* and *Language and Style*.

RGF

Subaltern Was first deployed as a critical term by the Italian communist thinker Antonio Gramsci. As he uses it, the term refers to the non-elite classes, including but not restricted to the proletariat. In this, he departs from the economic determinism and historical teleology of orthodox Marxism by considering the 'politics of the people' as consisting of more than just a revolutionary, or potentially revolutionary, industrialized working class. Himself a native of the Italian south, where capitalization of the rural economy had barely taken root, he understood that the rigid frameworks of orthodox Marxism limited any full analysis of class society. Taken together with his more fluid conceptualization of class–state relations, his development of a methodological programme for studying the history of the subaltern placed greater emphasis on the cultural and ideological dimensions of hegemony and subordination.

Gramsci's work in general has had a profound influence on leftist thinking in the twentieth century both in Europe and the global South, but the trajectory of the term 'subaltern' was decisively shaped by its encounter with a group of Marxist historians in India in the late 1970s and early 1980s, who later became known as the Subaltern Studies collective. Recognizing the importance of Gramsci's thinking for analysis of partially capitalized societies in which the peasantry remains the largest non-elite sector, these historians adapted Gramscian ideas about hegemony, subordination and subalternity within a methodological programme designed to contest the dominance of elitist historiographies of colonial India. The politics of the 'people' – those who remained outside the mechanisms that produced colonial 'subjects' – was invisible in traditional colonial historiography; the agency of the subaltern was ignored and excised.

In his 'Preface' to the first volume of *Subaltern Studies*, Ranajit Guha, who was the founding spirit and editor of the first six volumes of the series, suggested that there were two political domains: that of the elite and that of 'the people', the subaltern domain. This latter domain was autonomous insofar as 'it neither originated from elite politics nor did its existence depend upon the latter' (Guha). It had its own modes of operation, which were themselves a result of the subaltern groups having their own consciousness and forms of behaviour. In order to recover the agency of subaltern groups and their contribution to the politics of colonial India, and their role in its decolonization, the task for the historian was to identify moments when the subaltern consciousness could be witnessed in action and, through a 'thick description' of such events, inscribe the subaltern as a political actor within a narrative that was not necessarily commensurable with elite narratives of colonialism and nationalism. Subaltern Studies was, therefore, an attempt to write history from below.

This attempt to recover the silenced agency of the subaltern groups attracted attention from the growing scholarship on colonialism and postcolonialism that was emerging in the Anglo-US academy in the 1980s. The term 'subaltern' has thus since passed into the lexicon of post-colonial studies. It is often used here with less theoretical precision than by the Subaltern Studies historians, referring in general to dominated or subordinate groups within colonial power relations and is sometimes applied to the colonized elite as well as non-elite sectors of colonial societies.

Ironically, this may be closer to Gramsci's own usage insofar as he used *subalterno* to refer to dependency, because he thought only the hegemonic groups had autonomy.

The Subalternist conceptualization of subaltern autonomy is a theoretical innovation that had led to much debate and, in time, a reorientation of the project itself. In particular, it raised the question of representation. If part of the reason that the subaltern consciousness is autonomous is because it exists beyond the reach of the discursive regimes that produced colonial 'subjects', that is, because it existed outside colonial representation, then how can one recover this consciousness when the only access to the past is through those very discursive frames? Gayatri Chakravorty Spivak, in her well-known essay 'Can the subaltern speak?' observed that one cannot do so; the subaltern consciousness eludes representation and exists only as an effect within elite discourses (Spivak).

This has led many in the Subaltern collective to engage more thoroughly with post-colonial theory and to contest Eurocentric systems of knowledge, of which historiography is itself a part. The encounter with post-colonialism by younger members of the collective who are primarily based in the US, where Subaltern Studies was received warmly as a major contribution to post-colonial studies, has gradually led to a 'post-structuralist' turn in which the major influences are Foucault and Derrida rather than Gramsci. Thus, just as post-colonialism has been profoundly altered by its encounter with Subaltern Studies, so too has the latter been transformed by the former. See also POSTCOLONIALISM.

See Ranajit Guha (ed.), *Subaltern Studies 1* (1982); Ranajit Guha and Gayatri Chakravorty Spivak (eds), *Selected Subaltern Studies* (1988); Vinayak Chaturvedi (ed.), *Mapping Subaltern Studies and the Postcolonial* (2000); David Ludden (ed.), *Reading Subaltern Studies* (2002); Gayatri Chakravorty Spivak, *The Spivak Reader* (1996).

AM

Subject See DISCOURSE.

Surfiction See FICTION.

Surrealism Grew directly out of DADA, its founder and chief spokesman, André Breton, having played an important role in Dada experiments. Yet, where Dada reflected a sense of dissolution, providing public displays of artistic anarchy and images commensurate with the absurdity and uncertainty of the age, Surrealism propounded its own coherent antidote to both nihilism and optimism. It did so with an evangelical enthusiasm which should have forewarned of its subsequent commitment to radical politics. Where the Dadaists had seen meaningless disorder, the Surrealists saw a synthesis which owed something to Hegel, the Romantics, the Symbolists. Breton was prepared to acknowledge that Surrealism could be seen as the 'prehensile tail' of Romanticism. Certainly it borrowed some of its methods – a concern with dreams, madness, hypnosis and hallucination, deriving in part from Novalis, Coleridge, Nerval and Baudelaire. But the Surrealists were less dedicated to seeking visible evidence of a spiritual world than to creating the marvellous. Their aim was to change the world, partly through social revolution but more centrally through a revolution in consciousness. The techniques devised or borrowed – automatic texts and paintings (created in an attempt to evade conscious control and tap the intuitive, alogical, power of the subconscious), works inspired and shaped by chance, written accounts of dreams and paintings providing images of dream visions – were all designed to subvert aestheticism and precipitate a fundamental alteration in our understanding of 'reality'. To this end the Surrealists delighted in paradoxical images which mocked the process of rational thought and perception. They juxtaposed unrelated words and objects, thereby creating tantalizing images and iridescent verbal effects. Surrealism is concerned with reinvigorating language, expanding our definition and perception of reality to incorporate the insights of the subconscious, and extending our appreciation of the central and liberating role of chance, automatism and eroticism. It proposed the release of the imagination and stood as an implicit criticism of a restrictive rationalism in society and realism in literature. Though international in scope and influence, Surrealism is more firmly rooted in France than Dada had been. Its major writers and artists tend to be French (Breton, Soupault, Eluard, Aragon, Masson, Tanguy, Delvaux). Its impact in England came late (1936) and was largely ineffectual. But the United States benefited from the wartime presence of some of the leading European Surrealists, and its literature and art bore the marks of this cultural transfusion.

The standard history of Surrealism is Maurice Nadeau, trans. R. Howard, *The History of Surrealism* (1968). For a book which counterbalances his tendency to see Surrealism as a movement contained within the years 1922–39, see Roger Cardinal and Robert Short, *Surrealism: Permanent Revelation* (1970). See also Savone Alexandrian, *Surrealist Art* (1970); Ferdinand Alguié, *The Philosophy of Surrealism* (1969); C. W. E. Bigsby, *Dada and Surrealism* (1972); Raymond Spiteri and David LaCross (eds),

Surrealism, Politics and Culture (2003); David Gascoyne, Michel Remy (Introduction), Dawn Ades (Preface), *A Short Survey of Surrealism* (2000).

CWEB

Suspension of disbelief   See BELIEF.

Symbol   The literary symbol, defined straightforwardly by Kant (who, in his *Critique of Judgement*, 1790, calls it an 'aesthetic idea') in terms of the 'attributes' of an object 'which serve the rational idea as a substitute for logical presentation, but with the proper function of animating the mind by opening out for it a prospect into a field of kindred representations stretching beyond its ken' (his examples are the eagle that stands for Jove, and the peacock that represents Juno) takes on a special significance for Romantics, early (Coleridge) and late (Yeats). Yeats indeed goes so far as to maintain that a 'continuous indefinable symbolism' is 'the substance of all style' (*The Symbolism of Poetry*, 1900), and for him the excellence of a symbol consists in the suggestiveness that derives from the suppression of a metaphor's directly apprehensible terms of reference: 'as a sword-blade may flicker with the light of burning towers', so the symbol evokes unseen worlds.

Between Jove's symbolic eagle (and the symbolism of medieval literature, not always distinguishable from allegory), and Yeats's mysticism, lies Blake's idiosyncratic appropriation of the symbolic language of the Bible ('Bring me my bow of burning gold/Bring me my arrows of desire') and the major literary movement known as *Symbolism*, where the almost autonomous symbol reveals the hidden order that lies behind deceptive everyday reality.

The elaboration of a language of signs into what Arthur Symons (*The Symbolist Movement in Literature*, 1899) calls 'a form of expression... for an unseen reality apprehended by the consciousness', a quasi-occult mode of knowledge deliberately opposed to the positivism of the age, stems from the work of Baudelaire (his Swedenborgian poem '*Correspondances*', for instance) and from Gerard de Nerval's visions of a sentimental world lurking beneath natural forms, where ('*Vers Dorés*'):

> *comme un œil naissant couvert par ses paupières,*
> *Un pur esprit s'accroît sous l'écorce des pierres!*

De Nerval's active world of occult correspondences mocks the freethinking individual's inability to penetrate reality; Baudelaire's poem is devoted to the proposition that nature is a temple wherein the individual hears '*de confuses paroles*' offering an imitation of an order we are not equipped to confront face to face. For later Symbolist writers, the artist becomes a high priest of this temple, communing with, and communicating (to the extent that the profane multitude can comprehend) the occult truths hidden by the veil called reality. Baudelaire's highly sensuous '*Correspondances*', which draws attention to the elaborate pattern of synaesthesia by which it isolates itself from linear discourse, foreshadows an autonomous art which, in the work of Mallarmé, extends the ritualistic concern with the sacrosanct exactness of the incantation in the direction of an extreme preoccupation with technique: the connotative and associative functions of literary language and the evocative effects manipulated by the writer in the creation of a fictional world distinct from (often superior to) the world of everyday reality. The Art for art's sake of Gautier's *Émaux et Camées* (1858) had turned upon analogies between literature and the fine arts; the

new AESTHETICISM endorsed Pater's belief that 'all art aspires to the condition of music', praising Wagner's attempt to express the unconscious of his race in intricate structures of myth and symbol. The dedication of the Symbolists to the techniques of art, which, in Mallarmé's words, 'purify the language of the tribe', influenced many modern writers, including Eliot, Joyce, Valéry and Rilke, and engendered a literary criticism (that of the Russian Formalists and the English and American New Critics) which, stripping the Symbolist aesthetic of its late Romantic elements, evolved critical procedures delicate enough to describe the complex inner workings of modernist literature at the same time as it brought an unprecedented attention to bear on the linguistic devices of earlier writing. See also ALLEGORY.

See Maurice Bowra, *The Heritage of Symbolism* (1943); Guy Michaud (ed.), *La Doctrine Symboliste* (1947); Guy Michaud, *Message Poétique du Symbolisme* (1961); Arthur Symons, *The Symbolist Movement in Literature* (1899, reprinted 1958); Edmund Wilson, *Axel's Castle* (1935, reprinted 1961); Richard Candida Smith, *Mallarmé's Children: Symbolism and the Renewal of Experience* (2000).

GMH

Synonym See PARAPHRASE.

Syntax The ordering of words, phrases and clauses in the structure of sentences: the 'left-to-right' principle of linguistic structure. Meaning is abstract; it is therefore not transferable from person to person directly: the mediation of a physical channel is needed. Meaning has to be made concrete, spread out in time and space ('left-to-right') for speaker, hearer, writer, reader. It is the arrangements of syntax which are responsible for this space-time ordering of abstract elements of meaning. And syntax is a major influence on STYLE: the way meanings are concretized, through syntax, affects the way an audience responds to those meanings.

One property of syntax is its capacity to provide different word-orders for the same meaning. Even though word-order is not strictly 'significant', it is nevertheless valuable and potent because it can determine the sequence in which a reader apprehends the elements of the complex structure of meanings embodied in a sentence. For example, the second and fifth words of the sentence *She put the book down* form one single meaning (cf. *deposit*) but are, because of the word-order, experienced discontinuously. The meaning of put must be incomplete, provisional, until the sentence is completed by *down*. This interrupted or delayed perception of meaning does not occur when we listen to the synonymous sentence *She put down the book*. Meaning is the same, but the mode of experiencing meaning is importantly different, because of the difference in syntax. Here, the meaning of *put* is immediately completed by *down*, there is no suspense, and no subsequent part of the sentence disturbs the firmly apprehended meaning' ('deposit'). A different kind of syntactic influence on the reader's reception of meaning is illustrated by the sentence *She put down the rebellion*. It is obvious, once one has read the whole sentence, that *put down* does not mean 'deposit' but 'subdue'. But this fact is obvious *only* after one has taken in the whole of the sentence (unless one guesses from context). In the temporal experience of reading, or listening, this figurative meaning for *put down* is supplied retrospectively, the basic, physical meaning being assumed first. Here the temporal sequence of mental operations demanded by the syntactic order is the reverse of that required for the processing of meaning. The ways in which syntax determines, assists or even impedes the reader's apprehension of meaning are manifold.

To proceed to a literary example, the indirect and interrupted first sentence of Henry James's novel *The Ambassadors* – 'Strether's first question, when he reached the hotel, was about his friend' – appropriately gives one time to wonder what this question is to be, sets up the tone of tentative enquiry which characterizes the whole narrative. (See Ian Watt's important paper in *Essays in Criticism*, vol. 10, 1960.) Syntax can be mimetic; as the following lines from *Paradise Lost* demonstrate, the contrast between action and guile is imitated in first direct, then contorted, syntax:

> My sentence is for open war. Of wiles,
> More unexpert, I boast not: them
>   let those
> Contrive who need, or when they
>   need; not now.

Because syntax is inevitable and, in a sense, imperceptible, critics may fail to attend to its power. But as Winifred Nowottny observes, we should not regard syntax as merely ' "a harmless, necessary drudge" holding open the door while the pageantry of words sweeps through' (*The Language Poets Use*, vol. 10, 1962). We must recognize that syntax exercises a continuous and inexorable control over our apprehension of literary meaning and structure – and that its influence is not limited to the spectacular grammatical games of Pope or Browning or Cummings.

The importance of syntax is acknowledged by the French pedagogic tradition of *explication de texte*. In Anglo-American criticism. Donald Davie's *Articulate Energy* (1955) is a brilliant exposition of different kinds of poetic syntax. Syntax has been more extensively and technically analysed in linguistic stylistics, using techniques drawn from transformational-generative grammar. See, for example, S. Chatman, *The Later Style of Henry James* (1972), and many of the papers in D. C. Freeman (ed.), *Essays in Modern Stylistics* (1981), in which it is often claimed or implied that artistic design is embodied in FOREGROUNDED syntactic patterns. Advocates of functional linguistics have made another bold claim that syntactic patterns encode a 'vision of things' (Halliday) or 'mind-style' (Fowler). See M. A. K. Halliday, 'Linguistic function and literary style: an inquiry into the language of William Golding's *The Inheritors*' in S. Chatman (ed.), *Literary Style: A Symposium* (1971); R. Fowler, *Linguistics and the Novel* (2nd edn, 1983), *Linguistic Criticism* (1986). There has also begun some interesting work on psycholinguistic implications of syntax for readers: for example, G. L. Dillon, *Language Processing and the Reading of Literature* (1978). See also LANGUAGE, STYLE.

RGF

Syuzhet   See FORMALISM, NARRATIVE STRUCTURE.

T

Taste See CLASSIC, CULTURE, EVALUATION.

Technique STYLE as a deliberate procedure; literary and artistic craft, connoting formal rather than affective or expressive values. Every writer has employed a (more or *less* conventional) technique, but the insistence on technique rather than on inspiration, or the reverse, has been related to changing modes of sensibility. Thus, René Wellek follows other critics in maintaining that the distrust of inspiration and an accompanying faith in technique are the major points which set off Symbolism from Romanticism. In this, there exists an unbroken continuity from Poe, Baudelaire and Flaubert to Pound, Eliot and Valery. Pound has declared that he believes in technique 'as the test of a man's sincerity' and Eliot has praised Valéry's *On Literary Technique* for projecting the image of the poet as a 'cool scientist' rather than as a 'dishevelled madman'.

NZ

Tenor See METAPHOR.

Tension Conflict or friction between complementaries, converses, opposites. In literary criticism, a much-used term relying on its context for whatever particular meaning it may have. Endemic in dialectic thought, it has been variously employed in the analysis of the Romantic sensibility, and in criticism involving such polarizing conceptions as the Classicism–Romanticism antithesis, the Freudian opposites or Lévi-Strauss's dynamic dualisms. It is particularly common in discussions of twentieth-century poetics, reflecting the contemporary writer's increased awareness of tension, whether psychological, social or that within the frame of the linguistic medium. Thus, Gottfried Benn describes the Expressionist's medium as that of 'tension-laden words'. Generally, tension has been located wherever opposing forces, impulses or meanings could be distinguished and related to one another.

The Russian Formalists and their followers described verse rhythm in terms of the tension between the force of the rhythmical impulse and that of the syntactical pattern (cf. METRE). Other critics have pointed to the tensions inherent in metaphor. Empson's types of ambiguity were studies in different manifestations of tension between simultaneous meanings, while Cleanth Brooks's theory of paradox posited the power of the tensions involved in poetry as an evaluative criterion, in accord with the notion of a poem as drama. John Crowe Ransom defined a tension between the logical argument of a poem and its local texture, W. K. Wimsatt implied a tension between the concrete and the universal or the particular and the general, and Allen Tate attempted a theory in which tension means the simultaneity of literal and metaphoric or figurative meaning (*ex*Tension and *in*Tension). Such preoccupations with tension were responsible for the critical bias in favour of such lyrical or dramatic poetry in which it prevails as against poetry of tensionless sentiment or narrative and descriptive poetry.

See Brian Lee, 'The New Criticism and the language of poetry' in Roger Fowler (ed.), *Essays on Style and*

Language (1966), pp. 29–52, and references.

NZ

Text We should beware of regarding the printed text of a literary work as 'the work itself'. Many interesting questions arise when we consider the process of recovering 'the work' from 'the text'. In *Principles of Literary Criticism* (1924) I. A. Richards attempted to describe the process of reading and reacting to a text, and his analysis is suggestive.

Descriptive linguistics has clarified certain aspects of the decoding process, as applied to written or spoken 'text'. Two important points arise for literary criticism. First, an adequate understanding of the language-system involves a recognition of the important role played by stress, speed, loudness, pitch and voice-quality in meaning. All these features are more or less effaced by transposition into the written code, and much of the writer's work is to find means of replacing or reorganizing them. Gerard Manley Hopkins resorted to modifications of the written system which are far from precious or irrelevant. Second, knowledge of how the members of a community learn the meanings of words (through their use in contexts of language and situation) leads to a distinction between subjective and intersubjective responses to the text. Subjective responses rely on meanings derived from the use of a word in special circumstances unique to the individual, while intersubjective responses rely on uses which are widespread throughout the community. Clearly there is nothing so simple as a dichotomy: some contexts are peculiar to a section of a community or to a family. The possibility of communication, however, in the community at large depends on the widest type of intersubjective response. And literary criticism, if it is not to be local or (at worst) autobiographical, must appeal to that wider system of meanings. It must also be remembered that since the socio-linguistic background against which we decode a text constantly changes through time, marks on paper and recorded sound give only an illusion of total stability. But then, as Gombrich shows in *Art and Illusion* (1960), the same applies to the apparent permanence of stone and pigment. Attempts to restore the past can be partially successful only and cannot govern our overall response to the text.

In his influential essay 'From work to text', Roland Barthes put forward seven propositions to distinguish between traditional understanding of the literary work and a new emphasis on 'the text' which has since come to inform all recent discussion of the term: (1) 'the work is concrete, occupying a portion of book-space (in a library, for example); the Text, on the other hand, is a methodological field.... While the work is held in the hand, the text is held in language'. The first is displayed, the second demonstrated. 'A text can cut across a work, several works.' (2) 'The Text does not come to a stop with (good) literature; it cannot be apprehended as part of a hierarchy or even a simple division of genres. What constitutes the Text is, on the contrary (or precisely), its subversive force with regard to old classifications.... If the Text raises problems of classification, that is because it always implies an experience of limits... the Text is that which goes to the limit of the rules of enunciation.' (3) 'Whereas the Text is approached and experienced in relation to the sign, the work closes itself on a signified... [the Text's] field is that of the signifier' the work is moderately symbolic, but the text is radically symbolic. (4) 'The Text is plural.... The Text's plurality does not depend on the ambiguity of its contents, but rather on what could be called the *stereographic plurality* of the signifiers that weave it.' The Text is 'completely woven with quotations, references and echoes'. (5) 'The Text…is read without the father's signature.' The author can only come back to the text as 'a guest' so to speak. 'The Text can be read without its father's guarantee: the restitution of the intertext paradoxically abolishes the concept of filiation' (p. 78). So, a text read in the weave of texts no longer is anchored in the author. (6) The Text 'asks the reader for an active collaboration'. The reader thus should produce the Text. (7) 'The Text is linked to enjoyment.' In brief, Barthes sees the work as 'closed' and the text as 'open'. Many literary critics have subsequently been influenced by the work of Foucault and Derrida on the status and composition of both text and *the* text. See also TEXTURE.

See Edward Said, *The World, the Text and the Critic* (1991); Stanley Fish, *Is There a Text in This Class?* (1980); Roland Barthes, 'From work to text' in Josue V. Harari (ed.), *Textual Strategies* (1979); Geoffrey Hartman, S*aving the Text* (1983).

AAAC

Texture Strictly, the word *texture* when applied to language, describes the tactile images employed to represent various physical surfaces, but by extension has come to mean the representation in words of all physical phenomena. The widespread use of the term is based on the assumption that words have an expressive or simulative aspect which helps to illustrate their meanings more immediately. This belief in the onomatopoeic properties of language has not always gone unchallenged, but the existence of techniques for producing particular sensory effects in the reader is undisputed, and it

is thus possible to describe the texture of language in terms of either of the means used or the effects obtained. Assonance (identity of vowel sounds), consonance (identity of consonant sounds) and alliteration (repetition of initial consonants) may each be used to produce such effects as cacophony (a sense of strain in pronunciation) or euphony (a sense of ease in pronunciation). All are exemplified in Alexander Pope's famous exercise 'An Essay in Criticism':

> When Ajax strives some rock's vast weight to throw,
> The line too labours, and the words move slow;
> Not so when swift Camilla scours the plain,
> Flie o'er th'unbending corn, and skims along the main.

Samuel Johnson, however, attempting to prove that the mind governs the ear and not the reverse, quotes more lines with similar textural qualities and demonstrates quite convincingly that not even 'the greatest master of numbers can fix the principles of representative harmony' (*Life of Pope*, 1779).

Many other critical theorists from Aristotle to I. A. Richards have disputed the possibility of any natural connection between the sounds of any language, and the things signified. Richards in *The Philosophy of Rhetoric* (1936) asks:

> what resemblance or natural connection can there be between the semantic and phonetic elements in the morpheme? One is a sound the other a reference. Is (fl-) {in *flicker, flash, flare*} really like 'moving light' in any way in which (si-) or (gi-) is not? Is that not like asking whether the taste of turkey is like growing in some way that the taste of mint is not?

One need not go quite so far as this to agree with his conclusion that most expressive words get their feeling of peculiar aptness from other words sharing the morpheme and supporting them in the background of the reader's mind. The relation of texture to structure is dealt with more fully elsewhere (see FORM), but it should be noted here that of all those critics and theorists who have disagreed with Richards about the nature of poetic discourse the most influential is probably John Crowe Ransom, the founder and foremost theoretician of New Criticism. Believing that Richards's attempt to discriminate poetic discourse from prose by its ability to tease dormant affective states into unusual activity, relegates poetry to a disreputable status, Ransom looked for a more promising differentia in the kind of structure exemplified by a poem. In its simplest form that organization can be described as 'a loose logical structure with an irrelevant local texture'. He goes on to discuss the difficulties of composing poems on what he calls the 'two ground basis' of (1) an intended meaning and (2) an intended meter (texture), an operation in which the argument of the poem fights to displace the texture and the texture fights to displace the argument.

See John Crowe Ransom, *The New Criticism* (1941).

BCL

Theme   Traditionally means a recurrent element of subject matter, but the modern insistence on simultaneous reference to form and content emphasizes the formal dimension of the term. A theme is always a subject, but a subject is not always a theme: a theme is not usually thought of as the *occasion* of a work of art, but rather a branch of the subject which is indirectly expressed through the recurrence of certain events, images or symbols. We

apprehend the theme by inference – it is the rationale of the images and symbols, not their *quantity*. There is a case for restricting the loosely formal use of the term; if we use 'theme' to mean a certain quantity of features in a work (iterative imagery or stylistic mannerism), we are confusing a symptom with a cause. For example, if we talk about the 'theme of drowning' in Dickens's *Our Mutual Friend*, we are only saying that it is a novel in which people are repeatedly drowned or drowning is frequently mentioned, whereas the 'theme of Christian redemption' offers an explanation of the *significance* of drowning. Recurrent local features are better designated by the term *motif*.

The degree of abstraction of the term depends on the nature of the work under consideration. It makes more sense, for example, to talk of the 'theme of waiting' in Beckett's *Waiting for Godot* (1956) than the 'theme of drowning' in Dickens, because the play offers the action itself as an important part of its subject matter, not simply one kind of event which becomes 'thematic' by repetition. The epithet *thematic* should thus mean 'symptomatic of the presence of a theme' rather than merely 'iterative' or 'recurrent'.

However, the term is sensitive and useful precisely because it admits of degrees of abstract reference; it is neither possible nor desirable to restrict all quantitative usages, because theme implies the linearity or extension of a work in a way that other subject matter terms do not. Compared, for example, with *thesis*, a qualitative term meaning the core of argument or attitudes a work promotes or reveals, theme is a more concrete and formalistic term with structural implications. We think of a theme as a line or thread running through a work, linking features which are un- or otherwise related (cf. PLOT). The thesis of a work is paraphrasable, but a theme might not be so. Thesis is also an intentionalist term, whereas theme may or may not be. Proust's themes, for example, modelled on the analogy of music, are a conscious part of his creative method; but in other, less self-conscious cases, to use the term is to talk about structure, not intended content. Thus, critics may use 'theme' to refer to those repeated parts of a subject which control aspects of a work which they perceive as formal as well as conceptual.

'Theme' is also used to refer beyond the individual work. We speak of 'perennial themes', such as the theme of the Fall. Here, theme pre-exists the individual work and borders on *archetype* or even MYTH. On the other hand works of literature may express themes which condition other works (e.g. the *carpe diem* theme) in which case the term is starting to overlap with CONVENTION.

VS

Threnody   See ELEGY.

Topos   See COMPARATIVE LITERATURE.

Tradition   A historical scheme made up of formal, stylistic and ideological attributes common to large numbers of works over a long time. It generally implies a causal nexus linking individual works. Literary historians may use the idea of tradition either in a strictly historical way or as an aid to criticism. In the first case, they will use individual works to demonstate a process of literary change; in the second, the procedure will be reversed to illumine the individual work.

Tradition tends to be defined either in formal and stylistic terms, or in terms of ideas and attitudes: the 'oral tradition' and the 'radical tradition', for example. Placing a work raises many questions.

Can styles determine ways of thinking? In what lies the newness of a work? How does the individual work contribute to the evolution of the tradition? How far do social changes contribute to changing literary forms? Paradoxically, placing a work in an intellectual tradition may draw one's attention to specifically literary problems to explain why one work is more effective than another when both express similar ideas. And vice versa: the extra subtlety of thought of one work may become obvious through comparison with other works in the same convention. Most basic of all, an awareness of tradition may be indispensable when trying to establish the original meaning of a text, especially if works are closely linked by literary influence or imitation, as in (say) an oral tradition, or in the 'Classical tradition'.

Two methodological problems arise. We derive our definition of the tradition from individual works, but we decide which works are relevant according to our definition. The way out is the dialectical process of measuring the works against the tradition, modifying the tradition in the light of the works.

The second problem concerns how the tradition works (if it works at all). The causal link between works may be the influence of a common environment, including a common literary environment of aesthetic conventions and the language itself. It may be ideological or religious. It may be the direct link of literary borrowing. The attempt to determine the varying proportions of such influences by placing a work in a tradition can help immensely to reveal the structure of a literary work.

Traditional is sometimes opposed to *original* (see ORIGINALITY), with corresponding pejorative or laudatory undertones. Such oppositions rest on misconception and misapplication. Few works, if any, exist in such a vacuum that they cannot be related to any sort of tradition. And 'traditional' should not be equated with the negative sense of 'conservative': there are radical traditions. 'Traditional' is more properly a neutral descriptive term, with approving or disapproving undertones depending on one's attitude to the tradition in question. See also CONVENTION, CREATION, DISCOURSE.

See T. S. Eliot, 'Tradition and the individual talent' in *The Sacred Wood* (1920).

EJB

Tragedy As a species of drama tragedy can be defined only in the most general terms, such as Aristotle's 'the imitation of an action that is serious...with incidents arousing pity and fear'. His *Poetics* attempts a classification of the elements proper to tragedy but, despite his inductive methodology, few Greek tragedies conform to his model. However, his concept of *hamartia*, the act of the hero which initiates the fatal process, suggests a basis for a more developed theory of tragedy. This hamartia may be anything from a mistake over identity to deliberate crime or sin, but is always horrifyingly out of proportion to the consequences of pain and destruction. The act of the hero, an individual 'better than ourselves', opens a gap in the fragile fabric of morality and civilization through which the primeval forces of anarchy and destruction pour. Tragedy is a dramatization of an individual's sense of life and society as constantly under threat from the arbitrary chances of fate and humanity's own innate savagery. In tragedy's heroic phase (e.g. Sophocles's *Oedipus*) the individual accepts a measure of responsibility for the destructive action and asserts against it a quality of heroic suffering and knowledge. But in its ironic phase tragedy emphasizes the arbitrariness of evil, rather than simply its disproportion to

human action, and moves towards a kind of savage farce (e.g. Euripides's *Electra*) in which the heroic stance degenerates into futile posturing.

The tragic gap and the shift from the heroic to the ironic phase are evident in Elizabethan and Jacobean tragedy. The fates of Marlowe's Tamburlaine and Faustus are consequent on their hubristic error – denial of human mortality – but the tragic structure of these morality situations insists on the hostility, even the malevolence, of the 'gods' or 'God' that exact their rights. In Shakespeare's heroic tragedies – *Othello*, *Coriolanus*, *Antony and Cleopatra* – the heroes' psychologies are involved in a destruction that is limited in scope – domestic or political, not metaphysical – and the hero, in a final speech, asserts an enduring *virtu* against the facts of defeat and death. But the psychological factors – pride, lust, jealousy – are the *données* of the action, not its significant *causes*; they provide a context in which the forces of destruction can work. Similarly, the tragedies of Racine are not really explorations of the psychology of 'passion'; in their world a monstrous primeval power infiltrates the social and moral order through the intoxicating irrationality of sexual desire.

The gap between human and ultimate causes widens in Elizabethan developments of the Senecan tragedy of blood; in Kyd's *Spanish Tragedy* and Marston's *Antonio's Revenge* the revenge structure becomes a metaphor for an irruption of evil. Whatever the superficial moral realities of the situation, and the calls of the revenger on nature, honour and blood, the acting out of revenge is a descent into a chaos of horror and savagery urged on by a malignant and insatiable ghost. The revenger can only carry out a sense of 'duty' by stepping back from the reality of the act by elaborate mimes, masks and plays. It is the unbearable knowledge of the nature of revenge that makes Hamlet a prisoner in his own play. T. S. Eliot's complaint that Hamlet's emotion was 'in excess of the facts as they appear' is unwitting testimony to the gap between human motive and action and the pressure of evil behind them that defines the tragic experience. In *Macbeth*, a revenge structure in reverse, the commitment to crime is specific and deliberate, albeit fearful, but the tragedy again lies in the enormity and universality of the evil that enters through the gap in 'nature' that Macbeth has opened. The darkness and chaos of Scotland are not *caused* by the murder of Duncan; the forces that the weird sisters testify to are given licence by it. The symbolism of evil is not merely explanatory or emblematic; similarly, in *King Lear* the tempest is not a symbolic extension of Lear's disintegration so much as an expression of the primeval chaos that now engulfs him and his action. But at least in *Macbeth* the act and the consequence are still clearly related; in *Lear* the gap is appallingly wide. An act of senile folly precipitates the disintegration of human society – the basic ties of kinship fall apart to reveal a chaos where humanity 'must prey on itself like monsters of the deep'. The causal element, the hamartia, has become almost incidental; evil is immanent and overflows from the smallest breach. In this phase of tragedy the protagonist is forbidden even the luxury of stoicism; Lear's pathetic submission to fate is merely the prelude to the final cruelty. Beyond this there is only the surrealist horror of Webster: in *The White Devil* and *The Duchess of Malfi* tragedy is a horrible and inconsequential farce relieved only by magnificent rhetorical gestures; insanity, disease and corruption inform a world in which the individual is an arbitrary actor.

If tragedy has not been an available mode since the eighteenth century this may have to do with the growth of rationalism and the bourgeoisie. The tradition of REALISM in the new form of the NOVEL was antipathetic to the extraordinary or inexplicable; the canonical English novels in this tradition lack a metaphysical dimension, a sense of active evil pressing on the edges of civilization. Evil is redefined as moral or social *error* and the scrutiny of psychology and motive becomes the animating structural concern. The tragic gap closes and individuals are wholly responsible for the disorder they create. In this situation the drama of external evil finds expression only in the melodramatic modes of the GOTHIC fantasy and, later, the ghost story; in these the evil is external to 'normal' society, whereas in tragedy it is inherent. Some of the dramas of Ibsen attempt to express a sense of tragic destiny with insistent symbolism, but even at its most impressive and dramatic, as in *Ghosts*, the requirement of realism, of explicability, inhibits the symbolism of transcendence. Hereditary syphilis is undoubtedly horrific, but as a symbol of evil it lacks universality, it is too specifically a disease.

A different sense of tragic structure informs the symbolic fictions of Henry James and Conrad. A comparison of the similar moral situation in James's *Portrait of a Lady* and George Eliot's *Middlemarch* and *Daniel Deronda* shows James's symbolic rhetoric creating a sense of active, immanent, evil where Eliot was content with terms of moral responsibility and guilt. And Conrad's work is full of pressures from the heart of darkness. Tragedy is a possible form for these novelists because they collapse the realistic opposition of the 'real' and the 'poetic'; their symbolisms of evil are not illustrative or exemplary, but functions of their language. As Jorge Luis Borges said, 'Conrad and Henry James wrote novels of reality because they judged reality to be poetic'. See also CATHARSIS, DRAMA.

See A. C. Bradley, *Shakespearean Tragedy* (1904); J. Jones, *On Aristotle and Greek Tragedy* (1962); Dorothea Krook, *Elements of Tragedy* (1969); F. L. Lucas, *Tragedy: Serious Drama in Relation to Aristotle's Poetics* (1927, repr. 1961); F. W. Nietzsche, trans. W. Kaufmann, *The Birth of Tragedy* (1967); G. Steiner, *The Death of Tragedy* (1961); N. Frye, *Fools of Time* (1967); R. P. Draper (ed.), *Tragedy: Developments in Criticism* (1980); R. B. Sewall, *The Vision of Tragedy* (1980); John Drakakis and Naomi Conn Liebler (eds), *Tragedy* (1998).

PM

Translations   The literary translator has at all times been extremely influential, and the branch of literary criticism concerned with translation brings close analysis of language to bear on cross-cultural literary questions in a way central to COMPARATIVE LITERATURE, since a unique creative energy is generated where languages converge.

The NEW CRITICAL insistence on the inseparability of form and content questioned the possibility of translation: and one could cite a number of poets, from Shelley's likening of translation to subjecting a violet to chemical analysis to Robert Frost's working definition of poetry as 'what gets left out in translation' to demonstrate that writers have had grave doubts about it. Yet, Shelley (e.g.) was himself an admirable translator: and it seems that he was primarily stressing the impossibility of exact correspondence between source and target texts, rather than rejecting translation; he believed that 'the plant must spring again from the seed, or it will bear no flower'. Some

elements in the source text elude the net of the target language: others stretch it and call attention to the device by which they are admitted: the process is controlled by the translator, who must be a scrupulous critic and a creative writer to locate the 'seed' and make it grow.

Dryden, regrounding the classics in a contemporary idiom, was much concerned with translation. Unaware of modern conceptions of the relation between form and content, he could happily advocate reasonable freedom, demanding that the translator should first 'know what is peculiar to the author's style', and then

'tis time to look into ourselves, to conform our genius to his, to give his thoughts either the same turn, if our tongue will bear it, or, if not, to vary but the dress, not alter or destroy the substance.

This kind of translation, called by Dryden paraphrase, is, however, sharply distinguished from impermissibly free imitations. Modern translators, not sharing Dryden's conviction that human nature is everywhere the same, and concerned, like modern critics, with the phenomenology of a given work, have paid more attention to imitation as a mode of translating at least lyric poetry, and have often worked in the territory between two languages, rather than offering to reconstruct one on the foundations of another. Lowell's 'Imitations' are representative of, fifty years earlier, Pound's 'Homage to Sextus Propertius'. Louis Zukovsky's recent translations of Catullus have created an even more striking synthetic language that mimes or mouths the Latin of the original in a way that is deliberately indecent. See also PARAPHRASE. See W. Arrowsmith and R. Shattuck (eds), *The Craft and Context of Translation* (1961); W. Benjamin, 'The Task of the

Translator', in *Illuminations*; S. Bassnett, *Translation Studies* (1980); R. W. Brislin (ed.), *Translation: Approaches and Research* (1976); G. Toury, *In Search of a Theory of Translation* (1980); George Steiner, *After Babel* (1998).

GMH

Travesty See PARODY.

Typicality Although types and typologies have long been traditional ideas in literary criticism, MARXIST CRITICISM deployed this notion in new ways. The Hungarian Marxist critic Georg Lukács, heavily influenced by the aesthetics of the German philosopher Hegel, used the idea of 'typicality' to indicate the process whereby, in classical REALIST literature, events and individuals are at once uniquely particularized, and representative of broader, deeper trends in history itself. A George Eliot character, for example, is neither an isolated 'personality' nor a mere emblem of some underlying reality; the peculiar complexity of such a character lies in its dialectical unity of the individual and the representative. For Lukács, such a fusion avoids at once an 'alienated' presentation of character which divorces it from its social context, and a pure reduction of individuals or situations to abstract 'symptoms' of impersonal forces. Lukács finds MODERNIST literature characterized by both forms of representation, and

dogmatically regards them as absolute errors. Characters in such fictions are either damagingly 'privatized', reduced to mere abstract consciousness, or allegorically presented. But the latter defect is also, for Lukács, typical of the 'socialist realist' literature to which he was privately hostile: socialist realism in this sense perpetuates the weaknesses of 'naturalism', which represents a declension from the major realist tradition. Scott and Baizac, writing at a period when the bourgeoisie was still a progressive force, were able to create 'typical' events and characters, sensing the shaping forces of history within particular phenomena. By the time of Flaubert, Zola and Conrad, the bourgeoisie had endured a crisis of political confidence, could no longer make living connections between individuals and their world and found itself confronted by an opaque, impenetrable reality. It took refuge either in dispassionate description of this supposedly immutable society (Flaubert, NATURALISM), or in the private recesses of consciousness (SYMBOLISM). In the work of such exceptional writers as Thomas Mann, Lukács found the great tradition of typicality perpetuated into the twentieth century.

See J. Bernstein, *The Philosophy of the Novel* (1984); G. Lukács, *The Historical Novel* (1962), *Studies in European Realism* (1950); R. Williams, *Drama from Ibsen to Brecht* (1968).

TE

U

Uncanny, the From Freud's translation of the German term *das Unheimlich*, the uncanny designates both a concept and a feeling and is primarily associated with a profound sense of unease about both ourselves and the world we inhabit. Precariously located in the liminal space of the in-between, it calls into question established norms and boundaries, especially those between the familiar and unfamiliar, imagination and reality, inside and outside (psychical and material realms) and self and other. As have so many others who have written on the uncanny, we must turn to the realm of literature in order to illustrate the disorienting effects of such destabilization. In chapter 16 of Charlotte Brontë's *Villette* (1853), Lucy Snowe – having collapsed in the street – awakens in a house that is rendered strange precisely through its familiarity. Caught between the states of sleep and wakefulness, she surveys her surroundings and struggles to reconcile the presence of objects long familiar and intimately associated with her own childhood with the unfamiliar context of a strange house in a foreign country. Such objects appear as ghosts of a past life and a former self, effectively splitting her identity while blurring the boundary between the inner realm of her own psychical existence and the real world. What makes this episode specifically uncanny, as opposed to simply frightening, is, in part, related to its setting. Uncanny effects are most likely to be produced where they are least expected, within, for example, the confines of a comfortable home where one would normally expect to feel safe and secure. But, above all, the uncanny effect of Lucy's experience results from the conjoining of the familiar and the strange. To subtract either element would be to rob the scene of its uncanny quality. Moreover, as this example suggests, the uncanny is intimately bound up with the mode of representation. If the same events had occurred within a fairy tale or ghost story, the effect would not be uncanny. In order to be experienced as such, they must be situated within a narrative of ordinary material reality.

The notion of the uncanny has received the critical attention of a range of influential thinkers from Karl Marx to the German philosopher Martin Heidegger, and, more recently, the French post-structuralist, Jacques Derrida. It is, however, associated primarily with the founder of psychoanalysis, Sigmund Freud, and his 1919 essay 'The "Uncanny"' is still the key text for anyone interested in the subject. Purporting to be a scientific investigation, it has an undeniably literary quality due both to his concentration on E. T. A. Hoffmann's 1891 novella, 'The sandman', and Freud's own poetic style. The essay begins with an extended etymological discussion of *das Heimlich* (the canny) and *das Unheimlich* (the uncanny). As Freud demonstrates – in a manner entirely typical of later post-structuralists – the two terms begin as opposites but come to resemble each other more and more closely until they are indistinguishable. This collapse into UNDECIDABLITY is central to Freud's argument as it allows him to conclude that the uncanny is 'nothing new or alien, but something which is familiar and old-established in the mind and which has become alienated from it only through the process of repression'. In short, an uncanny effect is produced by the return of the repressed. He also, however, lists a number of more specific sources of the uncanny including: intellectual uncertainty, doubles, déjà vu, coincidences and repetition, omnipotence of thoughts (recalling our surmounted belief in the power of thoughts to affect the material world), the blurring of the boundary between imagination and reality, being buried alive, ghosts and death itself.

Taken as a psychoanalytic treatise, Freud's essay is limited by his determination to trace the uncanny back to infantile desires and fears, especially castration anxiety (where a young boy fears his father will castrate him as punishment for desiring the mother). Recent critics, including the French feminist Hélène Cixous, have argued that this emphasis is based on a misreading of Hoffmann's narrative, one that ignores key formal and thematic features and, as a result, actually reduces the uncanny element of the story. Moreover, Freud's essay has itself been revealed as a text haunted by its own gaps and omissions. It is now widely recognized that the lasting importance of this piece resides precisely in such uncanny qualities. The significance of the uncanny to literary studies is similarly assured. Western literature has always been preoccupied with the uncanny effect of doubles and repetition while some would argue that the relationship between imagination and reality and, even more importantly, the familiar and the strange, is central to all literature and, in fact, constitutes its status as such (SEE FORMALISM).

See A. Bennett and N. Royle, 'The uncanny' in *Introduction to Literature, Criticism and Theory*, 3rd edn (2004).

JA

Undecidability   To offer a simple or stable definition of undecidability is to ignore the radical implications of this 'concept' and its ability to undermine the conceptual basis of definition itself. Associated primarily with the deconstructive critic Jacques Derrida, undecidability is best described as an *effect of writing* where the latter is conceived, by Derrida, as a system of spacing and differences that encompasses language in general. As a site where the effects of writing are writ large, the undecidable, in turn, effects a profound destabilization of meaning, interpretation and the possibility of decision itself. Within Derrida's own texts, we can see these effects most clearly in his reading of terms such as différance, supplement, *pharmakon*, hymen, etc. According to the editor of *Positions* (1981), what links each of these undecidable terms is that they 'are always different from themselves, they always defer any singular grasp of their meaning'. Thus, for example, the term *pharmakon* signifies, amongst other things, both poison and cure while, at the same time, suspending the possibility of simply deciding between these contradictory meanings on the basis of the context in which it is used. As Derrida argues in *Dissemination* (1982):

> The 'essence' of the *pharmakon* lies in the way in which, having no stable essence, no 'proper' characteristics, it is not, in any sense (metaphysical, physical, chemical, alchemical) of the word, a substance.... If the *pharmakon* is 'ambivalent', it is because it constitutes the medium in which opposites are opposed, the movement and play that links them among themselves, reverses them or makes one side cross over into the other

(soul/body, good/evil, inside/outside, memory/forgetfulness, speech/writing, etc.).... The *pharmakon* is the movement, the locus, and the play: (the production of) difference.

As this example suggests, the undecidable does not simply suggest a temporary inability to choose between two (or more) alternative meanings (AMBIGUITY). Nor is it a collection of stable and discrete terms. It is, rather, a site that opens up the possibility of differentiation while simultaneously resisting any attempt to master it on the basis of opposition itself.

Although the undecidability of terms such as *pharmakon* cannot be detached from the chain of textual relations in which they are embedded, its effects exceed any single text to infect the larger conceptual systems upon which they depend. For this reason, the notion of undecidability represents a profound challenge to the rational discourse of Western philosophy. Since its inception, Western philosophy has been organized by the law of non-contradiction. As articulated in Aristotle's *Metaphysics*, this law asserts that 'it is impossible that contrary attributes should belong at the same time to the same subject'. This, 'the most certain of all principles', allows rational discourse to be organized around a series of conceptual oppositions (presence/absence, speech/writing, intelligible/sensible, etc.) where each of the two terms is simply external to the other. In establishing the very possibility of truth (as opposed to falsehood) and of a pure PRESENCE untouched by absence, it allows for the possibility of self-present and self-authenticating knowledge.

In its broadest sense, DECONSTRUCTION represents an attempt to challenge all such notions of self-present knowledge and truth by revealing the fundamental undecidability of the conceptual oppositions on which they are based. Never content simply to reverse such oppositions (privileging, for example, absence over presence or writing over speech), its strategy is to destabilize the very ground of opposition itself by revealing how each of the terms is actually the product of difference (or writing), and thus inhabited by the trace of its other. In *Dissemination* (1981), for example, Derrida deconstructs Plato's distinction between bad memory (associated with external, technical signs and thus with writing and absence) and good memory (a pure truth or presence that has no need for signs). As Derrida reveals, Plato would like to maintain that good memory is completely separate from writing but, at the same time, he can only conceive of the former in terms of the latter (good memory is described, for example, as being '*written* in the soul of the learner' [italics added]). Thus the opposition between good and bad memory collapses into undecidability.

It is important to recognize that undecidability does not constitute a tool or strategy that can simply be applied to – or imported into – a literary text. As I have already suggested, the undecidable is inextricably bound up in the contexts in which it is produced. That said, this notion does represent an important reminder that no text is a unified entity. Indeed, whenever a reader or critic claims to have produced a totalizing reading, it will have been achieved only by ignoring, or suppressing, the inevitable presence of other features – textual or otherwise – that contradict it. See also DECONSTRUCTION, DISSEMINATION and LOGOCENTRISM.

JA

V

Value   See EVALUATION, REFUNCTIONING.

Variation   The calculated avoidance of uniformity of expression, seems to be a feature of all art-forms (music, literature, etc.) having a time dimension. A pervasive characteristic of literary language, it occurs on lexical, syntactic and phonological levels.

Lexical variation has its most commonplace manifestation in the 'elegant variation' of fictional and journalistic prose: avoidance of repeated use of the same expression by choosing an alternative expression having the same reference; for example, by successively referring to a character as *Parson Smith, the man of God, Mr Smith, our clerical friend*, etc. Lexical variation is also a stylistic convention of much heroic poetry, for example, Old English verse, where the use of variant coreferential phrases is an inseparable part of the technique of alliterative composition. *Syntactic* variation can take the form of repeating the same structure but with different ordering (often with a chiasmic, or mirror-image pattern), as in Whitman's *Jehovah am I/Old Brahm I, and I Saturnius am* (from 'Chanting the Square Deific'). *Phonological* variation can take the form of 'ringing the changes' on stressed vowel sounds (particularly long vowels and diphthongs) for euphonious effect (*Paradise Lost*, 3):

> Then   feed   on   thoughts   that
>   voluntary move
> Harmonious   numbers;   as   the
>   wakeful bird.

A further kind of variation is the breaking up of excessive regularity in parallelistic patterns, whether these are patterns on a metrical or a lexico-syntactic level. *Metrical* variation is an accepted licence of English verse whereby (under certain conditions) the positions of stressed and unstressed syllables may be reversed. A similar phenomenon is the final twist in the verbal pattern of (*Merchant of Venice*, 3,1):

> If you prick us, do we not bleed? if you tickle us, do we not laugh? if you poison us, do we not die? and if you wrong us, shall we not revenge?

Whatever the differences between the above cases, they all illustrate enhancement of the element of unpredictability in language, often where in ordinary language the orderliness of repetition might have been expected. It is notable that whereas verbal parallelism characteristically follows a strictly predictable pattern in compositions such as folk-songs and language games, it rarely does so in literature. Similarly, metrical variation is found in serious poetry, but not in doggerel verse or nursery rhymes. Such observations suggest that variation has a more significant role in literature than the mere negative one of avoiding the tedium of mechanical repetition. One possible explanation is prompted by the Russian formalist thesis that art 'makes strange' the experience it describes, and hence that the language of art has to be a 'twisted', oblique mode of discourse. Variation, unexpectedness, establishes a medium or 'scenario' of poetic heightening, in which daring departures from linguistic norms become acceptable. See also FORMALISM.

GNL

Vehicle   See METAPHOR.

Verbal irony   See IRONY.

Verisimilitude   See BELIEF, REALISM.

Vers libre   See FREE VERSE.

Verse   is the minimal condition of poetry if poetry is to mean anything even as a metaphor – 'Poetry is only in verse and nowhere else' (Vigny). The degree of expressivity of language depends upon the frame of mind in which we approach it and that frame of mind is in turn determined by conventions of presentation, lay-out, etc. Free verse might perhaps be printed as prose, but, printed as verse, 'the words are more *poised* than in prose' and 'are to be attended to, in passing, for their own sake' (MacNeice, *Modern Poetry*, 1938; 2nd edn, 1968).

Verse is the line of poetry; a line of verse differs from the line of prose in that it has an active relationship with the page on which it may be written; it asks the page to proclaim its self-sufficiency, to make it portentous and to make room for its mental and emotional extension, the infra-line (Claudel calls the primordial line 'an idea isolated by blank space'); the prose line merely undergoes the physical limitations of the page which thwarts its urge for continuous linearity (the paragraph is a concession to the page, the stanza collusion with it). And the poem differs from the shopping list in that the poem turns sequence into the formally consequential.

A line of verse will be a line of verse as long as it can point to an authority of a higher order than grammar. By this standard, many lines need the corroboration of others, derive their 'lineness' from accompanying evidence. This authority of course need not be metric or rhythmic; it may be as arbitrary as it pleases;

enjambment is enough to suggest an unseen entity imposing itself, to look like compliance with a formal structure. Indeed there is a sense in which in free verse enjambment is a psychological need for both writer and reader, and more a purely formal than an expressive device.

Perhaps the first line of a lyric poem is more line than any of the subsequent ones. Its formulation is an act of perfect faith, it is invocation, libation, abstracted utterance. It can be neither good nor bad, because however the poet came by it, it is the absolutely given, the only assumption the poem can allow itself. Many poems are a making sense of and a giving quality to the first line. And if the first line can so often stand for a title, it is because, while being part of the poem, it partakes also of a paradigmatic existence.

If we call prose 'poetic' we must recognize that it is poetic not for any intrinsic reason but because it alludes to itself in a verse context. Prose is a manner, verse a form; there is no language called poetry, there is only a poetic language in the verse instance. Verse is verse before it is anything else, meaning, vision, etc. If highly imaged language is called poetic, it is because verse alone has enough formal presence to give direction to the caprice of invention and equilibrium to semantic violence, just as it has enough formal presence to re-animate the semantically sedate. See also METRE, POETRY, PROSE.

See V. Forrest-Thompson, *Poetic Artifice* (1978); P. Fussell, *Poetic Meter and Poetic Form* (revised edn, 1979); Phillip Hobsbaum, *Meter, Rhythm and Verse Form* (1995); Jeffrey Wainwright, *Poetry: the basics* (2004).

CS

Verse epistle   One of the neo-classical forms of familiar and complimentary poetry which flourished in England during the seventeenth century. Imitating the epistles of the Roman poet Horace, such verse was addressed to friends, patrons and fellow-poets in a style that approximated to the informal candour and civility of conversation, allowing the poet to expatiate freely in a personal manner on moral and literary themes. Among the principal themes of the Horatian epistle, for instance, are the pleasures and virtues of friendship, the values of self-knowledge and integrity of mind, the praise of the temperate life in country retirement, and general or specific reflections on the art and status of poetry (Horace's *Ars Poetica* is in the form of an epistle). Many of the complimentary poems with which Jonson and his followers commended and appraised each other's work are related to the epistolary form in their tone of personal familiarity. The extravagance of Donne's epistles to noble ladies has not drawn much critical approval, but the epistles of Daniel, Drayton, Carew and Herrick are much admired. The full capacities of the form, however, are best exemplified by Jonson and Pope; like Horace himself they are also keen satirists, and the kinship between verse epistle and satire rests in a common emphasis upon moral and critical realism. The Horatian familiar epistle should not be confused with the Ovidian elegiac epistle (e.g. Drayton's *Englands Heroicall Epistles* and Pope's *Eloisa to Abelard*) in which historical characters are fictitiously supposed to lament their misfortunes.

See R. A. Brower, 'The image of horace', in *Alexander Pope: The Poetry of Allusion* (1959); D. J. Palmer, 'The verse epistle' in Bradbury and Palmer (eds), *Metaphysical Poetry, Stratford-upon-Avon Studies*, 11 (1970).

DJP

Voice See DIALOGIC STRUCTURE, FORMALISM.

W

Wit   The term first comes into critical importance applied to literature in the seventeenth century, though it was used in the previous century in a general way to denote liveliness and brilliance of conversation. 'Witty Jack Donne' is an Elizabethan man-about-town, but when he turns up in Carew's 'Elegie upon the Death of the Deane of Pauls' (1623) as

> a King, that rul'd as hee thought fit
> The universall Monarchy of wit

we are moving into a time when *wit* was a powerful if disputed critical concept or basis for value-judgement, though such a time was more surely after the Restoration. The clue to the reason for this may lie in a meaning of *wit* which is assigned to the Restoration years: 'the seat of consciousness or thought, the mind'. Dryden, living in this critical climate, defined wit as 'sharpness of conceit'. His emphasis is on self-consciousness on the part of both the poet and the audience. It is no accident, then, that at this time 'the wits' emerged – a group conscious of their nimble minds and cultural awareness. Apart from self-consciousness itself, there are several other characteristics of Restoration and eighteenth-century wit that come from such an in-group attitude. Comparison is stressed. The wit demands to be used in a context of accepted ideas and reading, though the opposite side of this is also valued, namely unexpected justness. Cleverness and quickness are parts of it, too, and the idea of the marshalled disposition of material. Lastly, ideas are important: the most famous characterization of wit, echoed by later critics and poets, is that of the most influential philosopher of the age, John Locke, who defines it as 'the Assemblage of Ideas, and putting those together with quickness and variety'.

Locke is here, however, acting as the spokesperson for the new highly developed and articulate consciousness of the self in moral thinking, scientific observation and poetry, which begins to assume special importance in England in the seventeenth century. The consciousness of the self as initiator, user and arbiter of ideas produced the problem of establishing a communal, standard judgement, a point of rest which became increasingly the goal of the succeeding Augustan age. The arrogance of wit was resisted. There was a backlash of sensibility, from individuals who followed their hearts; and there was a conservative backlash from those who distrusted unsupported human daring. Addison devoted several *Spectator* papers to discussing wit (see nos. 35, 61–3, 140 and 249). In No. 62, he elaborates his famous distinctions between 'true wit' and 'false wit' allowing an escape hole of 'mix'd wit' to avoid condemning writers whom he half admired. There is a see-saw between admiration for quick cleverness and admiration for the harmony of the assemblage. 'False wit' appears to Addison to be '*Gothick*', that is without proportion, fussy, entertaining but lacking overall control. 'True wit' he sees as majestic and 'natural'.

It would be possible to give a historical account of the use of 'wit' as a critical term. Pope, for example, makes it one of the primary topics of his 'Essay on Criticism'. Dr Johnson was himself a witty writer. His *Rasselas* depends for much of its powerful and moving moral judgement on the witty juxtaposition of ideas and judgements. At the same time, he is firmly committed to total control in literature. In his *Life of Cowley*, a 'witty' writer of the seventeenth century, he gave two of the most widely quoted critical definitions of wit: 'that which though not obvious, is, upon its first production, acknowledged to be just; a kind of *discordia concors*...'. It is perhaps more important, however, to see the prizing of wit in poetry and writing in general as one of the ends of an arc through which taste can swing, from admiring the unconscious, the area of FEELING. In the 1890s, the writers in the *Yellow Book*, very conscious rebels against a suffocating Victorian tide of feeling, cultivated wit. T. S. Eliot, later, developed a poetic which made use of wit and selected for admiration certain seventeenth-century writers such as Donne and especially Marvell, in whose work he saw the successful realization of wit, which he defines in his essay on 'Andrew Marvell' (1921) as 'tough reasonableness beneath the slight lyric grace': knowledgeable technical skill united with a total self-consciousness. Here wit is not arrogant as in the seventeenth century, but a defensive personal attitude. Cleanth Brooks was a member of a group of American writers and critics who seized on wit as a personal style of writing and of living, in defence against the blanketing megalopolis of American capitalism. In *The Well Wrought Urn* (1947), he refers to wit as 'an awareness of the multiplicity of possible attitudes to be taken towards a given situation'. This was also a defensive position against the mass 'feeling' of communism, or fascism. The value of wit as a personal protection and a weapon had

been recognized by earlier writers, though they also saw its divisive disadvantages. As Pope wrote:

> Thus wit, like faith, by each man is apply'd
> To one small sect, and all are damned beside

See A. Alvarez, *The School of Donne* (1961), ch. 6; W. Empson, *The Structure of Complex Words* (1951), ch. 3; Bruce Michelson, *Literary Wit* (2000), ch. 4; D. J. Millburn, *The Age of Wit: 1650–1750* (1966), useful bibliography, 315–16.

AMR

Womanist A term first proposed by Alice Walker (1944–) in her 1983 collection of essays, *In Search of Our Mother's Gardens: Womanist Prose*. 'Womanist' is defined at the outset of the collection in a definition comprising four different parts, three of which are long and will be summarized in brief: (1) from *womanish* (i.e. opposite of ' "girlish", frivolous, irresponsible, not serious'), a black feminist or feminist of colour; (2) 'A woman who loves other women, sexually and/or nonsexually. Appreciates and prefers women's culture, women's emotional flexibility [...] and women's strength. Sometimes loves individual men, sexually and/or nonsexually'; (3) A woman who loves everything, herself included. The fourth part of Walker's definition can be given in full: (4) 'Womanist is to feminist as purple is to lavender'.

Walker's best-known fiction *The Color Purple* (1982) is alluded to here and points to the ways in which the novel (which also won the Pulitzer Prize and was released by Steven Spielberg as a film in 1985) is informed by 'womanism', exemplified by the used and abused

African-American women who come into their own in the ways outlined in Walker's definition of 'womanist'. The paler 'lavender' which betokens 'feminist' as opposed to the rich and royal purple of 'womanist' is a swipe at some of the patronizing and universalizing theories of white, middle-class feminists, who fail(ed) to understand or see the specificity of black women's experience, particularly the experience of double discrimination – or, more accurately, doubly-determined invisibility (reminiscent of Ralph Ellison's classic 1952 story of black manhood, *Invisible Man*) – on the basis of race *and* sex. As Walker explained in 'In Search of Our Mother's Gardens': 'Black women are called [...] "the *mule* of the world," because we have been handed the burdens that everyone else – *everyone* else – refused to carry'. Similarly, the black-American writer, Bell Hooks, noted in *Ain't I a Woman?* in 1981: 'No other group in America has so had their identity socialized out of existence'. Thus, when in *The Color Purple*, one of the characters says that 'it makes God angry to walk by the color purple in a field somewhere and don't notice it', it is a hypothesis that could be extended to the failure to notice and respect black women in particular. Walker has been criticized from time to time for her treatment of black male characters, particularly in early work, such as *The Third Life of Grange Copeland*. Of her main male character in that novel, Walker explained in an interview with Claudia Tate, that she knew men such as him well and would not ignore characters like him: 'I want you to know I know they exist. I want to tell you about them, and there is no way you are going to avoid them'. Walker is also interested in analysing and understanding the ways that disempowered black men vent their frustration on black women, but she is not interested in a cover-up which keeps black women silent and unseen. However, she does represent scenes of reconciliation between black men and women; Celie and her one-time abusive husband, Mr (later, Albert) in *The Color Purple* are a case in point. A Womanist Studies Consortium was established in 1994 at the University of Georgia. It advertises itself as an interracial, intergenerational, regional affiliation of scholars' which 'supports and facilitates feminist research on women of color in all disciplines and at all possible stages of development'. It seeks to provide a service that 'bridges the isolation, social exclusion, silence and intellectual desuetude among women-of-color researchers, students, and independent scholars within their home institutions'. 'Womanist theology' is also establishing itself as a lively contributor to contemporary theological debates.

SS

Writing See DECONSTRUCTION.

Notes on contributors

New and revising contributors

JA Janice Allan, Lecturer in English, University of Salford

PC Peter Childs, Professor of Modern English Literature, University of Gloucestershire

GD Gary Day, Principal Lecturer in English, University of De Montfort

GG Gareth Griffiths, Professor of English, University of Western Australia

DL Daniel Lea, Senior Lecturer in English Studies, Oxford Brookes University

BCL Brian Lee, Emeritus Professor of American Studies, University of Nottingham

AM Anshuman Mondal, Lecturer in Modern and Contemporary Literature, University of Leicester

DGP David Punter, Professor of English, Research Director, Faculty of Arts, University of Bristol

SS Shelley Saguaro, Principal Lecturer in English, University of Gloucestershire

GS Gerry Smyth, Reader in Cutural History, Liverpool John Moores University

Original contributors

MJA Michael Alexander

FWB F. W. Bateson

CWEB C. W. E. Bigsby
EJB Elizabeth Boa
MSB Malcolm Bradbury
AAAC Anne Cluysenaar
JC Jonathan Cook
EC Ellman Crasnow
TE Terry Eagleton
JWJF John Fletcher
RGF Roger Fowler
AMG Arnold Goldman
GG Gareth Griffiths
MAH Michael Hollington
GMH G. M. Hyde
BCL Brian Lee
GNL Geoffrey N. Leech
TM Timothy Marshall
PM Peter Mercer
MO'T Michael O'Toole
DJP D. J. Palmer
MHP M. H. Parkinson
SGP S. G. Pulman
DGP David Punter
AER Allan Rodway
AMR Angus Ross
LS Lorna Sage
VS Victor Sage
CS Clive Scott
RWS Richard Sheppard
LSM Lorna Smith
TGW Todd G. Willy
NZ Natan Zach
NCPZ Nicholas Zurbrugg

Literary Theory: The Basics
Hans Bertens

Part of the successful *Basics* series, this accessible guide provides the ideal first step in understanding literary theory. Hans Bertens:

- leads students through the major approaches to literature which are signalled by the term 'literary theory'
- places each critical movement in its historical (and often political) context
- illustrates theory in practice with examples from much-read texts
- suggests further reading for different critical approaches
- shows that theory can make sense and that it can radically change the way we read.

Covering the basics and much more, this is the ideal book for anyone interested in how we read and why that matters.

0–415–35112–X

Available at all good bookshops
For ordering and further information please visit www.routledge.com

Semiotics: The Basics
Daniel Chandler

Following the successful *Basics* format, this is *the* book for anyone coming to semiotics for the first time. Using jargon-free language and lively, up-to-date examples, *Semiotics: The Basics* demystifies this highly interdisciplinary subject. Along the way, the reader will find out:

- what is a sign?
- which codes do we take for granted?
- what is a text?
- how can semiotics be used in textual analysis?
- who were Saussure, Peirce, Barthes and Jakobson – and why are they important?

Features include a glossary of key terms and realistic suggestions for further reading.

0–415–35111–1

The Routledge Companion to Postmodernism
2nd edition
Edited by Stuart Sim

What does 'postmodernism' mean? Why is it so important? Now in its second edition, *The Routledge Companion to Postmodernism* combines a series of in-depth background chapters with a body of A–Z entries to create an authoritative, yet readable guide to the complex world of postmodernism. Following full-length articles on postmodernism and philosophy, politics, feminism, religion, post-colonialism, lifestyles, television, and other postmodern essentials, readers will find a wide range of alphabetically-organized entries on the people, terms and theories connected with postmodernism, including:

- Peter Ackroyd
- Jean Baudrillard
- Chaos Theory
- Desire

- Michel Foucault
- Frankfurt School
- Poststructuralism
- Retro

Students interested in any aspect of postmodernist thought will find this an indispensable resource.

0–415–33359–8

Available at all good bookshops
For ordering and further information please visit www.routledge.com

The Routledge Companion to Feminism and Postfeminism
Edited by Sarah Gamble

Approachable for general readers as well as for students in women's studies and related courses at all levels, this invaluable guide follows the unique *Companion* format in combining over a dozen in-depth background chapters with more than 400 A–Z dictionary entries. The background chapters are written by major figures in the field of feminist studies, and include thorough coverage of the history of Feminism, as well as extensive discussions of topics such as:

- Postfeminism
- Men in Feminism
- Feminism and New Technologies
- Feminism and Philosophy.

Dictionary entries cover the major individuals (Aphra Behn, Simone de Beauvoir, Princess Diana, Robert Bly), and issues (Afro-American feminism, cosmetic surgery, the 'new man', reproductive technologies) essential to an understanding both of Feminism's roots and of the trends that are shaping its future.

0–415–24310–6

Available at all good bookshops
For ordering and further information please visit www.routledge.com

Cultural Theory: The Key Concepts
Edited by Andrew Edgar and Peter Sedgwick

An up-to-date and comprehensive survey of over 350 of the key terms in cultural theory today! Each entry provides clear and succinct explanations for students in a wide range of disciplines, including literature, cultural studies, sociology and philosophy.

Topics include:

- Consumption
- Epistemology
- Hermeneutics
- Methodology
- Semiotics

- Deconstruction
- Feminism
- Holism
- Postmodernism
- Sociobiology

Major entries are accompanied by suggestions for further reading and the book also includes a bibliography of essential texts in cultural theory.

"Thorough, well-written and accessible, this text should be an indispensable part of every library."

Professor Douglas Kellner, *University of California at Los Angeles*

0–415–28426–0

Available at all good bookshops
For ordering and further information please visit www.routledge.com